JAPANESE INWARD INVESTMENT IN UK CAR MANUFACTURING

To my wife, Suh Chang-Hee, *Prima et Semper*

Japanese Inward Investment in UK Car Manufacturing

YOUNG-CHAN KIM
Royal Holloway, University of London, UK

ASHGATE

Published by
Ashgate Publishing Limited
Gower House
Croft Road
Aldershot
Hampshire GU11 3HR
England

Ashgate Publishing Company
131 Main Street
Burlington, VT 05401-5600 USA

Ashgate website: http://www.ashgate.com

British Library Cataloguing in Publication Data
Kim, Young-Chan
        Japanese inward investment in UK car manufacturing
        (Explorations in Asia Pacific economics)
        1. Investments, Japanese - Europe 2. Investments, Japanese -
        Great Britain 3. Automobile industry and trade - Great
        Britain - Foreign ownership
        I. Title
        338.8'8952'04

Library of Congress Control Number: 2001096369

ISBN 0 7546 1614 2

Printed and bound in Great Britain by Antony Rowe Ltd.,
Chippenham, Wiltshire

Contents

List of Figures

List of Tables

Preface and Acknowledgements

Whilst the developed countries advocated a free trading system, there has been a growing economic regionalism. NAFTA, ASEAN, and the EU have been developed as single blocs. The single European market movement since the early 1980s put nonmember countries under pressure. Under the name of globalisation, Japanese companies flooded into the European Union. As contrasted with the strategy in the US, Japanese multinational enterprises movement towards the EU were harmonised with political action by the Japanese government. Dumping accusations and voluntary export restraints made the Japanese government urge on her MNEs more positive action towards the EU – a push factor for foreign direct investment. While the Japanese government pushed her MNEs into the EU, all European industrial problems such as the high rate of unemployment, de-industrialisation, and shrinking consumer markets were expected to be solved by the new wave from the East, the pull factor. Within the push factor, the Japanese government, especially MITI, was brought into action again as a business negotiator. Because of the strong incentive from member countries (pull factor), the policy towards inward foreign direct investment was matched to the Japanese push factor. There was a small pinhole in fortress Europe, namely Japanisation.

The UK has been favoured because of her strong pull factor policy toward foreign investors, especially Japan. Ironically, while the UK lost her nationalised car manufacturers, there are now three big Japanese car makers in the UK. The British car industry was in turmoil and government intervention toward car manufacturing sectors was not supported by a clear industrial policy for the sector itself. As far as Japanese car makers were concerned, the UK had, then, a weak nationalised car maker, open-minded consumer taste, relatively free market competition, well-organised components industries and most of all, a strong government incentive policy. The Rover and Honda collaboration, and the Nissan greenfield investment, show us good comparative examples of Japanese strategy toward the EU. Because of the failure of the successive inward investment from the components industry, the lack of technical collaboration, and mismanagement from UK government (Rover and Honda case), the Japanese car makers in the UK are just assembly warehouses rather than manufacturing sites.

Though I am responsible for what follows in this book, there are numerous people who have contributed in a variety of ways to its realisation. Two people made contributions without which the project would have been impossible. Professor John Turner was, despite a formidably full schedule, generous with his time and advice, having ploughed through numerous drafts. Professor Charles Harvey was an invaluable source of ideas, inspiration, imagination, invention and often pure intuition.

My deepest thanks must go to the various interviewees, from former Cabinet Ministers, representatives and staff of car and component industries in the UK, research fellows in various institutes, and members of trade associations to managers in local government. Quite patently, without their courteous attention and interest in my questions, none of the present study would have been even remotely possible and I extend them my warmest gratitude.

The comments and personal conversations with ex-Cabinet ministers, Sir Edward Heath (Prime Minister 1970–74), Lord Biffen (Trade Secretary 1981–82, Leader of House of Commons 1982–87), Lord Howe (Chancellor of the Exchequer 1979–83, Foreign Secretary 1983–89, Leader of House of Commons 1989–90), Lord Parkinson (Party Chairman 1981–83, Trade and Industry Secretary 1983, Energy Secretary 1987–89, Transport Secretary 1989–90), Lord Tebbit (Employment Secretary 1981–83, Trade and Industry Secretary 1983–85, Party Chairman 1985–87), Lord Walker (Agriculture Secretary 1979–83, Energy Secretary 1983–87), Lord Young (Employment Secretary 1985–87, Trade and Industry Secretary 1987–89), government technocrats in IBB, DTI and local government staffs have played significant roles in my study. I am, also, deeply indebted to individuals from Honda UK staff, Nissan UK and British and Japanese component affiliates in Britain.

On a broader front, due thanks must be extended to the staff of DTI Library, House of Commons Information Service, Press Association, TUC Library in North London University, European Union Library in London, London Business Library, KPMG Japan Desk, Japan Information Services at Japan Embassy, JETRO Library, Anglo-Japanese Institute Library, Diawa Anglo-Japanese Foundation Library, Swindon Local Library, Economic Development Thamesdown Brough Council, Northern Development Company, Sunderland University Library.

For the insights they provided, I am indebted to the speakers, the guests and the organisers of various seminars from the Anglo-Japanese Economic Institute, the Asia-Pacific Technology Forum and the Daiwa Anglo-Japanese Conference.

The editorial staff at Ashgate, especially Kirstin Howgate, Jacqui Cornish and Sarah Charters, have been very helpful throughout the writing process. Lastly, family were a welcome source of strength and support, and friends in

Korea, and in the UK, who always stood by me and supported me when I needed them.

My final thanks go to my wife, Chang-Hee Suh and two children, Seung-Gyum and Yong-Gyum, whose support and endless sacrifices were enormous. Especially, while my first son would annoy me during the day, my second son would do so at nights, the same as his brother had done before. I hope to be a nice father to them. Special thanks go to my wife, because she has made me what I am.

I have drawn much, both consciously and unconsciously, on the thoughts of others, to whom I am grateful. However, the judgements, conclusions and faults are naturally my own.

List of Abbreviations

ACP	Asian, Caribbean and Pacific
AEU	Amalgamated Engineering Union
BOJ	Bank of Japan
CAD	Computer aided design
CCP	Common Commercial Policy
CCT	Common Customs Tariff
COG	Cars Organisation Group
COP	Committee of Overseas Promotional
EPA	Economic Planning Agency
ETP	Executive Training Programme
GSP	Generalised System of Preferences
IBB	Invest in Britain Bureau
IBJ	Industrial Bank of Japan
JAMA	Japanese Automobile Manufacturers Association
JETRO	Japan External Trade Organisation
JIT	Just-in-time
MDW	Measured day work
MFN	Most-favoured nation
MITI	Ministry of International Trade and Industry
MOF	Minister of Finance
MOFA	Minister of Foreign Affairs
NMM	Nissan Motor Manufacturing
OEM	Original Equipment Manufacture
QC	Quality Control
REP	Regional Employment Premium
RSA	Regional Selective Assistance
SRA	Selective Regional Assistance
TQ	Total Quality
VERs	Voluntary export restraints

Chapter 1

Introduction

For thirty years after the Second World War, multinational enterprises (MNEs) have been recognised as one of the most effective agents for economic development. By the early 1980s, 200 MNEs accounted for a third of global GDP, or one and a half times the production of the world's less developed economies including Latin America, Africa, India and China.

MNEs have in this way profoundly changed the global framework in which policies are pursued by governments and international organisations. Yet most governments which are members of the big international organisations, such as the Organisation for Economic Co-operation and Development (OECD) and the International Monetary Fund (IMF), have failed to grasp the international implications of a world economy dominated by MNEs, whether in agribusiness, manufacturing industry, services or finance. Virtually no international agency other than the United Nations Conference on Trade and Development (UNCTAD) makes any sustained effort to account for the share of MNEs in the output, pricing, trade or payments of the global macro-economy.

'The MNE is an enterprise that engages in foreign direct investment (FDI) and owns or controls value-adding activities in more than one country.'[1] FDI is typically the overseas manifestation of the activities of MNEs, so consideration of FDI must start with why companies become multinational. Japanese MNEs, compared to those of other developed countries, have been distinctive since the mid-1980s. Their policy differentiates between developing countries[2] and developed countries.

> The difference between developing and developed countries is mainly based on the business system in Japan. The pattern of Japanese FDI is an outcome of a political economy crisis whose roots were deep in the structure of Japanese capitalism. Hence, compared to investment in the developing countries, Japanese MNEs in the developed countries have relied on the invisible support of government.[3]

The biggest emerging consumer market during the 1980s in Western Europe was one of the major targets of Japanese MNEs. As Alfred Dienst, chairman of the Council of the European Business Community observed:

> Looking at the Triangle of Europe, the US, and Japan, it is clear that the Japan-Europe side is the weakest link. I think people in Japan need to reassess this situation once more. There seems to be a feeling in Japan that Europe is over the hill.[4]

The emerging single market presented a different challenge to that of the United States, where Japanese FDI had been underway since the 1960s. European institutions were relatively weak, and member states' national policies dominated by national economic strategies required specific tailored approaches by investing MNEs. Hence the role of the Japanese government was vital to support her MNEs' FDI policy.

During the 1970s, on the other hand, the European economies had been vulnerable to competition at both macro and micro levels. At the macroeconomic level, protectionism, consumption at the expense of investment, and narrow nationalism, were symptoms of 'Eurosclerosis' or '*Eikokubyo*' (English disease).[5] At the level of manufacturing companies, low productivity, technological backwardness and the decline of the 'industrial spirit' in the managerial classes made things worse. The emerging Single European Market (SEM) was intended to provide an opportunity to regenerate the competitiveness of European manufacturing sectors with a real and a psychological impetus to governments and companies.

As compared with earlier decades, the position of MNEs in the Single Market had an even more important role to play in economic development. The increasing importance of MNEs coincided with the importance of foreign direct investment. Japanese business was a latecomer to direct investment in Europe. In the Single Market, Japanese MNEs tried to catch up with American MNEs in market share. There were two dominant methods among Japanese MNEs: one was to concentrate their products within one or two main sectors; the other was to use government channels to promote the globalisation of their business.

The main object of this thesis is to describe and analyse the relationship between government and MNEs in the 'host country' receiving foreign direct investment. The emerging Single Market during the 1980s showed two different sides of the MNEs' FDI policy toward the European Community. There were 'pull factors' within the host countries; on the other hand there were 'push factors' within Japan. In these circumstances, without government intervention Japanese MNEs would have faced enormous difficulties in maintaining their business in developed countries, which were hostile to Japanese penetration, especially in Europe.

I have used three different perspectives in the analysis of one manufacturing sector, the car industry. Within EU member countries, opinions differ sharply about the merits of inward Japanese FDI in the Single Market. Within favourable countries (such as Britain), I have sought to discover whether FDI worked in the interest of national government or in the interest of industry. In conditions of severe competition among member countries to attract inward FDI, what did politicians do? I have tried to answer the following questions with respect to Japanese FDI in the British car industry:

- Why did Japanese car MNEs choose the UK as their manufacturing base?
- What was the working relationship between the British government and Japanese MNEs?
- What are the differences between joint venture (JV) and greenfield investments?
- Did FDI work to improve the host country's manufacturing competitiveness?

This introductory chapter reviews some leading FDI theories, with particular reference to the Japanese car MNEs in the European Community. The main question is whether the existing theories of FDI are likely to be adequate in explaining the FDI strategies of Japanese car MNEs. To do this, this chapter is divided into two parts. One, there is a general review of the major theories of FDI in explaining mutual investment between developed countries. The other, an alternative model is suggested, which can help us to understand the phenomenon of FDI on the part of Japanese car MNEs in the European Union.

Some Leading Theories of Foreign Direct Investment

The economic prosperity of each nation has always been influenced by the terms on which it has exchanged goods and services with others. Historically, since the early nineteenth century, an active international capital market has existed, while the international flow of knowledge has an even longer pedigree, which dates back to the exodus of the Huguenots from France in the seventeenth century. It was said that world trade in goods and factors inputs has always affected the economic welfare of participating nations, and that several countries owe the timing of their take-off in development directly to the inflow of foreign capital and expertise. From then on, there have been many foreign direct investments world wide originating from Britain and later from the United States.

Generally speaking, a foreign direct investment (FDI) involves an investor in one country purchasing and/or acquiring controlling interests in assets in another country. Direct investment is usually undertaken to establish overseas branch operations by multinational enterprises (MNEs). The value of direct investment may increase not only through the investment of new funds, which may be remitted from abroad or borrowed locally by the foreign investors, but also through reinvestment of earnings, or the sale to a foreign affiliate of nonfinancial assets, such as a license or management services. According to Stewart: 'FDI generally takes one of three forms: an infusion of new equity capital such as a new plant or JV, reinvested corporate earnings, and net borrowing through the parent company or affiliates.'[6] FDI is usually distinguished from indirect investment, which consists of international portfolio investment. While portfolio investment abroad is made to a large extent by individual investors, FDI is made essentially by corporations. Also, 'direct investment is motivated by the desire to control a foreign company, while portfolio investment seeks a higher return or risk diversification'.[7]

Although the definitions of direct investment and indirect investment are commonly accepted, it is quite difficult to distinguish FDI from indirect investment because of the ambiguous terms used in the definition of FDI.

According to Kindleberger and others,

FDI is determined essentially by advantages that allow a firm to operate a subsidiary abroad more profitably than local competitors. These advantages may be classified in two broad categories: superior 'knowledge' and economies of scale. The term 'knowledge' includes production technologies skills, industrial organisation, knowledge of product, and factor markets. ... Superior knowledge as such, however, is not enough to justify direct investment: the latter must also provide to the firm the highest return among all alternative ways of exploiting the superior knowledge in the foreign market. These alternatives are, essentially, (a) exporting products that embody the knowledge; (b) selling the knowledge to local producers in the foreign market; and (c) producing abroad (through direct investment) products that embody the knowledge. ... Besides superior knowledge, a determinant of direct investment may be the opportunity of achieving economies of scale. Economies of scale may be internal or external to the firm: the former normally lead to horizontal investment, and the latter to vertical investment. Foreign investment in vertically related stages of production is common mainly in industries producing and processing minerals and other raw materials. The main advantage of direct investment here consists in reducing the costs and uncertainties that exist when subsequent stages of production are handled by different producers by coordinating decisions at various stages within one firm.[8]

Another survey by the IMF in 1977 described FDI as 'an investment which is made to acquire a lasting interest in an enterprise operating in an economy other than that of the investor, the investor's purpose being to have an active voice in the management of the enterprise'.[9]

Most existing theories of FDI were developed on the basis of FDI from the developed countries to the developing countries. However, there has recently been much FDI from the developing countries to the developed countries. Moreover, mutual FDI between the developed countries, to take advantage of the managerial skills of MNEs, is nowadays commonplace.

Agarwal gives an overview on how the theories of FDI have developed since the 1930s:

> FDI did not enter the domain of the writings of the classical economists. They were mainly concerned with the causes of trade between nations. The resulting theory of comparative costs assumed that factors of production like capital did not move internationally ...
>
> The inter-war period after the economic crisis of 1931 was marked by exchange controls, international financial crisis and the loss of mutual political confidence by banks in the countries leading almost to a cessation of international capital movements (UN, 1949). As Nurkse (1966, p.121)[10] puts it, by the time Ohlin's book *(International Economic Reconstruction)* came in 1933, the classical assumption of international immobility of productive factors had become a reality. Then came the Keynesian revolution, concerning economist's attention on the 'short run' rather than on the 'long run' with which FDI are really associated.
>
> The immediate post-World War II period, no doubt, experienced an acceleration of international transfers of capital, but they were primarily composed of portfolio lending and governmental aid coming mostly from the America for the reconstruction of Europe. It was in the fifties and sixties that FDI registered an enormous growth, which attracted the interest of economists in research on the causes of these investments.[11]

Economists started to take an interest in the causes of direct investment and to develop various theories of FDI in the early 1960s. Thus the following theories will be reviewed in this chapter: the Kojima-Ozawa theory (1978, 1979), the Dunning's Eclectic Theory (1977), the Currency Area Theory of Aliber (1970), and the Internalisation Theory of Buckley and Casson (1976).

The Kojima-Ozawa Theory

Kiyoshi Kojima and Terutomo Ozawa and other Japanese economists were strongly opposed to existing theories, which were largely derived from the

Table 1.1   Characteristics of developed countries' MNEs *versus* developing countries' MNEs

	Developed countries' MNEs	Developing countries' MNEs
Manufacturing facilities	Dispersed across geographic markets	Concentrated in home markets
Labour intensity	Less	More
Flexibility	Relatively inflexible	Relatively flexible
Output scale	Large volume	Small volume
Technology sources	Internally developed	Purchased
Level	World leadership	Followers
Production line	Broad breadth, long concentrated at mid and upper price points	Narrow, short, concentrate at lower price points
Modified for overseas subsidiaries	No	Yes
Market shares in overseas markets	Medium-dominant rarely small	Small-medium, rarely dominant
Marketing adaptation	More standardised: moving to global approach	More tailored to local conditions Country by country or region by region approach
Use of third party distributors	Low	High
Usual marketing strategy	Pull	Push
Branding	Branded products	Private label products for resellers: few branded products
Lifecycle	Growth	Mature: growth if can use known technology or available manufacturing competence
Structure and size of overseas ventures	Large	Small
Vertical integration	More	Less
Legal/ownership	Wholly owned subsidiaries	JV/Licensing, technical agreements

Source: Verdon-Wortzel, H. and Wortzel, L.H. (1988), 'Globalising Strategies for Multinationals from Developing Countries', *The Columbia Journal of World Business*, Vol. 23, No. 1, Spring, p. 27.

US experience, and were in their view inadequate in explaining the pattern of Japanese FDI. In order to explain the Japanese model of FDI, Kojima attempted to identify the characteristics of two different types of FDI: trade-oriented foreign investment which was exemplified by the Japanese model and anti-trade-oriented foreign investment exemplified by the US. The Kojima theory was quite different from that of conventional theory such as the Eclectic theory, the Currency Area theory and the Internalisation theory. According to Giddy and Young,

> this explanation for Japanese FDI is quite different from conventional theory. In the first place, the 'advantage', which is usually assumed necessary to enable MNEs to compete successfully abroad, is not immediately obvious. Indeed, it is argued that the smaller the technological difference between the investing and host country industry, the easier it is to transfer operations. Moreover, what is being transferred is general technology, covering a wide range of production activities such as assembly techniques (e.g. cars, TVs, refrigerators); material selection, mixing and treatment techniques (e.g. dyes, inks and paints); machine operation and maintenance techniques (e.g. weaving and spinning); training of engineers and operatives; plant layout; installation of machinery and equipment; and quality, cost and inventory techniques. Secondly, the type of firm involved in foreign manufacturing activity is the smaller, marginally efficient operation rather than the large, innovative corporation. Thirdly, oligopolistic or monopolistic market structure need not prevail in either home or host countries.[12]

Ozawa sees Western MNEs as the outcome of an evolutionary process by which firms increase in size and organisational sophistication. The motivations underlying the overseas growth of Japanese firms were basically macroeconomic in nature, arising from domestic factor shortages, insecurity of supply of industrial resources and environmental constraints. Multi-nationality, according to this view, is a reflection of the collective way in which corporate objectives are set in Japan. Given their macroeconomic circumstances, it is concluded that the more competitive the industry (that is, the less monopolistic or oligopolistic the industry, and the less technologically sophisticated the product), the greater the need so far for Japanese industry to resort to overseas production.

Although this model is applied solely to Japan, it does represent a challenge to any claims of universality in conventional theory.

The Kojima-Ozawa theory suggests that:

> Comparative profitabilities in trade-oriented FDI conform to the direction of potential comparative costs and, therefore, complement each other. In other words,

FDI going from a comparatively disadvantageous industry in the investing country (which is potentially a comparatively advantageous industry in the host country) will promote an upgrading of industrial structure on both sides and thus accelerate trade between the two countries.

In comparison, the American model of FDI does not conform to this comparative profitabilities formula, mainly due to the dualistic structure of the American economy – the dichotomy between the new, oligopolistic industries and the traditional, price competitive industries. This type of FDI is anti-trade-oriented and results in balance of payments difficulties, the export of jobs, the prevention of structural adjustment and trade protectionism.[13]

Based on this approach, Kojima classifies the motives for FDI into resource-, labour- and market-oriented investment. Natural resources-oriented investment is obviously trade-oriented or trade generating, for it results from the investing country's desire to increase imports of its natural resources which are not available or not produced in sufficient quantity domestically, and increases vertical specialisation between producers of manufacturers and primary products. It flourished during the 1960s and the early 1970s in the Middle East Asia and Latin America.

Labour-oriented investment is also trade-oriented or trade-reorganising. Its main purposes are to utilise cheap labour, to establish an export base, rather than import-substitution, or the development of exports to the investing country and other markets. This is still an important part of the Japanese FDI programme in developing countries.

Market-oriented investment can be subdivided into two categories. The first type of FDI arises from the recipient country's interest in promoting import-substituting activity, not necessarily intended to be competitive in the international market. However, if the import-substitution industry grows successfully towards export-orientation, then FDI of this type turns out to be labour-oriented investment. This thesis argues that it is exemplified by Japanese FDI in the EU during the emerging Single Market period. However it has not been proved that it developed from market-oriented investment to labour-oriented investment. One of the major foreign direct investments in the EU, the manufacturing plant established by Nissan UK, showed no moves towards labour-oriented investment.

There is another type of market-oriented investment, which may be called oligopolistic FDI. This is typically found in US investment in new manufacturing product industries in recent decades, as will be seen presently, and is anti-trade-oriented.

The Kojima-Ozawa theory has a strong point in that it emphasises the importance of the role of the structure of a country's comparative advantage in trade such as resource and factor endowments and firm specific advantage, in determining the flow of direct investment. However, Dunning has made the following criticism of the Kojima theory:

> However, even as a prescriptive macroeconomics model, the Kojima approach is deficient in two major respects. First, since it is neo-classical in its stance, it can neither explain, nor evaluate the welfare implications of those types of FDI prompted by the desire to rationalise international production and to benefit from the common governance of cross-border activities ... Second, and related to the first, Kojima largely ignores the essential characteristic of MNE activity – that is, the internalisation of intermediate product markets – and where he does take this into account, he always seems to assume that the allocation of resources is less desirable than that which would have been dictated by the market (Kojima, 1978, Ch.9). This is because Kojima is locked into a neo-classical paradigm of perfect competition which negates the very possibility of market failure. In his scenario, the MNE can never be the most efficient agent for transferring resources across national boundaries, simply because its very existence implies a second best transactional situation.[14]

Giddy and Young further point out that:

> The 'Japanese theory' makes a spurious distinction between trade and anti-trade oriented foreign investments and between the motivation for US and Japanese investment. It may be true that much of US direct investment abroad replaces US exports, but there is no reason why this should work against the structure of comparative advantage. Provided US MNEs are able to appropriate the returns from their investment in R&D, this will permit further technological advance and a continuous upgrading of the US' economy. Moreover, it is contended that the motives of US firms are to maintain an oligopolistic market position, while those of Japanese firms are to upgrade the industrial structures of both home and host economies. However if Japanese motives were so benign, then licensing would be a more satisfactory method of transferring technology from the host country viewpoint. Direct investment occurs to retain control and appropriate the returns from intangible factors.[15]

More recently, Petrochilas has observed that:

> It is by no means clear that growing Japanese outward direct investment will continue to develop along present line, or along the line of comparative advantage advocated by Kojima. Since there is a discerning wish by Japanese businessmen

to follow the 'American type' in order to maximise profits. Kojima's model is not so much a theory explaining FDI but rather the use of such investment as a prerequisite for establishing foreign trade.[16]

The Kojima-Ozawa theory is consistent with the development of the Japanese economy in the take-off stage during the 1960s and with the progress of Japanese FDI during the 1970s. However, during the 1980s, the business behaviour of Japanese MNEs was more similar to the US style of the 1950s and 1960s. In particular, with respect to Japanese MNEs' FDI in the European Community, the Kojima-Ozawa theory would rather describe a trade policy than an investment policy. As Petrochilas points out, the Kojima-Ozawa theory is more suitable to an explanation of Japanese foreign trade than Japanese FDI.

With respect to Japanese car makers' FDI towards the European Community, the Kojima-Ozawa theory confronted two problems. The EU is not well endowed with natural resources. Low investment in technology, and lack of primary manufacturing skills, do not favour the interests of Japanese car manufacturers in 'lean production'.[17] Moreover, despite the strength of the *yen*, labour costs were not lower than those in Japan. In recent years (since the 1980s) Japanese foreign investment has shifted from the once typical trading company-manufacturing firm partnership towards fully-fledged direct investment abroad. The new wave of market penetration by Japanese MNEs, commonly named globalisation, shows the limitations of Kojima-Ozawa theory. After the mid-1980s, Japanese car makers' FDI toward Europe was not intended to promote exports but to reduce trade conflict. At the same time, exports to developed countries have partly been replaced by FDI. This trend can not be fully explained by the Kojima-Ozawa theory.

Dunning's Eclectic Theory

The eclectic theory, which is based on the existence of market imperfections, was first expounded by John Dunning in 1973. It was elaborated in 1988 in his book *Explaining International Production*, in which he explained that:

> The eclectic theory is based on a firm, which will engage in foreign value-adding activities if and when three conditions are satisfied;

> 1. It possesses net ownership advantages *vis-à-vis* firms of other nationalities in serving particular markets. These ownership advantages largely take the form of the possession of intangible assets or of the advantages of common

governance, which are, at least for a period of time, exclusive or specific to the firm possessing them.

2. Assuming condition 1 is satisfied, it must be more beneficial to the enterprise possessing these advantages to use them (or their output) itself rather than to sell or lease them to foreign firms: this it does through an extension of its existing value added chains or the adding of new ones. These advantages are called internalisation advantages.

3. Assuming conditions 1 and 2 are satisfied, it must be in the global interests of the enterprise to utilise these advantages in conjunction with at least some factor inputs (including natural resources) outside its home country: otherwise foreign markets would be served entirely by exports and domestic markets by domestic production. These advantages are termed to local advantages of countries.[18]

Concerning Japanese FDI specifically, he argued that

1. A favourable growth rate (which may be demand or supply led) for the output of the sectors in which Japanese firms have the greatest advantage, both absolutely, and *vis-à-vis* their European and non-European competitors;

2. the advantages offered by an EC relative to a Japanese location (L) as a production base for either creating or adding value to these advantages are becoming more pronounced;

3. the organisational modality for creating and exploiting these ownership (O) advantages favours hierarchies (internalisation, I) rather than market transactions because of increase in market failure and/or falling transaction costs of hierarchies;

4. that given these OLI variables, the strategy of Japanese firms favours production in the EC. One example of such a strategy would be the desire of one MNE to follow an oligopolistic competitor into the EC to protect its own position; another would be to diversify its foreign exchange or political risks.[19]

The eclectic theory suggests that all forms of international production by all countries can be explained with reference to the above conditions. It makes no *a priori* prediction about which countries, industries or enterprises are most likely to engage in FDI. The merit of the eclectic theory, according to Petrochilas is that 'the eclectic theory draws freely from different branches of economics, such as industrial organisation, the theory of property rights and vertical integration, and the theories of location and trade'.[20] However, the eclectic theory has its own limitations. Petrochilas also concludes that 'the eclectic theory is not an operational model capable of explaining all FDI at the firm, industry and country levels, though it represents a potent analytical

Table 1.2 The adoption of Kojima and Dunning FDI theory into Korean, Japanese and US FDI

Extended Dimensions of Kojima's Hypothesis

	Korean FDI	Japanese FDI	US FDI
Market orientation	Export-oriented	Domestic and export oriented	Domestic oriented
Choice of industry	LL group	LH. KL. and KH. groups	KH group
Firm size	Small	Medium	Large
Ownership	Wholly owned and majority owned	Joint ventures and majority owned	Wholly and majority owned

Notes

LL – Labour intensive, low technology
LH – Labour intensive, high technology
KL – Capital intensive, low technology
KH – Capital intensive, high technology

Application of Dunning's Eclectic Paradigm

	Korean FDI	Japanese FDI	US FDI
Firm-specific advantage	Access to market Economy of scale	Access to market Technology Capital Economy of scale	Technology Capital Management skill
Internalisation advantage	To ensure stability of support Transaction cost Economies of vertical integration	Same as Korea	Same as Korea
Locational advantage	Low labour cost Resources	Low labour cost Resources Market	Market resources

Source: Lee, K.C., in Sinhh, D. and Siregar, R.Y. (eds) (1995), *ASEAN and KOREA: Emerging Issues in Trade and Investment Relations*, p. 50.

tool and the best comprehensive efforts yet to the problem'.[21] Dunning himself admitted the eclectic theory's limitation in that 'it may well be that there are some behavioural-related variables of firms which have not been successfully incorporated into the eclectic paradigm'.[22]

In thinking about the application of the eclectic theory to Japanese FDI, it is difficult to relate the theory to the practice of MNEs because it is too general to explain each MNE's behaviour. The diversification of Japanese MNEs' FDI strategy is another reason. The eclectic theory does not mention the role of government. Since the increase of trade friction with developed countries, the direct or indirect role of the Japanese government in business strategy has been strengthened. Moreover, as far as Japanese car MNEs in the UK were concerned, Japanese car makers possessed better technology and had made greater R&D-related investments than British makers. And the UK is not a country to ensure stability of component supply, which Japanese MNEs have needed. Under the eclectic theory, the UK is not a place for which (I) and (L) advantages help to explain Japanese car MNEs' direct investment.

Currency Area Theory

Aliber is the architect of the currency area theory. He reasons as follows:

> FDI could be explained even if the market in advantages were perfect – that the source-country firm might pay a higher price for the same income stream that the host-country firm because the source-country firm had an advantage in the capital market. In the market for debt, the source-country firm may be able to borrow at a lower interest rate than the host-country firm. In the equity market, the shares of the source-country firm may be capitalised at a higher rate than the earnings of the host-country firm. Indeed the distinction between source-country firms and host-firms may be largely in terms of the difference between the capitalisation rate applied by their market to their shares ...
>
> In a world without an exchange risk premium, borrowers would incur the additional costs of denominating debt in a foreign currency, for the difference in interest rates would reflect fully the expected changes in the exchange rate.[23]

Aliber's theory reflects the point that the key attribute of a MNE is not the fact that it engages in foreign production, but that it finances at least part of this production in its home currency. The primary interest in the export of capital in the form of direct investment is seen as a means of financing capital expenditure rather than as a channel by which an enterprise transfers nonfinancial resources between countries, and controls the use of such resources once transferred. He believed that the extraterritorial expansion of firms *per se* raises no issues beyond those addressed by the theory of the domestic firm. Rather, the uniqueness of the MNE is its ability to dominate its geographically-dispersed assets in different currencies, and by so doing, to take advantage of structural or transactional imperfections in international capital and foreign-exchange markets, and particularly the existence of strong and weak currencies.

The merit of the currency area theory is that:

> it predicts well the direction of the post-war expansion of MNEs – in particular the American takeover of Europe in the fifties and sixties, and the Japanese take-over of Southeast Asia in the late sixties and early seventies. The recent decline in the strength of the dollar and the improvement in the D–mark may also explain the downturn in America overseas expansions and the resurgence of German multinationalism.[24]

However, the currency area theory has been criticised by Dunning, who argues that:

> Aliber's theory does not attempt to deal with many of the questions tackled by other scholars and should not therefore be judged by the same criteria. But neither does it have strong claim to be a general theory of FDI. It is difficult to see how it explains the industrial structure of foreign production or the cross-hauling of direct investment between weak and strong currency areas.[25]

Hood and Young have argued that:

> Aliber's theory predicts well the direction of FDI flows in the post-war period: the American invasion of Europe in the fifties and sixties on the strength of the dollar, and recent surge in German FDI as the mark gained on the dollar. Nevertheless, Aliber's model does not explain the continued growth of both American and British investment in spite of the weakness of their respective currencies, the presence of simultaneous investment cross flows, nor the existence of FDI within the same currency area such as the dollar or sterling areas.[26]

Buckley and Casson argue further that:

> While Aliber's theory explains both the existence and the direction of FDI between currency areas, it is unable to explain anything about capital flows within currency areas: the investment of US firms within the dollar area, for example. Neither can it account for cross-investment between currency areas – the fact that US firms

invest in Europe at the same time as European firms invest in the US. Nor does it explain why firms incur substantial costs in setting up factories abroad when they can profit from investor myopia simply by taking over going concerns. Indeed, Aliber fails to explain why holding companies have not been set up with the express purpose of capitalising on investor myopia; it may be that some firms have done just this under the cover of legitimate productive operations but it is certain that there are many MNEs that have not.[27]

The currency area theory has been a much more defensible explanation of Japanese MNEs' FDI since the appreciation of the *yen* in 1985. Many Japanese MNEs said that their new FDI policy toward the EU reflected the appreciation of the *yen* (survey result). However, the new trend of Japanese FDI since 1992, which has moved from the EU market to China and other Asian countries, is not fully explained by the currency area theory.

Since the European single currency movement after the Maastricht Treaty, the currency area theory is becoming an important factor in the FDI decision-making process of Japanese MNEs in the EU. However, as Buckley and Casson argued, the currency area theory explains some MNEs' FDI but not all of them. Japanese car makers' FDI to the EU is partly related to currency area considerations, because the strong *yen* was the one of main reasons to invest overseas. Compared to other Japanese MNEs, such as electronic goods, car manufacturers gain advantages from their relations with local component suppliers. Toyota's recent decision to locate a plant in northern France,[28] is a good example of a currency area-driven decision. Despite this, currency area theory only partly explains Japanese FDI and says nothing about the role of government.

Internalisation Theory

Internalisation theory is essentially directed towards explaining why the cross-border transactions of intermediate products are organised by hierarchies rather than determined by market forces. This was first applied by Hymer in his MIT thesis in 1960, and after that it was put forward in the mid-1970s by a group of Swedish, Canadian, British and US economists. Its basic hypothesis is that multinational hierarchies represent an alternative mechanism for arranging value-added activities across national boundaries to that of the market, and that firms are likely to engage in FDI whenever they perceive that the net benefits of their joint ownership of domestic and foreign activities, and the transactions arising from them, are likely to exceed those offered by external trading relationships. The essential prediction of internalisation theory is that, given a particular distribution of factor endowments, MNE activity will be positively related to the costs of organising cross-border markets in intermediate products.

Internalisation theory is based on three categories of argument:

1. Firms maximise profit in a world of imperfect markets.
2. When markets in intermediate products are imperfect, there is an incentive to bypass them by creating internal markets. This involves bringing under common ownership and control the activities which are linked by the market.
3. Internalisation of markets across national boundaries generates MNEs. ... The analysis highlights the fact that when there are time-lags in business activities their coordination requires future markets as well as spot markets and that, when activities are geographically separated, communication costs are a major constraint on market efficiency.

   Four main groups of factors are relevant to the internalisation decision; (a) Industry-specific factors relating to the nature of the product and the structure of the external market, (b) Region-specific factors relating to the geographical and social characteristics of the regions linked by the market, (c) Nation-specific factors relating to the political and fiscal relations between the nations concerned, and (d) Firm-specific factors which reflect the ability of the management to organised an internal market.[29]

Internalisation theory is primarily concerned with identifying the situation in which the markets for intermediate products are likely to be internalised, and hence those in which firms own and control value-adding activities outside their natural boundaries. Like earlier attempts to explain the growth of domestic firms, it seeks to explain the internalisation (horizontal and vertical integration of value-added activities) in terms of the relative costs and benefits of this form or organisation relative to market transactions. Certain types of transactions between certain types of buyers and sellers incur higher costs than others. Hierarchical organisational costs are also likely to be industry, country and firm specific. From that point of view, internalisation theory may be considered a general theory in so far it is able to predict the situation in which firms choose to internalise foreign markets.

However, the internalisation theory has its own limitations, in that:

The internalisation theory can not explain clearly the motives for internalisation. It explains that MNEs do bypass the market in intermediate products, through FDI. But, it is not certain that the motive for internalisation is the external market's inefficiency in terms of relatively high transaction costs and longer time lags or anything else. And also, the empirical evidence regarding the internalisation hypothesis is not very strong. Buckley and Casson have shown that the process of internalisation is concentrated in industries with a relatively high incidence of R&D expenditure, but this is a conclusion reached by many other studies.[30]

The internalisation theory can be used to explain the Rover and Honda collaboration in the 1980s, which is one of the two case studies in this thesis. Theoretically, the Rover and Honda collaboration exemplified the 'bypass' strategy[31] from Honda's side. Also, from Rover's point of view, the collaboration permitted improvement in the company's weak design capability and compensation for its lack of human management skills. However, collaboration and bypass are not traditional strategies for MNEs, and the Nissan investment, the other case study, is evidently not explained by internalisation theory.

An Alternative Model of Japanese Foreign Direct Investment in Europe

As discussed above, the FDI patterns of Japanese car MNEs in the EU are not easily explained fully by any of the leading theories now current. As an alternative model for Japanese car industries in the EU, a '*push and pull factors model*' is suggested here. Before analysing this model, we need to describe the general approach of Japanese FDI.

As far as Japanese FDI is concerned, there are three distinct phases: before 1975, the decade 1975–85 and since 1985. Before 1975, Japanese FDI was fully explained by the Kojima-Ozawa theory, in that it took particular account of the lack of natural resources in Japan. Japan's FDI at that stage was mainly directed to the US, South America, especially Brazil for its natural resources, and the Middle East for its oil. For example, in 1974, only about 10 per cent of the accumulated total of Japan's FDI was in the EU, in contrast to approximately 38 per cent in the US. Moreover, most FDI in the EU was in service sectors such as commerce, finance, and insurance, and those in manufacturing accounted for only 9.8 per cent at that time. The main motivation of Japanese FDI in the EU at that stage was clearly to secure a beachhead in the growing markets of industrialised European economies. Practically all Japanese FDI in the EU was designed either to promote exports or to reinforce trade competitiveness with partial local manufacturing if necessary. The role of the Japanese government at this time was to promote exports. Before 1975, the general trend of the Japanese FDI was towards trading rather than investment.

The Kojima-Ozawa theory was challenged after 1975 by the fact that the investment patterns of major Japanese MNEs came more and more to mirror those of their US counterparts. Between 1975 and 1985, increasing trade friction with the USA and the economic crisis in the Latin America, led the Japanese government to urge the diversification of Japanese FDI.

Japanese FDI in the EU, especially after 1980, attracted criticism from the European Commission, which protested that:

- Japanese enterprises are being established mostly in tertiary industries in order to sell Japanese products or to finance Japanese producers, not in order to produce in Europe.
- The share of local procurement is considerably lower than the Commission wishes. The often mentioned differences in the quality of locally produced parts is nothing but an excuse.
- Transfer of technology from Japan to the EC is insufficient, as seen from Japan's deficit balance of technology.
- All in all, Japanese investment in the EC is threatening European industries more than contributing to prosperity, employment and technological development in Europe.[32]

The Plaza Agreement of 1985 was another turning point in the history of Japanese FDI. It came about because of an international currency crisis (the undervaluation of the *yen*) and trade friction between Japan and other developed countries. The Group of Seven agreed to pursue realignments of the major exchange rates. There was subsequent appreciation of the *yen* against the dollar and to a lesser extent against the European currencies. The strong *yen* and pressure from the Japanese government induced MNEs to set up their affiliates in overseas areas, in a process described as 'globalisation'. Japanese government policy toward the EU, and that of MNEs, have been summarised under three headings (survey result):

i) There was a growth in costs associated with exporting from Japan, which was the result of the appreciation of the *yen* after the Plaza Agreement. Within two years Japanese MNEs saw the value of the *yen* double against the US dollar. The other reasons within Japan were increasing labour costs and land costs. Compared to the other OECD countries, Japan had had relatively low labour costs. Despite the increase in the cost of wages, Japanese workers received little welfare benefit from the government. Hence, the

Japanese government imposed lower taxation for welfare purposes compared to the other OECD countries, and Japanese industry was able to use its money instead to restructure and strengthen manufacturing sectors.

ii) Strong protectionist tendencies emerged in the EU. The Single Market manifested itself a number of ways including voluntary export restraint (VERs) agreements, formal quotas and tariffs toward some manufactured items originating outside the EU, especially cars. Moreover, Japanese products made in Japanese plants within the EU were counted as 'Japanese made' unless certain local content levels (usually 60 per cent to 70 per cent) were achieved. To deal with this situation, Japanese MNEs sought to establish themselves in member countries which could protect Japanese MNEs' business more strongly within the EU. For this, Japanese MNEs needed to exploit direct links between the Japanese government and the governments of member countries in order to support their FDI projects. The level of interest expressed by host countries' governments – arising from their 'pull factors' – were a major consideration in MNEs' decision-making. Globalisation was the only way to solve the chronic problem of trade friction, which was felt both by Japanese government and by the MNEs.

iii) For effective market penetration in the Single Market, Japanese companies needed to manufacture their goods in the areas where they were to be sold. This has been exemplified by the globalization or global localisation policy of Japanese MNEs. Between 1985 and 1990, the tendency was even stronger than before. The movement toward protective economic blocs, which was initiated by the US after the oil crisis of the 1970s, was accelerated and the Japanese government had to change its policy towards more proactive measures to deal with this tendency.

As far as the Japanese car-makers' FDI was concerned, the rationale for manufacturing in the EU is partly influenced by the firm-specific advantage discussed in the eclectic theory. Japanese car MNEs suffered more severe restrictions than they faced in the US market, largely because the single regulatory framework of the United States was easier to handle than the multiplicity of export restrictions against Japanese cars in the EU.

These restrictions are a good example of the nature of government direct intervention in car manufacturing. At that time Germany was the largest market, with over 40 per cent of total Japanese exports to the EU. The UK was second with 25 per cent. In contrast, the other three large EU countries (France, Italy, and Spain) together took less than 10 per cent of Japanese car exports.

Table 1.3   Restrictions on Japanese car exports to the EU, 1987

Italy	5,000 units annually
France	Restricted to 3% (bilateral)
UK	11% 'Gentleman's agreement'
Germany	No formal restrictions
Spain	0% limit without local assembly
Greece	No limit but assembly required
Portugal	Local assembly conditions
Belgium, Netherlands, Denmark, Ireland	No limit

Source: Nomura Research Institute (1988), p. 25.

Table 1.4   Shares of the European car market by producer

	Volume (thousands)	Share (%)
VW	1,741	15.2
Fiat	1,632	14.2
Peugeot	1,488	13.0
GM	1,361	11.9
Ford	1,333	11.6
Renault	1,126	9.8
Mercedes-Benz	370	3.2
Rover	343	3.0
Nissan	334	2.9
BMW	313	2.7
Toyota	310	2.7
Mazda	241	2.1
Volvo	204	1.8
Mitsubishi	151	1.3
Honda	137	1.2
Total Japanese	1,342	11.7

Source: *Financial Times* (1990), 19 November.

The distribution of market share shows the importance of locational decision making in the investment strategy of Japanese companies. Michael argued that:

FDI was the last stage of a process that began with exports, which meant that FDI would eventually substitute for exports. Firms start to enter into a foreign market with exports. But the firms may find if necessary to invest there when they face or fear tariff or non-tariff barriers from the foreign market or when their export volume reaches a critical size.[33]

The problems which Japanese car makers faced, explain why Japanese car makers needed new business tactics. The policy adopted was named 'globalisation', and came about because of 'pull factors' originating within EU countries and 'push factors' originating largely from Japanese government through the agency of MITI.

The 'pull factors' in the EU were based on a prolonged period of high unemployment throughout Europe after the mid-1970s. Governments were very anxious to reduce public (welfare) spending. As far as the manufacturing sector was concerned, the policy of attracting inward FDI was regarded as a means of cutting the Gordian knot. Since the mid-1980s, these 'pull factors' within Western European countries towards attracting East Asian FDI have been particularly prominent.

The results of a survey of Japanese MNEs in the EU, and two interviews with managers of Japanese car makers in the EU showed, that the major motive for moving into the EU was to avoid the protectionism which they expected to follow from market integration. The emerging Single Market was a principal reason for Japanese car makers to invest in the EU countries. On the other hand the 'pull factors', or external factor, from EU member countries was their desire to revive their de-industrialised manufacturing sectors. The UK and Spain were prominent in taking this position.

The 'push factors' were internal to Japan. The Japanese government, since 1985, had tried to avoid the political costs of an overlarge trade surplus. The Plaza agreement, in effect, forced Japanese car makers to move out of Japan. Increasing labour costs and the appreciation of the *yen*, but most of all the national antagonism towards Japanese goods in Europe pushed Japanese car manufacturers to 'globalise' by setting up their own affiliates in Europe.

'Push and pull factors' have one common factor: government. Strong relationships between MNEs and government have been quite common since the start of the globalisation process. During the emerging Single Market process, the role of government in business policy-making was strengthened. Owing to the political costs of decline in the manufacturing sector, each country within the EU tried to attract inward FDI in manufacturing sectors, using fiscal incentives from central government, government subsidy (often from local government), and direct negotiation with investing countries' governments. Generally speaking, some EU member countries have been significantly more successful than others. The author's survey has shown that the varying role of government is the determining factor in Japanese MNEs' final decision making. For that reason, this thesis has adopted a 'push and pull factors' paradigm to describe the FDI of Japanese car makers in the EU. (Figure 1.1)

Although there is a wealth of theory about Japanese FDI in developed countries, there have been few attempts to explain the role of government in this internationalized business process. During the period of emerging trade protection since the early 1980s, nonmember countries have faced the conundrum of how to invade 'Fortress Europe'. Japanese MNEs have had to secure access to the EU market. Their government has been a key player, just as it had been in the Japanese industrialization process. In this study, industrial policy and the relations between government and industry are surveyed in four major EU member countries. The car industry has been taken as sample case in an effort to understand each government's industrial policy and the reaction of the European Commission as a regulator. Within EU countries, it is a politically sensitive sector, partly because of its importance to objective national economies, and partly because of public attitudes towards the car industry as a symbol of national pride. The UK is the only country in the EU to have adopted open competition in the national market for cars. Unlike other EU countries, the UK attracted foreign investment in the 1980s in order to restructure its manufacturing base, combining this with a highly politicized representation of a flexible labour market, in which union strength was diminished by government action. Out of political expediency, the UK government invited Japanese MNEs into the UK as industrial troubleshooters. Japanese MNEs invested in the UK as either greenfield investors or in joint ventures with UK companies. For this study, Nissan's greenfield investment in Sunderland and the Honda-Rover joint investment at Swindon have been chosen as examples for closer investigation.

Notes

1   Dunning, J. (1993), *MNEs and Global Economy*, p. 3.
2   In this discussion 'developing countries' is taken to mean the Newly Industrialised Countries (NICs) such as Taiwan, Korea, Malaysia, Singapore.
3   Mr Yashhiro Shiraki: interview.
4   Dienst, A. (1989), 'Europe Inc.', *Journal of Japanese Trade and Industry*, No. 2, March and April.

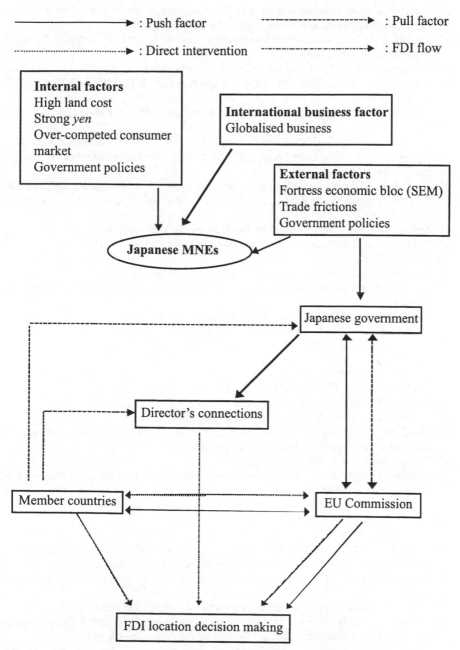

Figure 1.1   Push and pull factor model of Japanese FDI in Europe

Source: Derived by the author on the basis of original research.

5	'*Eikokubyo*' refers to the economics of decline and Great Power decadence that is showed by industrial problems, low productivity and economic rigidities.

6	Stewart, T. (1994), 'Trade Related Investment Measures', in *The GATT Uruguay Round: A Negotiating History*, p. 2003.

7	Yoshitomi, M. (ed.) (1991), *Japanese Direct Investment in Europe*, p. 2.

8	Ragazzi, G. (1973), 'Theories of the Determinants of DFI', *IMF Staff Papers*, 20, pp. 484–5, p. 488.

9	Thomsen, S. and Nicolaides, P. (1992), *The Evolution of Japanese Direct Investment in Europe*, p. 37.

10	Nurkse, R. (1961), *Equilibrium and Growth in the World Economy: Economic Essay*.

11	Agarwal, J.P. (1980), 'Determinants of FDI: A Survey', *Wettwirtschaftliches Archive*, 16, pp. 739–40.

12	Giddy, I.H. and Young, S. (1982), 'Conventional Theory and Unconventional Multinationals: Do New Forms of MNEs Require New Theories?', in Rugman, A. (ed.), *New Theories of the MNE*, pp. 65–6.

13	Kojima, K. (1977), *Japan and a New World Economic Order*, pp. 75–6.

14	Dunning, J.H. (1988), *Explaining International Production*, pp. 50–51.

15	Giddy and Young (1983), p. 72.

16	Petrochilas, G.A. (1989), *FDI and the Development Process*, p. 21.

17	It meant efficient use of resources, low inventories, and just-in-time production and delivery practices.

18	Dunning, J.H. (1988), *Explaining International Production*, p. 26.

19	Burgenmeier, B. and Mucchielli, J.L. (1991), *Multinationals and Europe 1992*, p. 159.

20	Petrochilas, G.A. (1989), p. 22.

21	Ibid., p. 23.

22	Dunning, J.H. (1988), p. 49.

23	Dunning J.H. (ed.) (1971), *The MNE*, pp. 51–2.

24	Buckley, P.J. and Casson, M. (1991), *The Future of the MNE*, p. 71.

25	Dunning, J.H. (1993), *MNEs and the Global Economy*, p. 74.

26	Hood, N. and Young, S. (1980), *European Development Strategies of US-owned Manufacturing Companies Located in Scotland*, p. 51.

27	Buckley and Casson (1991), pp. 71–2.

28	Toyota new factory for small car in the EU will be built in France, because of the delay of UK government's over the European single currency. At the initial strategy of Toyota UK was an extension of the Toyota plant at Burnaston, Derbyshire.

29	Buckley and Casson (1991), pp. 33–4.

30	Agarwal (1980), p. 754.

31	When Japanese MNE faced difficulties owing to national protection or government regulation, they turned their market penetration policy to more open countries. For example, Japanese car turned their policy from France or Italy to Holland or Belgium during the 1980s.

32	Trevor, M. (ed.) (1987), *The Internationalisation of Japanese Business*, p. 71.

33	Michael, T. (1973). 'Cross-Country Analysis of the Determinant of US Direct Foreign Investment in Manufacturing in Less-Developed Countries', thesis, p. 21.

Chapter 2

Japanese Industrial Policy and Foreign Direct Investment in Europe

Apart from a brief decline in the early 1980s, the foreign direct investment of OECD countries has increased dramatically. Between 1986 and 1990, the amount of global FDI grew at an annual rate of 24 per cent, rising from US$78 to US$184 billion.[1] Most FDI still originates from the OECD countries. In 1990, Japan, the US, Germany, France, and the UK were responsible for 69 per cent of the value of global FDI outflows. However, motivated by concerns with rising labour costs, environmental costs, and protectionism, some newly industrialised countries (NICs) have also begun to make more direct investment abroad. For example, Taiwan made US$12 billion of foreign direct investment in 1989–90, and Korea made US$ 1.3 billion in these two years and has increased its rate of investment in the EU market since 1992. This pattern reflects several recent and ongoing trends:

> First, rising FDI has signified the increasing importance of intra-firm trade – that is, transactions among the subsidiaries of the same MNEs – in world commerce. It has tended to displace arm's-length transactions, and thus to create comparative advantages due to domestic sourcing, economies of scale, transfer pricing, and 'captive' markets ...
>
> Second, the ongoing processes of globalisation[2] as well as regionalisation of national economies tend to spur FDI. The diffusion of production techniques, the standardisation of product designs, the easing of transport and communication barriers, and the conventions of subcontracting and local sourcing have facilitated this investment, especially of the export-oriented kind. At the same time, shifts pointing to possible regional trading blocs in Western Europe and North America have raised the prospects of protectionism, and the consequent fears of being excluded from lucrative foreign markets have fuelled defensive investment of the tariff-leaping kind.[3]

The main question addressed in this chapter is the approach of the Japanese government to the FDI policies of Japanese MNEs. It consists of an overview of the Japanese FDI policy since 1980, a study of Japanese industrial policy, and an examination of the decision-makers within Japanese government.

Japanese FDI and Europe

Japanese FDI since 1980

FDI is the main constituent of the globalisation strategies of Japanese MNEs. For this reason, we have to define 'globalisation' in Japanese business. Two leading businessmen who have globalised their business at the early stage indicated their own definitions. Mr Akio Morita of Sony stated in 1995 that 'The best way for Japan to meet its responsibilities as a leader of in the free world is to ensure better management of external relations through internationalisation of Japanese society',[4] while the president of Matsushita Electric, Mr Toshihiko Yamashita, said in 1986 that:

> Japanese corporations can no longer just conduct business in Japan, among themselves. Given their huge export volumes and their heavy dependence on foreign markets, companies that fail to follow international norms are bound to run into problems. Matsushita know full well that local production in the US is not going to be easy … But the issue at stake here is something bigger. Unless Japanese corporations like ours can succeed in US under the same conditions as American companies, we will never graduate from the level of Japanese business playing by special Japanese rules. Until we can pull this off, our companies will never truly be international.[5]

The transformation of Japanese business in this direction stimulated FDI policy, the gross value of which had been less than $1 billion until 1965. During the five years from 1965 to 1970 FDI value reached $3.6 billion and it grew even more explosively through the early 1970s. After the first oil shock, Japanese industries made strenuous efforts to rationalise and managed to avoid raising export prices despite to the appreciation of the *yen*.

After the early 1980s, many Japanese industries brought to a close the long period of adjustment, characterised by a search for stability, that had continued since the oil shock and ushered in an entirely new period. In addition, when it was clear that the high-valued *yen* had become a permanent feature of the Japanese economy many industries transferred their production bases overseas.

> The greening of Japanese companies in the international arena has advanced to the stage of all-out production operations overseas. And the companies that are producing overseas find themselves naturally drawn into much closer relationships with the host countries in which they operate, economically, socially, and otherwise.

In the process of transferring technology and production system, and even management methods, it will be necessary for Japanese corporations to become more international and to break away from rigid Japanese ways of the past.[6]

When business globalised, there were increasing demands from business groups for government support for their business strategy. Accidentally or not, the Plaza Agreement turned a trend into a rush. After the Plaza Agreement,[7] the Japanese Ministry of Finance (MOF) pursued expansionary monetary and fiscal policies, which sharply reduced interest rates and set stock, land, and real estate prices soaring and domestic demand booming. While MOF rearranged domestic policies, the Ministry of International Trade and Industry (MITI) sought to strengthen the international position of Japanese business.

Initially, MITI gave up its right to intervene in private business and allowed companies to invest without government regulation. For private business, mainly the automobile, electronics, and precision machinery industries, the economic logic of economic regionalism encouraged foreign investment. From the point of view of international trade, the strategy of manufacturing abroad and re-importing to Japan tended to decrease trade friction between the developed countries and Japan. Moreover it has been very profitable for Japanese business. As business globalised, FDI was vital for the government because it decreased trade friction, and for business because it permitted greater market penetration. The difference between the FDI of Japanese MNEs and that of other developed countries is clear:

> Japanese FDI is a mixture of politics and economics. When they make their FDI programmes, *ad hoc* meetings take place between the president of the company, the *keiretsu*'s banker, and a member of government. Even Honda, which is regarded as a 'nonpolitical' group among Japanese MNEs, has close relations with the Ministry of Foreign Affairs.[8]

A critical development in December 1980 was the amendment of the Foreign Exchange Control Law, which shifted the consideration of FDI projects by the Ministry of Finance from an approval-based system to a notification-based one. Within one year of the change, Japanese FDI jumped from an annual average of $4 billion for the fiscal year 1978–80 period to $8.9 billion in fiscal year 1981.

An Industrial Structure Council was set up in December 1981 as an advisory body under MITI. In April 1982, a subcommittee released an interim report which was expected to provoke debate toward the building of a national consensus.

The report emphasised the importance of a comprehensive approach encompassing economic, diplomatic, cultural, and educational means and, *inter alia*, made the following recommendations:

1. Japan should remove the remaining trade and investment barriers as much as possible, further liberalise its domestic financial institutions, and take initiatives to strengthen and broaden the GATT provisions as instrument of promoting free world trade.
2. High technology should be the engine to boost and revitalise the now-stagnant world economy. To this end, the fruits of R&D in high technology need to be internationally shared instead of monopolised by each nation. Japan should encourage, and actively participate in, joint international high-technology research with other advanced countries …
3. The government should continue to play a developmental and cooperative role *vis-à-vis* private business in generating and disseminating new technologies as well as in facilitating structural transformation of the nation's industries.[9]

It is clear from a comparison of economic policy development and the progress of Japanese FDI that government had a key role. The pattern of Japanese FDI can be divided into five broad phases.

On this scheme, the trend in Japan's FDI after World War II is marked by major differences in the factors behind investment in each decade. In the 1950s, Japanese FDI was extremely limited due to the trade deficit. Even in the 1960s, a large proportion of the FDI was in Asia for resource exploitation. There was very little FDI in manufacturing or service sectors. Major projects included the development of oil in Northern Sumatra in Indonesia up to the early 1960s, the iron ore of the Philippines and Malaysia, and the natural gas of Brunei in 1968. FDI, during the 1960s, was characterised by a prevalence of investment of a resource-development type in the developing countries, mainly in Asia, and the small size of the investments per project.

Throughout the 1970s, Japan became stronger in international competitiveness and began to enjoy a steady trade and current accounts surplus. From 1969 to 1972, the government liberalised FDI in four separate stages and came out with other measures to ease FDI such as lowering the interest rates on funding by the Export–Import (EXIM) Bank of Japan. As a result, Japan's FDI surged, starting with a first wave around 1972 with money flooding into the textile and electrical machinery industries of Asia. During this period, trade friction broke out between the US and Japan and forced the establishment of voluntary export restraints (VERs) in the fields of ferrous metals, colour TVs, and machine tools. It caused acceleration in FDI in the US in the late

Table 2.1   The factors and growth of the Japanese FDI since the 1950s

1950s to 1960s
–   Natural resource development in South East Asia
–   Government projects of industrialisation focused on import substitution
–   Trade friction with US about textile products

1970s
–   Foreign market expansion strategies e.g. export drive policy based on R&D
     intensive, assembly-based, higher value-added goods
–   Trade friction over ferrous metals, colour TVs, machine tools

1980s
–   Foreign market expansion strategies diversified from the US to the EU
–   First appreciation of the *yen*
     MITI guided the strengthening of cost competitiveness and the expansion of
     the production base in Asia
–   Trade friction in automobiles and VTRs

The early 1990s
–   Second revaluation of the *yen*
     MNEs struggled to reduce cost and increase intracompany trade
–   Strengthening of the world economic bloc tendency (the EU, AFTA and
     NAFTA)
–   Japanese investment draws back from USA and EU and moves towards
     China and SE Asia

Source: Derived by the author on the basis of JETRO reports, various years.

Table 2.2   Japanese FDI between 1981 to 1991

Area	Manufacturing	Non-manufacturing	Total (US$)*
Asia	44.2%	55.8%	52,300 million
North America	29.8%	70.2%	171,424 million
Latin America	10.0%	90.0%	42,547 million
EU	24.1%	75.9%	76,111 million
Rest World	11.8%	88.2%	29,634 million
Total			372,016 million

Note: * – cumulative amount.

Source: Derived by the author on the basis of JETRO reports, various years.

1970s. In 1972, Japanese FDI rose to US$2.3 billion, which was 2.7 times the level of the year before. This was followed by a steady growth in FDI in all regions. From 1978 on, there was major growth in FDI in the US, primarily in the commercial sectors so the overall value of FDI expanded considerably. This was regarded as the 'second wave' of Japanese FDI. This second wave was characterised by a shift from a traditional 'Japanese' style of FDI focused on the export drive to a 'US style', in which the emphasis was on localisation of production, though in Japan, unlike the US, the government took an important part in business policy.

In the early 1980s, Japan's trade surplus swelled even further and new frictions arose over cars, VTRs and so on. The pace of FDI continued to accelerate as it had in the late 1970s. By region, FDI in the industrialised countries of the Western Europe rose in significance; and the financing and insurance and the commercial sectors gained in prominence by comparison with manufacturing and the primary sector. In the US, Honda began manufacturing cars in Marysville, Ohio in 1982, Nissan in Smyrna, Tennessee in 1983, and Toyota in Torrance, California in 1984. Japanese car makers' FDI in the US coincided with increasing concerns about dumping of Japanese cars in the US market. This showed how Japanese business style changed under increasing pressure from host countries: the Japanese government guided Japanese companies towards establishing their affiliates in host regions. The same thing happened in the EU market.

FDI in the EU[10] also grew in the 1980s, with particular large increases seen in the manufacturing sector in the latter half of the decade. Preparations for the Single European Market (SEM), were accompanied by a heated debate on what the external trade barriers surrounding the SEM would be. 'Fortress Europe' stemmed in large part from the concerns felt by EU members about Japanese imports. As a result, the US and EU accounted for 70 per cent of Japan's FDI in 1989.

> One of the strongest controls exercised by government over business was financial tightness. The [Plaza] Agreement revealed that there is a limit to government's ability to use financial policy to control private business. While the MOF relinquished their involvement through financial policy, MITI developed specific FDI policies for selected industries. After that, the Japanese government's policy toward MNEs moved from direct involvement to private advice. The invisible *ad hoc* meeting between government and senior directors is getting more important. The power of directors in Japanese MNEs was the most important factor in their decision-making about FDI, but government intervened strongly at an informal level.[11]

The key point of the late 1980s was that trade friction and the appreciation of the *yen* spurred FDI, which was regarded as the 'third wave'. This not only held true for the manufacturing sectors, but also had implications in the financial sector and even real estate. The ability of Japan to export capital, engendered by its booming economy and huge trade surplus, added fuel to this.

The other particular trend of the period after 1985 was rather 'global localisation' than 'globalisation'.[12] 'Globalisation' could be seen as a first stage in Japanese foreign manufacturing investment, where Japanese manufacturers set up manufacturing operations overseas in a relatively basic form, where the investments are essentially final assembly operations closely controlled by the parents in Japan and where few components are sourced locally and little R&D are carried out. 'Global localisation' can be seen as the next stage of the FMI process where the investment deepens and Japanese manufacturers attempt to become insiders in foreign markets, as US companies such as Ford, 3M and IBM have done in Europe. Global localisation is essentially a market driven policy, and the result of trade friction. Japanese MNEs are increasingly seeing a need to produce in the markets that they are selling in, and the only effective way to complete is by following a global localisation strategy and opting for full manufacture. In this way, these companies can be flexible to meet local market demands without having to wait for months for orders to appear from Japan or to wait for design changes from the corporate R&D centres based in Japan.

Compared to globalization, global localisation cannot be controlled by a company alone, because it depends on direct assistance from the host country. Hence, Japanese companies had to cooperate with their own government to succeed in negotiations with host governments. The leading global localisation MNEs are all companies which were excluded from MITI's manufacturing restructuring process during the late 1960s, such as Honda and Sony.[13] Hence, the global localisation of these manufacturers was a reasonable response to their difficulties at home. Companies with large and secure shares of the domestic market undertook globalisation projects; companies with difficulties at home were more likely to attempt global localisation. However, there have been no obvious differences of approach by the Japanese government towards globalisation or global localisation projects: the nature of interaction between government and company has been the same.

In the early 1990s, Japan was hit hard by the collapse of its inflated real estate and stock markets. FDI in the US, particularly, suffered. FDI in the EU also shrank, but some was made in anticipation of the SEM in 1992 so the decline was not as great in the US. In Asia, FDI in ASEAN (Thailand, Malaysia, Philippines and Indonesia), in particular increased and remained strong as a whole. This increased production in East Asia was designed to offset the decline in competitiveness caused by the appreciation of the *yen*. The expansion of production in East Asia also led to growth in exports and imports between East Asian subsidiaries and their Japanese parent firms. FDI in China benefited from the expansion of the Chinese domestic market from around 1991 and accelerated rapidly thereafter. In 1993, the *yen* once again began rising against the dollar; and FDI as a whole increased, though slightly, in 1993 and 1994 despite the sluggish state of domestic business. A characteristic of Japanese FDI since 1993 has been its different motivation. FDI is not being made to deal with trade friction or increase the ability to export capital, but is being made more in order to circumvent higher costs in production in Japan caused by the appreciation of the *yen*. Further, it is being made to deal with the rise of regional economic alliances such as AFTA, NAFTA and the EU.

One of the interesting points about Japanese MNE's FDI policy is that the oligopolistic nature of industries such as car manufacturers, electronic goods, and computer and office equipment have been a sufficient motive for MNEs to launch FDI projects although the companies were not as experienced as their American counterparts in operating manufacturing facilities throughout the world.

The FDI strategies of Japanese MNEs in the 1990s have been increasingly oriented toward reducing costs through shifting operations overseas and international procurement and moving with the flow of liberalisation in regional economic alliances, and the role of the Japanese government has been reduced.

Japanese FDI towards the EU

Japanese business in the EU ran into difficulty in the early 1980s. When EU delegates met Japanese businessmen in Tokyo in 1981, they demanded that Japan should decide immediately to stem the flood of its exports to the EU. An eight-point programme was agreed.

> The programme includes the monitoring of imports from Japan of cars, colour TV sets and picture tubes and machine tools. This surveillance would require the Common Market countries to pool their information on a monthly basis instead of once every six months as formerly, and monitoring may be extended to other products.[14]

Table 2.3   Devolution of responsibility to 'globalised' affiliates by Japanese MNEs

Scale 1–5 MNEs 1986	1978	1985	1990*	1995**	Western
Planning	3.7	4.0	4.2	4.4	4.6
Organisation	2.6	2.6	3.3	4.0	4.2
Logistics	2.3	2.3	2.6	2.6	5.0
Status of expatriates	3.7	3.6	4.5	4.3	5.0
Promotion of locals	1.6	2.3	2.6	2.6	4.2
Marketing	2.8	2.8	3.0	3.5	2.8
R&D	2.7	2.7	3.0	3.0	2.8
Finance	2.6	2.5	3.0	3.0	3.7

Note: Unit: MNEs are scored (somewhat subjectively) on a scale from 1–5, with 5 indicating total local control and 1 indicating total headquarters control.

Sources: M. Trevor (1987); *interview with Malcom Trevor 1997; **author survey.

Moreover, there were dramatic changes in the methods of the EU Commission, in that rather than accepting voluntary price restraint agreements from Japanese industries, the Commission increasingly imposed protectionist antidumping duties on goods which it alleged were being dumped on the EU market, although the Japanese government repeatedly objected to the Commission's way of ascertaining whether such dumping was taking place.

Despite an apparently unified reaction to Japanese market penetration, the EU Commission and the member states failed to harmonise their policies, for political reasons.

> Although the Community member countries were often divided between 'natural protectionists' (France and Italy) and 'the ideological free traders' (West Germany and the UK), the Community itself had 'introduced an overtly political element into antidumping actions'.[15]

Four major motives for Japanese FDI in the EU were now emerging. First, the appreciation of the *yen* reduced the cost advantage of Japanese goods. Second, the several protectionist measures threatened Japanese market penetration. Third, despite increasing intra-trade between member countries, and thus stronger competition from European manufacturers, the emerging

SEM was big enough to be worth penetrating. Fourth, the Japanese government needed to show that Japanese companies were manufacturing in Europe rather than exporting Japanese-made goods. It was clearly shown in a JETRO survey that during the 1980s, about a third of the FDI in the EU was in electronics. Except for the car industry, the electronics industry showed the largest rate of local employment, which was eagerly expected by EU member countries.

Table 2.4   Motives for Japanese manufacturing investment in the EU

Number of responses

Part of globalisation strategy	235
Shift from exports to local production to meet increased demand	128
Meet consumers' needs	94
Benefit from growth from 1992	75
Concern about protectionism	60
Sell to Japanese MNEs in Europe	58
Avoid quantitative restrictions	53
Investment incentives	42
Carry out R&D	40
Anticipation of Eastern Europe	35
Avoid infringement of antidumping regulations	32
Avoid exchange rate risk	31
Reduce production costs	27

Source: JETRO (1991)

From this part of the investigation there is no single, clear explanation for the rapid growth of Japanese FDI. But if attention is turned to considerations about the country, a clearer picture emerges. The breakdown of responses showed the close relationship between the level of exports to a particular country and the rate of FDI. This strongly suggests that a major reason to invest was export replacement policy.

A detailed breakdown of location choices in the EU failed to show a clear pattern of incentives for the Japanese investors.

From the MNEs' viewpoint, though, the price index showed clear differences between FDI industries and the others. The volume of Japanese FDI received by different countries within the EU varied significantly. The UK has been the single largest recipient, followed by the Netherlands and

Table 2.5   The distribution of Japanese FDI and exports

Share of each country in the EU

	FDI (%)*	Exports (%)
UK	27	23
France	18	12
Germany	15	31
Spain	9	6
Italy	7	7
Holland	6	9
BLEU	6	7
Ireland	4	2
Portugal	2	2

*   Manufacturing establishments based on JETRO Survey.

Source: JETRO (1991).

Table 2.6   Motives for the inward investment countries

	Market size	English	Labour costs	Location	Worker's skills
UK	6	15	8	12	11
France	13	3	4	14	10
Germany	16	4	0	11	12
Holland	2	21	0	26	8
Belgium	2	15	2	19	15
Ireland	0	27	7	4	20
Spain	17	3	14	9	9
Italy	24	3	7	7	7
Portugal	0	5	35	10	10
Europe (average)	9	11	6	12	11

Notes: Per cent of companies mentioning each factor for each country.

Source: JETRO (1991).

Luxembourg in terms of all investments. When only manufacturing investment is considered, four countries are significantly represented: the UK, Germany, France and Spain. The level of market share and of FDI tended to coincide.

While FDI in Spain was dominated by joint venture investment, owing to protectionist legislation, greenfield investment has been major method of entry into the rest of the EU. Joint ventures have been suitable for the strategies of smaller Japanese companies. In particular, the first or second tier Japanese car component industries set up joint ventures with indigenous component makers. Acquisitions by Japanese MNEs were quite unusual, because of actual or feared local hostility to foreign takeovers.

A survey by the Toto Keizai Inc., JETRO, and EXIM Bank elucidated the common features of Japanese FDI in the EU:

i) There was a broad range of motivations for establishing operations in the EC, with the primary ones being: 'Preservation and/or expansion of market share in the host country', 'Building an international production and distribution network', 'Transition from export to local production' and 'Development of products adapted to the local market'.

ii) Broken down by country, the greatest number of Japanese firms have entered the UK, Germany, and France. A breakdown by industry reveals that the leaders were electrical machinery, general machinery and chemical products manufacturers, and that they were concentrated in the UK and Germany.

iii) The reasons for establishing a base in the EC countries were dominated by: 'Good geographic conditions for distribution', 'Existence of a viable infrastructure', 'Ability to hire English speaking managers' and 'Comparative quality of local workers when compared with other nations,' etc.

iv) A look at specific measures of Japanese firms to cope with the single EU market reveals that localisation of the entire range of production, management, and R&D formed the basis for their approach to the single EC market. Through this spectrum of activities Japanese firms have been attempting to make themselves Europeanised.[16]

In contrast to US and European MNEs' FDI, which has historically been directed at the developing world, Japanese companies were investing in advanced economies, many of whom already had indigenous makers in the sectors which the Japanese were entering, such as car, electric and chemical industries. The very variety of responses from the indigenous industries made any prediction of Japanese impact difficult. On the EU side, while the EU benefited enormously from the learning experience of having the Japanese industrial experience, many Japanese goods were profoundly threatening to existing EU industrial structures. Without substantial R&D facilities, it was feared that the future of EU would be as a warehouse for Japanese manufacturers. According to the Mitsubishi Research Institute survey in 1991, there was a clear pattern that:

> FDI by Japanese firms in Europe started in sales, followed gradually in the manufacturing area. That is, the number of newly-established sales facilities peaked in the early 1960s but gradually decreased after the late 1970s, whereas direct investments in manufacturing started in the early 1960s and then accelerated in the 1980s. Investment in R&D facilities started in the late 1970s, but the number so far remained negligible.[17]

The challenge for the EU was to find policies, which would allow key European industries to learn from the Japanese technologies without being annihilated in the process. Hence, the governments of EU member states had to have open competition policies toward Japanese investment, lest the companies should turn away from Europe. The intervention of the Japanese government was demanded by MNEs' because they needed the agreement of these host governments before their decision-making could be completed.

MITI and Business Groups in Japan

There are many arguable explanations of Japan's successful economic and industrial performance. First, it has been said that the success of Japan is culturally-determined; crudely, that the Japanese are different. Such explanations emphasise, *inter alia*, Japan's historical isolation from the West, ethnic homogeneity, Confucian ethics and ideology, and the absence of religious and class divisions. Secondly, other explanations emphasise 'unique' institutional arrangements which national cultural characteristics have helped to evolve. Among those identified are enterprise unions, lifetime employment, the 'dual economy', management-labour relations, and such characteristics of industrial organisation as cartels and monopolies, weak antitrust legislation, and discriminatory practices. A third set of explanations, drawing upon elements of both, emphasises the close, often collusive, relationship between governments, bureaucracy, and private industry. These 'triadic' relationships have been characterised variously, but most famously, as a conspiracy in the public interest, dubbed 'Japan Inc'. Here MITI is assigned the role of Chief Executive of a national public/private company, whose directors are drawn from the governing Liberal Democratic Party (LDP), the large manufacturing firms, and key parts of the bureaucracy. Fourthly, there are those who have argued that the secret of Japan's economic success is the leadership provided by the bureaucracy, and its domination of the government and the private sector.

> Perhaps Japan can be characterised as a 'network', a 'relational' or a 'societal' state in the sense that government power is intertwined with that of private sector. The government's power hinges on its capacity to work effectively with the private sector, with each side making an effort to take into account the needs and objectives of the other. Political power in Japan is thus exercised through a complex process of public-private sector interaction, involving subtle give and take, not frontal confrontation that results in the forceful imposition of one side's will on the other.[18]

As far as Japanese economic and industrial policy is concerned, MITI has been able to play the main role in the interdependence of state and industry and has been leading the Japanese economy to its relative success. Japan's industrial policy is wide-ranging in nature and has wide-ranging targets such as macroeconomic goals, the protection and bringing up or nurturing of infant industries, the prevention of excessive competition, the conversion of industrial organisation, and regional policy, all at the same time. In order to achieve these targets, MITI has used various measures: discriminatory treatment of permission to import, restrictive laws, financial subsidies, guidelines, presenting a perspective on future industrial organisation. So called, *gyosei shido*, the administrative guidance has always been included. MITI's industrial policy has been characterised by its ambiguity of definition and the variety of means.

As the motor industry case[19] showed, in the first stage of Japanese industrial policy, MITI treated almost all modern industries as 'infant industries'. It has been said that this kind of policy was successful before the maturity stage. Despite the failure of some industries,[20] MITI's industrial restructuring process has been successful. MITI was a part of a developmental state, where government policy was dominated by the objective of industrial growth. As a late entrant to industrialisation, Japan needed a political engine to lead private business. After the first oil shock, MITI shifted its fundamental policy attitudes from 'strengthening economic power' to 'good utilisation of economic power'. This meant that it concentrated on 'the knowledge-intensive industrial structure', instead of 'the modernised capital-intensive industrial structure'. Owing to the balance of trade, MITI had to think about the diversification of its policy. As far as government industrial policy was concerned, it was expected that the knowledge-intensive structure would be more important after ten years, and also, that knowledge-intensive industry would not attract the hostility from Japan's industrial competitors which had been associated with the 'dumping' of traditional manufactured goods. MITI's new vision attached importance to industrial structure policies, which emphasised such industries as:

1) R&D-intensive industries: Computer, Aircraft, Industrial Robot, Atomic power-related industries, Large-scale integrated circuits, Fine chemicals, Ocean development.
2) High processing industries: Office communication equipment, Numerically controlled tools, Pollution prevention machinery, Industrial housing production, High-quality printing, automated warehousing, Educational equipment.
3) Fashion industries: High-quality clothing and furniture, Electronic musical instruments.[21]

However this kind of guideline created some conflicts within the big business. Big business does not expect MITI to act as an authority. They hope that MITI's role will be as an arbitrator between rivals in order to minimise their loss of profits when cooperation in investment and production is necessary. Since the growth of economic regionalism, the influence of government has been declining even in Japan.

> It is undeniable that Japan's many important export industries still remain under the formal jurisdiction of MITI. Nevertheless, other ministries deserve more attention for two reasons. One reason is that MITI will lose some of its importance in the economy as many industries which formerly benefited from MITI's industrial policy reach maturity and services industries overtake manufacturing industries. MITI may find new sectors to nurture but as Japan's style of state-led industrialisation has come under international criticism, MITI may not be able to implement the explicit industrial policy it did in the past. Next reason is that, given that Japan's trading partners are frustrated with closed Japanese markets, a wide of sectors will be placed on the agenda of international economic negotiations. Therefore, ministries other than MITI which have jurisdictions over these sectors will be drawn to the front line of international disputes.[22]

After the 1970s, when international criticism of MITI's direct role in Japanese business was strongest, the work of MITI was diverted from direct intervention into 'shadowing' the decision-making processes of private business. Since the strengthening of economic regionalism, however, Japanese

MNEs have been asking MITI for increasing government involvement in negotiating the inward investment policy of host countries while MNEs tried to penetrate into the Single European Market.

> The differences before and after 1980 is its involvement in their policy toward private business. Before 1980, MNEs were eager to ask government for support for their own business policies, despite the government's 'free hand' policy. After 1980, MITI advised their intentions to MNEs' directors. There was internal and external pressure to make MITI's work informal. Since the regional trends in the world economy have strengthened, MITI's position has changed from that of industrial policy makers to that of foreign investment policy negotiators. Despite the decline of MITI's power, Japanese MNEs' relations with MITI will continue, so long as they have FDI plans.[23]

While MITI set out the general picture of industrial policy towards FDI, the *keiretsu* tried to match their own policies to those of the government. Despite increasing pressure from foreign countries, the role of *keiretsu* in coordinating Japanese business activity has not substantially changed. Mr K. Yamamoto, director-general of the machinery and information bureau of the MITI said that 'Without the development of technology, we can't assure the progress of living standards. This kind of technological development doesn't pay in the short term, so we have to support it (*keireitsu* organisation).'[24]

Keiretsu groups are the other key element in the interdependence of state and industry. Under the Allied Occupation control, *zaibatsu* were abolished and *keiretsu* were sanctioned by MITI.

> Prior to the World War II, *Zaibatsu* such as Mitsui and Mitsubishi were expanding as large trading companies. These companies had been increasingly seen by the Americans as an economic threat that breached American anti-trust laws and other anti-monopoly laws. After Japan's defeat, therefore, the Americans took steps to reduce Japan's potential economic strength, including the dismantling of the *Zaibatsu*, and to re-pattern Japanese markets, in order to better serve America's (and the West) needs. Subsequently, a new form of trading company emerged, the *sogo shosha/keiretsu*. These massive trading companies are engaged in almost every form of legitimate economic activity and straddle the world, but are no longer family dominated as were the *Zaibatsu*.
>
> The six largest *sogo shosha* are C. Itoh, Mitsui, Sumitomo, Mitsubishi, Nissho-Iwai and Fyuyo Group. They account for roughly 4 per cent of world trade and collectively they are the largest purchaser of US exports in the world, accounting for 10 per cent of overseas sales.[25]

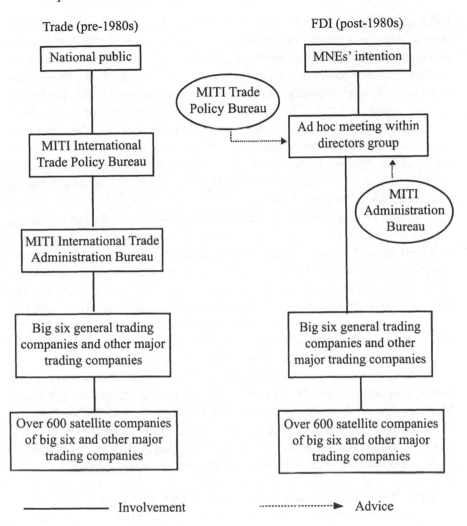

Figure 2.1   Vertical coordination pattern for international trade and FDI

Source: Derived by the author on the basis of original research.

Within the *keiretsu*,[26] membership of a group normally means reliance on the group-bank for external financing, stable but not exclusive internal business transactions, and extensive intercorporate share-holdings. That kind of structure gives a mechanism for diffusing and diminishing risks in the Japanese industrial system. Within the *keiretsu*, risks and profits are shared among members.

Keiretsu structures facilitate communication with government, and help to impose order on market competition. Its networks can be connected into the bureaucratic and political networks with reciprocal benefits and advantages. Within the business areas, *keiretsu* carry out two particular functions. One, intercorporate share-holdings inhibit mergers and takeovers by foreign MNEs or other Japanese MNEs. That is why there are no mergers or takeovers of Japanese companies by MNEs from other OECD countries. The other, the preference for intra-*keiretsu* trading and business transactions provides an informal but effective barrier to the entry of foreign MNEs into the Japanese market. Actually, the interfirm trade in Japan is dominated by long-standing reciprocal ties among companies.

The relationship between government and *keiretsu* has been strengthened in the mature stage of the Japanese economy. In the promotion and regulation of industry, the bureaucracy has incorporated *keiretsu* into the making and carrying out of agreed policies. The participation of business leaders in government R&D projects bring together firms from each *keiretsu*. For example, the Fifth Generation Computer included electronics firms from all of the six main groups. The intention is to finance and promote R&D and allow the firms to compete subsequently and more effectively with IBM.

Keiretsu has a greater significance in overseas matters than in Japan.

Although *keiretsu* constitute less than 0.1 per cent of all companies in Japan, they account for 78 per cent of the value of all shares on the Tokyo Stock Exchange. When we consider FDI in US, more than half of the Japanese manufacturing MNEs in California are owned fully or partly by *keiretsu*. *Keiretsu* MNEs accounted for 68 per cent of Japanese FDI in the US, high-tech manufacturers since late 1989. The picture is similar in the EU.

> I think the share of FDI in the EU by *keiretsu* is at a higher rate than that in the US. Lack of confidence, quite closely related subcontracting relations between assemblers and component industries, and relatively low support from government, make it more difficult for non-*keiretsu* manufacturers to invest in the EU. As far as car makers are concerned, the EU is dominated by members of *keiretsu* component industries. Government led inward policy, large manufacturing sites for car MNEs, and the difficulties of competing with other Japanese or European component industries, will prevent non-*keiretsu* component industries from establishing themselves in the EU within a decade. The relative weakness of the relationship between Honda as an assembler and its component industries shows this well.[27]

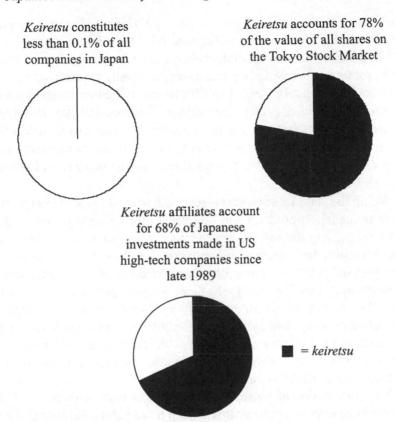

Figure 2.2   The comparative power system of the *keiretsu* in Japan and overseas

Source: *Fortune* (1991) 15 July.

Elite and Decision-making in Japan

It is strange from the Western viewpoint that key positions in the government and business elite group are occupied almost entirely by the so-called '*kakubetsu*', mainly graduates from Tokyo university. The *kakubetsu* occupy main government posts in MITI, MOF, the Economic Planning Agency (EPA) and the Bank of Japan (BOJ). Since the Meiji period, this educational elite has been strengthening its hold, because the elite from Tokyo university mainly lived near Tokyo and their fathers had quite similar occupations, such as senior managers in big business or leading positions in the bureaucracy. While at university, the elite group, who are usually members of the Department of

Law, absorb a cohesive conservative ideology. Their studies prepare them for the competitive examinations which determine their future careers.

The examination are essentially held for three professional career brackets: class I for future middle and top managers (university graduates or candidates from graduate school), class II to fill clerical and administrative positions, essentially for university and a few college graduates, and class III for manual and maintenance tasks (high school graduates). These exams are held annually, containing written, oral, aptitude and physical tests and, particularly for class I, are extremely competitive. The qualified examiners for class I are usually the members of *kakubetsu*.

Within the class I, the typical career path is as follows: i) after success in the examination, candidates will be selected for a ministry, and go through extensive training and advance together as a cohort; ii) when these bureaucrats reach their 40s, their career mobility options begin to narrow, as there are few section-chief positions, fewer bureau chief positions, and only one vice-ministership for each ministry; iii) those who are promoted to bureau chief are still in the running for vice-minister, and those who are not promoted are compelled to resign and seek a lucrative job in a private industry or public corporation; iv) ultimately, everyone must 'descend' because of the unrelenting pressure from cohorts advancing from below. The usual retirement age for a vice-minister is slightly over fifty.

The organisation of Japanese bureaucracy is very hierarchical. The 'life employment system' confirms this system more tightly. Few reach the top of the pyramid. This scarcity puts elite together under the same umbrella.

The interactions and interpenetrations of the government bureaucrats and businessmen are manifest in a myriad of multiplex relations and processes, but one of the most basic is *amakudari* (descent from heaven). The *amakudari*, the process by which top ministry bureaucrats retire to senior management positions in private enterprises, is pivotal to the overall strategic planning and coordination of the Japanese economy. The government bureaucrats, upon their retirement, move from high government positions to high-level positions in private enterprise – a direction of elite mobility that is opposite to the general pattern found in the US, though quite common in the UK and elsewhere in Europe.

The *amakudari* services several functions that lubricate, and indeed fuse relations between the state and economy. It provides a basis for informal policy networks transmitting information between the state and business and a vehicle for conflict resolution and consensus building on issues of industrial and FDI policy. It also serves to consolidate close relations and mutual trust between

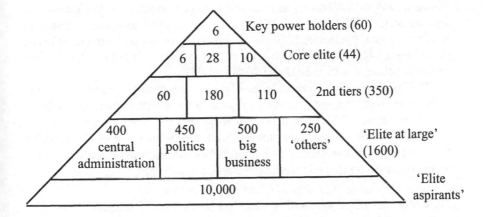

Figure 2.3   The membership of power pyramid in Japan

Source: Rothacher, A. (1983), *Economic Diplomacy between the EC and Japan 1959–81*, p. 2.

business group and bureaucrats. It is a mechanism of interpenetration extending and disseminating the spirit of corporation and accommodation to fuse private and public interests into industrial policy.

The *amakudari* works to consolidate the structure of government-business ties and the interpenetration of the public and private sectors through the network of intermediate organisation. During the period of transformation of Japanese industries' position in the world, the role of key figures within the government and business was important to decision-making. The main role of the bureaucracy is that

First, the developmental state is 'plan-rational' as opposed to 'market-rational' of regulatory states such as the US. Secondly, there is an explicit industrial policy aimed at producing and sustaining 'high speed economic growth'. The pursuit and achievement of that growth is part of an over-arching set of goals for society, upon which there is general consensus-the third element. Fourthly, a 'natural corollary of plan rationality' is 'the existence of a powerful, talented, and prestige-laden economic bureaucracy'. The role of this bureaucracy is explicitly instrumental. Although influenced by interest groups, 'the elite bureaucracy of Japan makes most major decisions, drafts virtually all legislation, controls the national budget, and is the source of all major policy innovations in the system'.[28]

Johnson reported that

Between 1963 and 1972 there was an annual average recruitment of 154 bureaucrats into industry. In 1990, out of 39,382 directors of all 2,086 corporations listed on the Tokyo Stock Exchange, 1030 (or 10.7%) were former government officials. Out of these, 144 were from the Ministry of Finance (MOF), 123 from the Ministry of Construction, 114 from BOJ and 96 from MITI ...

The influence of bureaucrats on management is difficult to quantify, as is the effect of a firm's decision to comply or not to comply with ministerial guidance on future business. However, given the scope and relevance of administrative guidance in business regulation on the one hand, and the high number of *amakudari* board members on the other, it is obvious that ex-government officials constitute an important factor in the Japanese governance structure.[29]

Bureaucratic influences within the Diet (Japanese Parliament), the LDP, even the new Coalition Party, and industry reinforces the strength of its historic modernisation role. Most legislation is drafted in the ministries by bureaucrats, and couched in general, often vague terms which enable them to regulate activities by decree, ordinance, and through the use of *'gyosei shido'* (administrative guidance). For example, Kerbo and McKinstry said that 80 per cent of bureaucracy-sponsored bills pass the Diet, compared to only 30 per cent of Diet-sponsored bills. A recent survey which was held by the *Nihon Keizai Shimbun* revealed that:

> a majority of senior bureaucrats think they must make policies, not politicians. Among 147 career bureaucrats who answered the questionnaire, close to 70 per cent supported the statement that bureaucrats must make policies instead of politicians because politicians are unreliable.[30]

During the Japan-EU summit meeting in the Hague in 1991, even Jacques Delors, the president of the EU, said that 'I consider that the politicians of Japan do not really govern. Behind them there is an infrastructure of business which governs, whose motives are not always the best in the world.'[31]

The problem of economic regionalism has been difficult to solve by business alone. Globalisation or global localisation is one of the most important tasks for Japanese MNEs. The growing harmony between government and business over FDI policy making during the 1980s was regarded as one of the most important factors in the development of that policy.

Conclusion

Over the last decade, major changes occurred in the global economic setting faced by Japan. This has required changes in Japanese foreign economic policy. During the transformation of the world economy, Japanese MNEs and government have no option to choose except FDI in each region. As the international activities of MNEs through FDI expanded, developed countries have felt strongly the need to strengthen international cooperation in order to decrease the risks of FDI, secure international business activities, and set up dispute settlement mechanisms, and are working to decrease the risks of FDI through measures such as opening negotiations at the world economic organisation such as OECD. Hence, the role of government in Japan is getting important to guide her MNEs' FDI policy toward other developed countries effectively.

Japanese FDI, at first, was a kind of political accident. When the Japanese government faced dumping accusations or other export restriction from developed countries, she pushed her MNEs out of Japan. The growing pressure from internal factors, such as the government push policy, shifted the MNEs' attitude towards overseas investment.

> For Japan ... overseas production has suddenly emerged as a national requirement encompassing practically the entire spectrum of her industries and enterprises, small and large alike. The segments of industrial activities that are no longer suitable, environmentally or otherwise, for the Japanese economy need to be transplanted abroad, and overseas resources must now be developed more directly to insure [sic] supplies. Furthermore, overseas investment is now viewed as an essential device by which to upgrade Japanese industry.[32]

However one of the strong points of Japanese government policy toward the FDI of manufacturing sectors is its specific focus on certain areas, such as electric goods, car manufacturing, and office equipment only. These manufacturing sectors have a good reputation in the consumer market. The economic recession in the EU was an important reason for each member state to develop an inward FDI policy. Moreover, these national-dominated inward policies gave more opportunity for Japanese government to intervene at the EU negotiation table.

The vertical organisation of Japanese industry has emerged as a factor of importance in the trade and FDI behaviour of Japanese car makers. The first or second tier component makers are found to follow the assemblers in investing in the EU in order to supply the assembler with locally produced components. Subsequent investment took place in response to the EU's local content regulations imposed on Japanese cars. The evidence on Japanese affiliates' procurement behaviour generally shows a preference to keep control over component production abroad, either through in-house production or through procurement from long-standing Japanese suppliers. The relationships with tiers and long-standing suppliers are part of an organisation of production characterised by 'lean production' system, just-in-time deliveries, and joint development of components for new products. This type of production management is widely seen as constituting a competitive advantage of Japanese car manufacturers, and the manufacturers faced with local component regulation have pursued a strategy to transfer the system abroad.

At the government level, Japanese bureaucracy has advantages in policy formation: its essentially meritocratic recruitment system and its information assembly capability compared to that of private business. Experienced in the US negotiation, Japanese government prefers multilateral conflict resolution to unilateral measures within the EU market.

The Japanese MNEs' approach to the EU market is explained in various ways. However, there is common idea that Japan feared economic regionalism.

According to a study by Fortune magazine and Ernst & Young in the late 1980s, over half the US executives and nearly two-thirds of Japanese polled saw Japan as most likely to be affected by potential protectionism. In particular, Japanese executives believed their products would be denied access to the EC though anti-dumping measures, import quotas, and local content provisions. Most major Japanese companies had developed special European strategies, which included building or acquiring new European manufacturing facilities, or at least establishing senior level task forces. Japanese firms went out of their way to be seen as 'good Europeans' and many chose strategic alliance with EC partner to hedge against the risk of protectionism.[33]

Establishing new strategies, while Japanese government examined a host government's support and attitude toward Japanese FDI, the Japanese MNEs were looking for bureaucratic support for their FDI plans, leading to connections between governments. By mutual agreement, FDI plans were concerned with government policy rather than business strategy. The objective of FDI programmes was to engage with the policy needs of Japanese and host countries.

Notes

1   UN (1992), *World Investment Report 1992*.
2   'Globalisation' is the term used in this thesis to refer to a process which is variously referred to in the literature as 'internationalisation', 'transnationalisation' and 'multinationalisation'.
3   Chan, S. (eds) (1995), *FDI in a Changing Global Political Economy*, pp. 2–3.
4   Morita, A. (1985), 'Japan: Where to go from here', *The Japan Times*, 12 March.
5   Yamashita, T. (1986), 'Making VTRs and Friends in the USA', *Economic Eye*, Vol. 7, No. 1, March.
6   Toyota Motor Co. (1984), 'The Wheel Extended', *A Toyota Quarterly Review*, Vol. XIV, No. 4.
7   In 1985 the Group of Seven agreed to pursue realignments of the major exchange rates. There was subsequent appreciation of the *yen* against the dollar and to a less extent, against the European currencies.
8   Mr George Bull: interview.
9   Ozaki, R. and Arnold, W. (1985), *Japan's Foreign Relations: A global search for economic security*, pp. 12–13.
10 In the EU, the year 1985 was the initial year to create EC Single Market by the end of 1992, by the publication of the Lord Cockfield's White Paper on European Integration.
11 Mr Atsushi Yamakoshi: interview.
12 Despite the differences between globalisation or global localisation, Japanese MNEs normally used its terms as same meaning, except few companies such as Honda.
13 Despite Yawata and Fuji's case, the MITI's intention to integrate the car industry into two groups, Toyota and Nissan, and the computer industry into three groups, Fujitsu-Hitachi, NEC-Toshiba, and Oki-Mitsubish Electric failed by Honda in cars and Sony in electric industry. Except there few cases, the general picture of restructuring process under political consideration has been successful.
14 *The Japan Stock Journal* (1981), February.
15 *Financial Times* (1985), 20 December.
16 Hirata, M. (1993), 'Japanese Overseas Investment in Recent Years and Corporate Responses to the Single EC Market', *Hitotsubashi Journal of Commerce and Management*, No. 28, pp. 35.
17 Mitsubishi Research Institute survey (1991), mimeo, p. 2.
18 Okimoto, D.I. (1988), 'Political Inclusivity: The domestic structure of trade', in Inoguchi, T. and Okimoto, D. (eds), *The Political Economy of Japan: Vol. 2, The Changing International Context*, p. 314.
19 MITI set up a plan based on consensus with the motor companies in 1951. It was:
    1) protection of domestic makers from car imports and investment by foreigner (tariff barriers, quantity quotas and a discriminatory commodity tax);
    2) favourable treatment for introducing technology from advanced countries;
    3) low-interest loans and favourable finance (particularly, financed by Nippon Developing Bank): Matsumoto, G. (1992), 'The Work of the MITI', Cowling, K. and Sugden, R. (eds), *Current Issues in Industrial Economic Strategy*, p. 149.
20 Honda and Sony case: they were not allow to enter car and electric sector. Despite MITI's ignorance, they have succeeded in overseas markets.
21 Matsumoto, G. (1992), 'The Work of the MITI', p. 151.
22 Mikanagi, Y. (1996), *Japan's Trade Policy*, p. 26.

23 Mr Yaushiro Shiraki: interview in Japanese.
24 *Fortune* (1991), 15 July, p. 52.
25 Taplin, R. (1995), *Decision-Making and Japan*, p. 72.
26 There are two unique differences in the *keiretsu*: horizontal and vertical *keiretsu*. Horizontal *keiretsu*: this is six core and biggest ones all revolve around a financial core, which always includes a major bank. The six largest banks are Dai-Ichi Kangyo, Sakura, Sumitomo, Fuji, Sanwa, and Mitsubishi, and the leading long-term credit bank, the Industrial Bank of Japan (IBJ). Vertical *keiretsu:* many of the biggest vertical *keiretsu* lie inside the borders of the Big Six. Almost all the Big Six companies are also the heads of their own vertical *keiretsu*. Beneath Toyota, Toshiba, Sumitomo Chemical, Mitsubishi Heavy Industries, Mitsui Bussan and all the rest, there are hundreds and thousands of smaller firms. It is unique pyramid subcontracting system. The vertical *keiretsu* is most important sectors within the car and electronic goods manufacturing sectors.
27 Mr Toyohiko Shimada: interview in Japanese.
28 Wright, M. (1989), *Government–Industrial Relations in Japan*, p. 8.
29 Schaede, U. (1994), 'Understanding Corporate Governance in Japan', *Industrial and Corporate Change*, No. 2, p. 319.
30 *Nihon Keizai Shimbun* (1993), 5 November.
31 *Japan Times* (1991), 31 July.
32 Ozawa, T. (1979), 'Multinationalism, Japanese Style', readopted in Morris, J. (1991), *Japan and the Global Economy*, p. 30.
33 Egan, C. and McKiernan, P. (1994), *Inside Fortress Europe*, p. 160.

Chapter 3

EU-Japanese Economic Relations and Car Manufacturing in Europe

The European Union[1] (EU) was responsible in 1989 for 15.6 per cent of world trade (average of exports and imports), compared with 13.8 per cent for the US and 8.1 per cent for Japan. This proportion has been increasing since the inauguration of the Single European Market (SEM). Excluding trade between EU member countries, the EU accounted for about 20 per cent of world exports in 1993, and is the world's largest single trade unit, surpassing both the US (16.3 per cent) and Japan (8.2 per cent). Despite moves towards SEM, and the desire for cohesion, trade policy in the EU has remained heterogeneous. In any industrial sector, the interests of member countries will differ depending on the structure of the sector concerned and its competitive position. This is highlighted by the case of the car industry.

This chapter is concerned with EU trade policy and its relation to Japan in terms of antidumping and voluntary export restraints (VERs) policy. It also describes the car industry within the EU, and the approach taken by the Japanese car industry to the EU market. The chapter is organised into two parts. The first provides the general picture of EU trade policy and its relationship with Japan; the second covers the car industry in the EU and the market penetration policy of the Japanese industry.

EU Trade Policy

The legal framework of the EU trade policy is the Treaty of Rome, which sets out the aims and obligations of the members countries. Article of 110 the Treaty requires member states: i) to work closely together to free the movement of manufactures, services, labour and capital within the Union; ii) to formulate and apply common policies for trade, agriculture, transport and competition; and iii) to coordinate their macroeconomic policies. Article 110 has two implications for EU trade policy objectives.

The EU is, first of all, committed to a liberal approach to trade – it supports a free multilateral trading system in the world (as established by GATT) with the most efficient producers supplying markets (trade creation). A logical outcome of supporting free multilateral trade would be avoiding protection of trade in whatever form. But Article 110 also, embodies a second principal policy objective: the formation of a customs union resulting in a common market, which discriminates against third countries.[2]

The external policy of the EU is based on free trade, or the aspiration to achieve it. The conditions of the trade with nonmember countries were to be regulated by a Common Commercial Policy (CCP) and the main point of the CCP was to be a common external tariff – the Common Customs Tariff (CCT). The CCT made sure that products entering the Union would be treated alike, without regard to the particular member country through which they were imported. Also, the agreement of the CCT meant that national tariffs, and the freedom to adjust them, had to be given up. All trade policy measures can be decided on the basis of majority voting. Because 'there is no single mechanism of formulating coordinating and implementing the broad range of trade-related policies in the EC'.[3] Trade policy authority will be bestowed on the European Commission, and some part of the policy which is more sensitive to each member's interests, will be shared between the Commission and member states. Within the SEM, the Communities expected to speak with a single voice in bilateral or multilateral trade negotiations with nonmember countries.

A particular example of EU trade policy in the early period was a network of preferential tariff arrangements for Union trade in manufacturers with the countries of the European Free Trade Association (EFTA), with Mediterranean countries and with Asian, Caribbean and Pacific (ACP) countries under the successive Lomé Conventions. In particular, a Generalised System of Preferences (GSP) was established for developing countries. Figure 3.1 shows the preferences for the trade in manufactures. However, there was a sharply increased rate of intra-European trade.

The high rate of intra-trade caused nonmember countries to invest in the EU. In the EU, trade policy can be seen at the national-level and at the EU level. Even after the Maastricht Treaty, it is said that there is still no truly common EU external trade policy. The 1992 programme was concerned with Union's domestic trade issues and it clearly concentrated on internal rather than external liberalisation of trade.

1   The Budding Stage (1958–68)

Since the agreement of the Treaty of Rome, which was influenced by the earlier rounds of GATT, the Union was able to speed up the economic and

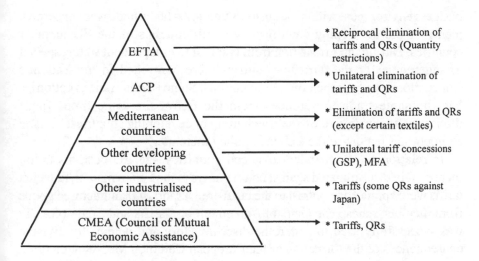

Figure 3.1   The pyramid of EU preferences for trade in manufacturers

Source: Mobius, U. (1991), *Einfuhr von Industrieprodukten* (mimeo).

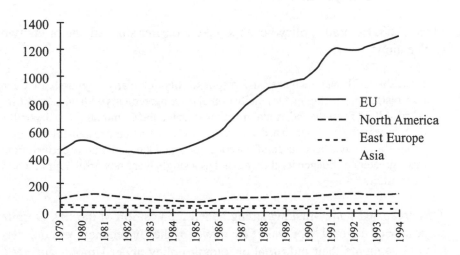

Figure 3.2   The EU trade paradigm

Source: EU facts (1993) (mimeo).

business environment within the customs union. As far as trade was concerned, plenty of the developing countries were still colonies of the EU member countries. During their transition from colonial to independent status, special arrangements for the African countries were continued in the Yaounde Conventions and later the Lomé Conventions. Some Mediterranean countries had the same trade preferences from the EU at the same time. Tariff discrimination, in favour of a selected group of developing countries, became an important feature of the EU trade policy thereafter.

In relation to nonmember advanced countries, the EU customs union increasingly discriminated against nonmembers in the Union market, to which tariffs were applied, in contrast to the tariff-free import of manufactured goods from member states. The General Agreement on Tariffs and Trade (GATT) was successfully used to soften the discriminatory and potentially divisive consequences of the formation of the European Common Market at this first stage. At the first phase of the EU integration at this time it was said of the Kennedy Round conference (1963–68), that 'the US saw the Round as a means of ensuring that the creation of a common market would not result in the EEC turning in upon itself'.[4] At this stage, Japan's role in world trade was quite small compared to that of the other developed countries.

2   The Enlargement (1969–74)

Since 1968, EU trade policy began to take a clearer shape. Hine offers two explanations:

> First, the CCT was in place, and responsibility for many key areas of trade administration – including the negotiation of trade agreements with other countries – had shifted from the individual member states to the Community … Secondly, the Kennedy Round – which had helped the EEC custom union to gain international acceptability – had been successfully concluded, and the Community derived from this a greater confidence its ability to act as a single, very powerful, unit in world trade affairs.[5]

This organised policy-making strengthened the position of the EU. Despite some lack of national approval of the power of the Union, member countries tried to negotiate their industrial or trading policy under Union's auspices. The 1973 enlargement of the Union was the turning point of its trade policy. The membership of the UK in the Union showed the difficulty of compromising between national and Union level trade policy.

On the one hand, the UK, with its long-established global trade links, could be expected to oppose a too inward-looking CCP. On the other hand, the chronic low growth and (pre-North Sea oil) balance of payments problems of the UK promised powerful support for a protectionist response to the trade difficulties of declining industries.[6]

Joining the Union, the UK and Denmark made a new move towards EFTA and the UK Commonwealth countries. The Commonwealth countries (except Asian countries) occupied the same position in EU trade as the African and Mediterranean countries since the Lomé Convention. The conflict between Union members and the rest of the Western European countries brought about the establishment of a new free trade area covering all Western Europe. During this stage, the members of the Union took a more active role in world economic relocation, and tried to harmonise their relations with their main trade partner, the US. When the UK joined the EU, the widening of the EU trade areas weakened the unified trade policy towards nonmember countries. Ironically, while the EU enlarged, the gap between member countries started to widen.

3   The Retardation (1975–84)

During these periods, the major problems that were confronted by the Union were the economic recession in Western European countries, and fierce competition from Japan and the Asian countries such as New Industrialising Countries (NICs). The oil crisis weakened the position of the EU countries even more, and caused the massive balance of payments deficits (especially in the energy-importing countries) and an upsurge in inflation. Hence, the trade policy of the EU became more protective. After that, the EU tried to set up new trade arrangements, such as the limitation of concessions from the EU to African countries under the renewed Lomé Convention in 1979, and the more restrictive application of the GSP against the NICs. This kind of protectionism spread to the developed countries, mainly Japan. In particular, the VERs between the EU and Japan, and a series of trade disputes involving agriculture, steel and East-West trade, began.

Before the oil shock, the position of Japan among the developed countries was often underestimated. Japan, on the other hand, did not try to compete strongly in industrial sectors. Some imports of Japanese goods, which were treated as dumping by the EU Commission, were reduced by the Japanese government's positive intervention in the industries concerned. Japanese FDI in the manufacturing sectors, during these periods, was mainly focused in the

US, owing to the strength of dumping accusations in the United States, and because of market-led FDI policies. In spite of increasing FDI towards the EU, Japanese manufacturing FDI in this region was still quite low in absolute terms and was directed towards specific manufacturing sectors only.

The economic recession in Western Europe led to the dominance of national government in trade policy compared, as opposed to the European Commission. The fully liberalised intra-trade between the EU members could cause trade distortions such as the import of low-cost products from Third World countries to the more liberal countries such as West Germany and the Netherlands. EU trade policy, during the Retardation period, moved strongly towards 'Fortress Europe'. The move was criticised by the members of GATT, which was to set up to promote an open trading system, for its protectionist tendencies. It was said that the Japan and NICs were treated as scapegoats by the EU members for their own internal failures. It was also alleged that EU policy-makers had failed to take account in their policy of the major changes in the international trade environment caused by the energy price shocks.

4   New Europe (since 1985)

This period can be divided into two parts. The first part was focused on the enlargement of the EU and the economic negotiation with the EFTA countries. The second part of this period saw the emergence of the Single European Market (SEM).

> There is clearly a coincidence between the Uruguay Round and the creation of a single market in the EC. Although the GATT round was scheduled to end in 1990, two years before the EC's programme, key decisions on the shape of the EC regulatory regime post-1992 were in fact taken during the period 1987–90.[7]

Producing the Single European Act (SEA), a series of treaty amendments was designed to speed up decision-making on the internal market. The main objective of the SEA was the extension of the scope of majority voting in the Council to include most of the decision required for completion of the internal market, and to give the European Parliament the right, under a new cooperation procedure, to a role in relation to those decisions that went some way beyond consultation. It also defined a Union competence in the fields of environment, technology, and conditions at work, set monetary union as a Union objective and gave the European Monetary Union a basis in the treaties, formalised the system of foreign policy corporation, and extended it to the political and economic aspects of security.

More positive trade policy was carried through by Jacques Delors, who was elected president of the EU Commission at the Milan summit at June 1985. Agreement was reached on a seven-year timetable to remove 300 barriers to the internal market,[8] and it was agreed to consider amendments to the Treaty of Rome. With the economic success of the EU in the mid-1980s, the European Council in June 1988 drew up proposals for an economic and monetary union (EMU). EMU got strong support from the business community who was the supporters of the SEA and it came to represent the other pillar of the SEM.

The enlargement of the EU brought in Spain and Portugal as new members in January 1986, and the negotiation began between the EU and the EFTA states to form a European Economic Area (EEA). SEA, and the enlargement of the EU would give more stable intra-trade conditions for the member countries. In December 1991, the Maastricht summit agreed on the Treaty on European Union which included detailed arrangements for a single currency, common foreign policy and security policy (CFSP), and a European Central Bank, together with a phased programme for establishing them by 1997 or, at the latest, 1999, even if not all member states would then participate. Owing to unexpected results in the UK and Danish Maastricht Treaty referendums, the intention of moving towards a federal Europe was delayed.

> The desire of at least a core group of member states to strengthen the Union and its institutions will, however, remain; and the economic and political circumstances may be more favourable for this in the second half of the 1990s than they appeared to be in the aftermath of Maastricht.[9]

Leon Brittan explained the SEM in two ways: 'There is a frontier-free market for goods, for services, for capital. There are more effective (and more firmly used) rules on state aids and competition, to guarantee fair competition.'[10] The SEM was expected to be a turning point in the EU trade policy towards countries outside Europe. The EU would depend on intra-trade more strongly. The SEM also would increase total demand and create greater imports from outside; after some restructuring, strengthened protectionism would exclude outsiders and divert imports from them to member suppliers.

One of the most striking features of the EU economy has been the growth in intra-trade that has taken place since 1985. Although the EU's trade with US and Japan increased during the 1980s, this was matched by a decline in the value of trade with other parts of the world. It is clear that the most rapidly expanding element of the EU's merchandise trade flows occurred within the region rather than between the EU and other regions. The increasing intra-trade has been one of main reason for overseas investment by nonmember countries in the EU. Japanese MNEs' market penetration policy will be achieved when they establish their affiliates in the EU. From the government side, global localisation negotiations during the 1980s were more favourable to the intentions of Japanese MNEs, because national governments were easier to deal with than the Commission.

The EU treated Japan as a developing country for the purposes of trade policy, because Japanese imports from the EU were comparatively low. In contrast to the general pattern of trade between developed countries, EU–Japan trade is to a great extent based on interindustry rather than intra-industry trade. Competitive pressures in intra-industry trade between the developed countries, can be handled by a given enterprise through a relatively mild process of seeking a new place in the same market. By contrast, Japanese competition seems to require an all or nothing response, and to threaten the extinction of whole industries and whole lines of technological development, and seems therefore to be comparatively more supported by the Japanese government. Japanese business tactics, which have flourished within the EU, have been criticised by EU businesses, because the market approach was not 'fair' compared to that of EU MNEs.

To reduce this kind of perceived trade imbalance, the EU has adopted two particular kinds of measures: antidumping regulations and voluntary export restraints (VERs). The EU made common antidumping regulations, against dumped or subsidised imports from non-EU member countries in 1968, although they were not used until 1976. The rules that the EU has developed for dealing with dumped imports have been derived in accordance with the EU's international trade obligations. The specific rules governing the EU's antidumping legislation were laid down in Council Regulation No. 2423/88 of 11 July 1988. The Regulation permits the EU to take antidumping measures provided there is 'evidence of dumped imports, – industry in the EU has been injured or threatens to be injured by the dumped imports, – intervention is in the EU's interest'

How important are antidumping duties for EU trade policy? The latest trade policy review of the EU carried out by GATT suggests that the EU has been making frequent use of antidumping actions. According to the GATT report, the EU is the most intensive user of antidumping measures in the world. Between 1988 and 1992, the number of antidumping measures used fluctuated between 152 in 1988 and 139 in 1990. Table 3.1 shows the specific details of the antidumping measures applied to Asian countries:

Table 3.1   Number of antidumping duties of the EU

	1987	1991	1995
Japan	7	14	8
China	–	20	26
Korea	5	9	10
Thailand		5	12

Source: Annual Report of the Commission on the Community's Anti-dumping and Anti-subsidy Activities.

That means that less than 1 per cent of all external imports into the EU tended to be affected by antidumping duties. The antidumping policies have led EU trade policy into protectionism. First, the dumping margin tends to be complicated by possible ambiguities surrounding the export price used in the calculations. Second, there is a different method used in assessing the export price between the EU and other countries, and even between EU member countries. Third, it is difficult to prove the fact of dumping. If dumping has been happening, the EU needs to prove the existence of a threat to the EU members' products caused by the dumped items. Fourth, the Commission has extended its antidumping regulations to the 'screwdriver' plants, lest exporters circumvent antidumping duties by setting up assembly plants within the EU and manufacturing products using a high proportion of imported components and parts. However there is no common agreed definition about that. This is likely to cause another 'Fortress Europe' movement towards other nonmember countries. On the other hand, it will be expected to be solved by government intervention. Since the antidumping process began, the Japanese government has tried to move Japanese MNEs' affiliates into the EU, while they negotiated unfair trading agreements.

A VER is the outcome of a negotiation between two governments which results in the exporting country limiting its export supply to the importing country. Although it is the exporting country that decides to restrict its exports, VERs often result from the exporting country yielding to pressure from the importing country. Cars, steel, machinery, electrical and electronic household equipment and textiles are the major products that have been affected by export restraint arrangements.

Table 3.2　　VERs in force toward Japanese goods in the EU

Product (other than MFA)	EU-wide	National	EU total	World total
Steel	14	1 (UK)	15	52
Agricultural and food products	36	4 (France, Eire, Italy)	40	55
Cars	2	11 (France, Italy, UK, Spain, Portugal)	13	17
Textiles and cothing	18	3 (Germany, UK)	21	72
Electronics	5	11 (France, Italy, UK)	16	19
Footwear	1	10 (France, Italy, UK)	11	14
Machine tools	2	1 (UK)	3	7
Others	10	10 (Benelux, Denmark, France, UK)	20	25
Total	88	51	139	261

Source:　GATT (1988), *Review of Developments in the Trading System.*

If there is economic growth, falling unemployment, and relatively healthy profits, the EU will remove protectionism, and VERs may be abolished as labour and capital are reallocated to expanding parts of the private sector or to a growing public sector. Hence, car investment in the EU has been expected to reduce VER regulation. Antidumping or VERs are regarded as a key test of political success in policy-making. Within the EU Commission, the continuous trade deficit with Japan had to be reduced or stopped. It was indicated by the EU Commission that Japan would have two options; either local manufacturing within the member countries, or restriction of Japanese exports to the EU.

EU-Japanese Economic Relations

The EU's trade relations with the developed countries are supposed to be conducted under the GATT rules and regulations. However relations with Japan have been strained, mostly because of the discriminative trade policies and the trade deficits.

　　EU-Japan relations have unfolded through five phases since 1945. Between 1945 to 1965, the first stage, Japan attempted to secure first membership in GATT[11] and get most-favoured nation (MFN) status with all the major

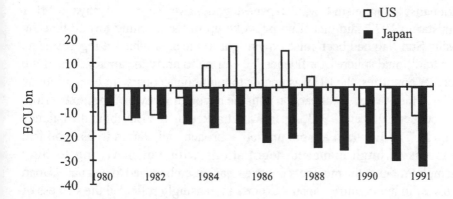

Figure 3.3   EU trade balance with US and Japan

Source: Eurostat, various years.

economic powers. At the first stage, the EU tried to block Japan's GATT membership and MFN status. Rothacher gives the historical explanation that:

> In April 1955 a UK White Paper on Japan's GATT membership predicted an Anglo-Japanese trade war as the result of MFN relations and proposed the conclusion of a bilateral long term Treaty of Commerce and Navigation instead. Although no longer opposing Japan's GATT membership in principle, Britain had decided to invoke GATT's Art. 35 withholding MFN treatment from Japan. When an increasing number of other GATT members appeared to follow the British example, those countries willing to open their markets to Japan became afraid of becoming the sole and therefore concentrated outlet of a desperate Japanese export drive.[12]

1965–73 saw Japan's increasing trade and investment penetration and a trade surplus with Europe. The EU has run a continuous trade deficit with Japan since 1969. Since that year, Germany has surpassed the UK to become Japan's leading trade partner in Europe and for the first time Japan's exports to Germany edged above its imports. The real problem facing the EU was the deteriorating trade system. Japan sold high-value cars, ships, consumer electronics and machinery, while buying lower-value agricultural products, basic chemical resources, and raw materials. During this time, the EU began to attack recurrent Japanese dumping assaults in sensitive products like textiles, TV, steel, ships, cars, tape recorders, radios, and motorcycles.

The continuous antidumping accusations were regarded as the result of nationalist antagonism toward Japanese goods. Mr Naohiro Amaya, a MITI Minister in 1977 said that 'Europe woke up in the morning to find that the Rising Sun flag had been raised overnight in the area which it regards as its own traditional sphere of influence.'[13] Failing to unify the approaches of the member countries, the EU was unable to maintain a consistent or continuous policy. This is a good comparison with the negotiation style of the next period.

Between 1974 and 1983, Japan was attacked by the EU about the balance of trade. The EU tried a more unified approach and started to use political solutions through managed negotiations with Japan. Owing to high unemployment in the member countries, each member tried to persuade Japan to invest in her country. Japan's exports increasingly reflected the success of its industrial policies in promoting such high value-added industries as machine tools, cars, steel and microelectronics, while the EU continued to sell mostly primary products such as raw materials, agricultural products and chemicals. The EU, in the eye of Japanese government policy makers, was an over-matured declining industrial empire. The approach of individual countries, such as Germany or the UK was much easier to negotiate.

In June 1978, bilateral relations became deadlocked over the interpretation of GATT Article 19 allowing safeguard clauses. The EU insisted on its unconditional right to impose restrictions against foreign trade predators, while Japan said that it would accept a selective safeguard clause that would allow retaliatory restrictions only if the exporting nation or GATT agreed. However, Japan said that it would accept the EU's position if the EU abolished its seventy remaining quotas on Japanese goods. From the Japanese side, their trade strategy, during this time, revealed by Mr Takashi Kosaka, the Director General of Japan's EPA, was that:

> For Japan, the relationship with the US is much more important. The Community is one large organisation with which we have a relationship. But basically that amounts to a series of bilateral relationships between Japan and West Germany, France, etc. We feel, therefore, that we should address problems in a bilateral manner.[14]

Between 1983 and 1992 there were some vital changes in understanding about the penetration of Japanese goods into the EU, while the emerging single market within the Western Europe was regarded as the biggest consumer market. The mutual interests of Japan and the EU during these times smoothed away their negotiation difficulties. Some goods were considered so vital to the EU's economic dynamism that the EU imposed trade barriers. Although the EU and its members have gradually reduced their quotas on Japanese goods, in 1989, of 131 EU imports quotas, 113 applied solely to Japan while the remaining 18 applied to Japan and to other countries. The Commission concluded its debate on the external dimension of the 1992 SEM, and announced the mutual relations with Japan that:

- in cooperation with the Japanese government, seek ways of facilitating industry's participation in mutually beneficial cooperation;
- further examine possibilities of facilitating the adoption by European parts suppliers to the requirements both of the Japanese market and of Japanese companies in Europe;
- maintain and extend its Executive Training Programme (ETP) to broaden and deepen industry's understanding of Japanese and the Japanese industrial economy;
- together with the Japanese government, strengthen the EC-Japan Centre for Industrial Cooperation;
- advocate the establishment by the Japanese government of new, coordinated business facilities for Community industrial newcomers to the Japanese market, especially small and medium sized enterprises.[15]

The SEM led to the adoption of a quite different strategy by Japanese businessmen and politicians towards the EU, because the real SEM meant that there would be a huge consumer market.

Since the first movement towards the 1992 SEM during the mid-1980s, the Japanese government was worried about the latter possibility on various occasions and warned against any move toward strengthened restrictions. However, the Japanese MNEs' strategy towards the SEM was quite different that of the government. If Japanese MNEs could be part of the SEM from the beginning, there would be no divergence between their interests and those of the EU. Japanese MNEs' viewpoint about the SEM, was much less pessimistic than was indicated by their government's expressed concerns.[16] Expecting over-competition between Japanese manufacturers within the SEM, Japanese MNEs asked their government to rearrange their FDI policies and to select member country which, seemed to favour Japanese FDI.

Before the SEM, the Japanese MNEs' strategy towards the EU market was dismemberment and subjugation. Japan always tried not to deal with international blocs such as the EU, NAFTA, ASEAN, or APEC, but rather to deal at the national level. Their international strategy was to play off one country against the others to strike the best deal they could. For example,

Japanese business have succeeded in the French or Italian market, which were characterised by their strong protectionism within the EU market, by sneaking in additional imports via more favourable countries such as Germany, and the UK. This strategy, however, faced real difficulties since the development of the SEM. It was forecast by the Community's chief delegate, Willy de Clercq, at the special session of the GATT contracting parties at Punta del Este in September 1986 that

> One of the aims ... is to ensure the mutual advantage of, and to bring increased benefits to, all participants ... The Community feels that many of the present tensions affecting world trade find their origin in the fact that concessions negotiated between the various contracting parties have in reality not resulted in effective reciprocity. It is therefore essential that the Ministerial Declaration should establish the objective of achieving a genuine balance in the benefits accruing to the contracting parties from the GATT.[17]

The EU's policy towards Japanese MNEs changed from a practice of separate approaches by individual member governments to one of coordination by the EU Commission, especially after the Maastricht Treaty. Before the mid-1980s, trade friction between Japan and the EU member countries had been dealt with mostly by negotiation between Japan and each European country separately. Since then, the EU rather than individual member countries, has often acted collectively over a specific issue such as office equipment or electric goods. Some specific areas, such as car manufacturing were however still a source of major difficulties for member governments.

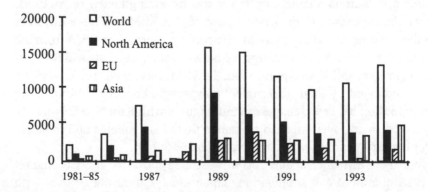

Figure 3.4   Japanese manufacturing FDI

Source: Ministry of Finance, 1996.

After seven years of dynamic growth of Japanese FDI, it slipped in 1990, and then was retarded after 1992. The real downturn of Japanese FDI led to a dramatic change in Japanese business strategy. From 1990 to 1992, Japanese FDI fell sharply due to the sharp decrease of stock in 1990 and land prices in Japan, and low levels of growth, which was combined with the continued rise in the *yen*'s exchange rate in 1994. The *yen* rose above 100 per dollar and 80 per dollar temporarily in 1995. Hence, FDI into the developed countries, especially the EU, decreased the most significantly, in part because business in the EU slowed down as large scale FDI projects were completed, because non-manufacturing MNEs, which were the main FDI components in the EU, were weakened by the stock market's instability, and, also as a consequence of the declining performance of Japanese parent companies.

The decline made the Ministry of Finance seek to find out why Japanese MNEs were not sustaining the pace of FDI in the EU. Four reasons were discovered:

1) Many enterprises feel they have completed the process of getting established abroad, although others believe they need to continue to invest overseas to counter trade friction.
2) The relative weakness of the *yen* has hindered some enterprises from raising the necessary funds for expansion abroad.
3) Investment capital is considerably harder to get.
4) The global recession has dampened the urge to seek new markets.[18]

However, the SEM did not meet these expectations. Ms Noriko Hama, Chief UK Representative, Mitsubishi Research Institute, said in an interview that:

In retrospect, the term 'SEM' is very much of a misnomer because, even though it deregulated markets, and eliminated the trade barriers between national markets in the EU, the EU did not eliminate the local differences, the local diversities, the individualistic traits of the existing local markets within the EU. Hence, this local diversity within the EU market causes difficulties for Japanese businesses – manufacturers and financial institutions alike.[19]

From the EU viewpoint, Japanese FDI in the EU is double-edged:

While the jobs, capital, technology and competitive stimulus the Japanese brought was, and is, very much desired, there was also the fear that this invasion would disrupt European industries and markets, causing a net loss of jobs as domestic firms fell victim to the new transplants. In addition, Japanese firms were criticised for not doing enough R&D in the EC.[20]

Under this chaotic situation in the EU since the mid-1980s, Japanese government and MNEs have succeeded with a market penetration policy, which is well illustrated by Nissan UK's invasion of the continental car market.

Despite the illusion of unity created by a SEM, however, the interests of the Union's 15 member states are still far too diverse and uncoordinated for any comparable moves by Brussels. Playing governments off against each other is an old Japanese sport, *Sumo* to which there is really only one solution: total European Union. The difficulty in achieving a more unified stance is that, while some countries seek protection from Japanese imports, such as France and Italy, others are eager to attract Japanese investment, especially the UK and Spain.

The European Car Industry

The car industries in the EU are more prominently in the public's mind than any other manufacturing industry. About 8 per cent of total manufacturing employment is in car manufacturing sectors only, and as many again in components and materials supply.

During the late 1980s, car manufacturing accounted for:

- at least 25 per cent of the UK trade deficit;
- about 29 per cent of the EU's positive trade balance;
- the direct employment of 1.7 million people in the EU;
- one in 10 jobs in the EU, directly or indirectly.

Hence, car manufacturing has always attracted government intervention, whether its value is good or bad, in the form of:

- investment;
- protectionist measures curbing imports;
- incentives to overseas investment;
- debt write-off.

As Donald Stokes, former Chairman of BL at the time of the company's collapse, said 'everyone is an expert on the motor industry'. The car industry is the largest manufactured item that the typical household ever purchases, a fact, which partly explains the popular interest in the product and in the industry which produces it.

Table 3.3   Car-manufacturing per employee after 1979

	France	Germany	Italy	Spain	UK
1979	7.3	5.9	5.5	–	3.1
1980	–	–	–	7.4	–
1981	6.6	5.4	5.3	6.8	3.3
1982	7.2	5.6	5.5	8.9	3.7
1983	7.6	5.7	6.5	9.2	4.4
1984	7.3	5.5	7.1	9.5	4.0
1985	7.7	5.9	7.5	10.5	4.9
1986	8.7	5.9	9.1	11.5	4.9
1987	9.8	5.9	9.6	12.3	5.5
1988	10.5	5.9	10.4	13.5	6.0
1989	11.4	6.2	10.7	14.3	6.3

Source: Eurostat and SMMT various years.

Despite the inherent dangers of overproduction, the car manufacturing sector has been forced to make as much as it can. The car, moreover, has become an international product and it illustrates as well as anything the economics of European integration. Between the 1950s and 1970s, car manufacturing was part of *national* economic calculations. Since the 1980s, as car manufacturing has become globalised, there are two types of development.

One is a form of localised production, i.e. parts and components, as well as end products, are manufactured in a local site. In this case, a project for manufacturing semi-finished products and sub-components should naturally be included in this localisation program.

Another case is a form of advocacy for the advancement of international corporation or international work-specification, where international planning is widely carried out for production ranging from parts and components to complete cars. These projects include capital co-operation, sales-route alignments, production tie-ups, and sharing of technology.[21]

The globalisation of EU car-makers has coincided with the Japanese car-makers' invasion of the EU. The emerging single market, overproduction by US makers, relatively weak European car-makers, and, most of all, conflicts between member countries' industrial policies towards the car industry, fuelled Japanese FDI in this region.

Table 3.4   Japanese cars' move into the EU

1962   Honda inaugurates its first moped factory in Ghent, Belgium.
1972   Toyota signs a contract for local assembly of light trucks (Dyna, Hiace, Hilux) and the Land Cruiser 4x4 with Salvator Caetano IMVT SA in Ovar, Portugal. Toyota owns 27% of the company.
1979   Honda signed a technical collaboration agreement with Rover.
1980   Nissan takes a minority interest in Motor Iberica, Spain.
1982   Nissan becomes the majority shareholder (67.6%) in Motor Iberica.
        Suzuki takes a 49% interest in Land Rover Santana (Linares, Spain) to manufacture Samurai small 4x4's.
        Mitsubishi acquires 50% of the equity of Univex (Vila Franca de Xira, Portugal) and starts production of L200 and L300 light commercial vehicles from CKD kits.
1983   Production of the first Nissan Patrol 4x4 at Motor Iberica's plant in Barcelona Zona Franca.
1984   Foundation of Nissan Motor Manufacturing Ltd (UK) in Tyne and Wear.
1985   Motor Iberica commences production of Nissan Vanett light vans.
        Opening of the Nissan Motor Parts Centre in Amsterdam, Netherlands.
        GM and Isuzu create IBC Vehicles, a 60/40 joint venture founded on the remains of GM's Bedford trucks operation, to produce Midi minivans, Suzuki SK410 and Super Carry light commercials and the Vaxhall/Opel Frontera 4x4 in Luton in Britain.
1986   Nissan Bluebird enters production at NMMUK.
        Honda opens a pre-delivery inspection plant at Swindon in Britain.
1987   Motor Iberica becomes Nissan Motor Iberica (NMISA).
1989   Foundation of Nissan Europe NV and Nissan Distribution Service (Europe) in Amsterdam.
        Nissan open European technical centre (NETC) at Zaventem in Belgium.
        Opening of an engine plant by Honda UK Manufacturing Ltd. at Swindon.
        Toyota sign accord for production of Hi-Lux pickups as the VW Taro at the VW factory in Hanover in Germany.
         Bertone commence production in Turin in Italy of the Daihatsu Rocky 4x4, powered by a BMW turbo-diesel and renamed the Free-Climber.
1990   Honda UK (HUM) and Rover take cross-share-holdings of 20% in each other's companies.
        Creation of Toyota Motor Europe Marketing and Engineering in Brussels in Belgium.
1991   SMMT recognises Nissan (NMMUK) as a British manufacturers. The Sunderland-built Primera is launched.

Table 3.4 cont'd

1992	Opening of the Nissan Europe Technology Centre (NETC) at Cranfield in Britain. Nissan MISA launches the Serena minivan, using an engine produced in Sunderland. Launch of the Sunderland-built Micra. Foundation of Nissan Design Europe GmbH in Munich in Germany. Honda plant in Swindon commences production. Toyota plants at Deeside in Britain producing engines and Burnaston in Britain producing Carina E saloons, start production. Production of Swift saloons starts in the Magyar Suzuki Corp (40% Suzuki/60% C. Itoh) plant at Esztergon in Hungary.
1993	Daihatsu and Piaggio from P&S SpA, a joint venture (49% Daihatsu/51% Piaggio) company for the production of the Hijet 'microvan' at Pontedera, near Pisa in Italy. Formation of Mitsubishi Motor Europe in Amsterdam. Inauguration of a Mazda Training Centre at Puurs in Begium. 60% of the Nissan sold in Europe are produced in Europe.
1997	Toyota engine investment in Northern France.

Source: Derived by the author on the basis of various sources.

1   The EU Car Industry during the 1970s

By the early 1970s, the prospects for the car industry in the traditional car producing countries of Western Europe and the US had begun to look extremely inauspicious. The first oil shock of 1973–74 brought energy shortages and higher petrol prices, resulting in a need for substantial investment in fuel economy, and the ensuing general economic crisis was bound to reduce purchasing power and depress further the demand for new cars.

Japanese car-makers, however, with their superior production system and with products of unmatched price and quality that uniquely suited the changed consumer preferences, were beginning to mount their export offensive, and lurking over the horizon were the newly developing countries with their huge supply of cheap labour.

The Japanese invasion of the EU market hit Western car-makers with a wave of product and process innovations in what had been seen before as a mature mass-production system. A restructuring process was undertaken, involving a very high level of investments from government and the private sector. New methods of supply management and work organisation were introduced. The relations between suppliers and assemblers were reorganised and a number of joint ventures were set up among Western and Japanese makers.

Despite the restructuring process, total employment in the big five countries France, Italy, Sweden, the UK and Germany did not decline much from the level of the early 1970s. In the early 1980s, there were policy changes in car employment. There were huge job cuts in Italy, France and the UK, while Sweden and Germany increased their employment in their car sectors. The different trends in employment in the sector reflected car export rates. Sweden and Germany were strong exporters as more than a half of total production went abroad. Italian export was one-third of total production throughout the 1970s and the early 1980s. The UK export share in 1970 was about 40 per cent and declined to 27 per cent in 1983.

One of the obvious things during the 1970s was that the better invested and export-led countries' car-makers survived in the more competitive world market. Domestic-dominated car-makers suffered a more severe restructuring process. The losers had to allow their management strategies to depend on government intervention in the industrial restructuring process, while the winners enjoyed an increasing market share in the EU. The gap between winners and losers, which was revealed during the 1970s, caused direct government involvement in the car manufacturing sector.

Compared to the restructuring process of the 1980s, this adaptation was mainly internal restructuring. Domestic-dominated marketing, new model development changes in the production line and in relations with components industries, proved to be unsuccessful in improving the competitiveness of the car industry in the EU. Traditional production methods lost ground in a period of rapidly developing technology.

The EU car industry since the second oil shock, clearly suffered in comparison to Japan's successful market penetration. During the 1980s, the EU car manufacturers, such as Rover, Fiat, Peugeot and Renault disclosed their weaknesses. Too much wasted capacity, over-investment, too many employees – these problems needed an unprecedented wave of rationalisation enforced by government intervention. All the EU car manufacturers, and their host governments put into effect a policy that a reasonable volume in the manufacture of medium to large-sized cars was essential for survival and that overproduction was a risk in the EU market base. In the first half of 1980s, productive capacity representing about one million units per annum was closed down, and major car manufacturers in each country were rationalised. During this period, 420,000 employees left the car industry, and this meant that over one million people needed governmental support through social security. One

Table 3.5   Market share in the EU

Maker	1979	1980	1981	1982	1983	1984	1985	1986	1987	1988	1989	1990
Ford	12.0	11.1	12.3	12.4	12.6	12.8	11.9	11.7	12.0	11.3	11.6	11.6
Fiat	10.0	11.8	12.7	12.5	12.3	14.5	13.7	14.0	14.9	14.8	14.8	14.2
VW	12.2	11.8	12.6	11.8	11.7	13.6	14.4	14.7	14.9	14.9	15.0	15.5
PSA	17.1	14.6	13.2	12.4	11.8	11.5	11.5	11.4	12.1	12.9	12.7	13.0
GM	9.6	8.7	8.4	9.7	11.2	11.0	11.4	10.9	10.6	10.4	11.0	11.9
Renault	13.5	14.9	14.0	14.7	12.8	10.9	10.6	10.6	10.6	10.2	10.4	9.8
Rover	5.4	5.1	4.7	4.2	4.0	3.9	4.0	3.5	3.4	3.5	3.1	2.9
Japan	7.3	9.8	9.2	8.9	9.4	10.3	10.8	11.7	11.3	11.3	10.9	12.6

Source: SMMT, EUROSTAT, various years, *Financial Times*, 22 Jan. 1990 and 21 Jan. 1991.

particular consequence of the oil shock in the EU was that the mass manufacturers such as Rover, Peugeot, and Fiat became dependent on their home market share. Growing high competition between foreign makers and nationalised makers weakened indigenous makers owing to their dependence on the home market only.

2   The EU Car Industry during the 1980s

During the 1980s, car-makers faced an even more stringent restructuring procedure. New technology investments, increasing research, high technology electronic parts, and most of all the development of close relations with other makers, specially, Japanese makers were added.

> Compared to the restructuring process in the 1970s, it has been more direct, profit based, globalised.

> • Competition between manufacturers intensified because the costs of research, design, development and production had to be met from increased volume of sales; the manufacturers adopted very aggressive marketing policies in external markets while temporarily maintaining the profit levels in their home markets.
> • It followed that systems of marketing had to be modified because of the need to cover markets more efficiently (an increase in the number of sales outlets, reorganisation of import subsidiaries, development of new marketing services); at the same time, the manufacturers wished to take precautions against the entry into the sector of new firms specialising in distribution.
> • Commercial advantage now began to favour suppliers, with component producers achieving a very high degree of technical and commercial autonomy; it followed that commercial relationships were acquiring a much better balance. This situation seems likely to be a lasting one in view of technical and technological developments in vehicle manufacture, although specialist firms (notably in electronics) are now making major interventions as suppliers. Manufacturers are thus confronted by firms doing business world-wide. They have to negotiate with them over improvements in productivity and they have to learn to live in their industrial culture.[22]

Even a brief surge of sales in the late 1980s in the EU proved insufficient to save some industries from a further round of rationalisation. Peugeot gave up Talbot, which was acquired from Chrysler in 1978; Rover, Alfa Romeo, and SEAT failed to survive on their own. Volkswagen bought SEAT in 1986 and Fiat took Alfa Romeo in 1987, Rover sold 20 per cent of its stake to Honda in 1990, and was finally taken over by BMW in 1994. After a string of successful years in the US market, the European specialist manufacturers such as Saab and Jaguar were taken over by GM and Ford respectively. Excepting VW, Fiat, Renault and PSA, the only other European manufacturers left are the specialist makers Mercedes Benz, BMW and Porsche, as well as Volvo, which ended its collaboration with Renault in 1994. BMW's acquisition of the Rover UK has turned the 'Big Six' into the 'Big Seven' EU car manufacturers. Even after the SEM, the individual markets are still dominated by domestic manufacturers. The manufacturers tend to have larger distribution infrastructures in their respective domestic markets and preference for locally produced cars still plays a significant role in some markets.

Table 3.6   Percentage of total Big Six European cars shares in the home market

	1987	1991
Rover	73.2%	65.3%
Fiat	67.5%	63.9%
VDA	53.9%	57.5%
Renault	49.3%	43.8%
PSA	47.1%	45.5%
SEAT	40.1%	32.6%

Source: SMMT, various years.

During the 1980s, relations between governments and car manufacturers became more distant. Alfa Romeo and SEAT were the first to be sold off, while the German government sold its stake in VW in 1987, the UK government privatised Jaguar, which was then taken over by Ford in 1985, and sold Rover in 1988 to BAe. The French government ended its special relationship with Renault and sold some shares to Volvo in 1990. This privatisation was forced by the escalating costs of sustaining weaker manufacturers in the industry, and the intervention of the EU Commission in vetting state aid and other forms of subsidies that might distort competition. Even after the privatisation of the car industry, the industry is still largely organised on a national basis in the EU. There are many intentions to collaborate in R&D and to remove many formal obstacles to collaboration, which were caused by nationalist manufacturing environments. However France and Italy still maintained their policy of resisting any attempt by foreign manufacturers to set up their affiliates in the country.

3   *SEM and EU Car Industry*

During the early part of the 1990s, EU car manufacturers have increased their collaborations with other companies or other countries. Many car manufacturers in the EU have entered into joint venture production agreements, such as the Ford-VW, and Fiat-PSA multipurpose vehicle projects. One particular collaboration is the Volvo-Mitsubishi agreement to produce two different car models on the same production base in the Netherlands. It is significant that it will produce one of Volvo's core models, rather than the niche models that have typically been the result of other manufacturers' joint ventures.

The EU car manufacturers have confronted one main challenge since the 1990s. The main problem is insecurity, which comes from the absence of unified economic control within the industry and political intervention at the regulatory level. The big four car manufacturing countries, Germany, France, Italy, and the UK, which have nationally-based assemblers, have sought management strategies of cost reduction without finding a competitive advantage. Hence, they are not able to recover their costs as they face the productive threat of competition from nonmember countries such as Japan, and US against a background of worsening internal-market problems. At the regulatory level the problem is that the EU cannot become an effective supranational state and the industry will be the victim of 'negative integration'. The assemblers have lost the protection of their national governments without gaining the protection of the EU. In the absence of appropriate political regulation of a united government, the resolution of the insecurity problem will take the form of a vicious process of restructuring.

According to Mr Franciscus Andriessen, the Commission vice-president, addressing the World Automotive Forum on 23–24 February 1990, the Commission researched how the car industry would work in the SEM, and concluded that:

> There are three principles of the car industry's external relations. The first is that the national restrictions that some Member States impose on imports from third countries, in particular Japan, must be eliminated by the end of 1992. A single market implies uniform Community rules for trade with which national restrictions are inconsistent.
>
> Our second principle is that Community industry needs a period of transition to adapt to an unified market and to open competition with Japanese companies. This period must be limited and clearly defined.

Table 3.7   The Progress Report on Project 1992 SEM

AREA	RATING	GOAL	PROGRESS REPORT	COMMENT
AIRLINES	☐	Totally open skies, including freedom of pricing, entry of new airlines, and access by foreign carries to routes within individual countries (known as cabotage).	Free pricing and licensing of new airlines begins 1 January 1993. Cabotage will be phased in between then and April 1997.	The ambitious plan should fully deregulate air travel – reduce fares – by 2000. In the next few years, though, EC members will use loopholes to protect their own carriers.
BANKS	☐	Freedom to provide financial services in any member country, including checking accounts, mortgages and business loans.	Many changes have already been phased in and the rest will take effect 1 January 1993.	Banks have begun moving into other countries but customers are sometimes cautious about trusting their money to foreigners. Many banks are looking for strong local partners.
INSURANCE	☐	Freedom to sell insurance in all member countries.	Some changes have been made, the rest will take effect 1 January 1993.	Like banks, big insurance companies have begun to move into neighbouring markets. But they also are finding it better to operate with partners.
STOCK MARKETS	☐	Investors in any member country should be able to buy and sell shares and bonds in any other.	Most restrictions have been lifted. All will disappear 1 January 1993.	Cross-border investing is steaming ahead across Europe, though much of the action remains in London.
CAPITAL MOVEMENT	⊙	Abolish all restrictions on movement across borders of capital owned by EC residents.	Eight members states have approved all directives. The others will do so by the end of the year.	Cross-border capital flows are increasing, but tax laws can still impede them in some countries.

Table 3.7 cont'd

		Aim	Status	Comment
MOBILITY	◉	European residents should be able to cross border without passports, and workers should be allowed to move any EC countries, base on Europe-wide recognition of professional or other qualifications.	By 1 January 1993 all professional worker directives will be passed by six states. These will have passed some, three will have passed none. No agreement on movement of individuals yet.	In theory, very exciting. In practise, language barriers and nationalism could delay free movement of workers for a generation. And no sensible European is throwing away his passport.
PHARMA-CEUTICALS	◉	Deregulate prices and bring standards and test procedures of all EC countries into line with each other and with the US and Japan.	Half of all directives have been adopted. Approval on the rest is expected by 1 January 1993.	Harmonisation of procedures is going well, but there has been no progress on deregulating prices.
TECHNICAL STANDARDS	◉	An end to restriction of foreign manufacturers on safety and technical grounds, assuming those manufacturers meet minimum standards.	Implementation so far in toys, pressure vessels, and safety clothing, among other areas.	Many small companies that can't meet the new standards, particularly in Greece and Portugal, will go out of business. But it will be some years before all barriers fall.
AUTOMOBILES	☒	Removal of all quotas and tariffs by the mid-1990s.	Original aim scrapped in 1991 when European car-makers asked for barriers against the Japanese until 1999.	Cars in Europe, already the most expensive in the world, are not getting any cheaper. Those built by the Japanese in Europe are not subject to quotas, but even that could change.

Table 3.7 cont'd

TELEVISION	[X]	Satellite broadcasters should be allowed to transmit anywhere in the EC.	Although this goal was adopted by the EC, no country has officially adopted it into national law.	Put that dish purchase on hold. Individual governments have been unable to reach agreement on decency standards, advertising regulations, and national program quotas.
PUBLIC PROCUREMENT	[X]	Open all bidding for public projects, including transportation and telecommunication.	Adopted by the EC, but no country has passed it into local law.	Though EC law in theory supersedes national law, it is hard to enforce. Fewer than 20 per cent of public projects have been open to bidding.

Notes

[ ] All measures agreed on by all 12 countries.
[⊙] Progressing satisfactorily.
[X] Not progressing at all.

Source: Fortune (1992), 14 December.

Finally, our third principle is that only the general rules of international trade will apply at the end of the transitional period. Let me come back to the transitional arrangements which have been the subject of much discussion. What we propose is to come to an understanding with the Japanese whereby they would monitor their exports to the Community for a clearly limited period after 1992. This will require exports corporation of the Japanese authorities.[23]

The SEM had a definitely positive impact on the car manufacturing sector. The free movement of goods has opened up new market opportunities, which the major manufacturers seized by spreading their production facilities throughout the EU. Car manufacturers' operations with subsidiaries have been also eased by the achievement of free movement of capital and progress on the front of cross-border payments. For that, the EU needs harmonisation of the taxation system and national regulation formalities i.e. a car whose technical specifications are approved in one member country must be approved all over the EU.

The Commission urged EU manufacturers to collaborate with overseas manufacturers in order to improve their competitiveness. According to Leon Brittan, addressing the Cambridge City Conservative Association Business Club on 9 February 1990, there were dangers of protecting the EU car industry from the nonmember countries' market penetration in that:

First, it denies European consumers an unrestricted choice, and it tends to force up prices ... A recent survey by the European Bureau of Consumers' Unions has drawn attention to the great variation in prices between different Member States for the same model ... But the root lesson is clear: market restrictions work against competition, and against the consumer interest.

Second, the effective maintenance of separate national car markets after 1992 reduces the credibility of the SEM, and this has knock-on effects in other sectors.

Third, any attempt to segment the Community market after 1992 would involve either the maintenance of frontier controls on trade or an acceptance of market segmentation practices which would be messy and unsatisfactory.

Fourth, a protected European car maker encourages a little-Europe view at a time when car production only makes sense as a truly international undertaking.

Fifth, so long as our market remains divided and restricted, European producers, including component-producers, will seek the prolongation of national quotas, and put off the hard decisions necessary to render European industry truly competitive on international markets.

Sixth, so long as we maintain restrictions, we will encourage Japanese producers toward strategic decisions which may or may not be in the European Community's long-term interests. For example:

- We encourage them to move up-market in their production, because their cars are being sold at a premium in Europe.
- We encourage them to produce within the European Community.
- We encourage them to produce in third markets such as Eastern Europe or EFTA against which we do not maintain restrictions and where 500/0 local content confer origin.[24]

Moreover, the competitive potential of the EU car manufacturers was affected by various elements.

- Several manufactures have a scale, profitability, and financial capacity, which are inadequate for a fully integrated European market.
- National champions dominate national markets. There is a strong national bias in purchasing patterns in Italy and France. For example, Fiat commands a large share of the Italian market, but the Italian market also absorbs 68 per cent of the Fiats sold in the EU. Almost half of Peugeot and Renaults sales are in France.
- Competition between the major European producers is fierce.
- Imports from abroad increase competitive pressure.
- Japanese imports and production by transplants represent a special threat because they have a competitive edge in productivity, quality, and the updating of models.
- European share in outside markets is declining.[25]

Hence the car manufacturers in the EU had faced an advantage, on the one hand, from the market expansion by intra-trade, and disadvantage, on the other, from Japanese FDI in the EU.

According to the EU Commission's research, on the other hand, the EU big four car manufacturers demonstrated a number of strengths, leading to the statement that management capacity of EU car-makers can be regarded as generally positive. Moreover, Leon Brittan commented about the Commission's role in the strengthening of the car industry that it was important:

First to press ahead urgently with our efforts to eliminate the technical and administrative barriers to a Single Market … The Commission has already tabled the main legislation required to eliminate such obstacles, and we must see the process through by the end of 1992.

Second we must sort out our environmental requirements.

Third we must continue to monitor and control state intervention. The car aid framework provides a necessary discipline which was long overdue. As a result, since the beginning of the last year we have required prior notification of proposals

Table 3.8   The strengths and weaknesses of the car manufacturing sector in the EU

European strengths	European weaknesses
General economic performance (also true for USA, Japan, Korea)	Time to obtain building, operating and environmental permits (mucher shorter in the USA, Japan, Korea)
Protection of intellectual property (legally also provided for in Poland)	High corporate income tax rates (much lower in the USA, Korea)
Excellent transport infrastructure (also offered by the USA, Japan, Korea)	High labour cost (the prime advantage for Korea, Poland)
Skilled labour availability (also valid for Korea, Japan)	Lack of work time flexibility (advantage for the USA, Japan, Korea)

Source: Commission (1996), *European Automobile Industry* (mimeo).

to grant national aids, to ensure that they do not distort competition between companies. Even in areas of regional priority we must balance development benefits against potential problems of over-capacity and unfair competition.

Fourth the Community must do all that it can to promote R&D on a European scale. Under the present R&D Framework Programme the Community is already seeking to promote relevant research, for example in such programmes as BRITE, ESPRIT or JOULE. The Community has drawn up a block exemption from the competition rules to cover corporation between companies in basic research. We must absolutely essential that the European motor industry should remain in the forefront, technologically. The primary effort must come from the industry itself, but insofar as the Commission can help to stimulate corporation which is compatible with fair competition, we must do so.

Fifth we must make a similar and parallel effort on the vocational training side.

But sixth – and this is the greatest single contribution we can make – we must have the courage of our Single Market convictions, and drive on towards a totally open market towards the middle of this decade.[26]

In all the explanations for the restructuring of the EU car industry, Japanese FDI is the most visible and competitive business challenge in the EU. In respect of the EU car manufacturing sector, it was an important coincidence that other EU manufacturers regard the arrival of Japanese volume assembly operations in the UK as a major threat to their established producers, while there has been a growing criticism within the UK of the economic benefits of the Japanese inward foreign investment in the UK.

Japanese penetration in the EU was supported, but only under the following conditions, by the EU Parliament in 1990:

1. a Japanese obligation with respect to local content
2. guarantees on access to the Japanese market
3. a review of the accord if at the end of the transitional period the total trade balance of the Community with Japan show a deficit[27]

The EU-Japan car agreement in July 1991 between Mr Andriessen, and Mr Eiichi Nakao, the MITI Minister, achieved a 'consensus' on the conditions of import of Japanese cars from 1993 onward. It promised

> facilitation of a move towards the full liberalisation of the EU car market with a transition period until the end of 1999. Before that year, the EU car industry will be restructured to adjust towards adequate levels of international competitiveness and to avoid market disruption.[28]

Under the consensus, the EU undertook to abolish all national import restrictions, and, from 1 January 1993, not to apply Article 115 to cars imported from Japan. Japan agreed to monitor the growth of export of cars to the EU as a whole and to the five more restricted markets, which are France where the estimated total exports of Japanese cars would reach 150,000 units by 1999, i.e. 5.3 per cent of the national market, Italy, 138,000 units, 5.3 per cent, Spain 79,000 units, 5.4 per cent, Portugal, 23,000 units, 8.4 per cent and the UK, 190,000 units, 7 per cent, on the assumption that its export would reach 1.23 million units in 1999 in a total EU market forecast at 15.1 million units.

Concerning this agreement, there is an important question about the production by the Japanese car affiliates in the EU. The Commission explained that 'the agreement covers only the shipments of automobiles from Japan to the EEC and does not extended to the existing Japanese investment in the EEC'.[29] If affiliates in the EU were not covered by the consensus, then their production could render restrictions on direct Japanese exports meaningless. However, there are two reasons why this may not be so in practice.

> First, transplants production is expected to be constrained by installed capacity. As Preusse states, production capacity of Japanese transplants in the EEC was 260,000 units in 1990 and would be 587,000 in 1993, 824,000 in 1994, 1,003,000 in 1995, and 1,420,000 in the year 2000. According to the Commission, production would not surpass 1.2 million by 1999. The Commission expects Japanese cars to raise their share in the EEC market from 11.3 per cent in 1992 to 16 per cent by

the year 2000. The Commission's working assumption is said to have been that, by 1999, such plants would be producing almost as many vehicles as would be imported from Japan. Secondly, it is possible that Japanese production within Europe is deemed acceptable, either because it is not perceived to be a competitive threat or because of the benefits it confers on the European economy.[30]

The agreement about the presence of Japanese affiliates in the EU industry was the target of the FDI policy of the Japanese government and Japanese MNEs. Japan regarded the agreement as a turning point in its market penetration strategy.

The agreement of the free hand for Japanese affiliates in the EU was a political victory. Multilateral manufacturing investment in specific countries with financial support from host governments, and unified market penetration strategy, are all that the Japanese government hoped for and did. Compare to the globalisation strategy of MNEs, the political solution showed a more direct effect on the car industries, as in the case of Nissan UK.[31]

Japanese Car Sales in Europe

For a decade, Japanese car-makers have continually increased their market share in the EU. After having successfully entered the US market through affiliates, they transferred this strategy to the EU. The big three Japanese car-makers invested particularly in the UK, and their English-made cars were exported to the European continent. The Japanese approach, consisting of lean production and group management, causes anxiety to EU car-makers. The EU's supremacy in the world market for cars, which they shared for a long time with American car-makers, seems to be jeopardised. The EU makers will be expected to restructure their management. The EU car-makers produce at higher cost than the Japanese. In order to reduce the cost gap, the EU makers are increasingly adapting Japanese production methodologies and building Japanese-style supplier relations.

With the start of the SEM, Japanese car manufacturers are faced by a slowdown of a sort never before experienced. A saturated domestic market, and political mismanagement in the EU, has forced Japanese MNEs to rethink their global strategy. In 1992, Nissan was sliding toward its first pre-tax loss in 45 years and even Toyota, the top Japanese car maker with a domestic market share of 42 per cent is facing a downturn. Despite current difficulties, Japanese car manufacturers are achieving their strategic targets. Their intention

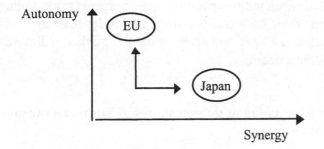

Figure 3.5   The manufacturing trends between EU and Japanese car-makers

Source: Richter, F. and Wakuta, Y. (1993).

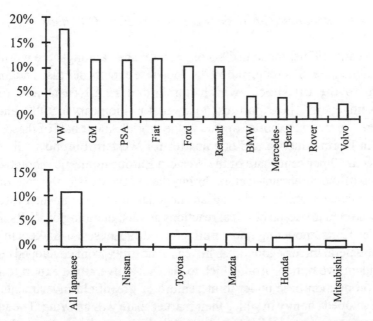

Figure 3.6   Market share within the EU by Western makers and Japanese makers

Source: *Fortune* (1993), 11 January.

in the EU has moved from setting up an assembling process to expanding into component sectors. Table 3.8 shows that the reality of Japanese globalisation programme, which is a 20 per cent share of the EU market, will have been accomplished within a decade.

Table 3.9   The expectation of market shares of European car market within a decade

	1990	2000
JAPANESE (total)	12.6%	19.5%
Imported	12.0%	10.5%
Made in Europe	0.6%	9.0%
EUROPEAN	64.6%	55.0%
AMERICAN	22.8%	25.5%

Source: *Fortune* (1992), 4 May.

1   The Japanese Car in the EU since the First Oil Shock

By the early 1970s, Japan had become established amongst the world major car manufacturers. Through the 1970s, Japanese exports increased dramatically owing to the oil shock, which demanded small cars, and to price competitiveness. The export rose to about 4 million cars in 1980, and Japan became the largest exporter of cars in the world. About half of these exports were in North America and one quarter for Western Europe – this amount reached a 10 per cent share of the Western Europe domestic market.

One of the important factors during these periods was the role of MITI. Well surveyed, scanned marketing, and negotiation at government level allowed Japanese cars to escape political reactions against dumping or VERs. Despite MITI's efforts, mounting trade profits forced Japanese car-makers to engage in multilateral trade negotiations. Increased hostility from developed countries gave them two options from which to choose: a diversified export route, or a local production base under joint venture or greenfield investments within the developed country in which their market share was growing. The Japanese government and car MNEs tried to find the solution during the early 1980s.

The role of government in business strategy was strengthened during the early 1980s. There were good examples of government negotiation, such as the Honda and Nissan projects in the UK.

Table 3.10   Japanese penetration of the EU car market

Country	Market penetration (%)				
	1970	1975	1980	1985	1990
Ireland	–	11.6	30.5	33.8	42.2
Netherlands	3.2	15.6	26.4	22.3	26.7
Sweden	–	–	13.5	16.1	24.9
Germany	0.1	1.7	10.4	13.3	15.9
UK	0.4	9.0	11.9	10.9	11.7
France	0.2	1.5	3.1	3.0	3.4
Spain	–	–	1.3	0.8	2.2
Italy	0.02	0.1	0.1	0.2	2.0
EU	0.6	4.8	9.0	9.4	12.6

Source: JETRO Annual Report; EU Commission Papers; *Financial Times*; SMMT Report
Paper, various issues.

In the early 1980s, the Japanese government tried to find outlets for their trade profits, which were causing international trade problems. Globalised Japanese business was one solution. But the emerging problems were where, when, how, and who? Since then, the direct involvement of the Japanese government with business has moved from salesman to broker. Under the Thatcher government, the UK was regarded as a good partner.[32]

Japanese exports to the EU continued in the 1980s, but the imposition of European restrictions effectively braked or sharply restrained Japanese market share growth in many Union markets during this decade. Although Japan's market share in Germany increased from 10.4 per cent to 15.2 per cent and in Italy increased from 0.14 per cent to 1.14 per cent during the years 1980 to 1989, the UK and France declined from 11.9 per cent to 11.3 per cent, and 2.9 per cent to 2.8 per cent. Despite these restrictions, Japanese car manufacturers maintained their shares of the total EU market. In 1989, Japanese car had about one-tenth of the overall EU market supplied almost entirely by exports numbering some 1.23 million cars.

When the Japanese government proved to have been successful in their approaches to individual member countries, the Commission tried to move multilateral negotiation towards unified EU level talks. The Commission of the EU issued a report about Japanese government as a guideline paper about cooperation with the EU. In July 1991, the EU and Japan reached a consensus on the conditions for the import of Japanese cars from 1993 onwards.

It is no part of the duties of government to take decisions on behalf of industry. Instead, both Member States and the Community should work to create a favourable climate in which industrial cooperation can thrive. In particular, the Community should:

- in corporation with the Japanese government, seek ways of facilitating industry's participation in mutually beneficial cooperation;
- further examine possibilities of facilitating the adaptation by European parts suppliers to the requirements both of the Japanese market and of Japanese companies in Europe;
- maintain and extent its Executive Training Programme (ETP) to broaden and deepen industry's understanding of Japanese and the Japanese industrial economy;
- together with the Japanese government, strengthen the EC–Japan centre for Industrial Cooperation;
- advocate the establishment by the Japanese government of new, coordinated business facilities for Community industrial newcomers to the Japanese market, especially small and medium sized enterprises.[33]

However, the agreement had its own weakness in that the agreement covers only the shipments of cars from Japan to the EU, and does not extend to the existing Japanese investment in the EU. If Japanese affiliates in the EU are not included by the consensus, then their production could render restrictions on direct Japanese exports meaningless. The global localisation programme of the Japanese car MNEs worked successfully within the EU without the agreement between the Japanese government and the Commission.

2   *Japanese Car's New Strategy in the EU*

The establishment of Japanese car affiliates in the EU was begun by Nissan Motor Manufacturing (NMM) in 1986 in the UK, and has been steadily increasing over the past decade. There are currently 12 Japanese affiliates in operation in Europe with an anticipated production volume of 1.63 million units by the mid-1990s. The big three (Nissan, Toyota, Honda) affiliates in the UK are crucial to this process, and these represent the bulk of overall production. There are also 35 auto component affiliates in the EU, mainly in the UK, compared to 300 in the North America. Japanese investment in the EU clearly follows the pattern of market penetration in the US.

The motive for Japanese affiliates in the EU is to access the largest car market. At the same time, there were strong 'pull-factors' from the EU Commission. Mr Brittan said that:

I say 'may or may not be in our long-term interest' because this is a subject of vigorous debate. My own view is that Japanese investment in the EC – whether Sony in France, Fujitsu in Spain, or Minolta in Germany – is a good thing, just as the wave of American investment in an earlier generation (which also provoked defensive European reactions) was a good thing. In the motor vehicle sector, such investment – and I am talking here about true manufacturing and not mere assembly – brings us knowledge of successful production and management techniques.

It promotes European product design skills, and R&D. It may well provide a new base for European exports, as illustrated, for example, by the recent announcement from Nissan UK that they will be shipping many thousands of their cars to Japan.[34] I utterly reject the absurd and defensive thesis that every European worker employed in Japanese-financed car production in Europe is putting others out of work. The same has been said, of course, about improvements in productivity in almost every major industry over the past century or more.[35]

The current protectionism about car industry in the EU is extremely *ad hoc*, varying enormously from member country to member country. The EU trade policy for car imports from Japan has changed, from individual country VERs or quotas to an EU-wide agreement with national supply forecasts. Before the agreement, parallel imports were prevented from disrupting the operation of national VERs by the use of administrative measures such as car registration procedures, based on differences in technical regulations, or explicit border controls.

The Japanese car manufacturers' global business plans call for increased local operations in the EU, as has been the case in North America. Beginning in 1996, Nissan is localising production of rear axles at its UK affiliate. The other makers are following suit, with plans to add production of new models and major components at their European affiliates. In 1995, production by Nissan, Toyota and Honda increased by 16.1 per cent, to 397,069 units, mainly due to the increased output from Honda's Swindon affiliate. Overall EU production amounted to 600,994 units, registering a growth of 20.9 per cent over 1994.

Exports to the other EU member countries are the main operation of the Japanese UK affiliates. Nissan's exports from the UK, which began at 11,080 units in 1988, increased 163,148 units in 1995. Exports accounted for 75.8 per cent of Nissan's UK production in 1995. To become fully Europeanised operations, Japanese car manufacturers set up nine R&D and design technical facilities in the EU. With the duties of overseeing compliance with local regulation, these facilities are concerned with market research and production planning. The arrival of Japanese makers and engine plants in the EU, to be followed as in US by Japanese product development, finally puts to rest any idea that protection against Japanese imports can be effective. In retrospect, the sealing off of the French, Italian and Spanish makers from the Japanese meant that the local manufacturers were never challenged to improve their product quality and productivity. As a result, they lost the top end of each segment of their own markets to the German manufacturers.

Conclusion

EU trade policy has two different approaches towards nonmember countries. The Commission's FDI inward policy has been a *'pull-factor'* expressed towards nonmember countries. FDI by US MNEs, since the late 1960s has mainly dealt with host countries one by one. US MNEs have changed their approach to Europe from a policy of establishing local affiliates to a policy of setting up independent manufacturing bases. Japanese FDI in the EU has been regarded as a key solution of the balance of trade problem. Since the late 1970s, Japanese companies set up their affiliates worldwide. US FDI and Japanese FDI in the EU were therefore quite similar. Despite differences of timing, US FDI in the EU was mainly undertaken by the manufacturing sector, such as cars, oil, and chemicals so on. However, Japanese FDI in manufacturing sectors toward EU is, even now, just 23.9 per cent of total FDI. While US MNEs' undertook their globalisation policy as part of autonomous company strategies, the role of Japanese government was enormous in the decision-making of Japanese MNEs.

Ironically, tariffs, VERs, and antidumping accusations have all worked to encourage Japanese car MNEs to invest in the EU. Such policies have not only accelerated FDI that would have taken place in any case, but they have also increased Japanese manufacturing investment substantially above the level it would otherwise have reached. Japanese FDI has been more likely to substitute directly for exports of the final products targeted by the EU trade policy measures. Car manufacturing investment, in particular, is more likely to be limited to assembly-type operations dependent on imported components, despite local component regulations. Empirical investigation of the UK case showed this clearly.

When the Japanese MNEs started to respond by investing in EU manufacturing operations in order to bypass trade disharmony, the EU amended its antidumping law to make it applicable to Japanese assembly manufacturers as well. The so-called 'screwdriver plant' amendment was effectively administered as a relatively strict local content rule. However, further investment from the first and second tier component industries limited the effect of the local content regulation.

In conclusion, to what extent can EU policies be seen as assisting EU-owned car-makers in competition with their Japanese rivals? Restrictive policies, such as antidumping and local content measures, targeting Japanese manufacturers can be seen as alternative cost strategies, improving the competitive position of EU makers by increasing the costs of Japanese manufacturers. However, the rapid technological advances in manufacturing capability gave Japanese makers competitive advantages in price. It became clear that the EU policies have been less than effective in reaching a major objective of strategic trade policies; protecting the EU makers. It is not to say that the EU policies have not been instigated to protect European companies, but the Japanese strategy of market penetration has been overwhelming. A good comparison between the EU makers and the Japanese ones was in their respective relationships with government. While Japanese affiliates enjoyed capital incentives for greenfield investment, the EU makers were muddling through a chronic restructuring process.

Moreover, the FDI response to antidumping reduced the effectiveness of antidumping challenges and local component regulations. The UK case study showed that Japanese car-makers reacted to the latter by producing components in-house in EU factories, inviting first or second tiers in the *keiretsu* to invest in the EU, and procuring components from independent Japanese components makers in the EU. Hence, Japanese car-makers' FDI in both assemblers and components makers will have enabled them to limit the EU car-makers' cost advantage from EU policies. On the other hand, the local component regulations have largely failed to promote local component manufacture by EU companies. Paradoxically, the regulations may have reduced sales of EU component suppliers to Japanese car-makers. Since the successful involvement of new components suppliers in the supply chain involves time and effort, the time pressure put on Japanese assemblers to increase local content is likely to have spurred transfer of components production from the UK to the EU in order to comply with the rules without loss of reliability and quality. The EU policies encouraging supply links between EU suppliers and Japanese assemblers would have been much more effective than local content regulations, which do not specify the source of local procurements.

While the EU trade policy measures have supported the EU car industry, there is no guarantee that EU car-makers will be competitive on world markets and viable in the absence of trade barriers. The real reason for the success of the Japanese invasion in the EU, explained by Louis Hughes, head of GM Europe is that 'The Westerner is like the hunter. He shoots and retreats. The Japanese is like the farmer. He endures.'[36]

Notes

1   There is a long history of the name of Western Europe's organisation. The ECSC (European Coal and Steel Community) in 1951, EEC (European Economic Community) since the Treaties of Rome in 1957, EC (European Community), in 1967 after Maastricht Treaty in 1991 EU (European Union).

2   Heidensohn, K. (1995), *Europe and World Trade*, p. 51.

3   GATT (1991), *Trade Policy Review: The European Communities*, p. 51.

4   Story, J. (1993), *The New Europe*, p. 300.

5   Hine, R.C. (1985), *The Political Economy of European Trade*, p. 6.

6   Ibid., p. 7.

7   Story, J. (ed.) (1993), p. 300.

8   A programme devised by the UK EU Commissioner, Lord Cockfield. It proposed that the virtual removal of all internal Community barriers to the free movement of people, goods, services, and capital, completing the internal market and creating an economic area without frontiers by 1992.

9   Pinder, J. (1995), *European Community*, p. 21.

10   Brittan, L. (1993), 'Shaping a Framework for Global Trade: The challenge for the EC', *European Access*, No. 3.

11   The application firstly, submitted in 1951 strongly supported by US. It was more political than the economic reason that the increased trade by Japan with the West was supposed to strengthen the anti-Communist forces in the Far East Asia and to cure Japan's chronic payments crisis which would be caused the other political crisis.

12   Rothacher, A. (1983), *Economic Diplomacy between the EC and Japan 1959–81*, p. 86.

13   Wilkinson, E., readopted from Rothacher, A. (1983), *Economic Diplomacy between the EC and Japan 1959–81*.

14   *Newsweek* (1979), 16 April.

15   The EU Commission (1992), *A Vonsistent and Global Approach: A Review of the Community's relation with Japan* (mimeo), p. 7.

16   At the Anglo-Japanese Conference 28 March 1996 at Cardiff, Wales, many Japanese MNEs' managers thought that the real problem, which their are faced since 1992 SEM, was the struggle between Japanese MNEs own. Because, some manufacturing sector, such as electric goods, car, office equipment competed with Japanese MNEs for a fixed market. The competition between the Japanese goods and the EU's have been stabilised during the 1980s. Throughout the 1980s, the Japanese MNEs have changed their strategy from exports to direct investment in local manufacturing sector. This was the second market penetration strategy. It have been abolished the anti-dumping, VERs and other quantitative restriction. However, it caused the struggle between the EU goods and Japanese ones for the free competition under the perfect market.

17   Willy de Clercq (1986), *Bulletin of the European Communities*, September, p. 15.

18   NIKKEI (1992), *Japan Economic Almanac*, p. 30.

19 Ms Noriko Hama: interview.
20 Egan, C. and McKiernan, P. (1994), p. 160.
21 Hirata, M. (1988), 'Internationalisation Strategy and Globalisation of European Car-makers', *Hitotsubashi Journal of Commerce and Management*, No. 23, p. 1.
22 Salvadori, D. (1992), 'The Automobile Industry', in Mayes, D.G. (eds), *The European Challenge*, p. 55.
23 Forum Address (mimeo).
24 Brittan, L. (1990) (mimeo).
25 Andersen, C. (1992), *Influencing the European Community*, pp. 302–3.
26 Club Address by Brittan, L. (mimeo).
27 Andersen, C. (1992), *Influencing the European Community*, p. 309.
28 GATT (1993), *Trade Policy Review of the European Communities*, pp. 46–7.
29 Ibid., p. 172.
30 Mattoo, A. and Mavroidis, P. (1995) 'The EC-Japan Consensus on Cars', *The World Economy*, May, Vol. 18, p. 349.
31 Mr Shimada: interview.
32 Mr Malcom Trevor: interview.
33 Commission of the EC (1992), *A Consistent and Global Approach: A Review of the Community's Relation with Japan* (mimeo), p. 7.
34 BBC that Nissan UK car start its export to Japan in 17 February 1997 reported it.
35 Brittan, L. (1990), Ibid.
36 *Fortune* (1993), 11 January.

Chapter 4

A Comparative Analysis of Industrial Policy and Inward Investment in Four European Countries

There are many reasons to invest in other countries. The host government's trade policies, FDI environments, and various incentives offered by individual EU member governments are said to be very important factors in influencing the investment decisions of firms from non-EU member countries. From the investors' viewpoint, the history of economic and industrial policy in the host country will be another factor taken into consideration. According to the OECD survey (1989), however, the '*specific incentives*' of MNEs have played an important role in influencing the location of FDI in particular countries, although they have not, in general, been a major determinant of the general decision to invest in the EU. This trend showed more strongly for Japanese investment in the EU. What is *specific incentive* for Japanese investment? The role of inter-government relations will be discussed here as a vital factor: the '*pull and push*' factors already discussed.

At government level, it is expected that there will be pre-negotiation between the Japanese government and the host government. 'Japanese investment is different, because there is strong intervention from the government during their decision-making procedure.'[1] While the host government expects to restructure its manufacturing sector, Japanese investors look for '*specific incentives*' at every level from firm-specific incentives to commitments at the level of industrial policy.

Inward investment implies the acquisition of productive assets in a country other than one's own.

Direct investment may take various forms:

(1) a new venture by a company with no previous interest in the UK;
(2) an extension of an existing subsidiary;
(3) a take-over of existing assets.

Two points are worth noting. First, both costs and uncertainties are probably intrinsically higher in the case of (1) than in the other two cases, and hence incentive scheme may have greater influence on this type of direct investment. But, once established, a new enterprise is normally expanded through retained earnings so that the initial public expenditure in the long run has a multiplied effect. Second, (1) and (2) might appear to offer greater employment and production opportunities, but so too would (3) if, in the absence of take-over the firm cease to operate.[2]

Owing to increasing demand for foreign inward investment, government policies towards foreign investment in the EU showed distinctive national characteristics. As Table 4.1 shows, compared to the US situation, the political effect in the EU was wider and the role of government stronger.

Industrial Policy and Investment Incentives

France

After the War, France experienced four particular stages of economic growth, following the destruction of its main industrial areas during the war. Between 1945 and 1958, France restarted its economy in a context of shortages, rationing, and import and export licensing under the aegis of the Planning Office. The period 1958–73 was a golden age for France. It started with the creation of the Common Market and the return to external convertibility of the French franc, and ended with the first oil shock. Growth was faster than in the immediate post-war period, and was accompanied by a marked increase in the labour force, both in manufacturing and in the service sector.

France adapted with difficulty to the wages and oil shocks during the period 1974–81. Overall growth slowed down very markedly, and employment grew only in the government sector, declining fast in the manufacturing sector. Since 1981 France has embraced market principles forcibly for its goods markets. Yet labour markets remain highly protected and, as productivity growth has not recovered from its post-1973 decline, limited growth in public employment is insufficient to prevent a massive rise in unemployment.

It is quite interesting that during this period, in three EU member countries, France, German, and the UK, government policies took similar turns towards the free market. France, under the pro-European F. Mitterrand, nevertheless pushed for more protective policies towards nonmember countries of the EU.

1 French industrial policy Under global economic instability, fluctuation of the currency, and declining export market share, France has lost more ground

Table 4.1   The impact of inward investment in the EU and US

EU	US
Economic effects	
• Acquisition entry and expansion an 'issue' in specific cases only	• High level of acquisitions and acquisition price a concern for some writers
• Wages and value added generally higher in foreign firms	• No systematic differences
• Impact of inward investment in LFRs a cause for concern (linked to effects of SEM and progress to EMU)	• Inward investment reinforcing growth of Sunbelt states
• Long-term developmental impacts of inward investment limited at country/ regional level	• Little discussion or evaluation
• Focus on the natures of the MNE subsidiary and its impact	• Little discussion
• Japanese investment has had a favourable demonstration effect on	• Concerns over Japanese *keiretsu* procurement practises, and displacement effects on indigenous industry, *e.g.* in autos
• Limited comment on transfer pricing or tax avoidance issues management practices in EU industry	• Results of some work consistent with transfer price manipulation
Political effects	
• Discussion of political economy of inward investment varies between EU countries	• Political influence of foreign firms a potential source of economic costs
National security effects	
• Little systematic discussion or evaluation	• Important concerns relating to technology dependence

Source: Burton, F. et al. (1996), *International Business and Europe in Transition*, p. 236.

than its main developed competitors, except the UK. From the industrial policy perspective, France's relative decline in the last 10 years has resulted for four major reasons;

- France had less raw materials for production of energy or basic industrial commodities than its competitors, at a time when their prices had soared;
- France became exposed to new competition in low wage-rate business;
- France was more vulnerable to open competition in complex-factor business;
- France had less strategic restructuring of industry at the national level.[3]

The government, on the other hand, significantly diminished potential governmental control over the economy by instituting a vast array of deregulatory reforms which went far beyond what the Left wing government had begun. Since 1988, as far as French industrial policy was concerned, bureaucrats and businessmen agreed that an industrial policy was no longer possible at the national level, and that it could and should be done at the European level. Moreover, there has been a shift in the government's industrial policy from large scale manufacturing industries to medium and small sized industries. During the Left wing government, French business experienced a new attitude on the part of government, that:

> Business as well as government leaders are convinced that industry needs leadership that only the state can provide, given its ability to take a long-term view. French business, although increasingly independent of the state as a result of continuing deregulation as well as increasingly interdependent, given the *noyaux durs*, nevertheless continues to look to the state for leadership, albeit of a kinder and gentler variety than that of the past.[4]

Mitterrand's industrial policy was presented as a 'tangible sign' of the change of government, and as 'a means of escaping from the crisis', by 'breaking with the traditional rules of capitalism'.

Despite positive French government intervention towards manufacturing sectors, industries were faced by four major problems during the 1980s.

> First, the country was in the throes of recession. The depth of the economic crisis can be gauged by the level of unemployment, which had already reached 7.2 per cent of the labour force. Two other indicators are equally striking: inflation (13 per cent) and the chronic balance-of-payment deficit ...
>
> Secondly, the turn of the decade was a time of great political uncertainty. True, the right was in power and was intent on accentuating the free-market orientation of the regime ...
>
> Thirdly, the recession and the uncertainties of politics established an entirely different social context, as the 1980s got under way, from, that which had underlain the 1960s and 1970s ...

Fourthly, in this relatively unstable political and economic context, one nonetheless discerns a number of elements having all the hallmarks of being virtually irreversible points of reference as early as the end of the 1970s.[5]

The economic and industrial problems were not peculiar to France at that time. Moreover, some part of the government's intention of restructuring industrial sector was more stringent than that of the UK. The implication of Mitterrand government's approach was rather more dangerous than that of other governments. The antagonistic approach toward big industries by politicians hindered further investment. As the Edith Cresson case[6] showed, French politicians could make France unattractive to foreign businessmen. Despite 'push factors' from Japanese government, France did not have 'pull factor' incentives for Japanese business.

2 French inward FDI policy Generally speaking, the attitude toward foreign direct investment in France was negative, even though rhetoric far outstripped reality. France has been associated, in the eyes of most Japanese businessmen, with strong protectionism, particularly directed against Japan, tight government control on foreign trade, foreign direct investment and foreign currency transactions, troubled industrial relations, undisciplined workers, and unpredictable social explosions. As the US case showed,[7] inward investment in France was quite difficult until the mid-1980s. Moreover, the Foreign Investment Commission, which was an agency of the Treasury Department of the Ministry of Finance, similar in function to IBB in the UK, had no common policy toward foreign investors. Cases of rejection of foreign investment application were extremely rare, but this may have been due to prudence on the part of foreign enterprises who submitted approval applications only when they believed their projects did not present any problems, preferring to hold back in the case of projects on which they felt, from prior contacts, that the Administration was not very keen.

Recognising the economic benefits arising from inward FDI, particularly with respect to the creation of employment, France has actively encouraged inward FDI from both EU and non-EU member countries since the early 1990s. The causes for this sudden turn in the situation were multifarious. When the French government realised the failure of industrial policy founded on the *solution française*, it was obliged to revise radically its restrictive and selective screening policy on Japanese direct investment. Approval of a joint venture between Toyoda Machine Tools and the French HES was a good example. The high rate of unemployment was another important reason. Benefiting from such a favourable change in attitude, coupled with various fiscal, financial, and other forms of incentive, several Japanese MNEs made direct investments in such depressed areas as Alsace-Lorraine, Bretagne, and southern France.

At this time, most importantly, French government and industry tried to acquire advanced technology from Japan. This was in line with the government's established policy of *renovation industrielle*, or modernisation of French industry. The above shift of the French government as regards Japanese direct investment culminated in the statement by Laurent Fabius, then Industry and Research minister, during his visit to Japan in July 1984, to the effect that France will adopt a more receptive stance to Japanese investment, provided that it is beneficial to both countries.

France's share of total inward investment rose steadily, from 4.5 per cent in 1984 to 5.6 per cent in 1986, and 6.5 per cent in 1990, to a peak of 14.5 per cent in 1992. At the same period, French inward investment was 27.7 per cent of total EU inward investment. With accumulated FDI valued at FF 100 billion, France ranks fourth in the world among foreign investment host countries, behind the US, the UK and Germany. On a per-country basis, the US is the principal investor. There has been a substantial increase in Japanese FDI since 1985. France now ranks second in Europe, after the UK, for Japanese investment, which comprise 80 industrial units. The general picture of inward investment is primarily to service sectors. The leading areas are finance such as banking and insurance, and trading goods, which is accounting for 44.7 per cent of total investment in 1991.

Despite increasing inward investment, the manufacturing sectors accounted for only one-third and the main industries are electronics, engineering, chemicals, and pharmaceuticals. Manufacturing investments are commonly carried out through joint venture with French companies, for example, Toroy and Elf, Toshiba and Rhone-Poulenc, JVC and Thomson, or take-overs, such as Dunlop by Sumitomo. Greenfield investment is quite rare (only Canon) compared to the other EU countries. Why was France not able to get greenfield investment? An explanation lies in the Toyota case. Under Mitterand there had been little direct encouragement to Japanese companies to invest: but after the distinct change of policy under Chirac, one of the major reasons for Toyota to establish its engine assembly from Derbyshire to northern France was the policy of French central and local government towards attracting investment, which had been lacking before. 'The uncertainty of British government towards the single monetary policy, and the strong encouragement from the French government led Toyota in Northern France.'[8]

As far as Japanese MNEs were concerned, the industries restricted by the French government matched the leading Japanese investment sectors. Despite the strong national car industry in France was EU member countries major foreign participators in the car market. The lack of government enthusiasm towards Japanese investors, tight regulation, and national-dominated consumer market, held little attraction for Japanese investors, especially in the car industry.

3 Japanese MNEs in France Grouping FDI by Japanese MNEs toward France since 1980 shows that most of them involved non-manufacturing sectors, which is quite common within the Japanese FDI in the EU.

Table 4.2   Japanese FDI in France

	1990	1991	1992	1993	1994	1951–94
Case	171	132	82	62	26	1,630
Value	1,257	817	456	545	418	6,392

Value: US$ million.

Source: JETRO in France Report, various years.

Table 4.3   Japanese FDI by industrial sectors (1951–94 accumulation)

Real estate investment: 1,228   Financial and insurance investment: 420
Trading investment: 1,160   Natural Resource investment: 355
Service investment: 889   Electronics investment: 285
Machinery investment: 603   Chemical investment: 259

Value: US$ million.

Source: JETRO in France Report, various years.

A number of reasons are given to explain why France remains a relatively less attractive country for FDI. Mediocre foreign language skills, lack of mobility, shortages of certain categories of highly skilled labour and inadequate training facilities for categories of labour below the '*grande ecole*' elite are often cited in the labour area. The administrative apparatus of central and local government is often perceived as being unfavourable to incoming investment. Despite the efforts to speed up administrative procedure since the mid-1980s, the government system is still seen as *'dirigiste'* and burdened by complex interpreted by a multitude of compartmentalised civil servants.

4 The car industry in France The French car industry has been protected by strong government regulation. It is remarkable that there were no Japanese car or automotive component affiliates in France until the Toyota plant in 1997. Even of transport equipment industries, there is only one Japanese affiliate in France, compared to eleven in the UK, and three in Spain. From the nonmember investor's viewpoint, access to the French car industry is highly restricted partly by the industry itself and even more by the government. The Renault and Volvo collaboration showed the limitations. The collaboration with Renault offered Volvo the use of existing plants in other parts of Europe, and pressure on the workforce through production comparisons throughout Europe. Moreover, Volvo's reputation for sound engineering, quality and reliability was expected to compensate for Renault's association with the faults of a nationalised company – inefficiency, poor quality and slow innovation.

The collaboration was not without its weaknesses. Each firm was reluctant to lose control of its own organisation, with Volvo in particular not liking the idea of letting car production go. By stopping short of full merger, they risked non-achievement of economies of scale, particularly through plant rationalisation. The acknowledged areas for gain lay in R&D programmes. The main weakness accepted by the two firms related to the threat from Japan, but this was seen as an industry issue, requiring protective measures. Amongst chief executives of European car companies, it was agreed that the process of uniting Europe's car industry must continue behind common barriers against the Japanese.

However, the collaboration between Renault and Volvo was thwarted by the refusal of Swedish shareholders to accept the deal in 1994. The main concern was that the French industry could not be adequately valued while it remained nationalised. Moreover, it was not acceptable that a French nationalised company should own a significant proportion of an independent Swedish company. The collapse showed how difficult it is to translate the economic logic of rationalisation and international mergers to the real world of shareholders and vested interests. While the Honda-Rover collaboration ended when Rover was denationalised, the Volvo-Renault deal collapsed when the government intervened in industry. It revealed an important characteristic of the industrial environment within the EU, that the car industry is one of the fragile industrial sectors, and that its needs will tend to hinder the process of industrial integration.

Conclusion France, during the 1980s, was one of the EU member countries in which Japanese MNEs would not have thought to invest. Compared to other EU countries, specific sectors of industry were prepared to invest in France, such as trading in primary foods, antiques, and mainly, the service sector. The real problem which French government faced was the low rate of manufacturing investment. Worse, the inward investment has not followed the upturn in the rates of further investment for French manufacturing sectors. Despite increasing Japanese manufacturing FDI in the EU, France is still below the average. The JETRO sectional manager in Paris explained that:

> France was a minor investment partner for Japanese industry in the EU. There were three reasons: national antagonism toward Asian countries, antagonism towards Japan in particular, and the lack of government support. National antagonism is a very important factor in manufacturing sector investment decisions. Moreover, because of the difficulty of market penetration owing to the national antagonism, no companies will invest in such a situation.
>
> Compared to the UK, the French government can not give any confidence to the investing companies. There was severe competition between member countries for inward investment since the mid-1980s, so there was no reason for Japanese MNEs to invest in an unwelcoming country. The Cresson case was a good example of French attitudes towards Japanese FDI.[9]

Germany[10]

Since the War, no other industrialised country has gone through such dynamic and fundamental structural changes as Germany. Germany's economic performance, when compared with that of other industrial countries within the EU such as the UK, Italy, and France, has been outstandingly strong. As a nation with relatively few natural resources, the economic miracle in Germany after the War mainly depended on the ability to create advanced and specialised factor conditions, such as highly educated skilled, and motivated workers as well as a very effective structure for commercial R&D. The picture of Germany's growing economic power is quite similar to that of the Japanese.

> There are two caveats to the first market-driven interpretation of German supergrowth. First, the disproportion between human and physical capital should be considered carefully ... Second, it is questionable whether the role of surplus

labour in maintaining the profitability of investment can be considered a purely war-related effect … Reserves of unemployed labour have long been identified as a source of exceptional growth in the Golden Age.[11]

Since 1973, the serious oil crisis and the growth of world economic protectionism made Germany strengthen its intra-trade with other EU members. Domestic economic policy boosted industrial production. Hence, among all of the developed countries within the EU, Germany had the largest industrial sector. In 1985, 41 per cent of the civilian working population was employed in industrial sectors. Manufacturing sectors were the engine of Germany's export-oriented economy and thus the foundation of its national prosperity.

1 German industrial policy[12] Germany has no strong tradition of industrial policy or selective government intervention. Compared to most other EU member countries, the involvement of government in industrial policy is moderate. Nor are there much public ownership in the industrial areas, and where the Federal government does hold shares in manufacturing companies, it does not use them as an instrument of economic or employment policy. The Ministry of Economic Affairs has a German version of liberal supply-side policy under which the principal responsibility of the government is to safeguard the functioning of the market, in part through free international trade and promotion of domestic competition. The privatisation of the majority of VW shares in 1960s was in line with this philosophy.

The government's lack of enthusiasm about industrial policy is clearly not shared by the trade unions. Moreover, the unwillingness of the government to intervene in sectional restructuring and the weakness of both unions and trade association as agents of industrial policy have placed the burden of adjustment exclusively on the individual enterprise and the shopfloor.

From the foreign investors' viewpoint, on the one hand, German industrial policy is characterised by the spirit of free enterprise tempered with controls and other bureaucratic measures to prevent abuses. On the other hand, most German industry is dynamic and except in the depressed areas, expansionist. The government does not encourage the development of specific industries as a deliberate act of policy, but does offer substantial subsidies and other support for, in particular, R&D to lead to new marketable products. In its government and private industrial environment, Germany has a quite different industrial mind from that of most EU members.

In German industrial policy, the 1970s could be regarded as a decade of the unions. In turn, the 1980s became a decade of the employers. This was mainly due to the fact that the conditions of the labour market had deteriorated remarkably since the mid-1970s. Since the early 1980s, there were four main development tendencies.

First, there is enduring mass unemployment that negatively influences the bargaining power of the trade unions and their representatives in the firms. The sensitive shift from a sellers' market to a buyers' market has enlarged the room to manoeuvre for management concerning allocation, remuneration and qualification of the labour force. Secondly, the employers are launching various strategies to combine labour more flexibly with new technologies. Flexibility and deregulation are attacks on the traditional functions of trade unions. Thirdly, the question of shortening the working week has come a crucial issue in the power struggle between employers and unions, culminating in 1984 in the biggest industrial dispute of the post-war era. Fourthly, relationships between the trade unions and the employers' associations are by and large still characterised by a relatively high level of corporation and willingness to compromise.[13]

One of the emerging questions is whether the changes really work to foster inward investment policy?

2 German inward FDI policy One of the particular features of German inward or outward foreign investment is that a few segments of industries such as chemical, machinery, electrical engineering and transport equipment industry are concentrated in investment strategy. A distinctive feature of the German economy is its openness and its pronounced international orientation. It means not only those German industries face strong competition with foreign manufacturers in the domestic market, but also that they have to develop foreign markets and actively seek investment opportunities overseas. This aggressive policy closely matches Japanese investment policies.

As Figure 4.1 shows, Germany is not an inward foreign investment country. There are many reasons for this. Labour costs in Germany are among the highest in the world. Strong labour regulation and social benefits are another burden on investors. Between 1992 and 1993 inward investment in Germany increased moderately from DM 4,614 to DM 5,086 million. This was mainly invested by neighbouring EU member countries. The major investment is property agencies. According to a survey by the Institute of the German Economy, 'investment by foreign companies in Germany is mainly triggered by market-seeking objectives'.[14]

The role of government is one of the important elements in the 'pull factors' for inward investment policy. Germany, however, has no foreign trade ministry

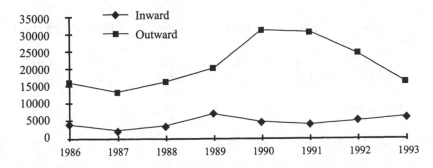

Figure 4.1   Inflows and outflows of German FDI, 1986–93

Source: Dunning, J.H. (ed.) (1997), *Governments, Globalisation, and International Business*, p. 339.

or organisation such as IBB in the UK or the Foreign Investment Commission in France. Moreover, overseas economic relations are seen principally as the responsibility of industries, not of the government. There are no authorisation requirements for FDI, nor for investment by established foreign affiliates, except for some strategic sectors subject to special conditions. Despite a liberal inward investment framework, there are various informal and indirect mechanisms to protect national industries in certain key sectors from foreign take-overs. With strong social requirements, the influence of employee representatives is a major impediment to taking over a German company.

3 Japanese MNEs in Germany   Germany is Japan's largest export market. Total trade volume between the two reached a high of over $43 billion in 1986 with Japanese exports accounting for $29.6 billion, since then it has been reduced $31 billion in 1991 exports $20 billion, and $34 billion in 1995, exports $20 billion. Despite the high rate of trade relations, FDI in Germany was fourth in 1987, and third in 1996 after the UK and France. At the first stage of Japanese FDI in the EU, Germany was the first among the EU members at 37 manufacturing affiliates, compared to the UK, 34 and France 22 in 1983.

Germany is regarded as a real competitor within the EU member countries, able to compete in the Japanese market, especially in the car, high-tech electronics, and chemical industries. Japanese FDI in Germany after World War II, was started by leading trade houses (*sogo shosha*) in the mid-1950s. The Mitsubishi Corporation established affiliates in Dusseldorf in early 1955. By 1960, almost all of the other trading MNEs had followed suit and in 1978

Table 4.4   Japanese FDI in Germany

	1990	1991	1992	1993	1994	1951–94
Case	134	119	65	61	19	1,451
Value	1,242	1,115	769	760	727	8,061

Value: US$ million

Source: JETRO in Germany Report, various years.

Table 4.5   Japanese FDI by industrial sectors (1951–94, accumulation)

Trading investment: 2,887

Financial and insurance investment: 1,239

Electronics investment: 846

Chemical investment: 795

Machinery investment: 554

Service investment: 429

Real estate investment: 376

Textile investment: 101

Value: US$ million

Source: JETRO in Germany Report, various years.

their early FDI in Germany was represented by nine affiliates incorporating an equity capital of DM 105 million. Investments in Germany by Japanese MNEs were initially made through joint venture partners. In almost all these cases the affiliates handled only sales while manufacturing sectors were an exception to the rule. One of the four leading Japanese bearing producers and the international zipper firm YKK were among the first to establish production affiliates in Germany.

Since 1980 the activities of Japanese MNEs in Germany have increased rapidly. According to a JETRO survey in 1987, over 50 per cent of all known affiliates of Japanese MNEs in Germany in 1987 were set up after 1980, and the total volume of FDI reached a total of DM 6.4 billion in 1987. This meant about 5 per cent of total Japanese FDI abroad and around 6 per cent of all FDI in Germany. Since then, the decrease of Japanese FDI in the EU has been matched by the decline of FDI in Germany.

The initial leading role of Japanese MNEs' FDI in Germany has not changed. The Japanese percentage of total manufacturing FDI in Germany has fallen to about 10 per cent in a period when FDI in general has risen. Compared to the other EU members, Germany has not been interesting to

Japanese MNEs. If we think about the mutual market penetration policy between Japan and EU, Germany is not a welcoming country in some industries such as car, car components, and high-tech electronics. According to the JETRO surveys in 1983 and 1987, the most important motive for FDI in Germany was import substitutions.

> For most firms defending the West German export market, which was henceforth threatened by restricted trade measures and frictions, was the paramount factor for starting operations. In the later survey the development of new market was also mentioned as an important consideration for investing in West Germany.[15]

Among manufacturing industries, the electrical and electronic MNEs continued to lead the list with 37 per cent of the FDI, and these were followed by synthetics, general machinery, and rubber.

4 The car industry in Germany There are many complexities in the domestic market in Germany: VW and Daimler (domestic producers), Ford and GM (foreign producers), VW, Ford, and GM (mass producers), and BMW, Porsche, and Audi (speciality producers). During the 1950s and onward, German car industries have been successful, by the standards of most of its industrial competitors, despite the VW crisis in the mid-1970s. Since the late 1970s, the German car industry has faced new challenges to which it is responding vigorously. The revolutionary impact of microelectronics on production technology, advances in the organisation of the production process, well-organised labour management systems made the German car industry vulnerable to the Japanese car MNEs, and the car industries of NICs. The spread of protectionism, and the sharp recession of the early 1980s car market have created a new and uncertain future for the industry.

The globalisation of the car industry since 1980s presented huge restructuring difficulties for the car industry in the EU. The German car industry was no exception. Globalization is described as an increase in the number of competitors in international trade, coinciding with a decline in institutional stability and the willingness to comply with free trade rules. As far as the EU car industries are concerned, the restructuring of the car industries needed two sorts of support, one from each member country's government, the other from the EU Commission. Compared to the French, and Italian car industries, the domestic market of Germany car industries received little protection. Despite weak government regulation on imported cars, there are nevertheless certain functional equivalents to formal market protection in Germany, which explain why German manufacturers have still been able to hold on to such a large market share.

One example that has been mentioned is the absence of an Autobahn speed limit. More generally, one might point to the high quality consciousness of German consumers, which is matched, again, only by that of their Japanese counterparts. The high market share of the extremely expensive Daimler Benz passenger cars is only one characteristic of an automobile culture for which quality engineering counts more than low prices, and whose members are willing to wait up to one year for delivery of their custom-made Mercedes or BMW. The diverse and sophisticated model range of the German manufacturers is well adapted to these preferences, and it is above all this match that accounts for the apparent consumer nationalism that has up to now kept the West Germany automobile market largely in the hands of West German manufacturers.[16]

The increasing export of German cars to Japan showed the success of industrial restructuring. As far as the car trade is concerned, German manufacturers are increasing their balance of trade benefit from Japan. In 1992, Japan exported cars to Germany worth $2,710 million, and imported from Germany cars worth $2,942 million. In 1995 the figures reached $4,421 million for export to Japan compared to $3,346 million of imports.

Conclusion Germany presents Japanese MNEs with two faces. One face is its potential power within the EU and its large consumer market; the other is the concern that the need to balance imports with exports will have a ratchet effect on German exports to Japan. German export to Japan is highest of any EU member country, despite the trade deficit. In particular, the car industries have been a key export-driver into the Japan market. The growth of imports from Germany will cause another flood from the EU.

Germany is a perfect country in which to invest. Despite tight social regulations, good labour attitude, favourable local government inward policy,[17] and skilled workers, were all attractive factors to Japanese MNEs. However, there were two basic problems. Too good is sometimes not good. If there were increased exports and FDI in Germany, there will be increased imports to Japan, *vice versa*. This will not welcomed by MNEs. Mutual competition will, in the long term, weaken Japanese competitiveness. The role of central government was too weak. As the Nissan case showed, powerful government support toward Japanese MNEs was a vital factor to consider when making investment decisions.[18]

Spain

Spain, unlike the other European countries, had experienced periods of dictatorship after World War II. In post-war Spain, government intervention was perceived as a crucial instrument for the post-war recovery. The lack of international manufacturing competition was the main reason driving forward industrial development. However, firstly, indiscriminate protectionist policies were the main obstruction on the road to industrial expansion. Secondly, heavily regulated government intervention in the economy hindered industrial restructuring. The economics of early Francoism can be summarised as:

> an attempt to achieve rapid industrialisation based upon indiscriminate import substitution, with severe restrictions on imports and capital inflows, a complex exchange rate structure, internal regulation and direct intervention. This set of policies led to a highly overvalued currency, a current account deficit, low reserves of hard currency, inflation (consumer prices increased by an average of 13 per cent per year in the 1940s, and 10 per cent in the 1950s), and a small and inefficient industrial sector.[19]

The arrival of the Socialist Party in government in 1982 strengthened the Moncloa Agreement, which was a set of structural reforms and economic policy measures supported by the consensus of the main political parties. The reform of the industrial sectors such as steel, textiles and shipbuilding, most affected by the crisis, and the opening of the economy, became the top priorities of the new government. During the transition period from Franco's death to Spain's EU membership, Spain experienced comparative retardation. For example, Spain's industrial output from 1974 to 1979 rose only 5.7 per cent in total, compared with around 10 per cent in France, Germany, Italy and the UK, and 18 per cent in the US and Japan.

Joining the EU, and opening itself to the global economy, Spain went through a fast economic recovery. From 1986 to 1990, real GDP grew at an average rate of 4.4 per cent, the outcome of cumulative efforts to fight basic disequilibria associated with integration into the EU, and of a closer link to the foreign markets. In turn, Spain faced a balance of trade deficit of -2 per cent of GDP, caused more by excessive imports than by inadequate exports. However, 'the external deficit was largely due to the private capital inflow (mostly direct investment) that was required to renew and expand the productive capital stock. In fact, the current account deficit was more than offset by long-term capital inflows due to its high return over 1986–91'.[20] The most important structural changes in the Spanish economy during this time were the further opening of the economy to international trade and the avalanche of inward FDI supported by new legislation and membership of the EU.

1 Spanish industrial policy Industrial policy in Spain has been shaped by a political economy in which the market mechanism was constrained by a high level of protectionism and government intervention. Restructuring of the manufacturing sectors has brought increased integration into the international economy, especially through the corporate networks of MNEs, which have themselves been reorganising on a European and often global basis. Changes in the relations between employer and employee since 1980s have coincided with industrial restructuring. While protectionism and extensive intervention was still considered necessary in the mid-1980s to bring Spain into line with other EU developed countries and to promote the further development of industry, industrial policy since then has shifted away from support to traditional industries, towards producing an economic environment conducive to the emergence of new industry. Since the late 1980s, the emphasis in policy has shifted to measures affecting the competitiveness of the environment and to upgrading factor inputs.

In comparison with Germany, France and the UK, the absolute size of the industrial sectors is small, though its relative size is broadly in line with that in other EU countries. Moreover Spain has few big MNEs: only 24 out of the FT-500 top European companies, compared with the UK's 179 and France's 75. Even the Netherlands and Sweden have more. In 1990 the number of people working in manufacturing sector was 2.98 million, 24 per cent of the total occupied population, contributing about 29 per cent of the GDP. Relatively weak within the EU, Spain needed an industrial policy more closely focused on high technology and competitiveness.

According to Espina there are five main dimensions in Spanish industrial policy:

- macroeconomic stability and the creation of a climate favourable to competitiveness
- active intervention to upgrade human resources
- support for R&D and for the diffusion of technology
- improvements to the quality and marketability of products, including attention to environmental concerns, design and products standards
- pressure to internationalise Spanish business via strategic alliance, commercial networks and foreign investment as has happened elsewhere[21]

2 Inward FDI policy Inward FDI in Spain, similarly to the rest of Europe's western and southern fringes has historically exceeded outward FDI by a wide margin. Spain, during the 1980s, was one of the most dynamic countries in terms of economic growth and FDI activity, consolidating its position as an attractive host country and as an emerging source of FDI. In 1991, Spain received $10.5 billion in FDI, the fourth largest inflow in the world surpassed only by the US, the UK and France. However, the rapid increase in inward FDI in Spain has been mainly due to non-manufacturing sectors, such as finance, and service-oriented industries.

The extend of overall foreign control in a particular industry often bore little relation to the quantum of external investment flowing into it. Between 1959 and 1973, 26.3 per cent of total inward investment went to the chemical industry. However, foreign concerns held only 36.8 per cent of the paid-up capital of large chemicals companies. In the car industry, vice versa, they received 9.2 per cent of total investment, 56.7 per cent of the paid-up capital from outside Spain. Penetration of inward FDI in manufacturing sectors has varied between sectors. In the late 1970s and early 1980s, the major destination of FDI in Spain was transport machinery sectors. GM's assembly affiliate in Zaragoza and the acquisition by VW of SEAT showed this. Since the late 1980s, the service sector, especially financial services, became the most important focus of inward FDI. The major investors in Spain in the late 1980s have been the EU countries, especially Germany, the Netherlands, France and the UK. This contrasts with the position in the late 1960s and early 1970s when the US tended to dominate, with inward investors such as Ford and ATT. In 1989 Germany had the largest industrial presence in Spain, but the UK was the largest single source of direct investment. The US and Japan continue to be a source of investments, but Spain's proportion of total FDI is generally small compared with that from the EU countries.

There were many weak factors in Spain. Industrial relations have long been poor. Despite its high unemployment, Spain has Europe's second-worst strike record. Basic skills of management and marketing have been slow to develop. For example, over a third of Spain's olive oil is exported in bulk to Italy, where it is put in bottles for re-export. Spanish bureaucracy is another burden for foreign investors. Generally it is said that the Spanish government's response to any idea is to regulate it. Anything an entrepreneur wants to do entails getting a permit from the local authority, the region or the central government in Madrid. High-tech industry is weak. They spend only 1 per cent of their GDP on R&D, half the OECD average.

3 Japanese MNEs in Spain Japanese FDI in Spain has been considerably lower than in the other EU member countries. According to the JETRO in Madrid:

> Spain is one of the major inward FDI countries within the EU. However, political instability, labour attitudes on the shopfloor quite different from that of other countries, low rates of infrastructural investment, and bureaucratic regulation are main hindrance to Japanese MNEs. The Sanyo case in 1992, in which a project to set up their battery affiliates in Barcelona was withdrawn, was a reaction to these problems.[22]

Table 4.6   Japanese FDI in Spain

	1990	1991	1992	1993	1994	1951–94
Case	43	34	27	26	13	420
Value	320	378	332	207	184	2,968

Value: US$ million

Source: JETRO in Spain Report, various years.

Table 4.7   Japanese FDI by industrial sectors (1951–94 accumulation)

Transport machinery investment: 653   Trading investment: 263
Electronics investment: 391   Machinery investment: 187
Chemical investment: 266   Real estate investment: 177
Service investment: 262   Steel and other metal investment: 115

Value: US$ million

Source: JETRO in Spain Report, various years.

Japanese FDI in Spain has been mainly focused on the transport machinery industry. There is increasing FDI in non-manufacturing sectors, however Spain still remains an unpopular country among Japanese MNEs owing to poor labour attitudes and cultural differences. The unsung hero of Spanish industries, however, is the car industry, which is entirely foreign-owned, but Europe's third biggest. In 1995, Spain made 2 million cars, roughly half a million more than either the UK or Italy. GM's Saragossa and Ford's Valencia plants are among the six most productive in Europe. The motor manufacturing industry did not begin to unfold until the 1950s when Spain achieved two prerequisites. 'An industry capable of producing the quantity of the special steels and alloys required, and a large enough market to make a domestic car industry worthwhile.'[23]

4 The car industry in Spain In 1959 Spain's car production accounted for only 0.4 per cent of world output but from about 1964 onwards production increased rapidly. By 1978–79, its share had risen to 3.2 per cent, an improvement surpassed only by the Japanese car industry whose market share soared from 0.7 to 19 per cent over the same period. However, there were considerable differences between Japanese and Spanish car manufacturers. In contrast to Japanese car MNEs, Spain's car industry started with the purchase of licences for the assembly of cars of foreign design and technology.

During the 1970s and the early 1980s, the American car MNEs such as Ford and GM and the Japanese manufacturer Nissan set up their affiliates in Spain. Ford started its Spanish affiliates as export bases. Authorisation for a factory at Almusafes was given in 1973 on the basis of the level of investment involved and the guarantee of exporting a specified quantity. In 1989 the Ford plant was producing 1,460 car units a day and had a capacity to produce about 1,935 engine units per day. Production was concentrated on small cars such as the Fiesta, Escort and Orion models, and on engines under 1300cc. Ford has extended its plant in Valencia and has built a new car electronics factory near Cadiz. GM followed Ford into Spain with the same management strategy. The Figueruelas plant was built as an export base for small car production, mainly the Corsa model, in Europe, producing on average 365,000 cars a year. GM in Spain is one of Spain's largest exporters.

Compared to American car industries, Japanese manufacturers have concentrated on the production of commercial vans. Nissan entered Spain in 1977 through a joint venture with Motor Iberica. Nissan increased its holding in Nissan Motor Iberica to 75 per cent in 1987. The Suzuki–Land Rover joint venture is the other Japanese car in Spain.

There were four characteristic changes in car sector during the 1980s.

1 SEAT passed through a serious crisis when Fiat decided to pull out for good in 1981. Since that time, it has been launching models designed within the company and by VW.
2 It was necessary to lay off a minimum of 20,000 workers in companies throughout the sector, with a view to bringing production levels more in

line with demand in the least costly way possible, and to introduce robots
to bring manufacturing costs down to Japanese levels.

3   It was necessary to reduce the number of models manufactured and enlarge
the series, which means signing complementarity agreements between
firms.

4   The car industry crisis has inevitably dragged down ancillary industries
with it. These are faced either with outright closure, or with difficult
reconversion plans or with the risk of being absorbed by stronger industries,
as occurred with Femsa (specialising in electrical parts for cars and other
vehicles), which was swallowed up by the Spanish subsidiary of the German
firm Bosch.[24]

Car manufacturing in Spain now symbolised the modern, international
face of industry, incorporating the latest automated and robotised production
techniques in factories linked to multinational production systems. About
70,000 were employed in car assembly in 1986, but if the number employed
in other automotive and automotive parts is added, the figure was closer to
350,000; adding the number in related activities may take the total closer to
half a million. The car industry also makes a significant contribution towards
exports, with six of the leading ten Spanish export companies in 1988. After
SEM in 1992, there were increasing numbers of local government incentive
policies towards car manufacturing MNEs, for example Navarra's policy in
1990 of offering 25 per cent subsidies to inward investors.

Conclusion During the 1980s, Spain was an emerging market for Japanese
MNEs' interests. When Spain joined the SEM, its position as a recipient country
for investment strengthened. However the position of Spain is still lower than
the other big three with regard to Japanese investors. Compared to the other
EU member countries, the weak infrastructures, peripheral position, different
labour attitudes, and political instability are the main reasons. To globalising
MNEs, cheap labour costs do not offset these disadvantages. Despite increasing
FDI in Spain, there are withdrawals as well. Spain is regarded by Japanese
businessmen as a country for the passer-by.

At first glance, Spain looks like a favourable place to invest. When time passed,
we needed to learn to live with Spanish labour attitudes, and more importantly,
Spanish political instability. With growing competition (for FDI) among EU
member countries' during the 1980s, the role of the Spanish government was too
small.[25]

Japanese FDI in the UK

Outward and inward foreign investment policy has always been important to the UK. The contribution of foreign and domestic MNEs to gross national product, capital expenditure, employment, exports and profits, are considerably greater in the case of the UK than in that of any other EU member countries. After the Conservative government came to power in 1979, deregulation, privatisation, and the restructuring of the handling of labour disputes were driven by a clear philosophy concerning the role of the market and the negative economic and social effects of certain types of market distortions.

Compared to other EU member countries, the cost of the greater internationalisation of the UK economy may have been the loss of some structural autonomy on the part of the UK, as MNEs may encourage more corporate globalisation between different parts of their operations and sectoral or cross-sectoral integration within the UK. This may have the effect of reshaping both market and economic structure, and the incoming Conservative government sought foreign help for this. According to an OECD survey (1987), MNEs had adjusted to recession and technological changes more speedily than indigenous industries. The MNEs, moreover, were at the forefront of such changes which have far-reaching implications for both positive and negative interventionism by government. The new government did not have a worked-out industrial policy, but rather expected MNEs to exploit their Midas touch. The general approach of the Margaret Thatcher government's inward FDI policy will be explained in this section.

UK Industrial Policy

The relative weakness of UK industry has been a subject of intense historical and political debate since the mid-1970s. De-industrialisation, rapidly increasing unemployment, and strong Trade Unions power were an important part of the contemporary image of the UK held by outsiders. The chronic economic disease, on other arguments, was caused not by economic or political factors but for social and cultural reasons. Dahrendorf said of UK economic performance that 'economic performance and cultural values are linked. An effective economic strategy for Britain will probably have to begin in cultural sphere'.[26]

Generally speaking, however, the decline of Britain was mainly related to economic policy mis-judgements and to disdain for industry among elites. When the Thatcher government came to power, weak industrial competitiveness prevented the achievement of recovery through the creation and exploitation of markets. Traditional antagonistic relationships between senior managers and trade unions prevented managers from dealing effectively with the shop floor. Lower R&D spending for high-tech industry and heavy support for the defence industry created imbalances in investment, and the collapse of Communist Russia made the UK defence budget fruitless. Manufacturing restructuring during the 1970s was frustrated by either too much government intervention or too little. The lack of an adequate skilled labour supply for manufacturing industry and employment policies dominated by political considerations moved workers from skilled manufacturing sectors to part-time service sectors.

Table 4.8   Unemployment rates in selected OECD countries (%: total labour force)

	1964–73	1974–79	1980	1981	1982	1983	1984
USA	4.4	6.6	7.0	7.5	9.5	9.5	7.4
Germany	0.8	3.2	3.0	4.4	6.1	8.0	8.6
France	2.2	4.5	6.3	7.3	8.1	8.3	9.7
Italy	5.5	6.6	7.4	8.3	9.0	9.8	10.2
Japan	1.2	1.9	2.0	2.2	2.4	2.6	2.7
UK	3.1	5.0	6.9	11.0	12.3	13.1	13.2

Source: *OECD Economic Outlook*, various years.

After the oil shock the great increase in non-manufacturing employment and the accompanying increase in non-manufacturing investment took resources away from the balance of payments and industrial investment in the UK. The squeeze on manufacturing investment was the most serious effect of all, because manufacturing growth has often been described as the 'engine of growth'. Since then, UK economic policy has had two devastating consequences for the economy. First, the reduction in the share of investment has greatly reduced the rate of growth of industrial capacity. When demand increased after the oil shock, industries could not fulfil the economy's requirement for goods. As a result of the consequent growth of imports, UK manufacturing industries lost their competitiveness. Weak competitiveness led to declining industrial investment. Declining investment produced unemployment in an economic 'domino effect'.

When she was in opposition, Mrs Thatcher said at the Conservative Party Conference in 10 October 1975 that:

> We Conservatives hate unemployment. We hate the idea of men and women not being able to use their abilities. We deplore the waste of national resources and the deep affront to people's dignity by being out of work through no fault of their own.[27]

However, her industrial policy based on employment considerations was wrong. Worse, she took such a domino effect as a matter of course. In the House of Commons in 1986, she said that 'the number of people in work has increased by 700,000 since October 1983 ... Yes, many of the jobs have been part-time, and what is wrong with that?'[28] Under an employment policy based on such statistical interpretations, the fall of world competitiveness of the UK industrial sector was hard to avoid.

Second, the Thatcher government's economic and industrial policy was little more than 'muddling through'. It was alleged by Sir John Hoskyns that:

> The prevailing establishment view at the time of the 1979 election seemed to be that, since the country had been in relative economic decline since the 1870s, there was really no point in talking about policies for recovery.[29]

Lord Young and Lord Tebbit also said that:

> There is no industrial policy, though maybe there is a monetary policy for industry. Under free competition, there will be a clear divide between advanced companies and the others. As Thatcher said 'if you can not compete with the company from the Far East, you should give up your business'. This was the real industrial policy during her era, whatever she did.[30]

Owing to tight monetary control, price inflation was low, but unemployment stayed very high and growth remained relatively poor. Despite high unemployment, a collapse in manufacturing output, and the fall of the international competitiveness of manufacturing sectors, the basic features of government spending were able to remain unchanged, owing to North Sea oil. While the social costs of these economic policies were made possible only by oil revenues which paid for unemployment benefit, and wage rises and cheap imports which kept those with a job in rising real living standards, the competitiveness of the manufacturing sector worsened. Rather than solving the problems, the Thatcher government shuffled along through changing ministers. During her terms in government, there were three Chancellors of the Exchequer but 9–10 ministers at the Department of Trade and Industry.[31] The strength of the Treasury under her cabinet forced industrial policy under the control of the Treasury. Tight money control made industrial restructuring harder. Moreover, the responsibility for industrial mistakes moved to ministerial level. As Nicolas Craft said:

> International comparisons suggest the UK is relatively weak in long-term investments, including human capital and R&D, the factors emphasised by new growth theory as engines of long-term success and which have positive externalities. Policy efforts should increasingly be directed towards reforming institutional structures to reduce short-termism and to strengthen human capital formation whilst retaining the disciplines of competition.[32]

However, Mrs Thatcher lacked confidence in the manufacturing sector and just tried cover up current difficulties. The House of Lords Select Committee on Science and Technology concluded that 'The present lack of Government commitment, support and assistance to industry are damaging to our national interest.'[33]

Accidentally, a flourishing inward FDI policy tactically provided the government with a means of escape from de-industrialisation and above all, a solution to the balance of payments deficit. Without causing political crises, MNEs could provide jobs, contribute to a surplus in the balance of payment, and above all, especially in the UK, help regional development.

FDI in the UK since 1979

The UK has been a favoured location for nonmember countries' FDI. Mr Hiroshi Kitamura, the Japanese ambassador to the UK between 1991 to 1993, gave a clear account of the UK's position in the eyes of nonmember investors.

> I think there are four factors, which played an important part. First, there is the English language, the most accessible foreign language for most Japanese people. Secondly, there is the infrastructure reflecting Britain's status as an industrial nation of long standing – particularly in the financial field, as symbolised by the City. The third factor is the availability of a high-quality, diligent and productive labour force at a relatively reasonable cost. Finally, there is the welcome shown by the British Government as well as by local authorities and communities to Japanese inward investment. Nonetheless, there are a few sources of concern that could affect our mutually beneficial economic relations.[34]

Table 4.9   Japanese FDI in UK

	1990	1991	1992	1993	1994	1951–94
Case	270	222	197	139	59	2,751
Value	6,806	3,588	2,948	2,527	2,169	33,830

Value: US$ million.

Source: JETRO in UK Report, various years.

Table 4.10   Japanese FDI by industrial sectors (1951–94 accumulation)

Financial and insurance: 13,824   Trading investment: 3,270
Real estate investment: 5,620   Transport investment: 1,827
Electronics investment: 2,592   Service investment: 1,680

Value: US$ million.

Source: JETRO in UK Report, various years.

The entry of the UK into the EU in 1973 made British government policy change. The Republic of Ireland seized the opportunity of EU entry to industrialise, setting up a powerful Industrial Development Authority and offering tax exemption for foreign MNEs on profits from exporting. Hence there was some switch of investment from Northern Ireland to the Republic of Ireland.

Inward investment responded more positively to government policy than domestic industry.

First, it argues that inward investment brings jobs – currently an estimated 10,000–15,000 a year – to manufacturing industry. Second, inward investment projects have shown themselves to be relatively responsive to regional incentives and therefore there is some likelihood that these jobs will be created in areas of particularly high unemployment. Third, most projects are seen to bring with them valuable managerial and/or technical expertise, which has spin-off effects throughout British industry. Indeed, with the growing awareness of Britain's need to equip itself with competence in the new technologies and the bias of inward investment towards high-technology products, the technological spin-off from inward investment is receiving increasing emphasis.

Two other advantages that are seen to derive from inward investment are (a) that the projects are less likely to embody 'dead-weight' assistance (this is a term used to refer to assistance paid to firms for investment which they would have undertaken irrespective of the assistance on offer), and (b) that on balance they are less likely to displace other British output than are domestic projects receiving assistance (*i.e.* foreign investment frequently replaces imports rather than domestic production).[35]

The creation of the Scottish Development Agency and the Welsh Development Agency at the beginning of 1976 led to a marked upturn in the Scottish and Welsh inward FDI promotional efforts. In 1976 the Secretaries of State for Scotland and Wales began to administer regional selective assistance which allowed the Scottish and Welsh Offices to negotiate assistance packages directly with investors from overseas.

From the DTI down to local development agencies, there is a network in place that seeks to attract inward investment from foreign MNEs. At the government level, inward FDI is perceived as a positive opportunity for the creation of jobs and trading opportunities, often in poorer regions of the economy. Hence, the need for a UK national promotional effort to match the efforts of its international competitors led to the establishment of the Invest in Britain Bureau (IBB)[36] within the Department of Industry in 1977, and early in 1980 the Committee of Overseas Promotional (COP) was set up to coordinate the territorial and UK promotional efforts. IBB became the Secretary and, for practical purposes, the mentor and conscience of COP. COP's role is to keep under observation the distribution of resources, prevent clashes between agencies, develop corporate activities, act as a forum for discussion and promote mutual trust and discourage unnecessary secrecy and wasteful competition.

Within the total inward FDI in the UK, about 20 per cent were classified as manufacturing sector during the 1990s. At 1979 there were just under 975,000 people employed by foreign affiliates in the UK. By 1987 this figure had fallen to just fewer than 625,000 before recovering to just over 775,000 by 1990. This latter figure represented around 16 per cent of UK manufacturing employment, and was distributed among 1443 separate enterprises.

Traditionally, a large part of inward investment came from the US, although in recent years the share of the EU has increased remarkably. The share for Japan has been increasing since mid-1980s. Compare to the other foreign investors, Japanese investments was often financed from local sources, which biases the figures downwards and underestimates the importance of Japan as an international investor. On the other hand, US investment had traditionally been concentrated in manufacturing industry, whereas EU and Japanese investment had been biased towards the services and finance industries. Since mid-1980, there has been an interesting change in the relationship between Japan and US investment in UK. Whereas American investment has moved into service sectors, Japanese investment has moved from service sectors to manufacturing industries.

In terms of the international source of this manufacturing investment, the US accounted for about 47 per cent of the individual affiliates, and over 58 per cent of total employment. The EU accounts for 27 per cent of firms but only 20 per cent of employment. The largest contributors from the EU were Germany and France, whose investments together accounted for just over 90,000 employees. Japan is becoming more prominent as a UK inward investors. In 1990, Japanese affiliates employed 5 per cent of total workforce of foreign owned manufacturing, and accounted for around 6 per cent of net foreign manufacturing output. Some indication of growth in investment from this source, however, was provided by the fact that during 1990 alone, Japanese manufacturers accounted for nearly 9 per cent of net capital expenditure committed by foreign manufacturers.

According to Steuer Report, which was sponsored by the DTI and published in 1973 on the impact of FDI on the UK, there were negative and positive impacts in the host country.

The allegedly negative considerations were summarised as (i) if foreign investment involved the acquisition of British firms, the research achievements of these companies might be lost to the British economy either because foreign interests acquire the property rights or research organisations are disbanded; (ii) foreign MNEs may not undertake R&D in Britain; and (iii) the country might in a general sense become technologically dependent.

On the positive side: (i) affiliates may draw on the research efforts of the parent company at low or zero costs; (ii) new products are made available at lower costs and marketed more effectively; and (iii) linkage effects diffuse the benefits of new products and processes throughout the economy.[37]

Despite the Hitachi case, Japanese investment in UK tended towards type (i) a new venture by a company with no previous interest in the UK. Under the Conservative government, there were a lot of type (i) Japanese investments in UK. There were interactions between 'pull factors' from the UK government, and 'push factors' within the Japanese government. Compared to the other EU members' 'pull factors', the UK had a free market competition policy, with government incentives to investment. Moreover, the investor had security in the domestic market owing to the weakened state of the inward country's competitiveness. The car manufacturing sector was a good example.

Despite the impact of American technology on UK industry since the 1960s, in some industries, especially car manufacturing, it was insufficient to ensure survival. Collaboration between the Rover and Honda since 1979 was shown, by the take-over of Rover by BMW in 1994, to have failed as well. Did FDI really strengthen the host national economy and/or allow its industry to survive? If not, was it the responsibility of any government or of foreign MNEs? Why did any government within the EU try to use attract foreign investors into its country? This will be addressed in the next chapter.

Japanese MNEs in the UK

Inward FDI happens because of the mutual interests between a host government and foreign investors. Sometimes it will occur because of host government incentive subsidy or local government's strong support. If every option was clear, investors will also think about other conditions such as cultural affinity or the level of Japanese settlement in the host country. As far as Japanese MNEs are concerned, the UK has been the most favourable country within the EU. Within the manufacturing sectors, labour attitudes and the employment culture are also important considerations. As compared to other EU countries, the UK has some more specific incentives than the others.

> All Japanese MNEs' managers have to think about the host country's resident rates. Because we are social people, who is more emphasised within Japanese society. We needed wider educational chances, and a more favourable environment to live with other Japanese people. Racial discrimination, high rate crimes, and rapid social change will be discouraging to Japanese who have to work overseas.[38]

In 1995 there were about 1,271 Japanese residents in Wales, 764 in Scotland and 847 in Northeast England. Car investment has especially contributed to this process. Nissan in Sunderland, Toyota in Derbyshire and Honda at Swindon account for some of the largest concentrations outside London.

The history of Japanese manufacturing investment in the UK can be traced back twenty years to the establishment of YKK Fasteners (UK) Ltd by Yoshida Kogyo UK at Runcorn. Sony Corp. set up the Bridgend factory of Sony (UK) Ltd in mid-Glamorgan in 1973 and NSK Bearing Europe Ltd established its plant at Peterlee in County Durham a year later. These early developments marked out South Wales and Northeast England as key areas for further

Table 4.11 Population statistics of Japanese nationals living in the EU

	Total 1985	Total 1995	A	B	C	D	E	F
France	10,822	16,889	6,376	4,901	912	1,251	–	–
Germany	13,691	23,843	–	–	–	–	21,101	2,742
Spain	3,221	4,611	1,251	551	151	589	–	–
UK	21,931	45,671	20,404	18,601	636	538	–	–

Notes:

A Private company staff.
B Student/researchers/teachers.
C Working for government.
D Self-employed.
E Long-term residents.
F Germany passport.

Source: JETRO, various country data.

investment. Since the late 1970s, Japanese manufacturers spread into Scotland, the East and West Midlands, Derbyshire, Yorkshire and other regions. The 1992 SEM provided the impetus for a veritable flood of Japanese manufacturing investment into the UK, rising from 15 to 206 affiliates in the 11 years prior to January 1994. The UK has attracted over 40 per cent of Japan's total FDI into the EU and is today home to the largest of all its Japanese communities.

The other sub-motive for choosing the UK is the tax incentive. Toyota described the UK as having 'the lowest labour costs among major EU countries'.[39] Nomura Securities has put a figure that the UK is 44 per cent cheaper than Germany, 30 per cent cheaper than Italy, and 15 per cent cheaper than France. Similar differentials apply at the technical and managerial level. The UK managers at Japanese affiliates take average annual holidays of only 22 days, against 30 in Germany and 27 in France. Moreover the labour attitudes from shopstewards toward Japanese managers are more important things in industrial relations. If the Maastricht social chapter were to be ratified, many Japanese thought that they would lose the biggest advantage of their UK operations.

At the end of 1982, when the take off stage of Japanese FDI towards the EU began, the number of Japanese manufacturers in UK was in fact extremely small. The number identified varies somewhat from one source to another but there would seem to have been approximately 24 Japanese manufacturing affiliates in the UK (excluding the BL and Honda case). At this time, 16 of the 24 employed fewer than 100 workers. A further six companies employed between 140 and 420 workers but only two – Sony and the joint venture between GEC and Hitachi – employed more than 1,000 workers.

Although there was some diversity of product, including zip fasteners, PVC products, smoke detector alarms, industrial bearings, polyethylene products, spectacle lenses, industrial batteries, fishing rods, circuit breakers and analytical instruments, the major emphasis was quite clearly on consumer electronic goods assembly. Of total Japanese manufacturing employment in the UK, 72 per cent was in colour TV and other consumer electronic goods production. Why was the UK investment dominated by electronic goods' manufacturers?

> There will be two reasons, one, there were no competitors among British electronic goods makers and Britain was a good consuming market. Most of all, safe market share is important for Japanese investors. The other reason is that Sony's successful business in the UK gave confidence to the other investors who followed. Traditionally, Japanese business preferred to follow rather than to lead. Further Japanese car makers' investment in the UK followed Honda–Rover's successful collaboration.[40]

The ownership style in the UK was unusual compared to other regions. Eighteen of the 24 affiliates were wholly owned by their Japanese parents. Despite MITI data, which showed that only 10 per cent of Japanese FDI investments worldwide were wholly-owned, Japanese FDI in UK presented a different picture from that of the normal strategy. One question arising from this point is why the UK was dominated by Japanese greenfield investment compared to other European countries? 'The free environment of business in UK, and the government's policy toward investors have been crucial factors in the decision for greenfield investment.'[41]

However, greenfield investment has particularly flourished since the Thatcher government. At the initial stage of investment in the UK during the late 1970s and early 1980s, joint venture was one of the particular management strategies of Japanese MNEs.[42] The BL-Honda, GEC-Hitachi, and Toshiba-Rank cases showed the conservative market approach strategy of Japanese MNEs. The regional distribution was rather simple. The major concentration of Japanese manufacturing activity was in South Wales, which had seven of the 24 companies and more than two-thirds of total UK employment. Four of the seven South Wales companies were in consumer electronics, including two of the largest Japanese colour TV manufacturers; Sony at Bridgend and GEC-Hitachi at Aberdare.

The Thatcher government showed a positive attitude toward Japanese government, and its power within the EU Committee decision-making process, and, most of all, the appearance of an effort to solve industrial problems, impressed Japanese businessmen at this time. On the other hand, the Japanese government sought a reliable ally in the EU. One of the emerging questions at this point was how the UK achieved its success in attracting investment from nonmember countries? The UK stood top among EU member countries in its inward FDI. Was this really only because of industrial factors? If not, what kind of role did the British government play?

In 1988, Ambassador Kazuo Chiba told a Cardiff economic conference about the importance of the UK from the Japanese viewpoint.

Japanese (economic) leaders in increasing numbers see advantages in the UK from the adaptability, high productivity and historical dependability of your labour force, which is now proving very responsive, demonstrating a talent and loyalty which was only waiting to be unlocked. Certainly the excellent performance of the British economy in recent years and the death of the myth of Britain as a strike-prone casualty ward for industry have combined to make the UK a 'first' on the client list of Japanese companies eager to expand overseas.[43]

The detailed procedure of the United Kingdom's inward FDI policy was explained in the following terms by Mr. Young-Sang Yoo, Commercial Attaché in the Embassy of Korea.

Since 1990, there has been a lot of investment from Korean MNEs into the EU. Especially, there is a large amount of Korean investment in UK. I think there are many factors leading Korean companies to invest in the UK. However, as far as big investments in the UK are concerned, the favourable financial support will be critical factor. If the other conditions were the same, we would be investing in the UK. If there are more favourable conditions from the financial perspective, Far Eastern countries' MNEs should be in UK. The special relations between banks and manufacturers, particularly in the case of Japan and Korean MNEs, mean that they would be forced to invest in the UK.[44]

According to these remarks, the political and financial factors,[45] which were the result of the policies of the Thatcher government, made a favourable environment for investment in the UK. Her efforts to revitalise the ailing British economy, get rid of stagnation in the vast range of state-run industries by selling them off and encouraging the survival of the fittest, and crush the militant unions accused of holding British industry and the nation's economy to ransom, were regarded as good 'pull factors' by Japanese industrial leaders. Hence, two fifth of big investments in the EU since 1982 have been set up in the UK.

Conclusion

The Single European Market has been regarded by non-EU members as a 'fortress Europe'. Compared to the US MNEs, which have a long investment history and mutual understanding, Japanese MNEs have been regarded as a 'Trojan Horse'. Japanese affiliates were established in the EU with all their technology developed and management control remaining in Japan. The fears of technological dependence concerning US investment, warned of by Servan-Schreiber in his book, 'the American Challenge' could be used again towards Japanese investment in the 1980s.

> The infusion of ever larger amounts of American investment into key industries has the short-term advantage of sparing Europe expensive research costs. But in the long run it deprives the European economy of the possibilities of rapid expansion that exist only in these key industries.[46]

This fear among EU member countries has increased since Japanese FDI began flooding into the EU in 1985. Especially in the car industries, owing to dumping and VERs, the mutual relationship between investor and host government was demonstrated. The UK showed the real regional impact of Japanisation. The inward policy among the member countries changed from open competition to high protection. There is a common feature that the inward investment policies have coincided with host government's trade policies. From the host government's viewpoint, there are various different FDI incentive policies within the EU. The incentive policy is an important factor for nonmember investors.

Despite the relatively small amout of manufacturing investment compared to the US MNEs' investment in the UK, the Japanese had good reason to invest in the UK, as Garrahan and Stewart showed:

> The more than 130 Japanese-controlled companies now in business in the UK directly employ around 30,000 people, but whereas US-owned companies operating in the UK have forty times as many British employees, the significance lies in the fact that Japanese capital is expanding its interest in Britain while US

Table 4.12   The FDI incentive policy from the Big Four countries

	UK	Germany	France	Spain
Trade policy	Free trade Promoting export	Free trade related with EU Policy Domestic market control	Free trade related with GATT System 'Japan, C'est Possible' Movement	Following EU trade policy regulation of export and import
Industrial organisation	1st 1.7% Cons. 5.9% Manu. 25.4% Servi. 65.9%	1st 1.2% Cons. Manu. $\overline{36.7\%}$ Servi. 62.1%	1st 4.3% Cons. 5.9% Manu. 23.6% Servi. 66.2%	1st 3.5% Cons. 8.5% Manu. 23.8% Servi. 64.2%
Government regulation for inward FDI	Positive policy excluding rail and gas	Positive policy Permission for financial part	Positive policy mainly case by case ex. tele-com, military, car and semiconductor Based on high employment, increasing import, regional development and inward High-tech industry, were welcomed	New Regulation in 1992 Permission for ship, mining, oil, military, communication, transport system, and financial part

Table 4.12 cont'd

	UK	Germany	France	Spain
Inward policy	Since 1988 RSA set up Special support in NI Enterprise zone – more support such as tax, rent free for 10 years Government support for marketing and project. Free of remittance	1) Regional 2) Manu. 3) Export 4) Tax incentive policy 8% of total investment support (former East German is 15–23%)	Mainly regional development and employment Financial support for 1) Employment and regional support 2) Low interest 3) Reduce tax 4) Re-education employee	Permission from government over 500 million Fiesta
Merger and acqusition	Merger: under partnership law Acquisition: stock capital	M&A controlled by EU regulation	Employment reason, merger welcomed Acquisition: stock, capital, Fonds de Commerce	Permission from government

Source: Tokai Bank (Tokyo) European Countries Survey, various years.

companies withdraw in the face of global competition from Japan. In parts of the UK like the North-East, where traditional industries have declined and been discarded as smokestack industries, the reshaping of global competition between US and Japanese capital comes as a mixed blessing. Growing interest in the region during the 1980s by Japanese firms has produced thousands of new jobs, but during the same period many US companies have run down their operations or withdrawn from the region completely.[47]

Japanese MNEs seem to need more structural incentives, such as the ratchet effect in the domestic market or social conditions, compared to the other Asian MNEs which are mainly concerned about financial incentives. For Japanese investors, the approach to the host country is examined by the financial institutions and government organisations such as JETRO.[48] Government intervention in the investors' location decision-making is related the EU member's trade negotiation style.

Table 4.13   The comparative analysis of the motives for inward FDI among the Big Four countries from Japanese MNEs

	UK	Germany	France	Spain
Labour attitude	High	High	Low	Low
Social regulation	Middle	High	Middle and antagonism	Low and antagonism
R&D facility	Good	Good	Middle	Bad
Market openness	High	High	Low	Low
Rate of Japanese population	High	High but scattered	Middle	Low
The rate of push and pull factor	High	Low	Low	High

Source: Derived by the author and JETRO on the basis of interview results and various years reports.

Despite the decline of the Japanese FDI in the EU since 1990, the UK is still the most favoured country within the EU. For Japanese businessmen, an in depth understanding of the distinctive characteristics of management in the host country is an important factor. It requires that the Japanese undertake a serious study of management characteristics of both countries in comparative perspective. The UK advantage among the EU big four is that there have been many comparative analyses concerning British management style. Supplemented with the strong 'pull factors' from host government, Japan will not resist.

Mr Hiroshi Kitamura summarised that:

At every critical juncture in the process of EC integration, Britain has attempted to block moves toward a 'Fortress Europe' that would shut out the rest of the world. It has assiduously negotiated with those countries on the continent that sometimes seem to let Eurocentric tendencies rise to the role.

Britain's stance in this area matches Japan's interests perfectly. Japan will benefit greatly from openness in the integrated EC. As long as a Japanese company sets up an operation in Europe that employs local workers, purchases and uses a large volume of parts manufactured in the host country or another EC country, and achieves a high local-content ratio, its products should be considered European and allowed to enter other European markets freely. Our country can only hope that Britain will keep up its efforts in this direction.[49]

From the Japanese side, the UK has perfect 'pull factors' when Japan used her 'push factors' toward her own MNEs. For inward investment only, Thatcherism has worked successfully. However, there are two sides of the coin in inward investment policy. As the Steuer report mentioned above, the negative factors were overshadowed by her charismatic approach.

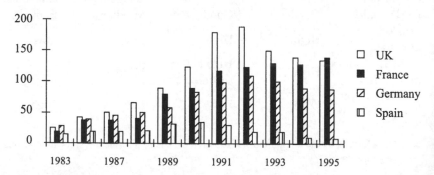

Figure 4.2   Japanese manufacturing enterprises in the UK, France and Germany

Source: Derived by the author and JETRO on the basis of survey from each country and JETRO paper.

Notes

1   Lord Young: interview.
2   Brech, M. and Sharp, M. (1984), *Inward Investment*, pp. 26–7.
3   TELESIS (1986), *Competing for Prosperity*, p. 32.
4   Ibid., p. 194.
5   Segrestin, D. (1990), *Recent Changes in France*, pp. 97–9.
6   Madame Edith Cresson, first woman Prime Minister of France and former Minister of Trade and Industry (1983–86), criticised Japanese investment in the EU. She said that 'Japan is an adversary who does not respect the rules of the game and whose overwhelming desire is to conquer the world ... Japanese investments are not like others. They destroy jobs. Those who can't see that must be blind ... We hear all to often that we must open up our markets which really means first to the Japanese. In the name of what must we abandon France?', *The Economist* (1991), 18 May. It was one of main reasons of transferring Nissan and further investment in the EU from EU main land to the UK.
7   When the Remington factory in Lyons closed, during the mid-1960s, it led diplomatic crisis with US.
8   Toyota press address (mimeo).
9   Sectional Manager JETRO in Paris: interview in Japanese.
10 West Germany only. There were few FDI in the East Germany before the Unification.
11 Crafts, N. and Toniolo, G. (eds) (1996), *Economic Growth in Europe since 1945*, p. 466.
12 Generally speaking, Germany did not have any particular industrial policy within the national level. It meant the industrial policy for the specific industry, especially car industry, in this research.
13 Baglioni, G. and Crouch, C. (1990), *European Industrial Relations*, p. 127.
14 Welge, M.K. and Holtbrugge D., 'Germany', in Dunning, J.H. (eds), *Governments, Globalisation, and the International Business*, p. 343.
15 Kumar, B.N. (1991), *Japanese Direct Investment in West Germany*, p. 220.
16 Streeck, G.B. (1989), *Successful Adjustment to Turbulent Markets*, p. 144.
17 Restricted especially East Germany region only.
18 Sectional Manager JETRO in Frankfurt: interview in Japanese.
19 Crafts, N. and Toniolo, G. (eds) (1996), pp. 367–8.
20 Ibid., p. 376.
21 Ahijado, M., Begg, I. and Mayes, D. (1993), 'The Competitiveness of Spanish Industry', pp. 102–3.
22 Section member of JETRO in Madrid: interview in Japanese.
23 Tamames, R. (1986), *The Spanish Economy*, p. 129.
24 Ibid., p. 130.
25 Sectional Manager JETRO in Madrid: interview in Japanese.
26 Dahrendorf, R. (1976), 'Listener 96', 14 October.
27 *The Times* (1975), 10 October.
28 *Hansard* (1986), 30 January, col. 1090.
29 Hoskyns, J. (1982), 'Whitehall and Westminster: An Outsider's View', *Fiscal Studies*, 3, November.
30 Lord Young and Lord Tebbit: interview.
31 Before the 1983 General Election, there were two departments: Trade (J. Nott, J. Biffen and A. Cockfield) and Industry (K. Joseph and P. Jenkin).

32 Crafts, N.F.R. (1993), *Can De-Industrialisation Seriously Damage Your Wealth?*, p. 77.
33 House of Lords (1991), *Report from the Select Committee on Science and Technology*, p. 43.
34 Kitamura, H. (1993), *Japan and Britain: The global context of a dynamic partnership*, AJEI (mimeo).
35 Brech, M. and Sharp, M. (1984), p. 11.
36 Its role is:

- information to enable firms to choose the best possible location for an operation taking account of all their requirements – availability of labour, transport, proximity to customers and suppliers and above all, particular commercial needs;
- information about how to set up an operation in the UK;
- information on the national, regional and local incentive available to encourage investment;
- help in any contact with public authorities: whether central government, local government, nationalised industries or essential services such as gas, electricity, water and telecommunications;
- arrange visits to sites and buildings available in any part of the UK;
- contacts with key private and public sector companies.

37 Young, S., Hood, N. and Hamill, J. (1988), *Foreign Multinationals and the British Economy*, p. 67.
38 Mr Shimada: interview.
39 Toyota Company Report (1986) (mimeo).
40 Senior Manager in JETRO: interview in Japanese.
41 Mr John Bevan Corporate Communications Executive in Sony UK: interview.
42 As Hitachi case showed the Labour government failed to get a confidence toward foreign investors. On the other hand, Japanese MNEs had to spend more money toward US investment plan than the EU from the financial part. The time gap between JV and greenfield investment had to cover by Plaza agreement.
43 Chiba, K. (1989), *Japan in Britain: The Challenging Partnership*, AJEI (mimeo).
44 Mr Young-Sang Yoo: interview in Korean.
45 One of most important financial grant was the Regional Selective Assistance (RSA). The size of any grant is limited to the minimum of three ceilings:

- a maximum internal Net Grant Equivalent (NGE), believed to be currently 30 per cent of eligible project costs in Development Areas, and 20 percent in Intermediate Areas;
- a maximum cost per job, believed to be 5,500 European Currency Unit (ECUs), per job in Development Areas and 3,500 ECUs in Intermediate Areas;
- European Commission limits on maximum assistance under competition rules.

46 Servan-Schreiber, J. (1968), *The American Challenge*, p. 39.
47 Garrahan, P. and Steward, P. (1992), *The Nissan Enigma*, p. 14.
48 Author survey result: about 50 per cent of Japanese affiliates in the EU answered for information reason, they still depend on government data.
49 Kitamura, H. (1993), AJEI (mimeo).

Chapter 5

Car Manufacturing in the UK, 1945–77

The car industry has been a highly important leading manufacturing sector in the British economy since World War II. Whether nationalised or not, it has been subject to frequent and extensive government intervention. After the War, British car companies have managed to do little more than muddle through, despite a wide popular interest in the industry and support for its products. There are many reasons to explain this. The core explanation, however, was the role of government. Compared to other Western car-makers, British car-makers have not had any national market protection from government. When we think about Japanese makers, once imitators of British industry, now the world's second largest car-maker, the British government's dereliction of its duty is clear.

There has been no particular difference between the Conservative and Labour governments' industrial policies towards the car industry. However, if we tried to find the difference between the two parties, Labour governments have rather been inclined to strengthen direct intervention to the industry through policies towards employment and the balance of trade, while a *laissez-faire* policy has dominated Conservative thinking.

Between 1945 and 1975, the UK car industry suffered a dramatic decline in efficiency, competitiveness and world market share. The lack of policies in the UK, to foster a stable growing domestic market, and the inability to maintain good labour relationships and thereby improve productivity were largely responsible for the deteriorating performances of the British car industry. A policy of government support to the industry required much continuity and relatively stable goals and programmes. Such continuity could be found in France, German, Japan and even Spain. Support also requires a large and rapidly growing domestic market, as well as government continuity and dedication.

Government and the Car Industry

The role of government between 1945–75 should be seen in three periods: the brief renaissance in 1951; turbulent times under Conservative rule, 1951–64; labour policies and industrial decline since 1964.

The Brief Renaissance in 1951

World War II gave a Janus face to the British car industry. The angel was that the car industry made a most valuable contribution to post-war exports, and proved to be one of the country's most capable foreign currency earners. The devil was its own ignorance of the chronic problems which had been faced before the war, such as too many manufacturers, models, and government regulations compared to other competitors such as the US, France and the other European countries. Technical weaknesses such as inadequate size and low-powered engines, fragile suspensions and insufficient dust-proofing worsened the basic competitiveness of the British car-makers.

Britain's car industry survived the war almost intact and was in a unique position to begin to satisfy the world demand for cars. It was possible to leave the companies to their own devices at this time, facing no competitors on the European continent, and a withdrawal of American makers from the European and British Commonwealth markets. Without industrial reassessment, the government forced car manufacturers to an export-drive policy. The policy was implemented through an export quota system.

Within the Clement Attlee government, the car industry was regarded as basic manufacturing sector, and exports were therefore encouraged. The Labour government exhorted the car-makers, which had previously looked at exports as little more than a distraction, to turn their attention to global markets.[1] Official opinion made it clear that:

> the present exceptional opportunity for securing overseas markets for motor vehicles should ... be exploited on an expanding scale. We feel that this must strengthen our long-term position in those markets besides providing a very significant improvement in our balance of payment position now.[2]

Also, Hugh Dalton, the Chancellor of the Exchequer mentioned to the manufacturers that:

> As I told you before I am anxious that the motor industry shall export at least half its output, but I should not wish to interfere if that target is reached. We intend that the choice of types of cars and export markets shall be left to the industry to decide.[3]

Even Stafford Cripps supported the export-drive policy that:

> the (export) target should be at least 50 per cent; the country should be content to go without cars in the interests of the export effort. These remarks were greeted

with boos and shouts of 'No!' and 'Tripe!' [From members of the SMMT] Cripps added, rather bitterly: 'I have often wondered whether you thought Great Britain was here to support the motor industry, or the motor industry was here to support GB. I gather from your cries you think it is latter.[4]

Demand inevitably outstripped supply for the industry's products during the early post-war years but there were shortages and restrictions and the 1937 peak, when Britain built some 493,000 cars, was not surpassed until 1948. Then the half million figure was exceeded for the first time. Yet within six years this had doubled, for 1954 was the first of the industry's million cars year. Successful exports in 1946 made the Labour government raise export targets for 1947. The high target had created shortages of natural resources such as fuel and steel. Despite sterling convertibility, the government pressed on with further efforts to stimulate exports. At first, car export quotas were raised to 75 per cent of production, but later the government reserved all output for export except that required to meet essential home demand. There was one obvious mistaken element in this policy: without a stable domestic market share, the foreign market was too fragile to continue.

By 1948 the pound had become overvalued and competitors from the US and France had expanded their markets into the other continent. In 1949, the government modified the quotas so that:

in order to give the manufacturers greater flexibility, they will no longer be required to keep rigidly within quarterly allocations for the home market so long as their exports over a reasonable period attain the required level.[5]

Whereas the growth of the domestic market was consistently encouraged by the governments' direct or indirect policies in other countries, the British government continued to concentrate on exports. The growth of the home market, for example, made it possible for Japanese manufacturers to become internationally competitive. In Britain, however, domestic demand was not covered by British car-makers, owing to the government's non-protective policy. The wide spread of US car MNEs, Ford and GM, and Germany's VW in Britain in the mid-1950s worsened the competitiveness of the British car. Britain's traditional reactive rather than proactive policy, made its manufacturers' domestic market share worse.

The Korean War and the British rearmament programme was regarded as the 'first objective of the government's economic policy'.[6] When the government was setting about to reduce its intervention in manufacturing sectors, the Korean War compelled the Attlee government to undertake a policy of rearmament and state control of industry. The Labour government's decision to rearm coincided with the end of a sustained export-led recovery in the immediate post-war boom period. Moreover, the rearmament caused a raw material shortage, which had been worsened by the US government's stockpiling policy. The price of raw materials rose from an index, which stood at 100 in December 1949 to 215 points by June 1951. This increased overall UK import prices by almost 60 per cent over the same period. The volume of UK imports in 1952 roughly equalled the 1950 level yet in value terms the imports cost an additional £900 million. The high rate of balance of trade deficit and increasing raw material prices exacerbated the difficulties of the UK car industry.

Compared to the other European competitors, such as French, German and Japanese car competitors, the British car industry had lost its manufacturing competitiveness owing to the shortage of raw materials during the take-off period. Despite impressive performance, Britain's place as Europe's leading car manufacturer weakened. What was worse, Germany's VW, or France's Renault, began to penetrate the European market when Britain did not have a single dominant manufacturer. On the other hand the domestic market was penetrated by US MNE car-makers. It clearly made sense for the two British car-makers to unite against the growing strength of the US-owned Ford and GM.

In its first years the Attlee government pursued the New Jerusalem without a clear manufacturing vision. Overspending on social policy led the government to need higher rates of tax on the middle class, who would be expected to be ideal car consumers. As far as the car industry was concerned,

> it [the car industry] was badly handicapped by government fiscal policy, because the weight of taxation hindered the growth of the home market while its type discouraged design of the kind of high-powered, larger vehicles that many foreign drivers wanted.[7]

In the second period of Labour government, according to Burnham, the decline of UK car industry was not substantially affected by rearmament. He argued '... the reasons for long-term decline must be sought in the market structure and practices of firms themselves in addition to looking at the effects of government policy'.[8] Apart from the government's policy's failure, there were five main reasons for the success of the car industry in overseas markets in the early post-war years.

1) Pent-up, war starved demand for vehicles in other countries.
2) An immediate concentration of resources upon the particular demands of export markets coupled with a vast extension of sales and service organisations.
3) Dollar shortage of importing countries and a high level of domestic demand in North America, which reduced US and Canadian exports; the US exported 4 per cent of output in 1950, compared with 11 per cent in 1938 and Canada 9 per cent instead of 35 per cent.
4) The slower recovery of continental competitors, especially Germany and France, due to serious war damage and general dislocation.
5) The rising standard of living in many countries.[9]

The export-led car industry had missed its chance to restructure. When world demand increased after the mid-1950s, Britain was overtaken by German and other European makers which had regenerated and expanded their capacity in the home market. In contrast, British makers had to fight their own government regulation to penetrate domestic markets. As the *Economist*'s anonymous writer argued: 'For fifty years, motoring has been overtaxed. Motor cars have been treated as if they were visible symbols of the selfishness of arrogant wealth.'[10]

Until the mid-1960s, car production was the foremost British manufacturing industry. Despite mediocre performance, manufacturing sectors, especially car manufacturing, employed the largest ever proportion of the workforce. Under these circumstances, the Labour government did not recognise the automatic restructuring wave which was carried on in the continental European car-makers.

Turbulent Times under Conservative Rule, 1951–64

The incoming Conservative government was lucky to have taken over when the Korean War was over, and US stockpiling policy was reduced. Whether pre-Butskellism or not, it is difficult to find the gap between the Conservative and Labour government's approach to the manufacturing sectors, most of all towards the car industries. The Winston Churchill government pursued the same policy as the Labour government.

In order to give motor manufacturers a greater incentive to export vehicles, I have agreed with the industry that the home quota should no longer be a fixed figure, but should be calculated as a proportion of output. The industry have undertaken to endeavour to export not less than 80 per cent of their output of passenger cars, 70 per cent of LCV [light commercial vehicles], and 50 per cent of HCV [heavy commercial vehicles]. Allocations of steel to the industry will in future be more closely related to export performance.[11]

The Conservative government seemed to be the bringers of good times. With the increasing standard of living, stable unemployment rate, and reasonable domestic consumption, it was a good time for British car-makers to penetrate the domestic market. However, the British car-makers had lost their opportunity: there were too many units and unions internally, and externally the seller's market had come to an end. Despite mergers and acquisitions among manufacturers, British car-makers suffered severe competition from US MNEs and the fast growing German and French car-makers in the home market. The lack of government protection towards national makers at this time stood in obvious contrast to that of other big car making countries. Not to mention the Japanese government, France and Italy restricted imported cars in their home markets. When the seller's market ended, unstable market share put British car-makers at a major disadvantage.

The incoming Anthony Eden government stood for a more traditional *laissez faire* policy. Hence the export quotas and steel quotas for the car industry were abandoned and the car industry was left to act in its own best interests. Since 1953, the Conservative government had taken a hands-off approach to manufacturing sectors, and pursued a 'stop-go' policy in macroeconomic management.[12] The stop-go policy damaged the car industry especially heavily.

First, as the country's major exporting industry, any decline in motor exports had a noticeably harmful effect on the balance of payments. Secondly, whenever it was necessary to improve the balance of payments, the government would reduce internal demand. Consumer durable demand, particularly demand for cars, was very susceptible to general restrictions. Hence the motor industry tended to feel the brunt of the country's balance of payments difficulties from two directions.[13]

The stop-go policy in the car industry showed cyclical trends in manufacturing and exports. During the 'go' periods there was little pressure on the industry to export. 'Stop' periods showed high intervention within the national market and pushed car industries to increase exports. The 'stop-go' policy hindered management forecasts of demand and weakened market penetration. The reluctant collaboration between government and manufacturers led the industry either to overproduce or to under-produce. The industry therefore lost a second chance to increase worldwide competitiveness during the 1960s.

According to the SMMT report 'Progress and the Motor Industry' in 1958:

A statement of government intention towards the industry, as suggested below, would do much to confirm and encourage the industry in this belief.

1. The government recognises that the motor vehicle is not only essential but socially desirable, and that the wider distribution of car ownership throughout the population can be a real move towards social advancement, and the higher standard of living that the government seek to promote.
2. The government believe that vehicle output should be steadily increased, both to meet home demands and the needs of a widening export market.
3. The government, whilst expecting the motor industry to bear its fair burden of general restraints and of taxation, recognise that at the present time, these fall more severely on the motor industry than an others – especially in relation to purchase tax, fuel tax and hire purchase restrictions – and undertakes to reduce these handicaps at the earliest opportunity, with a view to reducing road transport costs, expanding the output of the industry, achieving the right balance between home and export markets, and thus facilitating exports.[14]

All the car-makers wanted was strong government regulation against imported cars and to be allowed to improve quality using stable domestic market by themselves.

It is easy to say that Japanese success and British failure in the car industry were caused by differences in the governments 'role'. Whether they increased exports or not, all car-makers faced a second wave of take-off stage during the 1950s except for US makers. Compared to the first wave, multinationalised car-makers tried to find new markets. Without government restrictions on home markets, there were few car-makers who could survive. The real power of current Japanese car-makers originates from high government restrictions during the 1950s and 1960s. The reason for British failure is simple: they did not have strong government regulation.[15]

As Plowden argued '… there was nothing to choose between Tories and Labour; apart from Labour criticisms of the industry's failure to export, neither party officially made an issue of any aspect of the motor car'.[16]

The lack of confidence about the British car on the part of the Conservative government was made clear in the House of Commons when Maurice Edelman put to the President of the Board of Trade, Peter Thorneycroft the point that:

… the present crisis in the motor industry stems indirectly from the catastrophic decline in the exports of motor cars from 73 per cent in the last year of the Labour government to 43 per cent under present Administration? In view of that fact, will not change his furtive policy of exhortation and *laissez-faire*.

Thorneycroft replied that 'it is not for any government to export motor cars; it is for the motor car industry to do that'.[17]

Table 5.1   UK car exports 1950–55

	UK exports of new cars and chassis (£ million)	% of total value of production exported
1950	116.6	66%
1951	119.1	65%
1952	111.3	53%
1953	103.9	45%
1954	118.5	44%
1955	122.5	38%

Source: HCD (1956), 15 March, col. 530.

Thorneycroft, moreover, ignored the demand from the British car industry that '… we have here an open market, with just the same changes of competition as anyone else. There is no easy short cut to getting that motor car trade except by producing a better car at a cheaper price'.[18]

Why did the Conservative government not try to restructure the British car industry? One of the main reasons was their lack of confidence in the British car industry. They tried to encourage car-makers to depend not on the government's protective hand but on their market position.

The Conservative government thought industrial policy had to have an economic utility. Most politicians thought that the car industry would be the same as the steel or coal industry within a decade. Moreover, car companies were regarded as a centre of trade unions' militant power. The chronic problem, which British manufacturing sectors had been facing, was not a manufacturing issue but a change of British industrial tradition. Especially, industrial action in the car industry seemed to get worse. Compared to Mrs Thatcher's production-based national car industry, they hoped that the car industry would change on its own.[19]

Within the company level, they struggled to survive. The first action from the car-makers was a mergers and acquisitions (M&A) strategy.

Table 5.2   Historical M&A process of the UK car industry

1952   Austin and Morris formed the defensive alliance of BMC.
        First failure to achieve real integration.
        Jowett set up R&D programme which failed because it was too expensive.
1955   Rootes saved Singer with cash support.
1960   Jaguar bought BSA's Daimler cars and Transport Vehicles.
        Jaguar took over Guy Motors, a commercial vehicle producer.
1961   Ford introduced the Cortina as a first successful medium size car.
        The Cortina competed with BMC's new 1100 and Rootes's Minx which was
        the first defeat for UK manufacturers win medium cars.
1961   Leyland took over Standard-Triumph.
1962   Leyland took over its CV rival Associated Commercial Vehicles, changing
        its name to Leyland Motor Corporation (LMC).
1964   GM's Ellesmere Port plant, an investment of £120 million opened, the most
        modernised investment programme since the war.
1964   Chrysler saved Rootes which had failed to win ground in the small and
        medium car market.
        Leyland Motor which was concentrated on commercial vehicles only, was
        one of the most profitable manufacturers in the UK car industry.
1965   Rover bought Alvis.
1966   BMC and Jaguar merged to form British Motor Holdings (BMH)
1967   LMC bought Rover.
1967   There were two big car-makers in the UK, BMH and LMC
1968   BMH and LMC merged, and was named British Leyland, later renamed
        Rover.
1975   BL nationalised under the Labour government
1979   Rover signed a technical collaboration agreement with Honda.
1988   Rover was sold to BAe.
1994   Rover was taken over by BMW.

Source: Derived by the author on the basis of SMMT annual papers and newspapers various
           issues.

Under this business strategy, there were three main groups left: the 'Big Five' organisations – BMC, Ford UK, Rootes Motors, Vauxhall, and Leyland-Standard-Triumph – which manufactured quantity produced popular cars, specialist cars and commercial vehicles (CV); manufacturers of specialist cars only; and manufacturers of light, medium and heavy CV. Before the acquisition of Standard-Triumph, Leyland was the largest manufacturer outside the 'Big Five', which were responsible for over 95 per cent of the number of cars produced in Britain.

After the late 1950s, there was severe competition between BMC and Ford. The Mini was an innovative range of front wheel drive cars, while Ford produced its rival Cortina. Despite its long sales history, Mini was fatally flawed as far as its price, under £500, was concerned, which was to have devastating long term implications for BMC. Moreover, BMC was a company dominated by engineers who were contemptuous of what they perceived to be the evils of marketing. The Cortina started its sale with an impeccable exercise in timing, marketing and production planning, precisely the opposite to a BMC strategy.

The poorly technically based British car faced another problem within its own company. As Table 5.3 shows, there were too many models of car within BMC.

One of the ironies of this was that despite the number of car-makers, there were no popular models except the Mini, which was losing money. A worsening emerging problem since the late 1950s was deterioration in labour relations between the car-makers and their workforces. Strikes, both official and unofficial, became an all too frequent feature of these days and managers found that they were spending an increasing amount of time and money in countering the growing influence of the shop stewards. BMC, with its multitude of factories and makers, was particularly vulnerable in this regard.

Under the circumstances, the Conservative government's best policy towards the car industry was hand it over to the makers. However, public opinion about the car started to move into a new stage. Before the late 1950s, the car ownership could never become universal or even general. The car was widely regarded as a middle-class luxury. A Gallup Poll showed that 60 per cent of car owners voted Conservative, 19 per cent for Labour and 11 per cent Liberal. There were gradual changes in political attitudes towards the car. Between 1958 and 1963 the real price of cars fell by some 18 per cent. The number of car users increased from under 4 million in 1956, to 4 and a half million in 1958, and to 6 and a half million in 1962. When the Conservatives had come to power, almost exactly half the vehicles in the country had been cars; by 1962 the proportion was nearly two thirds.

Whether for political reasons or not, under the Conservative government, a three years boom began. Increasing exports coincided with revival of the world economy, and an enlarged domestic market enabled the car industry to increase production. As exports increased, the balance of payments improved. Hence the government was able to remove the purchase tax surcharge and lower purchase tax. This allowed government to speed up economic growth. With the cutting of purchase tax on cars from 45 per cent to 25 per cent, the

Table 5.3   Makes of cars produced by British manufacturers

Group	Company	Make of car	Make of CV
The 'Big Five', who manufacture quantity-produced and specialist cars and CV	BMC	Austin-Healey Metropolitan Morris MG Riley Vanden Plas Wolseley	Austin Morris
	Ford	Ford	Thames
	Rootes	Hilman Humber Singer Sunbeam Standard	Commer Karrier
	Leyland- Standard-Triumph	Triumph	Standard Triumph Leyland Albion Scammell
	Vauxhall	Vauxhall	Bedford
Manufacturers of specialist cars and CV	Jaguar	Jaguar Daimler	Daimler Guy
	Rover Jensen Reliant	Rover Jensen Reliant	Land-Rover Jensen Reliant

Table 5.3 cont'd

Group	Company	Make of car	Make of CV
Manufacturers who construct either specialist cars or CV (makes which differ from the firm's name are given in brackets)	Company making specialist cars	Company making Associated CV (AEC, Maudsley, Crossley, Thornycroft)	CV
	AC	Dennis	Dodge
	AFN (Frazer Nash)		ERF
	David Brown (Aston Martin, Lagonda)		Foden
	Bristol		Shelvoke and Drewry (SD)
	Fairthorpe		Trojan
	Lotus		Atkinson
	Morgan		Seddon
	Rolls-Royce (Bentley)		
	Turner		

Source: British Information Services (1962) (mimeo), British Motor Vehicle Industry.

relaxation on home sales coincided with a car boom in Europe and a revival of sales to the US. During this period, the industry was working at full capacity.

At the same time, however, Britain was overrun by European competitors and Japan. Between 1962 and 1964 the car industry experienced growth, and then, from 1965 to 1969, it showed a gradual decline in production, national market share and exports. Over the same period, Japanese car production increased tenfold whilst French, German and Italian output all at least doubled. The Conservative government was be rather luckier than Labour, because the heyday of the car industry lasted until the end of Conservative government. However, the real gap between the British car industry and the others emerged under the Conservative government. The government-led business strategy, in particular the stop-go fiscal policy, threw British car-makers into turmoil. There was only one government, apart from the US, which left the national champion car-maker to suffer severe competition without protection. One more important thing the Conservative government forgot, was the end of the British Empire. They still thought that British cars would export easily to Commonwealth countries. While the European makers turned their eyes on their neighbours, Britain still thought of their long distance old friends.

Labour Policies and Industrial Decline since 1964

The Harold Wilson government took power with ambitious plans for the restructuring of industry and faster long-term growth. After the 'thirteenwasted years', the government needed to put an end to the 'stop-go' policy. The new government set up an incomes policy with the cooperation of the trade unions, improving industrial efficiency by investment allowances for export industries and various kinds of industrial equipment, founding or expanding hi-tech industries with state help, and promoting R&D and industrial training. Most of all, the Labour government in 1964 enjoyed the advantage that there had been full employment for nearly a quarter of a century. Full employment at the time when Labour came to power was a never-ending dream for Wilson government.

Despite this reason for confidence, the Wilson government was soon involved in a day-to-day struggle to support sterling. On the other hand, they had the confidence about their industrial policy that 'state intervention in the market system was needed, but only in order to make private firms bigger than they otherwise would be'.[20] The British car industry, since the 1960s, was a core problem for British industrial policy. Exports sales were gradually lost to cheaper and more reliable foreign makers whilst, imports of foreign cars were on the increase, from around 3 per cent in 1960 to just over 15 per cent by 1970. Despite a decline of exports, the domestic sales of the product were relatively good, and many manufacturers allowed their existing model ranges to run on too long. Older models did not require modernised assembly processes, and the policy thus encouraged a general lack of investment in new plant. When this was contemplated, it met with considerable government interference over its location.

Compared to the former Conservative government's *laissez-faire* and stop-go policy, the two prongs of the Labour government's strategy toward car industry were regional distribution and the full employment policy. Despite criticism about overmanning in the car industry, Wilson thought the car industry was the engine of full employment.

> But we could ignore neither the cost to the balance of payments nor the effect on employment if Leyland were suffered to go under. Leyland's direct exports from Britain in 1974 had reached almost £500 million. Moreover, *the company employs over 170,000 people directly in this country, and the livelihood of several hundred thousand more is dependent upon it. I must tell the House that in this decision a million jobs are at stake.*
>
> As more Conservative back-benchers criticised the decision, I warned again about the loss of a million jobs. (emphasis my own)[21]

However, the politically based industrial policy led British car industry in an unstable condition.

The single-minded full employment policy under the Wilson government proved disastrous. The new BL inherited ineffective management, overcapacity, and a stable of barely profitable cars at best and money-losing models at worst. Moreover, BL was buffeted by rising imports, which increased from 10 per cent of domestic sales in 1969 to over one-half by 1978. The loss of home market share was a fatal blow to the British car industry.

> The best merit of the merger was the increase in domestic market share. However, the problem was not in a single model but in the whole of the manufacturers' business strategy, and the effect of merger was not as expected. The lack of popular models among British car-makers was too painful to ignore. One of the major mistakes under the Wilson periods was that they spent money in the wrong place. Full employment policy spending was not directed to technology and R&D investment but to promoting full employment. When the car industry globalised, they needed more capital investment and R&D spending. British car-makers, however, still mismanaged themselves under the name of full employment.[22]

Under this situation, badly needed reductions of the work force, resulting in layoffs, provoked strikes in the early 1970s. According to the Castle diaries, 'David Basnett made his parting shot, "Unemployment is the Achilles heel of the Social Chapter".'[23] All problems which British car-makers faced were made worse by Labour government policies. As a result of this turmoil, the company was unprofitable until 1973 and was nationalised by the Labour government two years later.

During the 1970s, Dunnett argued that:

> Government policy as regards the motor industry had to be sharply modified as the government did what it could to help the much weakened UK motor industry fight off intense international competition. To paraphrase J.F. Kennedy, it was no longer a matter of what the UK motor industry could do for the government and the country, but a matter of what the government and the country could do to make the motor industry viable.[24]

The 1970s were the time of the emergence of national car champion industries in the world consumer market. However a 1950s industrial spirit still flourished in the UK car industry. The emerging intense competition between car-makers within the Western Europe had moved from labour-intensive industry to high-technology automation systems and a high investment R&D based industry. Despite increasing spending, the British car-makers still had the 1950s manufacturing mentality. As Barnett argued:

> In March 1945 a special committee submitted a report on the post-war motor industry which identified virtually the same weakness as the 1975 report on 'The Future of the British Car Industry' by the Central Policy Review Staff (CPRS): too many companies; too many models; not enough standardisation of production and parts to ensure low costs; failure to design vehicles that could defeat the competition in overseas markets; limp export marketing and poor service and spares organisation – in sum, a picture of an industry that could thrive only so long as its main potential competitors remained knocked out by war and car-starved customers were will to buy anything with four wheels and an engine.[25]

Through merger, however, British car-makers increased their capacity not with high technology or restructuring manufacturing methods but in size and in the amount of money spent on employment policies.

Another fatal blow to the UK car industry was the oil shock. The oil crisis in 1973 caused a recession of the Western economies which had a disastrous effect on Britain's inflation rate and balance of payments. Moreover the UK car industry could not support the balance of payments owing to the loss of international consumer markets. One particular government mistake was the Heath government's 'dash for growth' policy. Under the Conservative government, British industry suffered considerably from the energy crisis. For the first two months of 1974, following a major strike by the coal miners, the government implemented a three-day working week to save energy. This policy created a steel shortage for the car industry which necessitated further reductions in production. According to the *Financial Times* on 20 February 1974 'BL claimed they lost production worth three million pounds a day.'

As far as regional policy was concerned, the Conservatives had largely neglected regional problems during the 1950s, and although they started to step up assistance to the depressed areas in the early 1960s, it proved fruitless. The Labour government in 1964 had a double incentive to bring down regional unemployment. On the industry side, the extra labour resources that had to be mobilised if the National Plan was to succeed mainly had to come from the areas where unemployment was high. There were also political incentives, because the majority of Labour's parliamentary seats were in the development areas of Scotland, Wales and Northern England.

With the introduction of the Regional Employment Premium (REP)[26] plan, the government tried two different approaches towards manufacturing sectors. Despite a rational approach to manufacturing sectors, the effect on the car industry was disastrous. Since the globalisation of car manufacturing, greenfield investment was a most important factor for British car-makers. When industry tried to initiate greenfield investment to compete with other European makers, there was an obstacle from the Wilson government. The government tried to guide British car-makers to set up their affiliates in the less-developed areas, such as the North England, and Scotland. In evidence to the Trade and Industry Sub-Committee examining the effects of regional policy the Chairman of BL, Donald Stokes observed that government intervention increased business risks. He said that 'You [the Government] have cost us a fortune by making us set up in places which are quite unsuitable to have factories.'[27]

Chrysler's Linwood plant, which was the only car manufacturing part in Scotland was, also, a good example. After the oil shock, the increasing cost of transporting parts was one of the biggest burdens on the assemblers. The policy which was inspired by political calculation made British car-makers suffer more. When the Chrysler crisis happened, the real problem was revealed from the government side.

He thought that Chrysler's share of the UK market had probably gone completely and we should concentrate on making BL a success. But 25,000 jobs were at immediate risk ... Willie then stormed away about the effect of closure on Scotland. Linwood was the only part of the motor industry Scotland had, he declared. 'This will be politically disastrous.'[28]

Despite good intentions, the effects of government intervention were usually adverse from the industrialists' point of view. Many companies complained that they found output per head in their Development Area plants to be lower than that of plants in other areas. Moreover, although the Wilson government had pursued regional policies, there had been little consistency in Government regional policy. It was stated in the House of Common's Expenditure Committee report that:

Much has been spent and much may well have been wasted. Regional policy has been empiricism run mad, a game of hit-and-miss, played with more enthusiasm than success. We do not doubt the good intentions, the devotion even, of many of those who have struggled over the years to relieve the human consequences of regional disparities. We regret that their efforts have not been better sustained by the proper evaluation of the costs and benefits of the policies pursued.[29]

Since World War II, the UK government had used the car industry as a policy measure to help achieve a number of overall economic aims. The increased exports in the 1940s helped the balance of payments, and the late 1950s achieved the regional relocation of the unemployment areas. It was the car industry, which helped to postpone devaluation. It was proved during the 1970s, that the UK government and industry recognised the real impact of misconceived government regulation and management failure. It was clear when compared to Japanese government policy. Barnett argued again that:

... let alone the kind of twenty-year development plan masterminded by the Japanese MITI in the 1950s, which transformed the Japanese motor industry from a workshop operation into the largest and commercially most successful in the world. Instead, British manufacturers were to be 'urged to collaborate more closely' with regard to overseas marketing and servicing; government financial assistance might be offered to induce manufacturers 'to embark on projects which they now regards as too risky'.[30]

When Japan used her car industry as a symbol of its high technology industrial sector, UK used it as a barometer of the success of government policies. When they enjoyed their heyday, the British government led the car manufacturers to hide real problems which British industry had traditionally faced. When the heyday was passed, the responsibility had been shifted from government to industry on its own. One of the objectives of the incoming government in 1979 was that should Britain solve her traditional industrial problems herself or through collaboration with foreign companies. They did not care about whether the white or the black cat caught the rat.

Conclusion

The government's industrial policy is normally seen as a vertical rudder within the manufacturing sector. As far as British car industry was concerned, each government failed to use that rudder properly. During this time, Bhaskar observed that:

> First, the car has always been treated as a luxury item. The Labour Party, for example, has always had a doctrinaire dislike for the 'luxury' symbolised by a car and the fact that cars are *private* as opposed to *public* goods. Equally, the Conservatives have done little systematically to promote the industry. Secondly, all governments have found it useful to conduct the demand management of the economy through demand for consumer durable and particularly demand for motor vehicles. This has led to very large swings in the demand for motor vehicles which in the 1950s and 1960s created cyclical employment in the industry and helped to stoke the inherent insecurity of the labour force ... Thirdly, such inconsistent government interference has had another effect. The UK motor industry has always been characterised by long lead times and high break-even points which make it difficult for the industry to react to external changes. Yet, as one manager of BL International is reputed to have said, 'In the period 1960-70, the initial growth period of the European and Japanese industries, the terms on which cars could be purchased – the rates of purchase tax and the conditions of credit payment – were altered on average every ten months ... Solely because of selective intervention on the part of the Government, the UK motor industry faced a period of seven year's decline and stagnation immediately following a period in which demand had leaped over 60% in three years. All this at a time when all its competitors experienced continuous and generally rapid growth in their domestic markets.'
> ... *One can only hope through the experience with the motor and other industries that the government will not again adopt such a short-sighted approach to industry.* (emphasis my own)[31]

More clearly, John Beswick, the director of the SMMT in 1975 said in the House of Commons that:

In all other countries of the world, without exception, their governments take a positive attitude towards their own domestic industry ... this is one factor we have been lacking in this country for many years; in short, a positive attitude by Government to the motor industry.[32]

Mr Nicolas W. L. Maclean, an adviser to Mrs Thatcher on industrial policy 1979 to 1982, told me that

Between Wilson and the incoming Thatcher government, there were two similar policies about the car industry. The car industry was treated as an employment and regional policy barometer. The difference was in approach. When Wilson tried to save the national car industry by maintaining full employment in the component industries, Thatcher preferred value-added competitive car-makers, in which the question of ownership is not a matter of concern.

As far as regional policy was concerned, while Labour spent money to improve labour relations policy towards multinational car-makers, the Conservative spent money to encourage foreign companies to make greenfield investment. That was expected to save British component industries, and on the other hand to improve the balance of trade within the manufacturing sectors. Hence, there were few options to choose. Because of the emerging SEM, there were new investors to get a foothold within the EU. With a flood of entrants moving towards Europe, the thing which governments have to do is just 'wait and wait'. And things happened suddenly, just like accidents.[33]

When the Thatcher government came to power, there was a sharply emerging question of the deep-seated uncompetitiveness of British manufacturing sectors. There were two options to choose; either to rebuild the manufacturing base by a positive investment strategy behind protective walls, or to rely on the devaluation of sterling to enable Britain to undercut its competitors. There was a determined policy that the Thatcher government would not use sterling policy, because she did not want to be the first Conservative Prime Minister injured politically by devaluation. She thought to rebuild manufacturing sectors with the help of foreign companies, who were eager to get market penetration, but without protective barriers. The policy began with Honda and ended with Nissan.

Industrial Relations

Industrial relations within the car industry were a barometer of British industrial relations practice. The industry had a reputation before the war for hire-and-fire practices. After the war, the poor performance of the car industry was blamed on troublesome labour relations. The labour problem was identified by both sides, from employer and employee. Managers complained that the 'decline of the industrial spirit' came about because there were too many trade unions which led to difficulties in negotiation, and also to wildcat strikes without negotiation between employer and employee, or among employees themselves. From the shop stewards' viewpoint, the knowledge gap between manager and employee was too wide. There was, moreover, no effort from either side to close the gap. Despite weak relationships between employers and employees, the government had no solution to industrial problems. Had any government since the War ever tried to solve the problem wholeheartedly? Would industrial relations problems have been a main reason for the decline of the British car industry, if there had been proper government intervention?

Government and Industrial Relations before 1964

The general picture of industrial relations, until 1964, was of noninterference by government in free collective bargaining. There was, also, no national agreement, covering the whole car industry, for the determination of basic wage-rates. Generally there were negotiations between the Allied Employers National Federation, which included BMC, Rootes and Leyland-Standard-Triumph, and the engineering unions. Compared to the other manufacturing sectors, earnings in car manufacturing were considerably higher than the basic minimum agreed rates, as a result of piece rates and bonus payments. Two American makers, Ford and Vauxhall were not members of a national negotiating body. Hence, there was variation between different manufacturers in wages, conditions of employment, labour relations and the machinery for settling disputes, and, moreover, procedures differed in different plants of the same company.

One of the main difficulties in the labour relations situation was trade union structure. Trade union structure in the car industry presented variations between companies and plants. Though almost all workers were represented by trade unions which were affiliated to the Confederation of Shipbuilding and Engineering Unions, the unions' interests were not mainly concerned with the car industry. The four largest unions were the Transport and General Worker's Union, the National Union of General and Municipal Workers, the Amalgamated Engineering Union and the National Union of Vehicle Builders. In addition, there were many craft unions such as the Electrical Trade Union, with a membership mainly of skilled workers. Generally, the shop stewards of the various unions represented in a particular plant established a joint body between themselves to conduct negotiations with the management.

During the Attlee government, there were few disputes in the car industry owing to the increasing level of export and the good external environment. When the Conservatives came to power, there emerged a gap between government and unions. Under the Conservative government, the Minister of Labour was concerned about the number of strikes and the increase in the number of working days lost. It had been unofficially estimated that in companies in the car industry during the period 1958–60, there were 62 separate strikes involving directly or indirectly 105,000 workers and resulting in the loss of 285,000 working days. In the previous three years, 1955–57, there had been 25 strikes involving 40,000 workers and resulting in the loss of 135,000 working days. Although wages had tended to be much higher than in other branches of engineering, a large proportion of disputes had still concerned wages. The claims from the unions at this time resulted from the good business turnover during the late 1940s and the early 1950s. When the harvest came in, employees' thought that they had lost out compared to their managers.

> I thought that the result after the War was too good for British car exporters to expect. When the Conservative government and the employees in the car manufacturing sector started to negotiate about the portion of cheese, neither government nor labour paid attention to the real problem, the decline of British car industry. A concession-hunting and subsequently 'stop-go' policy missed the chance to restructure industrial equipment and reeducate shop stewards.[34]

Hence, the Minister of Labour, in February 1961, set up a committee made up of leading representatives of the employers and unions, but excluding shop stewards, to examine the matter. The agreement was expressed after the committee that:

> The committee had agreed on a number of points on which action should be taken in our respective fields to assist individual companies, work people and trade unions in their day to day relations ... We have fully satisfied ourselves that these procedures are generally adequate if operated in the spirit.[35]

Despite the agreement, there was continuous strike action after then. The real problem, which was faced at this time, was the lack of mutual understanding between managers and shop stewards. The lack of mutual understanding between management and trade union was revealed by an interview in which:

A Ford Convenor told us 'the main barrier we have to overcome on both sides is mutual suspicion. There is still a long way to go in the field of communications between the management and trade union' and 'communication is a problem' said a Longbridge witness.[36]

From the managers' side, also, this kind of weakness had been recognised.

Asked 'Do you think your communications with your 70,000 employees are reasonably good?' Mr. Terence Beckett, the Chairman of Ford (UK), said 'I would give us not a very good mark on that score ... There is a great deal of scope for improvement. The improvement of communication and the flow of information was an essential part of the Ford industrial relations programme.[37]

Although many assumptions were made about the improvement of labour relations, there was no improvement. As a far as labour relation was concerned, the Conservative government had no familiarity with trade unions. The government through the 1950s and early 1960 had got along by muddling through.

Britain has two systems of industrial relations. The one is the formal system embodied in the official institutions. The other is the informal system, created by the actual behaviour of trade unions and employers' associations, of managers, shop stewards and workers.[38]

The incoming Wilson government tried to grasp the informal system, which had been getting stronger since the mid-1950s. The car industry was its barometer.

Government and Industrial Relations after 1964

The incoming Wilson government was the first Labour government, which was politically independent and free from outside pressure. Under the 'modernisation' policy[39] towards manufacturing sectors government tried to change labour relations in the car industry radically. The government's actions influenced labour relations with new labour legislation, courts of inquiry, a series of government reports and informal discussions at the Prime Ministerial level. One of the reasons for this positive government policy was the change in the Prime Minister's approach to the manufacturing sector, especially the car industry. Most of the interactions between government and the trade unions were dominated by strikes, conflict and confrontation. As Table 5.4 shows, the industrial instability of the UK car industry increased every year.

Table 5.4   Industrial action in the British car industry, 1949–78

	No. of strikes	No. of workers involved ('000s)	Working days lost ('000s)
1949	38	7.9	47
1950	53	24.3	132
1951	67	53.5	265
1952	44	38.1	457
1953	40	300.7	560
1954	46	33.4	98
1955	76	62.8	452
1956	48	87.3	361
1957	65	154.8	800
1958	84	72.8	160
1959	135	157.6	465
1960	129	186.3	515
1961	102	121.5	425
1962	116	508.3	747
1963	129	148.3	315
1964	165	150	429
1965	165	218.9	874
1966	170	134.2	344
1967	223	200.6	504
1968	233	402.5	898
1969	276	276	1,636
1970	336	271.4	1,105
1971	241	340.3	3,100
1972	217	247.3	1,355
1973	297	422.6	2,082
1974	223	296.6	1,255
1975	150	164.0	829
1976	191	206.0	785
1977	208	234.3	2,593
1978	194	366.6	3,495

Source: Ministry of Labour, *Labour Gazette*, various years.

Owing to the intensity of industrial action, the Prime Minister undertook a policy of informal discussions about car industry labour relations. A series of meetings was set up between the industry and union leaders, excluding shop stewards. According to the *Economist*, the result was clear that

... it is hard to discuss the futility of the government's latest industrial manoeuvre. Unofficial strikes cannot be abolished by cosy chats at Number Ten. These are workshop problems that fail to be settled at workshop level, a tiny minority of the disputes that arises every day throughout industry.[40]

Compared to other European makers, who had been developing automation systems, the British car manufacturing process was, still, mainly dependent upon labour-intensive technology. Hence, the emerging power group within manufacturing sector was not employers or trade unions but the shop stewards group. Despite the government's positive attitude towards car manufacturers, the policy bore no fruit owing to underestimation of the influence of the shop stewards. Although one of the main reasons for industrial action since the mid-1950s was the lack of communication between shop stewards and managers or unions' leaders, the Wilson government did not recognise this point. As the notorious Selsdon Park Hotel conference convened by Edward Heath in preparation for the 1970 election campaign mentioned:

> The point of industrial relations change is to redress the balance between employees and employers. Up to 1939 the balance was on the side of the employer. After 1945 the balance was on the side of the unions and it is still on the side of the unions.[41]

One of the Wilson government's mistakes towards labour relations during the first term was its method of approach. The origin of industrial action was often disharmony between members of different trade unions, which was exploited by shop stewards.

> The mistake during the Wilson government before 1970 was underestimation of the shop stewards' power. Since the 1951 Conservative government, the shop stewards in the car manufacturing sector had been strengthened. The government and managers made compromises and lost control of the shop stewards. Without the support of shop stewards, any compromise will not achieve good results between managers and employees.[42]

The IRIS New Survey in February 1966 emphasised the bad industrial relations on the shop floor:

> Many of these problems arise from the very nature of things, but good management are constantly looking for new remedies. Poor supervision is one of the major dangers, and it must be said in fairness that there is much reluctance among the

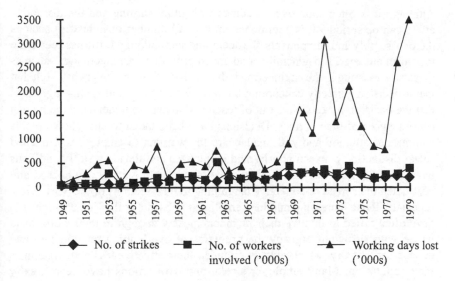

Figure 5.1   Industrial action in the British car industry, 1949–79

Source: Ministry of Labour, *Labour Gazette*, various years.

rank-and-file to accept the responsibility of the foreman and the shop steward. There may be for recruiting graduates for first line of supervisory jobs today, especially in time rate factories where the foreman is often in effect a manager's and there is also an urgent need for a much higher standard of training for the ordinary foreman at the lower supervisory levels.[43]

Without an exact understanding of the structure of labour relation within the factory, agreements between government and trade unions were not quite reliable. Even when there was government action towards strikes using agreements or court inquiries, such as in the Ford case in 1962, there was no sign of a decrease in strikes. This was mainly caused by the existence of too many trade unions for government to talk to, and the gap in mutual confidence between employers and employees.

In 1968, Barbara Castle, when preparing her paper *In Place of Strife*, wrote of the current situation that

The deficiencies of Britain's system of industrial relations are reflected in the character of our strike problem. It is true that, in comparison with many other countries, Britain's strike record, if measured by the number of employees directly involved and the number of working days directly lost, is relatively good ... The typical British strike is unofficial and usually in breach of agreed procedure.

Although it is often soon over, it comes with little warning and the disruptive effect can be serious. It is commonest in a small number of industries such as motor assembly and components, the docks and shipbuilding. Little has been done to reform outdated and generally condemned procedural arrangements – such as those now existing in the engineering industry. Too often employers have felt that major decisions directly concerning them were being taken at such a high level that the decision makers were out of reach and unable to understand the human consequences of their actions. Decisions have been taken to close down plants without consultation and with inadequate forewarning to employees. Outdated social distinction between hourly-paid employees and those on staff conditions have been perpetuated. At the same time, some employers have opposed and obstructed the spread of collective bargaining to new sections of the work force, especially those increasing numbers employed in 'white collar' jobs. Unions too have often failed to involve their members closely enough in their work, or to tackle with sufficient urgency the problems of overlapping membership and unnecessary rivalry, which always diminish their effectiveness and sometimes their reputation. Many employer's relations with unions have been greatly complicated by the large number of unions that may have members in a single factory.[44]

Although the paper exactly recognised the real problems within the industry which were inadequate structure and numerous trade unions, it was regarded as too hostile to the trade unions and too difficult for the Labour party to deal with.

The British government's attitude towards trade unions has been one of abstention. During the export heyday of the 1950s, all negotiation partners were over-mighty, except for government. The action by Wilson government was rather for political than for industrial reasons. If they wanted to succeed, they should have changed their political manifesto, especially 'Clause Four', first. Otherwise, all actions by a Labour government will be dependent on political considerations.[45]

As Castle mentioned in her report, 'The need for state intervention and involvement in association with both sides of industry is now admitted by almost everybody. The question that remains, is what form should it take at the present time?',[46] despite many emerging intentions from government to restructure the manufacturing sector, there was no government policy. Without the steering gear, it led to political defeat in 1970 general election, and revealed, moreover, the limit of government's role in manufacturing sector.

One of the emerging questions during the first term of the Wilson government towards the manufacturing sector was 'what did the government think about the manufacturing sector itself?' Under the 'modernisation plan', government-funded R&D programmes had been concentrated on such high-tech intensive industries as military and civil aircraft, and nuclear technology. Also, the Wilson government's Industrial Reorganisation Corporation encouraged the manufacturing sector towards merger with government support. The merger boom of the late 1960s coincided with an absolute fall in industrial R&D spending, and indeed a fall in the R&D/output ratio for manufacturing industry. The Wilson government's mistake in its first term (and indeed its second term) was that the manufacturing sector was used as a political instrument.

The 1970 Conservative government was characterised by a period of severe industrial disputes. The Prime Minister's effort to prepare the country for membership of the EEC by modernising its industrial capacity and strengthening regional infrastructure, needed radical movement, which was uncomfortable for industry. 'When I realised the real industrial problem, I was exhausted and the external stimulus in 1973 put the British manufacturing sector out of control.'[47] Within the car industry, the government's incomes policy between 1971 and 1972 made industrial relations worse. The policy, which was introduced at a time when the industry was still converting from a piecework to a measured day work (MDW)[48] system, hampered the establishment of a rational pay structure for car industry workers. MDW at BL and Chrysler was regarded as another major cause of disputes, even though the system had been operating successfully at Ford and Vauxhall for a number of years. Having received little help from government, the industry had put in a great deal of research into manning levels and output standards before MDW was put into operation. Within the industrial sector, BL and Chrysler had different systems from those of Ford and Vauxhall. Overmanning and consequent disputes, a decrease in productivity and the heavy demands on foremen in many cases ill-equipped to cope with unfamiliar pressure were serious problems in BL and Chrysler.

After 1970, one particularly prominent type of industrial action was strikes in the automotive component industry. During the 1960s, strikes in the components industry had tended to be short and sharp. Once the workers returned to work, piece rates and overtime soon had production booming and the backlog made good. Since then, however, the strikes had been longer and more bitter. Pilkington, Lucas and Sankey had been sole suppliers to much of the industry of glass, electrical equipment and wheels respectively. Because the industry worked with deliberately small stocks, it was not long before component shortages brought the lines to a halt. More tactical industrial action within the car and components industry made the British car industry relatively more vulnerable as manufacturers.

The Heath government, willingly or not, made worse the gap which had grown up between leaders and the shop stewards since the mid-1950. The policy which imposed ever-greater burdens on the shop floor to secure wage restraint in the public interest proved a failure. As Thatcher admitted in retrospect 'The philosophy of the Bill, the 1970 Industrial Relations Act was muddled. It was in part corporatist and in part libertarian.'[49] This was the industrial policy Heath government pursued.

The second Wilson government and trade unions leaders made efforts to create a new public policy through the so-called 'concordat' that laid out hopes for a future of coordinated pay bargaining based on the West German model.[50] But it lacked mutual credibility. The shop stewards, excluded during the negotiations, would not allow further settlement.

The main role of government intervention towards manufacturing sectors was expressed by a trade union official in 1966:

> the government's role was to improve the interests of workers only as the second best alternative to the development by employed people themselves of the organisation, the competence, the representative capacity to bargain and to achieve for themselves satisfactory terms and conditions of employment.[51]

No British government after the war could escape this phantom.

Conclusion

British management, since 1945, in all manufacturing sectors proved inept, and weak in leading its workforce, which served only to worsen the other great causes of lagging British productivity. There were continual industrial actions, mostly wildcat, and go-slows. Moreover, there was a near universal tendency to shorten shifts and lengthen breaks at both ends. These kinds of 'British disease' became notorious in the 1960s and 1970. The leading industrial actors were the car manufacturing and coal mining sectors.

> One of the main problems, since the mid-1960s, is that there have been too few engineers, who can compete with other Western manufacturers. The Wilson government's employment scheme was mainly concerned with employment policy not with the education of the workforce. Hence the car industry was regarded as one of the weakly-skilled manufacturing sectors in Britain. The general approach of trade unions was that 'the first overriding responsibility of all trade unions is to

the welfare of their members. That is their primary commitment, not to a firm, not to an industry, not to the nation. A union reflects its members' contributions and demands their loyalty specifically for the purpose of protecting their interests as they often see them, not their alleged 'true' or 'best' interests as defined by others.[52]

This trend in car manufacturing had more critical consequences. The industrial damage from the strong trade unions since the war, was noted by Dunnett:

There were several consequences of the unsatisfactory fragmented labour relations system on motor industry conduct and performance. First, it meant considerable resources and effort were wasted on labour relations problems which might better have been applied elsewhere. Secondly, poor labour relations tended to discourage research and innovation. Every time new methods and techniques were introduced into production they created a hazard for labour relations, and therefore the innovation of new research was slowed ... Thirdly, the existence and attitudes of the unions affected employment stability in the industry. The existence of unions meant the firms had to make greater efforts to avoid redundancies than before the war, so encouraging better production planning but also labour hoarding in times of weak demand. Finally, the labour relations system as it existed after the war had negative effects on the balance of payments: whenever the system broke down and strikes occurred exports were lost.[53]

One of the more severe weaknesses in British car-makers was the lack of mutual understanding between managers and shop stewards. The relation between employers and employees was made clear by Professor Gaetano Cortesi, the Chairman of Alfa-Romeo, who observed that:

a well-managed, profitable company that could afford to pay wages would solve most of its industrial relations problems. But even in the ideal company there will be differences of opinion between workers and management. We examine later how mutual understanding of problems can help to avoid resentment crystallising into strike action. Once such action has been taken, however, speed is the conditioning factors. The aim must be to resolve a dispute before attitudes become entrenched, bitterness is engendered, and the problem become still more difficult.[54]

The industry's post-war history of disagreement and dispute between management and labour fostered an atmosphere of mutual distrust and suspicion. The CPRS report said in 1975 that:

this not only leads to misunderstanding, confusion and mistrust, but also creates a more fundamental problem. Management is unable to communicate clearly and convincingly to its workforce the true competitive state of the British industry. Consequently, the workforce does not accept the urgency and the scale of improvements required, but rather sees management's efforts, for example, to reduce manning levels as an attempt to boost profits at the expense of the workforce … Bad work practises which obstructed efficient capital utilisation in the factories of BLMC and other British car producers.[55]

Industrial problems since 1945 had been one of the major difficulties that by British car manufacturers faced. The reluctant government intervention during the Conservative period and the mistimed or excessively radical solutions based on political calculations under Labour governments made labour problems worse. The various trade unions structures and multi-organised trade unions within the British car industry made things worse. The mutual lack of confidence between government and trade unions during the Conservative government lasted too long for a successful recovery, when Labour came to power.

Management Strategy

Management strategy has been an important issue for privatised companies in Western Europe since the globalisation of their businesses in the mid 1960s. One of the particular weaknesses of the UK car industry, however, was the dependence of its marketing strategy on the assumption that it was still part of the nationalised sector. High competition between car manufacturers in the world market imposed a need for high capital intensive R&D spending. The UK car industry faced wage disputes during the high-tech capital spending periods.

Marketing and the Productivity Problem

Car manufacturers have to offer a better car to the consumer. The competition is mainly driven by product quality such as more powerful engines, inventive design, cheaper prices, good advertising and most of all after-sales service. After the War, the British car was characterised by its weak and low-powered engine, which was suitable to road conditions in the UK. This was not a problem as long as the continental European makers did not have champions in their national markets. As Barnett mentioned above, the UK manufacturers did not need the change in their policy, which would become necessary within a decade. Within a seller's market, short supply in conditions of large demand was the main hindrance to the UK car manufacturers' market adjustment.

As far as car models were concerned, the UK manufacturers put on a variety show. Ford UK produced two basic models for several years. Ford's main medium size product, the Cortina, was dominant and was not seriously contested by other manufacturers. Despite periods of high expansion since the 1960s, Ford produced only five basic models. In contrast to Ford, BL made more main saloon models than any of its major competitors. Toyota had seven, Renault eight, Ford Europe, VW and Fiat only five models, when BL had nine models.

> One of the major mistakes of the British car-makers was the lack of a representative model. When the business globalised, each maker tried to concentrate on one or two basic models. Whether merged or not, British car-makers have suffered from the lack of a representative model line in their production system, except for Mini which had never made a profit. Marketing questions, on the other hand, were never considered by government or leading managers.[56]

Model specialisation was regarded as one of main sources of economic success of the Japanese car manufacturers. This was particularly evident after the oil shock. There were many reasons for the UK car manufacturers' reluctance to reduce the number of models offered:

> ... the failure to integrate after the mergers and encouraging subsidiary companies to produce models in competition with each other. This competition or duplication might have deterred entry to the industry by multinationals, or improved performance by a form of 'yardstick' competition. But as Williams has argued, BMC's constituent companies were chasing a declining, minority market. In contrast to Ford, BMC based its strategy on the mass production of small cars with low profit margins. BMC/BLMC failed to produce one car, which took 20 per cent of the small car market on which it was increasingly dependent. Consequently the company had to introduce or keep in production a variety of models which sold in small quantities to defend its market share. The Central Policy Review Staff (CPRS) in 1975 contended an insufficient range of inadequate models in the small car segment lost the British-owned industry market share. The product range provided less car for the money than foreign competitors. Performance, handling and road holding, dimensions, interior and comfort, additional refinements, fuel economy and seating were typically less than fully competitive. The problem was not model proliferation but failure to introduce satisfactory new models.[57]

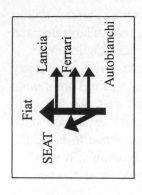
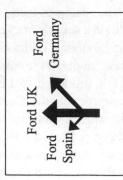

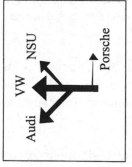
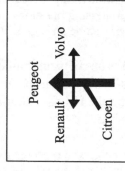
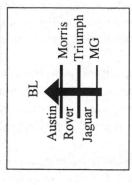

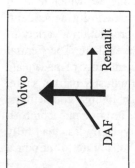
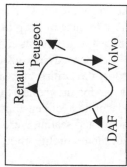
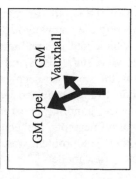

Figure 5.2　The car manufacturers in Europe

Source:　The Times (1976), 11 March.

Without a representative model, consumers ignored the British car after world car competition became significant.

One of the more important difficulties which British car manufacturers faced, was their productivity problem. From the early 1950s to the mid-1960s, car production trebled to nearly 900,000, but the number of cars produced per employee never rose much above the early 1950s level of around seven. The best productivity was around nine cars per employee in the years 1963 to 1965. Compared to the other major European competitors' standards, this was a very poor result. While BMC's output was more or less constant, other European makers, who started from lower levels, managed to double the number of cars produced per employee as they expanded production. Moreover, by the late 1960s, BMC not only lagged behind its direct competitors like Ford UK and Vauxhall who could produce 10 to 12 cars per employee in their UK affiliates but also behind other European makers such as Renault and VW.

Without any solution to this chronic disease, in May 1968, BL was created, when the two largest British controlled motor manufacturers, BMH and Leyland Motors, came together in one Britain's biggest mergers of industrial companies. Press Express said of the merger that 'Only the Heavyweights can win'.[58] The coming oil crisis forced BL towards a downsizing restructuring process. The oil shock ensured that 'compact and economic size are beautiful' among car manufacturers, as Honda showed. After the merger, BL had too many manufacturing facilities among their divisions without satisfactory new models. BL was the seventh largest industrial company in Britain and had been Britain's leading exporter since the War; exports in 1974 totalling nearly £500 million. All these statistics were for nothing when the oil shock and the 'world car' competition came.

> Marketing was the real weakness of British car-makers. After the War, with high demand from US and other Commonwealth countries, they did not need any marketing strategy. During the fifties and early sixties, the productivity problem was more important than other issues. Since the mid-1960s, while dealing with increasing internal problems they ignored any other external business behaviour. Moreover, the pendulum policy of nationalisation and de-nationalisation, missed all opportunity to restructure.[59]

Research and Development

R&D are correctly regarded as investment for the future, with no immediate return sooner than a decade. Competition between new products needed new

Table 5.5   BMC production

	Employees ('000)	Home produced ('000)	Export ('000)	Total ('000)	No. of cars per employee
1951–52	40	97	180 (est.)	277	6.9
1955–56	60	252	187	440	7.3
1959–60	76	383	286	669	8.8
1960–61	79	402	199	601	7.6
1961–62	80	377	224	600	7.5
1962–63	87	478	270	748	8.6
1963–64	93	539	320	859	9.2
1964–65	100	560	326	886	8.9
1965–66	120	531	314	846	7.1
1966–67	114	372	322	694	6.1

Source: BMC, Annual Report, various years.

investment, and investment needed financial support. However, money hungry managers and the policy of making demonstrations for political reasons induced short termism. This damaged the British car industry and the trend got worse when Thatcher came into power.

A significant feature of post-war development was the great advance in production methods and factory layout, especially among the largest vehicle and component manufacturers, which included some of the most up-to-date plants in Europe. Plants became increasingly automatic in their operations and there was a high degree of mechanisation. Despite the general trend towards highly-developed automation processes, British car assembly procedure still depended heavily on manually skilled workers.

During the early 1960s the expansion programmes of the constituent companies which merged to form BL were concentrated in Scotland and in Northwest England. Key features of investment during the 1960s were £45 million reconstruction of production facilities at Cowley, Oxford, which increased capacity from 5,000 to 10,000 cars a week; a similar £21 million programme at Longbridge to accommodate one of BL's new models; and a £20 million expansion scheme at the manufacturing and assembly plant at Speke. Modernisation and expansion of the Rover plant at Solihull, involving expenditure of £25 million on new assembly and paint facilities, and the Jaguar factory at Coventry began in 1973. However these were short-term projects again, and the plant installed was never properly used.

By the early 1970s, there had been an obvious lack of return on this investment by British car-makers. Government reports of the 1970s into the fortunes of the British car-makers focused on the relationship between technology and capital investment, and the industry's long term record of inadequate and under-investment, but failed to agree on the causal significance of investment.

> CPRS said that under-investment paled into insignificance in comparison with the company's history of unsatisfactory work practises. The House of Common Expenditure Committee agreed that the investment mattered, inadequate investment and the lower productivity of old plant have been the greatest contributors to the poor profitability of the mass production car side of the industry's, but added that this had been exacerbated by capacity under-utilisation, whether caused by industrial disputes, poor production planning or the uncertainties resulting from Government policies.[60]

The problem of R&D based technology is important for understanding Britain's relative decline in the car industry.

> First, it became crucial that large volumes of production at each stage in the production process were achieved in order to realise economies of scale. The British producers had problems achieving large output volumes. Second, access to large financial reserves were required in order to pay for the necessary capital expenditure ... Finally, the new technology made competition by annual model changes unviable given, for example, the high fixed costs of presses, which had to be spread over several years. The tendency in this period was to keep the same basic body shell for several years (for anything from 5 to 20 yeas), and to amend existing, rather than introducing new, models by modifying body panels. The pre-war practice of annual model changes thus ceased in the post-war period to be a feature of the industry.[61]

During the turbulent years, the British car-makers spent money to solve labour problems rather than on R&D facilities. Compared to Japanese car-makers, British car manufactures committed far less to R&D spending in proportion to the companies' turnover.

In the new wave of the high technology after the mid-1970s, the British car suffered its own 'winter of discontent' even in the domestic market. The liberalisation of car imports in the domestic market was the final blow to the British car-maker.

The Expenditure Committee analysed the reason for investment problems among British car-makers:

Table 5.6   R&D expenditure on car industry (unit: US$ million)

	1967	1969	1971	1973	1975	1977	1979
US	1250	1600	1600	2200	1700	2100	2500
Japan	250	300	450	600	650	800	1200
Germany	450	600	700	600	640	750	850
France	220	230	290	300	290	400	500
UK	220	210	190	180	170	160	220

Source: SMMT, 'The Future of Car Industry', press reports, various years.

> this means that until investment substantially increases the capital stock, productivity in the British motor industry will not be able to equal productivity abroad ... given roughly equivalent environments, the inefficient use of resources as a result of poor management, marketing, capacity utilisation or industrial disputes accounts for a very much lower proportion of productivity differences than might be imagined.[62]

Or, as Michael Edwardes recently observed: 'As far as I remember, we cannot say we have had any R&D programme since the War. We have just had re-programming and demolition procedures.'[63]

Car Exports and Imports

In the immediate post-war years, the British car was the key player in the export drive and any car made seemed to be sold. Between 1949 and 1951 Britain was the world's leading exporter of cars. During this period, the British export drive policy put Britain on the top of the world car exporters. Compared to Britain, the other European makers had to start to re-equip and restructure their manufacturing sectors. Modernisation of manufacturing sectors was a vital process to compete in the world market after a decade.

High technology and the computerisation of car making procedures after the mid-1970s, can be traced back to the result of the restructuring process after the war. When the British car enjoyed its relative export success, it lost markets in the future. The British car still depended on the labour-intensive methods rather than capital-intensive high technology. Increasing industrial action, and low manufacturing quality put British car-makers at a disadvantage between the domestic consumer and export markets. It became clear after the oil crisis. In 1976 the British car never returned to capture the domestic market. Table 5.7 shows the balance of trade of British cars since the war.

An SMMT report criticised British car-makers mismanagement concerning the relation between the domestic market and the model range, arguing that:

> the industry finds it difficult to accept the notion implied in the suggestion of a reduction to ten basic models, that British manufacturers should not compete against each other in various market segments. We do not believe that a healthy industry, internationally competitive, could be based on the concept of predetermined shares of the UK market.[64]

As Tables 5.8a and 5.8b show, one of the most notable features was the steep rise of the Japanese car in the world car market. Strong government intervention, high domestic market protection, and intensive industrial restructuring, allowed Japanese car output to be the fourth largest in the world, exceeded only by that of the US, Germany, and UK.

UK export markets changed significantly between 1955 and 1964. In the period 1957–61 Britain's share of world car exports fell from 30 per cent while Germany's rose from 35 per cent to 40 per cent. In the early 1960s, Europe had been a rapidly growing export market, owing to the increase in overall demand. UK exports to EFTA rose between 1963 and 1964, while exports to the EU fell, both by substantial amounts. Since then, the share of British cars in the world market has steadily got smaller.

The formation of the EU gave car MNEs the opportunity to penetrate into wider markets. For example, Ford had operated two affiliates in the EU from Germany and the UK until 1966. In 1967 Ford merged these two affiliates into a single Ford Europe. The Capri (1969), the Cortina/Taunus (1970) and the Granada (1972) were designed jointly and assembled in both Germany and Britain. In contrast to Ford Europe, British car manufacturers failed to focus on the popular models

As we find in Table 5.6, when the UK joined the EU in 1973, the British car consumer market was penetrated by foreign producers, especially Germany and Japan. The problems of British car-makers within the world market arose from internal and external factors. Lord Donald Stokes suggested that lack of product availability caused a variety of problems including increased import penetration. He argued that:

> What they [the importers] have had is something that we have lacked and that is availability. We have lost 150,000 cars a years due to industrial disputes and so on. With regard to our dealer or distributors, the position is just beginning to change now, but for the last five years one of them have had complete availability of motor cars. This has made it very difficult for them to sell. There is no doubt

Table 5.7   Export and import in the British car market

Year	Export no.	Export (£'000)	Import no.	Import (£'000)
1946	84,358	19,448	63	28
1947	140,691	37,347	222	128
1948	224,374	59,356	–	–
1949	257,25	72,505	1,868	581
1950	397,688	116,268	1,375	359
1951	368,101	118,802	3,723	1,134
1952	308,942	110,795	1,876	713
1953	307,368	106,045	2,067	761
1954	372,029	120,945	4,661	1,681
1955	388,564	127,816	11,131	4,053
1956	335,397	119,886	6,885	2,344
1957	424,32	157,053	8,828	3,055
1958	484,034	187,169	10,941	3,926
1959	568,971	222,532	26,998	8,991
1960	569,889	224,634	57,309	19,101
1961	370,744	147,874	22,759	8,511
1962	544,924	215,474	28,611	10,681
1963	615,827	237,205	48,163	18,768
1964	679,383	256,709	65,725	27,139
1965	627,567	250,859	55,558	22,986
1966	556,044	234,356	66,793	26,567
1967	502,596	211,413	92,731	39,144
1968	676,571	280,101	102,276	49,328
1969	711,634	340,939	101,914	53,495
1970	690,339	327,711	157,956	85,006
1971	721,094	368,843	281,037	174,465
1972	627,479	329,879	450,314	324,406
1973	598,816	327,818	504,619	436,901
1974	564,791	418,502	375,421	355,005
1975	516,219	483,261	448,747	514,047
1976	495,796	633,231	533,901	886,379
1977	474,826	751,926	698,464	1,323,878
1978	466,382	923,584	–	–

Source: SMMT, *The Motor Industry of Great Britain* (1978, 1993).

Table 5.8a   World production of cars and CV 1955–64

	1955	1960	1964	1964 as % of 1955	Annual rate of increase %
USA	9,169	7,869	9,307	102	0.2
UK	1,238	1,811	2,332	188	7.3
Germany	909	2,055	2,910	320	13,8
France	725	1,369	1,616	223	9.3
Italy	269	645	1,090	405	16.8
Japan	60	482	1,702	2,837	45.0
World total	13,500	16,312	22,069	163	5.6

Table 5.8b   World production of cars 1964–73

	1964	1969	1970	1971	1972	1973
USA	7,752	8,224	6,547	8,505	8,824	9,668
UK	1,868	1,717	1,641	1,742	1,921	1,747
Germany	2,650	3,437	3,528	3,692	3,514	3,650
France	1,351	2,168	2,458	2,694	2,993	3,202
Italy	1,029	1,477	1,720	1,701	1,732	1,823
Japan	580	2,612	3,179	3,718	4,022	4,471
World total	17,030	22,910	22,560	26,100	27,630	*
British % of total	11.0	7.5	7.3	6.7	7.0	*

Notes

Unit: '000
*   No figures

Source: UN Statistical Yearbook 1973 and SMMT, various years.

that people will not wait for a motor car for a year or eighteen months if there is another car available.[65]

With these difficulties, the new competitors from other European car-makers and from Japanese makers had easy access to UK car market. The joining of the EU without industrial restructuring, moreover, subjected British car-makers to more severe competition.

One of the emerging market penetrators after the mid-1970s was the Japanese car industry. Back in 1962, when Japanese cars were almost unknown

Table 5.9   List of largest car manufacturers in 1967

1	GM	6,489,973
2	Ford	4,145,912
3	Chrysler	2,328,741
4	Fiat	1,340,884
5	VW	1,339,823
6	Renault/Peugeot	1,060,421
7	BMH/Leyland	961,045
8	Toyota	635,451
9	Citroen/Berliet	520,087
10	Nissan	259,997
11	Daimler/Benz	245,293

Source: SMMT Report (1970) (mimeo).

outside Asia, Honda inaugurated its first factory in Europe, near Ghent in Belgium. Honda began to think seriously about car production in the late 1970s, even before Japan's MITI put its weight behind the idea of 'transplant' in a pamphlet published in 1980. The main reason to invest in the EU was that Japanese car-makers had relative freedom to invest in the EU to maximise taxpayer support, to minimise labour costs with young semiskilled non-unionised labour, and to leverage productivity with proven assembly practices and new equipment, thereby increasing the competitive advantage of their EU affiliates. While other EU car-makers did make efforts to increase their competitiveness by cutting costs within their traditional fully-integrated structures, Japanese investments in the EU, using very limited integration, achieved operating profits more quickly (because their capital costs were subsidised and they were able to import components from affiliated companies), and were able to compete on an even lower cost plane than their European rivals.

Conclusion

Car manufacturers after 1945 faced the strategic difficulty, which government and trade unions faced at the same time. There was limited preparation by the manufacturers to develop their technical or organisational methods to compete. Without improvements in production technology, British makers lost contact with consumers' taste during the 1960s. When the real competition started after the oil shock, British management in the car industry was far behind that of European competitors, even leaving aside the US and Japan. Lacking confidence towards the car manufacturers, the British government would have been muddling through even if the management strategy had been different. On the other hand, car-maker themselves had no will to survive, because of their long history of dependency on government.

Conclusion

Explanations about the decline of British car industry are varied. The inconsistency of government policies, obstructive labour relations, and managerial weakness are undoubtedly the major reasons. As Daniel Jones observed:

> Unfortunately, while the car-makers were making efforts to maximise short-term exports sales they paid less attention to the sales and service infrastructure. Government was no doubt partly to blame for this as the vehicle makers found it almost impossible to obtain foreign exchange to establish sales and service networks. The resulting reputation of British cars for poor reliability took a long time to overcome. The post-war boom with its problem of production rather than demand put the greatest emphasis on engineering. This meant that the three vital areas of industrial relations, marketing and AS services were virtually ignored – to the long-term disadvantage of the industry.[66]

Lord Donald Stokes commented on a different but equally important issue:

> I do not think we have ever particular been advocates of stopping other people coming into market, but we would like to have the same conditions in our domestic market that they have. If you take the Japanese, for instance, it was only in the Sixties that the Japanese market was opened up to imports. If we had had a protected home market since the War until the Sixties we would have a much healthier industry than we have today.[67]

As far as government policies were concerned, a comparative analysis is perhaps easier to understand. As Lord Stokes mentioned, tight government intervention in domestic market was needed. Since the war, however, the British government pursued not an industrial competitiveness policy but policy of backing winners during the Conservative governments or a policy of responding to political necessities under Labour. Neither policy had given much support to the car manufacturers. Under conditions of growing mutual misunderstanding between government and manufacturers, car-makers' management became steadily more vulnerable to pressure from the trade unions, while governments sought the help of foreign car-makers to save British component industries.

When government faced the reality of British industries, as Barbara Castle observed:

> Wedgie [Benn] thundered on 'We are endorsing the lame duck policy of Edward Heath. The truth is that the whole of Britain is a lame duck.' Harold [Wilson] suggested mildly that 'it was important to distinguish between a lame duck and a dead duck'.[68]

The second term of Wilson government had the option toward car-makers either of British investment or to encourage foreign affiliates to invest in Britain. When the programme of the Ryder report, designed for political rather than industrial reasons, supporting investment in British firms, was shown to have failed, the incoming Conservative government changed its policy from support of national makers to encouragement of foreign investment.

The crisis of British labour relations under the Heath government brought about dramatic increases in levels of worker militancy and strengthened the conviction of the new Conservative government that the trade unions had to be marginalised. This was not initially to be done in any crude or radical way but by the slow, incremental use of statutes that sought to avoid any confrontation with the trade unions in a trial of strength. For this, foreign management skills would be brought in to crack down on unions power. Moreover, the decline of skill levels among British workers was another important factor. As Edwardes mentioned:

> In the collaboration between Rover and Honda, there were many advantages, and one positive reason from the Rover side was that we hardly found skilled labour on the shopfloor. Since the Second World War, each government spent money not to reeducate employees but for the welfare of employees, who had weak ability. Hence, we had neither enough money to educate, nor enough time to learn. We found a way, which Japan found about two decades before. Japanization of our shopfloor was a short cut to success.[69]

The incoming Conservative government and the new management in Rover were forced to consider radical solutions for the future of the British car industry.

Notes

1 The meaning of global market is quite different that of late 1980s trend globalisation.
2 Tiratsoo, N. (1992), *The Motor Industry PRO BT64/2898*, Memo by H. Binney, 23 September 1946.
3 Ibid., PRO WO185/224, Copy of letter H. Dalton–P. Bennett, 1 May 1945.
4 Plowden, W. (1973), *The Motor Car and Politics in Britain*, p. 321.
5 *Hansard* (1949), 11 April, col. 2449.
6 Burnham, P. (1995), 'Rearming for the Korean War', pp. 346–7.
7 Tiratsoo, N. (1992), p. 164.
8 Burnham, P. (1995), p. 362.
9 Reference Division Central Office of Information (1955), *The UK Motor Vehicle Industry*, Quote no. R 2917, p. 4.
10 *Economist* (1952), 25 October.
11 *Hansard* (1952), 23 June, col. 135.
12 According to Pollard, S. (1992), 'British economic policy was dominated by short-term expedients reacting to short-term crises. Whatever major movements occurred were the result of the sum of short-term policies impinging on the underlying trends in a catastrophic rather than a clearly planned manner, and in the end sacrificing long-term aims for immediate needs', *The Development of the British Economy*, p. 354.
13 Dunnett, P.J.S. (1980), *The Decline of the British Motor Industry*, p. 61.
14 SMMT (1958), 'Progress and the Motor Industry' (mimeo), p.10.
15 Deputy Manager in Nissan: interview in Japanese.
16 Plowden, W. (1971), p. 357.
17 *Hansard* (1956), 8 March, col. 2295.
18 *Hansard* (1956), 15 March, col. 532.
19 Lord Biffen: interview.
20 Stewart, M. (1978), *Politics and Economic Policy in the UK since 1964*, p. 98.
21 Wilson, H. (1979), *Final Term*, p. 139.
22 Mr Roger King: interview.
23 Castle, B. (1980), *The Castle Diaries 1974–76*, p. 559.
24 Dunnett, P.J.S. (1980), p. 121.
25 Barnett, C. (1986), *The Audit of War*, pp. 274–5.
26 REP was an employment subsidy of £1.50 a week for adult men, and correspondingly smaller amounts for other workers, paid to manufacturing industry in the development areas. It was designed that this labour subsidy would lead to a fall in the price of goods manufactured in the North and West, diverting demand away from factories in the Midlands and South East. Moreover, it was hoped to reduce their politically embarrassing rate of unemployment.
27 HCC (1975–76), *Public Expenditure on Chrysler UK*, Eight Report from the Expenditure Committee (Minutes of Evidence), p. 147.
28 Castle, B. (1980), p. 545. 'Willie' is probably William Alan Lee, the Labour MP.
29 HCC Report (1973–74), Ch. 12, para. 170.
30 Ibid., p. 275.
31 Bhaskar, K. (1979), *The Future of the UK Motor Industry*, pp. 15–16.
32 HCC (1974–75), *Vol. 25, National Income and Expenditure Committee, 14th Report: The Motor Vehicle Industry*, 9 April 1975, p. 410, col. 1514.
33 Mr Nicolas W.L. Maclean: interview.

34 Lord Parkinson: interview.
35 Quoted by Dunnett, p. 108.
36 HCC (1975), *14th Report: Motor Vehicle Industry*, p. 83, col. 207.
37 HCC (1975), ibid., p. 83, col. 208.
38 Pollard, S. (1992), p. 281.
39 The policy was a strategy of state-led modernisation. Wilson made address January 1964 at Swansea that Britain needed for a range of structural changes, including support for exporters, selective encouragement for industrial investment, state involvement in restructuring and the formation of new industries, extension of the regional programme, and investment in education and training. At the heart of the strategy, however, was to be the extension of indicative planning coupled with policies to promote modern technology (Coopey, R. (ed.), *The Wilson Government 1964-70*, p. 79).
40 *Economist* (1965), 3 September.
41 Taylor, R., 'The Heath Government, Industrial Relations: Myth and reality', *The Heath Government 1970-74*, p. 168.
42 Mr Roger King: interview.
43 IRIS News Survey (1966), February (mimeo).
44 HCC (1968–69), vol. LIII, *In Place of Strife*, Command 3888, p. 8, col. 15–16.
45 Mr Roger King: interview.
46 *In Place of Strife*, p. 23.
47 Sir Edward Heath: interview.
48 MDW was the reform of pay system in the Cowley Plant. The management gave the right to choose between plant-level bargaining or company-wide bargaining. It was direct challenge to the power base of the shop stewards, who, under the piecework system, had the power to negotiate directly on the wages of each of their members.
49 Taylor, R. (1996), 'Industrial Relations', in *The Ideas that Shaped Post-war Britain*, p. 171.
50 At a certain, and unspecified size company had to co-determinated any kind of industrial proposal between employers and employees, so-called the principle of legislation on employees' participation.
51 Taylor, R. (1996), p. 89.
52 Ibid., p. 88.
53 Dunnett, P.J.S. (1980), p. 55.
54 HCC (1975), *14th Report: Motor Vehicle Industry*, p. 80, col. 199.
55 CPRS Report (1975), p. 102.
56 Dr Sue Bowden: interview.
57 Foreman-Peck et al. (1995), *The British Motor Industry*, pp. 139–40.
58 *Press Express* (1968), March, No. 41.
59 Mr Roger King: interview.
60 Foreman-Peck et. al. (1995), p. 148.
61 Ibid., p. 121.
62 HCC (1975), *14th Report: The Motor Vehicle Industry*, p. 36, col. 90.
63 Sir Michael Edwardes: interview.
64 SMMT (1976), Comments on the CPRS Report (mimeo), p. 3.
65 HCC (1975), *The 14th Report: Motor Vehicle Industry Evidence*, vol. I, p. 121, col. 315.
66 HCC (1975), *14th Report: Motor Vehicle Industry*, p. 9, col. 26.
67 HCC (1975), *14th Report: Motor Vehicle Industry Evidence*, vol. I, p. 122, col. 316.
68 Castle, B. (1980), p. 545.
69 Sir Michael Edwardes: interview.

Chapter 6

Government, Industrial Decline and Japanese Involvement in the UK Domestic Car Industry

In 1975 the British-owned car industry was nationalised as British Leyland (BL). Nationalisation is one of main political means to economic control. Immediately after the 1974 General Election, Wilson faced dual burdens from the previous government.

> Firstly, he inherited an appalling economic situation partly created by the policies of the 1970–74 Heath Government and partly inflicted externally by the world oil crisis. Secondly he inherited a Labour party which in opposition had moved further leftwards than Wilson had hoped, and which, now in office, expected immediate radical socialist solutions. Put bluntly as attending to prime ministerial policy determination in relation to the economic situation.[1]

Based on political reasons on the one hand, and envisaged as an economic solution on the other, the nationalisation policy was a rather simple and easy way to get political support. Wilson's appeal after the October 1974 General Election was to a new lower-middle class, and he therefore relied less on the professional politician's appeal to an established working-class party and more on his own personality. This tendency pushed him towards improvisation when a decision had to be made. The British car industry was good example of this.

The British car industry under the incoming Labour government was an immediate problem demanding solution. In the House, Tony Benn, the Secretary of State for Industry announced that:

> because of the company's position in the economy as a leading exporter and its importance to employment both directly and through the many firms that are dependent on it, the Government are informing the company's bankers that the approval of parliament will be sought for a guarantee of the working capital required over and above existing facilities … the Government also intend to introduce longer-term arrangements, including a measure of public ownership.[2]

The task of bringing back the 'ashes' in the world car industry was undertaken by the Labour government through BL. The initial action from the government was the Ryder Report, which aimed to solve the problems, which Tony Benn mentioned above.

Nationalisation and the Ryder Plan

The second term of the Labour government was marked by a huge nationalisation plan that was regarded as a solution to political problems rather than as an economic project. In 1977 nationalised industries had about 1,750,000 workers, who represented 7 per cent of total employment, and they were responsible for over 16 per cent of gross fixed capital formation, excluding housing. While the nationalised British Airways, electricity, telecommunication, gas and British steel industries invested between two and a half and five times as much per worker as industry and communication as a whole, BL and the National Freight Corporation (which ran road haulage) invested less than average.

Between 1973 and 1975 BL's production fell from 1,013,000 vehicles to 739,000 and its weighted output[3] declined by over 20 per cent. This was due to a contraction in the size of the market rather than to a fall in BL's share. Whether from the contraction of the domestic market or for other reasons, BL was in trouble. By 1974–75 gross operating profit had all but disappeared and there was a net loss of £300 million, though the picture would have looked slightly better but for the loss of £26 million at BL's Italian and Spanish subsidiaries, which it was decided to dispose of.

> Ryder emphasised the handicap of the company's outdated plant and machinery, its excessively centralised corporate organisation, and also criticised weaknesses in management-labour communications which contributed to a bad record of industrial relations. The Sub-Committee was also critical of a debilitating bargaining structure, but attached greater importance to overmanning and excess capacity, which reflected a failure to respond to consumer demand. The CPRS levelled similar criticism, but blamed lack of maintenance of plant and equipment and working practices, which showed workplace and restricted productivity.[4]

The Reports each had merits and faults at the same time. Compared to the other two, the Ryder report mainly emphasised internal problems and macroeconomic conditions. Since the oil crisis, however, the car industry had faced turmoil in its markets. During its restructuring process, BL needed a more proactive business strategy towards the world market. Until Edwardes' arrival, BL suffered similar problems under a series of different managers. The Ryder Report was mainly influenced not by industrial purposes but by political tactics. Wilson supported the report and summarised it as follows:

> The Report, I told the House, recommended that the vehicle production industry ought to remain an essential part of the UK economic base, and that BL should therefore remain a major vehicle producer. But urgent action was needed to remedy Leyland's weaknesses revealed in world markets. A capital investment programme was needed to enable new models to be introduced and also an immediate and massive programme to modernise plant and equipment. The report was highly critical of Leyland's organisational structure as being harmful to its efficiency and future development.[5]

In the House, there was common agreement about the Ryder report that:

> The government accept the Ryder Report as a basis of future policy towards BL and have already started upon discussions with the board of BL with the aim of putting these proposals into effect. The Government agree with the proposal that they should offer to buy existing shareholders and underwrite a new rights issue ... The government also accept that they may be required to provide £500 million of extra capital to BL between 1976 and 1978 if none is available from other sources: the question of funds beyond that date will be a matter for later consideration. In return for this massive investment of public money the Government intend that they should have a majority shareholding in the reconstructed company.[6]

Despite Wilson's support, there were many critical views of the Ryder Report. Even within the Cabinet, Barbara Castle objected that:

> Ryder's report was ruthlessly thorough. What was wrong with Leyland was poor management (Stoke would have to go), grotty machinery and bad industrial relations ... The alternative was to accept the unemployment of nearly one million people and the abandonment of a comprehensive motor industry. Harry Urwin had been an invaluable member of the Ryder Committee, accepting that there had been bad overmanning and that industrial relations had been partly responsible for the whole mess. And so, with very little opposition, it was agreed. Even Wedgie warned that we must be cautious and monitor each stage of the development carefully ... he [Harold Lever] said; it was like a 'bad Pharaoh's dream' in which we were not even promised seven fat years after the seven lean ones. But he did not cut much ice.[7]

The Ryder team regarded the under-investment as the main reason for the BL's difficulties. With massive cash investment, financial stability gave more room to restructure management strategy. However, the investment flowed to the wrong place. Within the same number of manufacturing sites, increasing demand from the employees, and a badly-focused policy toward design and R&D, any further investment would not work. As Wilson ordered Ryder, 'BL and all its jobs must be saved whatever the cost'.[8] Under the terms of this political instruction, the result was inevitably disastrous.

One of the ironic situations of the British car industry was that even after this instruction workers at BL had to be sacked.

> The latest crisis at BL is the old, old, story but with a new twist. Overmanning, strikes and the resulting low productivity are the familiar ingredients that for years kept customers waiting and enabled foreign manufacturers to move into our market.[9]

During the Wilson government, the British car industry was measured not as an industry for industry's own sake but as an industry for the government's interests. This was the major mistake Wilson's government made.

> The Ryder team took a naive protectionist view of the company's problems and committed the company to investments which were wasted when market limitations constrained the sales ability of the company's existing production lines ... similar strategic mistakes were made in steel.[10]

Also the *Economist* said that:

> the two main planks of the Ryder plan were (1) that BL should retain a 33 per cent market share in Britain and increase its exports, especially to the EEC and (2) that BL should put up the bulk of the £2.8 billion investment envisaged by Ryder, with the government contribution limited to £1 billion. Both planks are already riddled with woodworm ... BL's share of the British market has already slipped ten points (to 23 per cent) since the Ryder report was published. Apart from odd flurries, it shows no sign of reviving. Exports have fared no better. And far from generating investment funds internally BL has had to use taxpayers' money earmarked for investment, to pay its wage bills. Investment plans are in ruins.[11]

The incoming managing director in BL was selected for industrial reasons rather than as a political appointment, owing to the increasing criticism of Donald Ryder or David Stokes, who were regarded as 'Wilson's Poodles' 'The Ryder plan's assumptions about BL's long-term export potential were made by men playing politics, not by men making serious industrial analyses.'[12] In November 1977, Michael Edwardes decided to accept the chair and said that

'If BL fails to succeed it will have the most dire effect on jobs and investment prospects not to mention the reputation of Britain and British goods overseas.' The question you will ask is, 'Can you really hope to influence such a situation?' I don't know. The task is enormous; some people could even say impossible ... But I am going to try because I believe that BL does have a future. It is a company which has talent at all levels, talent that can and must be fully utilised. Given the right support from all in the company and the Government it is still possible to restore its growth and realise its full potential.[13]

His first movement was to free the company from political control. He said that 'I told Leslie Murphy that I needed to resolve the two questions: the need to have a free hand in running the company, which was up to him.'[14] Despite the government-supported Ryder report mentioned above, there was a wide gap between the view from outside and the view from the inside. Michael Edwardes asked himself:

it could be argued that both these subsidiary issues could have been dealt with by following the Cars Organisation Group (COG) recommendation, that is, merely by changing the people, rather than the structure. Yet, if the existing organisation really was workable, and the individual managers were presumably not advocating their own demise, why was the company in a state of chaos? Why was the quality of our products very bad indeed? Why were inventories out of balance and excessive in terms of money tied up? Why were deliveries of cars uncertain and unpredictable? Why were no factories achieving targeted rates of production? Why had disputes run at more than two million man hours for every single month in 1977? Why had managers in some plants abdicated major functions – such as recruitment – to shop stewards? Why was all communication with our employees only effected via the union system? Why were dealers defecting to competitors? Why were problems and confidential documents being leaked to the press with embarrassing regularity? These were some of the questions that I had debated with senior executives – and with my main Board colleagues, at less frequent intervals, but with equal frustration.[15]

Solving internal problems first, a British designed car was chosen as *European Car of the Year* by a panel of international journalists in 1976 and 1977. In 1977 it was the Rover 3500, which was produced at Solihull, Birmingham. These cars illustrate two crucial features of the car industry in the UK: its extensive technical skills and potential, yet half of it dependent on the whims of US-owned multinational companies. The other half of the industry was BL cars. It showed the limit of BL's position in manufacturing technology.

After successful negotiations within the executive group in BL, a second plan was made, to slim down its size. Almost one-fifth of all jobs in car manufacturers disappeared in 1981 alone. The most concentrated phase of rationalisation occurred between 1980 and 1983 when a total of 165,800 jobs were shed in the car sector. Within the three years 1977–80 BL halved its capacity. This had two consequences for BL's predicament. The chronic industrial friction between employees and managers at each manufacturing site was reduced, owing to the reduction in numbers. The gap, which was caused by the huge reduction of manufacturing employees, must be replaced by other means. Because of the component industries' labour problems, such as the Lucas strike in 1983, and the unexpectedly low technical standards in BL and its suppliers, Edwardes feared for the future of the British car industry without progressive action.

This situation showed the wide gap between expectation and reality, which was initially mentioned when Edwardes was, appointed BL managing director.

He was embarrassed, because there was a deep industrial and technical swamp. Moreover, the increasing demand from government for certain aspects of BL's revival was more crucial. There were some things, which could be solved by financial support, however others were incapable of solution by money alone. The latter emerged as more fatally damaging to BL's revival.[16]

Even Michael Edwardes said:

whether BL was nationalised or not, the current situation of BL was one of the government's major problems. I tried to stop the political ratchet effect, which was started by the first Wilson government. The internal solution was undertaken through restructuring processes such as job reduction, cuts in the number of manufacturing sites, increased R&D investment, and bridging the communication gap between managers and shop stewards. The external solutions, such as new model launches, reduction of the technical gap, and world marketing strategy, were supported by foreign collaboration. One of the reasons to choose Honda was that while BL focused on the volume and specialised car, Honda's technology would cover the small and medium size market.[17]

Despite concentrated efforts, Edwardes thought that BL needed a more practical restructuring process, such as collaboration. The reason for collaboration by BL with other car-makers was made clear in his book:

collaboration quite simply is the art of synergy, of joining forces with others to save funds, or to optimise cash and engineering resources; or simply to achieve a larger scale of purchases or production, to cut the cost of components and of complete vehicles.[18]

Most of all, it would solve all problems which BL could not handle by getting further financial support from government. The collaboration was expected to be an easier way to compete with other European makers within a decade, which was emerging as one of the government's demands.

Edwardes stood up to the unions, closed plants and gave his managers back the pride and commitment they were in danger of losing, inspiring their counterparts in companies all over the country. On the other hand, a politically aggressive new government under Thatcher, very hostile to the trade unions, hastened its collaboration programme. Edwardes was asked after the general election whether Thatcher's style of government made BL an important element in the new government's industrial policies. He predicted of the incoming government that: 'We may have thought we were picking our way through a political minefield under a Labour Government, but that was child's play in comparison to what was to come.'[19]

One of the special characteristics of the new government was its governing ideology. The general approach of Thatcher and her cabinet members was essentially nationalist and mercantilist. To meet her requirements about British goods in the EU market, British goods must be of the right quality and price to compete internationally. However, the British car industry stood at the far end of the scale. Pressed by the government for an increase in the competitiveness of British car-makers, Edwardes needed new models. The best plan was to find a collaborator among foreign car-makers.

Michael Edwardes and the Honda–Rover Collaboration Project

One of the longest-lasting joint venture projects within the car industry since World War II has been the Rover and Honda project. Rover, renamed from BL, faced a slump in turnover and market share during the 1970s and early 1980s, as imports increasingly penetrated the UK market. In 1981, Rover's car production was 347,500, almost half its 1976 figure of 688,000. Despite Edwardes' efforts, the survival of Rover itself was regarded as 'mission impossible'. The situation of Rover reached the point that the collaboration was a last chance rather than a preferred strategy. During the late 1970s and early 1990s,[20] there was a surge in the number of tactical international joint ventures. Collaboration provided 'a platform for organisation learning, giving partner firms access to the skills and capabilities of their partners'.[21]

Table 6.1   BL production, home sales and exports 1978–85

Year	Production*	Export allocation	% of output exported	UK sales	Total UK market	BL market share[+]
	('000s)	*('000s)*		*('000s)*	*('000s)*	*(%)*
1978	611.6	247.9	40.5	373.8	1591.9	23.5
1979	503.8	200.2	39.7	337.0	1716.3	19.6
1980	395.8	157.8	39.9	275.8	1513.8	18.2
1981	413.4	126.2	30.5	275.1	1484.7	19.2
1982	383.1	133.9	36.0	277.3	1555.0	17.8
1983	445.4	118.3	26.6	332.7	1791.7	18.6
1984	383.3	78.6	20.5	312.1	1749.7	17.8
1985	465.1	106.5	18.6	328.0	1832.4	17.9

Notes

*   Includes Jaguar for all years except 1984 and 1985 (Jaguar production in 1980 was 15,469, rising to 25,467 in 1983) because comparable figures to subtract from exports are not available.

+   Include Austin Morris, Rover and Triumph, but from 1980 excludes Jaguar (1978–79 figures include some 5,000 or 6,000 Jaguar saloons)

Source: *BL Annual Report* (1985), p. 32.

Clearly, Rover could not finance the next model range from its own resources, particularly since a replacement for the Metro was due in 1989. On the other hand, Rover needed a solution for industrial problems on the shop floor, improvement of poor design quality, and if possible, cost savings which Rover could transfer from the partner's components or other technical R&D. A precise specification for what Rover considered the ideal partner was drawn up and then matched against the world's manufacturers.

The first applicant was Renault, which was favoured for practical reasons. The collaboration would be difficult to manage with the necessary momentum and flexibility if the two partner's headquarters were a long distance apart. Renault regarded as having some important attributes as a collaborative partner, such as a well-managed company, with good products, based on a strategic and well thought out production plan. However, after the *Financial Times* antagonistic comment about the collaboration and the growing apprehensions of a Trojan Horse, the collaboration was in trouble. The *Financial Times* said that:

> The talks about this European solution to BL's problems have gone very cold since Mr. Edwardes took over 18 months ago. He maintains that BL simply could not fulfil its part of the proposed deal because it can not make enough Land Rovers, Range Rovers, Rovers and Jaguars to meet demand through existing overseas outlets, let alone provide extra vehicles for Renault's network. The emphasis in yesterday's statement about the similar size of BL and Honda making them compatible suggests that Mr. Edwardes' does not wish to get swamped by a group twice as large as BL-Renault's 1978 turnover was Ff. 57 billion (roughly £6.4 billion) compared BL's £3.07 billion.[22]

Even Edwardes objected that:

> Renault offered us one of their models to assemble in Britain. All the major components were to be made in France, and while BL would have had the right to sell this model, its market would have been restricted to Britain – and some Renault top executive envisaged that their version of the car would also be sold in Britain. In short, while it would have helped to reduce the inevitable paucity of the British market share while we developed our new models, its strategic implications were somewhat threatening in that the BL franchise would have helped to establish Renault in Britain without reciprocal benefits for us in Europe. It was not a two-way collaboration. Nevertheless, it warranted thorough consideration, and we put in a great deal of time before we finally decided that to join forces with our French colleagues would not be to our ultimate advantage.[23]

The component sector was a vital area for restructuring within British industry, hence there was no further consideration about the Renault negotiation. On the other hand, political considerations were important.

> Edwardes should have known that the collaboration between a French car maker and Rover was impossible. The relation between Thatcher and Edwardes had been good. The strong nationalist Thatcher would not give her national champion car maker over to a French manufacturer, and he knew that. The collaborative project between Renault and Rover was wrong from the initial stage.[24]

After the collapse of the Renault project, the Rover management started to think about a survey of world car manufacturer. The government's antagonism towards Western Europe tended to favour other areas, especially Asia. From Rover's side, the size and manufacturing facility of any collaborator was an important consideration. It must be an equal position, not a merger.

Table 6.2   The parties

	BL	Honda
Total sales	$5,386m	$4,646m
Sales of cars and trucks	785,000 units	685,000 units
Sales of cars and trucks as % of total sales	93%	57%
No. of employees	195,000	33,000

Source: *Financial Times* (1979), 4 April.

The choice of a car maker from the Far East was 'thinking the unthinkable'. As far as management strategy was concerned, the headquarters of collaborators had to be close, and perhaps should share the same cultural foundations. The approach to Honda was surprising and moved more swiftly than other European makers expected. According to Edwardes:

The result of this comprehensive survey of world competitors was Honda; we did the exercise from a different perspective and we still came up with Honda. Their size, their engineering skill, their remarkable track record, and a number of other key factors made Honda the most desirable partner. Perhaps they would provide the answer to our biggest single problem; how to fill the yawning gap until the long-awaited launch of Metro in early 1983?

Although Honda was the one company whose objectives seemed complementary to BL, at first glance there were major differences; on further study the fit was remarkable. Compare the two companies in 1978; BL had a large, complex and unprofitable range – 16 model families, no less. Honda had just two families. BL had more than 30 car factories, with no less than eight assembly plants. Honda had two assembly plants; it was altogether simpler and more workable. BL was and is state controlled; Honda was and is owned by individual shareholders.

These were some of the differences, but there were many similarities. Both were free of complex collaborative commitments. Both were leaders in front-wheel-drive technology. In the US, Honda was deeply involved in small volume cars and therefore they were complementary to our great strength there – the luxury Jaguar. Where Honda's other half is motor cycles, BL's is trucks, buses and Land Rovers. Overall the companies are comparable in terms of output. Both were open-minded about the desirability to collaborate in at least some aspects of their business.[25]

According to the Honda company profile, potential merits from the collaboration were that

In the late 1970s the world automotive industry was starting to stagnate after decades of consistent growth. All manufacturers were moving swiftly to find ways of adjusting to the new climate. They were looking to use R&D money more effectively, and looking to spread the risk associated with the manufacture of major components in a high volume plant. They were also looking at *ways of gaining access to markets which were difficult, or seemingly impossible, to penetrate.* Increasingly, manufacturers world-wide were reaching the conclusion that a joint venture was the best way of meeting these objectives and, at the same time, remaining independent. Rover also reached that conclusion. A precise specification for what we considered the ideal partner was drawn up and then matched against the world's manufacturers. Honda emerged as an ideal partner; a medium-sized company with an outstanding reputation for automobile engineering, particularly in the field of engine design. Honda also had a reputation for quality and high productivity serving their major markets in Japan and the Far East. Rover was ideal for Honda, having a reputation for innovative design, and ability to use interior space exceptionally effectively, an expertise in suspension systems, a dedication to high technology and a significant presence in the European market.[26]

BL's approach to Honda was quick and smooth. Despite Nissan's approach[27] to BL in 1979 , Edwardes made a proposal to Honda, and it was announced on 3 April 1979 to the press and BL employees. The press reflected Britain's hostile opinion that

The time to pronounce on the desirability or undesirability of a link between Honda and BL will be when their negotiations have gone further and the proposals are clear. Since the NEB is the major shareholders in BL, their approval, and that of the new Government, will be necessary. Meantime, it is surely premature to condemn the very idea of a link with Honda, as some of the MPs sponsored by the TGWU have seemed to do. Perhaps the negotiations will not succeed, just as the possibility of a link between BL and Renault has faded. But if there are positive advantages for BL, as well as for Honda, then the scheme may have more to be said for it than the ritual resort to calls for formal import controls to prop up the British motor industry.[28]

A critic from the *Financial Times* commented that 'After all, BL is the Trojan Horse bringing the Japanese manufacturers to Europe.'[29]

The new Conservative government had quite a different picture from that of the former government. As far as industrial policy was concerned, the election manifesto indicated its strongly antagonistic approach to the trade unions: '... by heaping privilege without responsibility on the trade unions, Labour have given a minority of extremists the power to abuse individual liberties and to thwart Britain's chances of success'. The 'Thatcherite' position towards industrial policy emphasised market competition. 'Selling the State' – privatisation – was seen as ideologically desirable and as a way of reducing state spending and waste. During the first six months the government took a number of significant steps towards rationalising the existing nationalised and state sector or towards ultimate transfer by sale to the private sector.

The real problem, which the new Conservative government faced after the election, however, was to strengthen their position for negotiation with the trade unions. At this time, specific industrial sectors were not targeted.

> With the Conservative victory in May 1979, I found myself to all intents and purposes dealing directly with the new Secretary of State for Industry, Sir Keith Joseph ... His intellectual integrity was helpful to BL because it made him a non-interventionist on commercial issues. He has no real interest in motor cars and did not see why he should struggle to understand them ... He knew the BL Board was in a much better position than his Department to exercise commercial judgement, and his departure to the Department of Education in September 1981, we enjoyed a period of minimal intervention by the Government on other than the broadest issues. We were therefore able to make great progress by concentrating on our proper business.[30]

The board and Edwardes rushed to make new models. On 27 December 1979, an agreement, which consisted of an original equipment manufacturer (OEM) system was signed, and gave birth to the Triumph Acclaim, a compact, four door saloon, assembled from 'knockdown' components. While Honda received a licence fee and earned profit from the import of major components, such as the engine and gearbox, the first approach involved little input from Rover.

The fruits for the BL had to be reaped within a limited time. In the House, John Silkin asked:

> Does he [Keith Joseph] agree that the key to BL's future lies in the new model programme? As a new model takes about four years to reach fruition, and as his plans end in 1980–81, how does he propose to guarantee that the new model

programme, should it be the right one, is able to continue? Joseph answered that 'it is true that new models are an essential part of the plan. It is intended that one new car model will be launched in 1980 ... however, while new models are vital, they are not the only component of success. There are also productivity and quality. As to disposals the judgement of them is for the management. Future success is up to the management and work force of BL.[31]

Neither Edwardes nor the government had any future plans within such a short time. The government wanted a quick return from its policies, and was looking for foreign intervention to achieve it. Edwardes wanted to solve his internal problems quickly, to demonstrate his success to the British government, and also looked for foreign help to enable him to do so. One of the best opportunities Rover expected was to put Japanese technology under the Rover badge. Mr John Butcher asked that:

> British car assemblers that there should be minimum percentage British component factor in all cars assembled in this country? Keith Joseph answered 'A substantial part of the car that will be built with Honda will be supplied by British factories, and component manufacturers are sensibly pursuing sales abroad as well as at home.' Mr George Park said 'he [Joseph] said that the BL-Honda car will be assembled mainly from parts made in this country'. Joseph said 'if I said "mainly", I was wrong'.[32]

For the British component industries, the collaboration had started in the wrong direction. The OEM, and 'knock down' agreement allowed unlimited component import from Japan and elsewhere. A politician-led management strategy ignored the current situation of indigenous component industries. One of the ironies of Thatcherite industrial policy was that one of the main strands of inward FDI policy towards car industry in the UK was to save the British component industry.

The second stage of collaboration was over the luxury range model, named XX. The Legend by Honda, and the Rover 800 project shared as equally as possible in order to draw on the respective strengths of the two design teams. While Honda covered electronics and engine parts, Rover made the interior, chassis and suspension system. As a result of the XX project, Honda gained more than expected, such as access to high quality design and its first penetration of the British luxury market. Rover had, also, the more modest goal of developing quality replacement models for an existing range. The fact that Honda appeared to move faster than Rover in getting its variant of the Legend model into the marketplace would seem to suggest that collaboration had done little to narrow its broad lead over the UK car manufacturing industry. Moreover, since the knockdown agreement, the increasing rate of component import had damaged the local economy.

Despite problems in specific areas, the collaboration carried on until the Rover-BMW merger. Its history is shown in Table 6.3.

Table 6.3   Rover and Honda: history of their collaboration

Aug. 1978	Edwardes asked Sir Fred Warner, who had been the British Ambassador to Tokyo, about collaboration with Honda.
Sept. 1978	Mr Kiyoshi Kawashima, the President of Honda put the proposal to his Board.
Oct. 1978	Mr Edwardes set about the real negotiation of terms with Honda in San Francisco.
Jan. 1979	Sir Fred Warner and BL's team started to talk about more practical subjects such as model, and products range.
April 1979	Information about the collaboration project was released to the BL trade unions and the press.
Oct. 1979	The draft agreement between two companies was settled.
Dec. 1979	Honda signed a technical collaboration agreement with BL, under which BL would produce a new car designed by Honda.
Dec. 1980	The corporate plan was approved by Keith Joseph and announced by Mr Kawashima.
June 1981	BL begins producing Triumph Acclaim cars under license with Honda.
Oct. 1981	BL launch sales of Triumph Acclaim cars under license with Honda.
Nov. 1981	Announcement that Honda and BL will jointly develop and manufacture new executive car. (Chief Executives were Mr Kiyoshi Kawashima and Mr Ray Horrocks).
April 1983	Rover and Honda sign an agreement for joint design and development of a new executive car.
April 1984	Rover and Honda sign a manufacturing agreement on the XX project.
April 1985	Honda construction work on an automobile inspection plant and parts assembly plant in England.
June 1985	Honda signs a collaborative memorandum with BL to increase joint activities, including development of new compact cars.
April 1986	Rover and Honda sign an agreement, under which Rover will produce Honda Ballade.
Dec. 1986	Rover and Honda sign an agreement for joint design and development of a new medium car code-named YY.

April 1987	Honda signs a joint-manufacturing and engine-supply agreement for a medium-sized car, code named YY (Concerto/R8) with Rover. Honda UK manufacturing planned to start production of engines in UK in 1989, announced.
Nov. 1988	Plans announced to launch a 5 billion *yen* project to construct an R&D centre in Europe.
July 1989	Rover and Honda make a new agreement, which includes plans for construction of a new automobile plant in UK.
Oct. 1989	Honda Motor Europe Ltd (HME) established in Reading, UK. Groundbreaking ceremony held for Honda UK manufacturing Ltd. at Swindon, automobile manufacturing facility.
April 1990	Rover signs agreement with Honda for joint shareholding 20 per cent each.
April 1990	Honda Engineering's (EG) branch office in England is incorporated into Honda Engineering Europe Ltd (EGE).
March 1991	American Honda Motor begins to export Accord Wagon to Europe.
Oct. 1992	Production of Accord by Honda UK (HUM) commenced.
June 1993	Honda import and sell 4-wheel drive Rover vehicles in Japan.
Jan. 1994	Rover taken over by BMW and Honda reluctant to move on further joint development.

Source: Derived by the author on the basis of original research.

Its first hindrance came in 1986, when Rover had take-over discussions with Ford. The approach made Honda move towards a project for independence, which was established in 1989 as the Honda Motor Europe Ltd. Despite the rejection of the Ford deal, Honda after then feared the government's intentions and the future of Rover. After the turbulent years, the two companies committed themselves to further cooperation in the YY project, which aimed to provide replacements for the smaller Maestro and Rover 200. During the 1980s, it was certain that Rover would not survive without this collaboration. If Rover had continued to make substantial losses, there would have been the possibility that its government support would falter and that it would be sold to another company. Under these unstable conditions, Honda made sure that its parts were supplied by import rather than by local manufacturing.

Within the EU car market, the collaboration was a bitter blow for the European car-makers. The *Financial Times* reported that:

European car manufacturers yesterday reacted with a little bitterness, some dismay and a modicum of surprise at the news that BL really is to collaborate with Honda of Japan. The surprise was about the timing rather than that the Japanese had chosen the UK as a base from which to operate in Europe. It has been widely expected that the Japanese would find a way of setting up some kind of manufacturing operation in Europe, either in a 'neutral' country like Holland, which has no major local car maker to protect, or in the UK, which is the volume market with the weaker national automotive business – BL.[33]

Honda's approach to the EU market was analysed by *Time*:

> Now Honda is adopting its US strategy to invade the EC with the made-in-Britain Legend. Beginning in September, the car will be produced in corporation with Rover Group, the British government-owned firm formerly known as BL. The goal is to circumvent voluntary quotas on Japanese imports in countries like Britain, where the limit has been set at 11 per cent of the total car market. The aim is also to avoid import barriers in such countries as Italy, where shipments from Japan are kept to a more 2,200 vehicles a year, and France, which imposes a 3 per cent-of-market limit …
>
> Honda's venture with Rover will bring mutual benefits: Rover gains from tapping Honda's experience in the US and Asia, while the Japanese company acquires a European manufacturing outlet.[34]

Since the end of the collaboration after the merger with BMW, there were emerging questions from the British car industries about whether Honda really did operate as a collaborator or just as a market penetrator. At the initial stage, Honda was in a weak financial position though market penetration into the EU was crucial. Compared to the other two makers, Toyota, and Nissan, Honda was (and still is) a relatively small maker. When their first move towards Europe was strengthened by their successful business in the US, Mr Atsushi Yamakoshi, the *Keidanren* US Representative told me:

> Honda is not a company with a strong financial basis from *keiretsu* partners. It is a rather technically dominated company. Between the late 1970s and the early 1980s, I think Honda could not afford to invest in two different countries at the same time. If I were a manager of Honda, I would try to find a proper collaborator within the European market. And as I say, they did it.[35]

The proposal from Rover must have been welcomed as an opportunity for market penetration (company profile) and as a means of access to new technology in the shape of the four-wheel Land Rover, which is an area which Honda had never tried.

Rover and Honda collaborated on a project-by-project basis. Under the project scheme, it is always likely that there will be poor relations between assembler and component makers. Each project made Rover into a local assembler rather than a vertically-integrated car-maker. This was clearly demonstrated by the predicament of local component industries in Swindon. The weakened competitiveness of British component industries made government lose confidence in the revival of British car industries. That was one of the major reasons why the British government favoured greenfield investment programmes after the Rover–Honda episode.

Despite the successful joint venture between Rover and Honda, the British government never believed in the revival of the British car industry.

> The Thatcher government never thought about the success of Rover. The most important thing for the car manufacturing sector was its component industries. The British component industries had world-standard competitiveness. If Japanese car-makers came in, they would help the revival of component makers. Whether we have a nationalised car maker or not, is a problem of emotion, not of economic utility.[36]

When the British government denationalised the car industry to make an integrated engineering industry under BAe, expecting synergic effects from the relationship between car manufacturers and the aerospace industries, there was in fact more severe competition between UK car-makers such as Nissan UK, Honda UK, and even, Toyota, not to mention US multinationals. As Edwardes remarked:

> The de-nationalisation of Rover is very important for industry itself. It has been our constant aim since the early 1980s. However, the timing and the choice of buyer under privatisation was quite bad. Once again, the British car industry was the victim under her style of government policy. The reason for failure was not industrial but political logic.[37]

Denationalisation and the Death Knell of the UK Domestic Car Industry

In March 1988 Lord Young, then the Secretary of State at the DTI, announced that there were negotiations between the government and BAe about the denationalisation of Rover. BAe was cash-rich after the Falklands war and saw profit opportunities in the Land Rover and DAF product lines. The government was anxious to be rid of a troublemaker. One of the ironies in the government's position was that when the former Labour government tried the nationalisation of BL, Michael Heseltine asked Tony Benn, the minister in charge, 'Why does he now believe that public ownership will solve problems that do not appear to have anything to do with the ownership of the company, but concern its internal difficulties?'[38] When the government tried to sell Rover, the same question could be asked vice versa.

Between 1985 and 1989 an unparalleled boom in British car industry gave the government confidence to put forward its de-nationalisation plan. A key indicator of the fragmenting British market, however, was the shrinking combined market share of the 'Big Three' – Ford, Vauxhall, and Rover – from almost 62 per cent in 1984 to 55 per cent in 1989. For Rover only, the current condition was worse still and continued to deteriorate.

Table 6.4   Changes in market shares in the British car market, 1970–90

	1970–77	1977–81	1981–85	1985–90
Rover	-13.8	- 5.1	- 0.9	- 4.3
Ford	- 0.8	5.2	-4.4	-1.2
GM	0.2	-1.8	8.0	-0.5
Japan	10.2	0.4	- 0.2	4.4

Source: Foreman-Peck et al. (1995), *The British Motor Industry*, p. 224.

One of the main reasons for BAe tried to buy Rover was the Land Rover. Many Land Rovers were sold to the British and foreign armed forces that accounted for most of BAe's sales. In 1986, 76 per cent of BAe's turnover was in military aircraft, weapons and space equipment. BAe already used converted Land Rovers to transport its Swingfire and Rapier missile systems around, and wished to have the vehicles to add to its package of hardware on offer to military buyers. BAe's chairman, Roland Smith, recognised that he could not buy Land Rover alone. One more profit opportunity, when BAe purchased Rover, was the 40 per cent stake in DAF, the Dutch holding company that bought Leyland Trucks in 1987. DAF was concerned with military business as well. There were, also, many car-makers that had moved or were moving into the aerospace business. Fiat's jet-engine accounted for less than 2 per cent of its revenues, while GM bought the Hughes Aircraft Company in 1985.

Roland Smith was a notable business figure during the Thatcher era. He was a visiting professor at the Manchester Business School; however, he spent more time putting his academic knowledge into practice. Government welcomed the deal between Rover and BAe, because the project seemed to promise the synergic effect, which had been pursued by Lord Young. On the whole, government's mistake in this transaction was to give BL to the wrong owner. As Terence Davis asked in the House: 'As BAe needed government help to fund its contribution to the Airbus development a year ago, how will BAe find the money to finance new model development at Rover Group in future?'[39] Kenneth Clarke said about the synergic effect in manufacturing sector in the House:

> As a result of the changed industrial climate and the Government's economic policies, we have seen a powerful manufacturing group emerge composed of what were fully unsuccessful nationalised industries only a few years ago ... that this great will go on to be a very powerful manufacturing force in the British economy.[40]

However, the synergic effect proved a failure and even Lord Young said:

> my intention (synergic effect) was mismanaged owing to the rapid change of the world industrial sector. Conditions were not the same as in the 1960s or 1970s, when MITI undertook its policy: moreover, the situation in the UK was quite different from that of Japan.[41]

The government's real intentions for the British car maker at this time were challenged in the House by the Labour shadow chancellor, John Smith, who observed that:

> Is it not the truth that the deal has been done not to further long-term interests of British car industry but to satisfy the short-term need of BAe for cash? The Prime Minister answered that 'we would have had the drip, drip, drip feed of public expenditure maintaining BL, not a privatised, world-beating company'.[42]

Despite successful collaboration with Honda, Rover's market penetration was quite far from balance of trade target. When the Japanese small and medium size car penetrated the UK market, other EU car-makers, owing to the single market, increased their market share of luxury models. At the time when Rover privatised, it was really hard for Rover to compete with other car-makers. Rover compared to other car-makers, did not have enough domestic market share.

There were criticisms of BAe's approach to BL, particularly that:

BAe can do little to help Rover in this precarious quest. It may have something to offer the Land Rover business the two share many customers in governments and armies around the world … Aircraft and cars are utterly different to make, utterly different to sell. Rover needs car-company skills, full stop. It is getting them from Honda and would need to hang on to this rather vulnerable partnership as much as ever under BAe's stewardship.[43]

North Sea oil replaced expensive net imports of oil by home production, leading to large current account balance of payments surpluses in the first half of the 1980s. The 'feel good factor' was expected to spread the consumer boom to the British car industry. Under this expectation, the government had the confidence to privatise BL. However, there was another side to the 'oil effect' on the British manufacturing sector. This was the strong pound. When the UK became an oil exporting country, the strong pound made it more difficult for the British manufacturing sector to compete. Compared to other developed countries, there were no direct government transfer payments from the proceeds of oil export to investment in the manufacturing sector. Moreover, the competitiveness of imported goods from the other developed countries worsened the British manufacturing sector's competitiveness. Its first victim was the car industry, under attack from Japanese and French makers.

There were many critics of the de-nationalisation of the British car industry at that time. The short heyday was achieved with foreign help, Honda, not by British makers alone. However, the government thought it would work as long as they maintained their policies to attract inward investment. When the real crisis happened after mid-1986, the government tried to escape the political cost. Since mid-1986, if there was an intention to save the British car industry, the government should have tried to set up its own restructuring process and market protection not sell out. I wonder if the Thatcher government had any practical policy towards the car manufacturing sector.[44]

In 1994, Britain was unique among the larger industrial countries in having no single national car producer. For BAe, the expected consumer bubble burst too early, and the end of demand for defence products with the collapse of Russia put the company in financial difficulty. As far as financial support was concerned, Rover was another cash-hungry business from BAe's viewpoint. New projects in the defence and aerospace sector were too much for BAe to support. Despite Honda and Rover's successful Rover 600 and 800 series, the future of the world car market and the domestic situation, which was dominated by more severe competition from Japanese makers, were both gloomy. It was the first time that the British car maker had the opportunity to choose its owner.

The first offer was made to Honda, to take more than a 48 per cent of stake in Rover. Honda, however, was not prepared to go that far, and offered to double its holding to 40 per cent, wishing to see the remaining equity floated on the stock market. One of the misunderstandings on the part of BAe was its conception of Japanese merger and acquisition strategy. Traditionally, Japanese companies favoured a three-stage M&A policy. 'The first stage is building up agreements. The second stage is stake-building, and the third will be friendly take–overs.'[45] Honda thought the collaboration with Rover was still at stage two. BAe, which was eager to get financial support by selling Rover, was clearly unwilling to wait until the company could display a balance sheet, which would have found favour in financial markets. After that, there were various potential purchasers including VW and Ford. The unexpected sudden announcement of the proposed sale by BAe of its 80 per cent stake in Rover to BMW for £800 million took everyone by surprise except the government.

From the government's optimistic viewpoint in the House was told that:

> For Rover, the new relationship with BMW offers some significant opportunities.
> BMW has stated that it will: maintain Rover as a separate enterprise, with its own
> manufacturing plants and its own design and development capabilities: be able to
> offer better access to the very substantial funds needed for investment in new
> models: encourage Rover to build on the progress it has made in developing long-
> term relationships with its suppliers, and be able to offer Rover additional export
> opportunities, which should increase volumes. BMW has also stated that it hopes
> that Rover will be able to maintain and to build on the existing links with Honda.[46]

Who was the winner or loser after BMW merged with Rover? Despite BMW's expectations, Honda started its own business in the UK. After the merger, the West Midlands suffered severe competition from foreign makers. Except for a few first tier component industries, an increased number of companies have been closed since the merger. It was not the real impact the Thatcher government expected.

As Table 6.6 shows, it is clear why the UK lost her national champion which was its top export item after the war, and on the other hand how the Japanese stood top of world car market at the same time.

The British car industry's relation to the government's industrial policy as a whole in the period was summarised by Edwardes: 'BL's struggle for survival presented a microcosm of the issues affecting British industry as a whole.'[47]

Table 6.5   British car industry: UK component share and trade balance

Makers	% of UK component			Balance of payments (£M)	
	1974	1984	1994	1984	1994
Rover	90%	90%	72%	£183 M	£66 M*
Ford	88%	46%	32%	£-600M	–
GM	89%	22%	Under 20%	£-500M	+

Notes

* Estimated.

+ All Vauxhall production in the UK has been in the form of kit assembly since 1986.

Source: MILAN report (1986), SMMT Annual Report.

Table 6.6   The comparison of governments' attitudes to the car industry between the UK and Japan

	UK	Japan
Balance of trade	Increased imports and reduced exports	Restricted imports and export-drive policy
Competition	Increased competitive pressure from other European manufacturers	Low stage development of the other Asian manufacturers
Labour problems	Multi-union negotiation	Single union
Economy of scale of competition	Too many models	Popular model policy
Government controls	Based on political or monetary reasons	Industry for its own sake
Automation process and R&D	Low	High

Source: Derived by the author on the basis of original research.

Honda in the UK

The reason for collaboration on Rover's part was clear. Mr Edwardes said that 'To find mutual synergy on a broader front is not easy at all, and so talks often come to nothing. You win some – but in the collaboration stakes, you lose some too.'[48] According to him, Honda, during their collaboration, found some advantages and some disadvantages. Rover was taken over by BMW in 1994, and Honda left without any future agreement. Is Honda really the loser? Despite BMW's positive approach towards continuing their collaboration, Honda started make efforts towards independence of marketing, manufacturing and R&D in the UK. Was the collaboration a lifebelt for Rover or a Trojan horse for Honda?

Honda's management strategy, called global localisation, laid the foundation for its FDI strategy since 1978 which was the year Honda of US Manufacturing Inc. established itself in Marysville, Ohio. Honda's international strategy had two sides in the approach to its market. One was the export from Japan of finished or assembled products. The other was to produce outside Japan, wherever there is a major consumer market. This was called 'global localisation', and consisted of the 'localisation of people', which means hiring and educating local people, who have not had any experience in the manufacturing sectors and assigning capable local employees to important positions. According to the Thamesdown report in December 1989:

> Honda have publicly indicated they will be training in-house largely, in line with company practice. Nevertheless the introduction of new systems will have a spill-over impact on manufacturing-related training in the Swindon area.[49]

Did it really happen? Its effect in Swindon will be explained in the next part of this chapter.

The 'localisation of money' means the maximum reinvestment of profit locally. Honda, compared to the other two large Japanese car companies, has few relations with any financial organisation within the same *keiretsu*. The financial independence created advantages for Honda overseas affiliates' R&D investment.

> I don't think they have a programme about 'localisation of money' in Swindon at this time. On the one hand, the Accord model failed to penetrate the EU market, in contrast to its success in the US. On the other hand, with a world recession in the car market, it will be a difficult time to make further investment in Swindon.[50]

'Localisation of people' and 'localisation of money' were the two pillars of Honda's global management strategy. Since the beginning of the globalisation of strategy, Honda has aggressively pursued its corporate activities from an international standpoint. Honda's global activities originated with the establishment of Honda Belgium in 1962. One year earlier, European

Honda (now Honda Deutschland GmbH) was established to carry out motorcycle sales. The approach of Japanese car manufacturing investment in the EU is both similar to and different from American behaviour. As in the US, Honda's approach to the EU is another localisation project which is the main manufacturing strategy. Within the EU, it has been shown that the SEM created another battleground for the emerging Japanese global big three – Nissan, Toyota and Honda.

In contrast to US car manufacturers, the European car manufacturers have a long history of separate national markets each dominated by one or two national leading car manufacturers that the government have supported and protected when necessary. Even with the SEM policy, some countries have severe restrictions on imported cars within their own markets. The collaboration between Honda and Rover was fast developing into the most ambitious relationship ever attempted between Japanese and a European car maker.

Following the successful approach to the US with the Accord model, Honda had to find its ideal partners within the European market. Honda had gained confidence from the market penetration, which followed the establishment of the Honda US manufacturing affiliates in March 1978, but its shortage of capital obliged it to find joint ventures or other collaborative partners in the EU. When Rover approached Honda, Honda had to consider its marketing strategy: hence, Rover was ideal for Honda, having a reputation for innovative design, and ability to use interior space exceptionally effectively, an expertise in suspension systems, a dedication to high technology and significant presence in the European market.

The Rover 200 was a further step in the partnership. While the design was basically Honda's, Rover injected engineering expertise for the European market with revised suspension and the option of a Rover 1.6 litre power unit. The project also marked the beginning of joint manufacturing as the Honda version of the car, the Honda Ballade, was made for Honda by Rover at the company's Longbridge factory. The success of the 200 series, which was voted Car of the Year (*What Car*, 1989) was followed by the upper medium sector 400 series, both built at Longbridge. The Rover 200 series was a £400 million investment by Rover in not just a new car, but in advanced manufacturing technologies to manufacture up to 100 different body specifications. Rover also manufactured the Honda Concerto for Honda in Europe, which shared the same basic design.

The next step was a momentous one for both companies. It led to one of the most far-reaching joint ventures in the history of the car industry – a truly joint project between East and West for the design and manufacture of a totally new car. Project XX, the Rover 800 Executive saloon, was conceived in the autumn of 1981 on the basis of equal partnership. It evolved a remarkable degree of trust, for each company accepted the design responsibility for particular aspects of the car. At the same time, each company retained its own manufacturing autonomy and product identity. The resulting cars – the Rover 800 saloon range and the Honda Legend – were designed so that visually they looked quite different, but shared under-the-skin components and a core body 'platform'. Rover developed the car with its own-designed Fastback variation, while Honda produced a two-door coupe.

With the success of these agreements, Honda agreed to put the 10-year project-by-project relationship onto a closer and more enduring basis. Honda invested more than £200 million in a car assembly plant at Swindon. A new upper medium car range – the Rover 600 and the Honda Accord were launched. At this time they assembled at different places. The Honda car was built at Honda's Swindon plant, while the Rover version was built at Rover's Cowley plant. Panels for both cars were produced at Rover's pressing plant at Swindon, and Rover also supplied further components from its other manufacturing plants. Additionally, Honda agreed to sell the Land Rover Discovery through its dealer in Japan, badged as a Honda.

On 14 April 1990, an agreement was signed giving a mutual 20 per cent cross-shareholding between Rover and Honda UK. This advanced the relationship to a more formal and permanent basis and helped both companies, while preserving their separate identities, to develop long-term strategies to meet the demands of an increasingly global market. In October 1991, Rover and Honda took a further strategic step forward with the formal announcement, not just of the previously mentioned OEM-made car, but of two further joint model ranges to be built at Rover's Longbridge plant. The two companies also formalised a joint strategy on purchasing and component supply for the expanded Honda and Rover model programmes to be built in the UK. 'After that, Rover escaped from the position of subcontractor. This started a real collaboration.'[51]

> This was another chance to regenerate our production capability. The high pressure of financial considerations drove the two companies into one path in R&D, component supply, and marketing strategy. The 'Theta project' was its core. This would be a real synergic effect of collaboration.[52]

The main justification for pushing two companies into one was also welcomed by Honda.

The strategy of marketing one car under two names was, however, severely criticised by the Honda headquarters in Japan.

> Within the managers group, they were surprised when they found out the unexpectedly low rate of sales of the Honda Accord in the UK. The Accord is one of best cars Honda ever made. One of the clear answers was to avoid market competition between Rover and Honda with the same model. The other was to increase share-holdings of Rover and Honda for further improving mutual relations. The effect was a cross share holding deal. The 'Theta' project, a new car to replace the 200/Concerto models was hoped to become one model for the same market. This was expected to improve the collaboration effect. The 'Theta' project is regarded as last stage of their collaboration *If the 'Theta' project worked, Honda would think about the merger with Rover*. However, its impact diminished owing to the BMW merger. (emphasis my own)[53]

As Japanese management philosophy said,[54] Honda showed their intention to set up an independent manufacturing site. According to Mr Peter McVeigh, General Manager Honda Collaboration for Rover:

> I think the motive for the independence of Honda UK was the announcement of de-nationalisation plans by government, because it was then that they announced their Honda Manufacturing Enterprise (HME) plan. The series of announcements about R&D and the expansion of the manufacturing facility in Swindon supported this hypothesis.[55]

Mr Yasushi Uno, Deputy Chief Representative of EXIM Bank in Washington, who was regional manager for EXIM in the UK during the collaboration period, said that:

> The approach to the foreign market is always started by Honda adventurism. Honda marketing in the US was regarded as a textbook example for the other two car-makers. In the UK, Honda needed its own affiliates, because its confidence in the US market encouraged Honda into a more positive global localisation strategy. I thought that in the late 1980s, Honda extended their management skill over Rover's part of the business. HME was not a sales operation, it was a manufacturing site. The collaboration always had two sides. There is no winner, or loser. When the collaboration had succeeded, Honda expected to put aside the collaborative relationship and move on. The privatisation threat was another good reason to think again, because the collapse of collaboration with the company when it was nationalised would have caused political difficulties with and for the Japanese government.[56]

According to the Thamesdown economic section's report, it was clear that:

> Honda had a policy of increasing capital outlays – $2,113 million in the 1988. As a part of the financing of this expenditure, Honda sold a bond issue on the Euro Market in March 1989.[57]

Whether Honda sold its bond for cross-share holding or for an independent project, Honda had been facing severe cash flow difficulties since the late 1980. The all-in-one project, named 'Theta', was expected to solve this.

In January 1994, Honda was suddenly shocked to discover that Rover was to be taken over by BMW without any consultation with the Japanese partner. BMW stated quite clearly that:

> it is not their intention to merge the two companies and that Rover will remain autonomous, under its own management and pursuing its previously agreed strategy. Rover managers appear to have confidence in this declaration, and have added their weight to reassurances from BMW to workforce that terms and conditions of employment will not alter. Notwithstanding the initial reaction of Honda to the BMW deal, closer consideration of the relationship between the Japanese company and Rover makes it clear that there are a series of complex agreements that can not be quickly or easily unravelled.[58]

Owing to the unexpected merger, Honda apparently lost a lot. The 'Theta' project was expected to lead the way in the design process, but 80 per cent production would be undertaken by Rover who had therefore met 80 per cent of the development costs. Honda would have had a new model for 20 per cent of what it would have cost to produce it alone. This was far more damaging for Honda's further production plans. It was not erased without trace, because of the long history of their collaboration. The future, however, looked bleak. According to Mr Akio Suzuki, the Liaison Manager from Honda:

> I did not hear any news from the Rover before the press told us. We were humiliated. We thought there would be a possibility, not a reality within a decade. Rover is surviving and Honda, of course, we will help them to get stronger. The collaboration has a long history. We do not want sudden death owing to the merger. However, it will have a limited life, I think.[59]

According to the Honda press briefings:

... in January 1994, everything changed when the majority shareholder in Rover, BAe decided to sell its shares to BMW of Germany. There followed a period of intense discussion and finally on 19 May, a new agreement was reached between Honda and the Rover Group, under which all the existing and projected collaborative projects are to be continued, but the cross share holding agreement would be terminated. The relationship between Honda and Rover has been unique in the automobile world. It has been responsible for the production of over 1 million cars and has helped the people of Rover to establish a new force in the European market. Honda has benefited from Rover's tradition in car manufacturing in the UK. The relationship will now continue until at least the year 2000.[60]

When we examine BMW's advantage from the merger, it reflects the negative effect on Honda:

... the principal advantages for BMW in the purchase of Rover as:

- instant experience of those aspects of Japanese production methodology which are known to be applicable in Europe;
- the opportunity to complete BMW's model range with small cars, front wheel drive and off-road technology and provide a 'fast route' to expansion into new market sectors;
- giving BMW an advance on Mercedes–Benz and putting it far ahead of Audi ...;
- BMW feels that Honda needs foreign engagement to counteract problems it is experiencing at home in Japan where there have been rumours of a take-over threat from Mitsubishi and will therefore be forced to co-operate;
- the advantages of bringing a competitor 'in house';
- the UK is a lower cost production location;
- BMW feels its world-wide image is very important and sees the purchase of Rover as an opportunity to enhance this.[61]

During the Major government, the industrial policy had been tied by previous decisions and the government had a good deal less room to manoeuvre than former governments.

Compared to his predecessor, Major had no intention of saving the UK car industry, nor any patriotism, which was an important feature of the Thatcher government. Unfortunately, BAe was keener on cash to save the high technology defence industry than on Rover. The British component industries had expected to be saved by the big three Japanese makers. But the dream never came true.[62]

One of most disputed consequences of the Rover and Honda collaboration since 1979 was the real impact of technical collaboration on the British car components industries. As far as design and human management were concerned, there were examples of good practice in the collaboration. Higher expectations from Rover, however, such as high qualified R&D and technical manufacturing skills were not achieved to the level of the initial agreement. According to Tadashi Kume, president of Honda:

> There are some technologies that we don't have, and sometimes it seems the cheapest thing would be to buy them. But when you buy technology from others, it remains frozen, a foreign thing that is not part of yourself, and in the end you don't know where to go with it … It is hard to develop ongoing technologies if you have not developed the basics yourself.[63]

This must work in reverse. However, Rover, from Honda's viewpoint, did not have enough basic technology.

According to the author's survey, moreover, Honda rated themselves in the top position for technology and the ability to adapt their competitive advantage. On the other hand, Honda thought that EU countries were not well equipped to acquire new technologies. As far as UK car manufacturing skills were concerned, Honda thought that the UK was not a good country into which to import advanced technologies, but it was a cheaper labour cost country within the EU. Conclusively, Honda's approach to Rover, regarding the technology and R&D facility has been neglected. It is best understood by a study of the local economy in Swindon.

Honda and Regional Economic Development

The car industry is of central importance to the West Midlands economy and its state of health is a major influence on the well being of the area as a whole. Since the privatisation of the Rover, car manufacturing within the West Midlands is mainly divided into two parts. In Oxford and Longbridge in Birmingham, Rover's car plant at Cowley is unavoidably linked to the state of the car industry in Britain. The other area is Swindon, which was expected to dominate after the collaboration between Rover and Honda.

In the mid-1980s the railway works, which although greatly reduced was still one of Swindon's largest manufacturing employers, closed for ever. This was a big blow for Swindon's economy, but the effects were softened somewhat by the decision by Honda to locate their European manufacturing plant in this area. This marked the initial phase of an on-going process of investment by the company in their operations in the town to the point where they now have a factory with the capacity to assemble 150,000 cars per annum.

The collaboration between Rover and Honda during the 1980s and the early 1990s was also crucial in safeguarding the 3,500 jobs, which exist in the Rover body pressing plant in Swindon. And also, it was expected to lead to further investment and increased employment from Honda's related automotive components manufacturers in that area. The car industry has thus been of particular importance to Swindon since then. During the 1980s, Swindon was widely described as the fastest growing town in Europe. Compared with other local areas, Swindon's dramatic development has been made all the more impressive by the fact that there have been no financial incentives, from central government such as IBB or England Partnership, for companies and organisations to locate in the town. Swindon has a major advantage over many other centres in that its communications are good, and this asset has proved to be a considerable attraction for 'clean' industries such as computer chips, and for highly capital-intensive industry.

The coming of Honda to Swindon was explained in a Borough report as follows:

> The decision to invest in Swindon was a direct result of Honda's collaboration with Rover group, which started in 1979. In order to satisfy the increasing European demand for Honda products it was decided that Rover should produce cars for Honda's operation. The choice of Swindon itself was based on four key points that: excellent people, excellent infrastructure, good communications and work facilities and greenfield site ... The 370 acre which was previously owned by Vickers Supermarine Ltd., was purchased in 1985, the advantages being proximity to Rover Group at Cowley Longbridge and Swindon, its excellent transport infrastructure, the large site and the warm welcome from the local community.
>
> A pre-delivery inspection plant was established in September 1986 for cars produced by Rover Group. In 1989, phase 2 of the development was completed with opening of the engine plant. The buildings then occupied 21,200 sq. metres. The car manufacturing facility, covering additional 72,000-sq. metres started volume production in October 1992, and completed phase 3 of the development.[64]

Compared to Nissan UK, Honda got very low government incentives – under 25 per cent (author survey result) – which were, mainly, land and premises, advice and planning permission. Honda regarded Swindon as an unexceptionable location for investment. According to the author's survey, they thought the labour ability, risk of strikes, and low wages were quite average for the UK.

Honda's initial investment in Swindon was expected by Thamesdown to be lower impact than the assembly plant proposals for Nissan in Sunderland, and Toyota at Derby.

> However, with a planned capacity of 100,000 units, the Honda proposal is half the size of the other two developments. Body pressing will be undertaken at the Rover plant at Stratton, not on site. Investment in a new press facility is currently underway, and is programmed to tie with the main plant development programme.
>
> There will be a relatively small amount of manufacturing on site, apart from the engine assembly. Major components such as seats, radiators, wheels, tyres and electronics instrumentation will be brought in from elsewhere. Already enquiries have been received from linked suppliers for sites near to the main assembly plants, and Semperit, a Honda supplier of tyres has relocated its UK activity to a site within one mile of Honda.
>
> There is a view, widely held amongst motor trade analysts that the present decision is merely an interim stage in the overall development plan for Honda, and that the ultimate plan will be for 200,000–250,000 units annually. The parallel experience of Nissan in Sunderland, and Honda in the US suggest that this incremental process will occur in Swindon. However, no planning approval exists for any expansion over and above the current development plans.
>
> The requirement to achieve 80 per cent local content will have a major impact on the need to manufacture components within the UK compared with Nissan where the majority of components have been imported and the plant to date has been largely a 'screwdriver' operation with local content largely derived from labour cost input. The recent announcement by Nissan to establish two technology centres in the UK indicates the route down which Honda should be encouraged to go.[65]

Despite the development of the Honda assembly plant in Swindon, it has not so far brought in the amount of additional inward investment from component manufacturers that was originally hoped for. There are two main reasons: one is the relative weakness of the Honda *keiretsu* components organisation in Japan; the other is the 'knock down' agreement. Hence, there are still few automotive components industries in Swindon compared to the other Japanese car manufacturing areas such as Derby for Toyota, or Tyne and Wear for Nissan. Compared to the Toyota and Nissan with 32 and 36, Honda has only 14.

Based on the closeness of relations between car manufacturers and components suppliers, Honda is rather weaker than the others. Worse, Honda does not have a first tier group of component industries but only core component parts suppliers. Tyne and Wear or even Derby have seen first and second-tier investment in the local area, while Swindon experienced only three car component-related investments.

The collaboration based on the OEM system led the assembly process to rely on imported parts. According to a Honda report:

> Honda is using 199 European component suppliers, 143 from the UK and achieves 80 per cent European content and 60 per cent British content. From 1995 when the plant reaches a production capacity of 100,000 cars, the anticipated spend on components will be approximately £500 million. Honda is committed to assisting European component suppliers to gain business from other Honda operations through the world.[66]

However, there was criticism of the inadequacy of both the quantity and the quality of local component content.

> The local components regulation was not important. The importance was the quality of components. The technology gap over engine parts requires a quite different explanation from that of tyres or other simple parts. Honda since the collaboration, has imported key parts from the Japanese HQ, or US affiliates, not from the UK. All the 80 per cent EU regulations have been treated as political camouflage, not used for the benefit of the component industries.[67]

It was confirmed by Ms Lorelei Hunt, manager of the local economic section of Thamesdown Borough Council that:

> An early misconception arose from the talk of 'local sourcing' of components for Japanese cars built in the UK. In reality this meant sourcing from Europe rather than from the immediate hinterland of the assembly plant or even from the UK. In order for the cars built by Japanese companies in Britain to be politically acceptable in other European countries they had to include components made in those countries. There appear to be only a small number of key components that are almost always manufactured close to the assembly plant, which include body panels, seats, paint and glass. Swindon has followed this pattern with the exception of glass which will be manufactured by a joint French/Japanese company at a plant in Belgium, although it is expected that the company will set up a buffer warehouse in Swindon as production at the Honda plants steps up.[68]

When author interviewed Ms Hunt she argued that:

Table 6.7   The relation between car-makers and component industries

Shares of equities	Less than 5%	5–9%	10–19%	20–29%	30–39%	40–49%	50% or more	Total car-makers
Toyota	9	7	4	7	3	2	–	32
Nissan	7	4	2	12	6	3	2	36
Honda	9	3	–	–	2	–	–	14

Source: Tokyo Business Today (1992), February, p. 51.

Table 6.8   List of Japanese companies in the Swindon area

Name	Activity	Parent company
Clarion Shoji (UK) Ltd	Distribution of car audio equipment	Clarion Company
Honda Logistics Centre	Car parts distribution	Honda Motor
NBC UK Ltd	Paint automotive manufacturers	Nippon B Chemicals
Nissin UK	Freight distribution	Nissin Corporation
Pentel Stationery	Distribution of stationery	Pentel Co.
Sakata Inx UK	Distribution of electronic components	Sakata Inx Corp.
Yuasa Battery Sales	Distribution of industrial batteries	Yuasa Battery Co. Ltd.

Source: Swindon Economic Development (1994).

... our expectation about Honda's impact within Swindon proved a failure. I think there are two reasons; one is the Rover's sudden death, which brought about Honda's direct components import from other industries which there are outside Swindon, outside the UK, and some of them outside the EU. It produced no further inward investment from other car component industries into Swindon. The other reason was the collaboration strategy. The OEM system collaboration allowed Honda to import high technology parts from Japan to save time and R&D spending. The government's catch-up policy and the Rover's hasty new model production programme allowed a Japanese invasion in Swindon without conditions about the local economy. Moreover, it had a fatal impact on Swindon's further development plans such as the local employment policy or further inward investment plan.[69]

Conclusion

The Conservatives came to power in 1979 promising to end a long period of relative economic decline in the UK by breaking away from the interventionist economic policies of the 1960s and 1970s, and by ending the trade unions' veto on economic reform. The emphasis of policy switched towards putting greater pressure on managers in both public and private industries to increase efficiency epitomised by the high-profile privatisation and deregulation programmes. The British car industry was the first test of the Thatcher government's industrial promises. The government's new policy towards the manufacturing sector and the strong support of a nonpolitical managing director in BL put the fresh air into the British car industry.

When Edwardes became Managing Director of BL, he had two emerging solutions within BL. While solving the internal problems, such as industrial disputes, low investment in R&D, and increasing market share using foreign help from Honda, he had to solve the external problems created by the government. Under political pressure, BL tried to gain managerial advantage by using the name of joint venture.

The joint venture was supported by Japanese government on the grounds that:

Japan owes its post-war growth to the free trade system. It is the duty of our nation to contribute to the maintenance and expansion of the free world economic order sustained by the tri-polar powers – Japan, the US and Europe – doing whatever we can to avoid falling into the pitfall of protectionism. It is necessary from this viewpoint to help solve the structural problems with industry in America and Europe, encourage its revitalisation, and form a harmonised international division of labour among them. Japanese industry is keeping up a good performance as compared with its counterparts in the Western nations. Not only should Japanese industry have trade relations with them, but it should also promote mutual exchange in wider areas such as capital, technology and know-how, and complement and strengthen mutual activity. 'Industrial collaboration' is a concept that encompasses industrial exchange in a wide spectrum between industrialised nations as described above.[70]

Under the Japanese government's international joint programme (push factors) Honda adopted its US strategy in the UK, and welcomed Rover's invitation with *Kyoei Kyozon* (prosper together, suffer together.)
From the Rover side:

... management can only promote industrial recovery on two further conditions: first, management must formulate a strategy which identifies and attacks the real problems of the business in a sensible order, and second, the enterprise must be operating in an environment where the relevant internal and external problems can be solved by management. Neither of these conditions was satisfied at Austin Rover or in British manufacturing as a whole.[71]

Edwardes' collaboration plan aimed to solve those problems at one time. While Honda was in the '*kyozon*' (suffer together) philosophy, Rover hoped for the '*kyoei*' (prosper together) policy only.

Compared to the close relationship between management and government in Japan, why did this not happen in the British manufacturing sector? There are two main reasons to explain this. The Japanese government since the 1970s has been focused on some specialised manufacturing sectors among her industries. Car manufacturing, electric goods, and office equipment are regarded as prime items to lead in world markets. The general waves of Japanese FDI towards the EU have followed this pattern. The high-cost industrial areas have allowed Japan to dominate world markets.

Compared to this specific method, British government adopted a more general approach to the manufacturing sectors. The manufacturing sector has frequently been at odds with the Thatcher government, while the financial sectors have prospered. The policy towards the manufacturing sector has been worse than in the Wilson government. The Thatcher government made two major mistakes when they dealt with the British car industry. The overestimation of Rover's strength and the failed de-nationalisation plan, expected to have a synergic effect on Rover, came at the wrong time. Despite the government's hard-driven export strategy, Rover's market share in the world declined every year. The dual manufacture between Rover and Honda of a single model damaged Rover's export effort as well as Honda's. Worse, the problem in the home market was that no one model could take a substantial market share and in such a fragmented market a producer could only obtain a reasonable overall market share if the maker had several models available. Rover had had too few and had been too optimistic about the market share that its models could win. Rover's financial instability, on the other hand, made it difficult to develop a range of models of sufficient quality and reliability to compare with the best models from their competitors.

Based on this mistaken interpretation, the de-nationalisation plan was undertaken at the wrong time and in the wrong place to have an effect on the British car industry. The emerging theory about denationalisation was that it would create synergy. The British car maker in the world market was too weak to compete. The restructuring process under privatisation was the idea of the 1960s when the Japanese did it under the guise of a government protection policy. Compared to the 1960s world market, the competition during the 1980s was more severe and more capital intensive. Moreover, there was no government determination to protect domestic market for British car-makers from foreign car-makers. Without a stable domestic market share, it was harder than the 1960s Japanese situation.

It has been always very difficult for an outsider to obtain enough information really to understand properly the prospects for a large corporation. Rover, despite government support and collaboration with Honda, failed to penetrate markets both at home and abroad so as to increase its sales by at least a third if it were to become viable. Increasing productivity was heavily dependent upon reductions in the number of employees. The Thatcher government, in spite of 'Thatcherism at work', failed to promote the manufacturing sector. This was proved when Rover was merged with BMW.

Within the Swindon local economy, there were two major criticisms from local government and local component industries. As far as the Thatcher government's policy was concerned, the MILAN report said

Inevitably, Government attitudes toward ARG (Austin Rover Group) were criticised. Earlier in the day, Management had also argued that recent Government action had created uncertainty and reduced market confidence in ARG. It was suggested that the key issue for local authorities was how to establish countervailing power to resist future negotiations between the Government and multi-national motor companies. This pointed to a local authority strategy with two strands:

- A short term strategy which is opportunistic and realistic, and which aims to provided benefits for the indigenous motor industry which the limits set by the existing political and economic environment.
- A longer-term strategy aimed at producing an alternative development plans for the industry capable of winning support from future governments.[72]

This was confirmed by a Cabinet source. 'I do not think the Thatcher government had a long term strategy towards manufacturing sectors. It just allowed things to happen, and reacted.'[73]

Worsened, Honda's impact has been lower than expected. It was explained by Ms Hunt that:

The 'Honda' effect on Swindon is far more diffuse and difficult to define than at first expected. The amount of inward investment by component suppliers is limited at present, although it is likely that further warehousing space will be taken as production at Honda increases over the next two years ...

The companies are not strongly linked together within the local economy, and it does not seem at this stage that just-in-time production policies have led to a spatial concentration of motor manufacturing in Swindon. It is now clear that it would be extremely difficult for local companies to break into the Honda supply network at this stage, as the first tier component suppliers are already in place. There may be opportunities further down the supply chain to supply those tier component suppliers, but few of those are located locally.[74]

It was further explained in the MILAN report that 'In common with the other Japanese affiliates in the UK, Honda has a policy of using European components suppliers where both quality and competitiveness can be assured. Much of this has been achieved by partnership, joint venture, and working closely with supplier companies. Many key components are still imported direct from Japan, although Honda either complies with or is close to the 80% European content as defined by the DTI.'[75]

During 1994, Honda faced their first difficulty since 1979. 'The big question now facing Honda is whether it should continue on its own, given that it is the weakest of the three. An industry analyst said 'Honda took the less expensive route into Europe by finding a partner, but that has now proved to be a disaster.'[76] After the 1994 merger, Honda embarked on a *Kyozon* (suffer together) period.

The House of Lords Select Committee concluded of the Thatcher government's industrial policy that 'Manufacturing industry is vital to the prosperity of the UK ... Our manufacturing base is dangerously small ... The present lack of Government commitment, support and assistance to industry are damaging to our national interest.'[77]

Notes

1　Holmes, M. (1985), *The Labour Government, 1974–1979*, p. 1.
2　*Hansard* (1974), 6 December, col. 2115.
3　I.e., its share of the total output in Western Europe.
4　Church, R. (1994),*The Rise and Decline of the British Motor Industry*, pp. 87–8.
5　Wilson (1979), *Final Term*, p. 137.
6　*Hansard* (1977), vol. 890, col. 1742–8.
7　Castle, B. (1980), *The Castle Diaries 1974–76*, p. 374–5.
8　*Economist* (1977), 22 October, p. 86.
9　*Daily Telegraph* (1979), 10 September.
10　Williams, K. et al. (1983), *Why are the British bad at Manufacturing?*, p. 263.
11　*Economist* (1977), 22 October, p. 86.
12　*Economist* (1977), 19 March, p. 87.
13　*Guardian* (1977), 26 October.
14　Edwardes, M. (1983), p. 44.
15　Ibid., p. 54.
16　Mr Chris Firth: interview.
17　Sir Michael Edwardes: interview.
18　Edwardes, M. (1983), p. 186.
19　Ibid., p. 221.
20　The European car industry had gone through four stages of development at these times:

   i)　cost cutting and new model development;
   ii)　competition between manufacturers on the basis of volume and revenue growth;
   iii)　emphasis upon marketing in order to attempt to match sales to new, higher output levels;
   iv)　consolidation of company positions, with the emphasis upon cost cutting rather than growth.

21　Hamel, G. (1991), 'Competition for Competence and Inter-partner Learning within International Strategic Alliance', *Strategic Management Journal*, No. 12, p. 83.
22　*Financial Times* (1979), 4 April.
23　Edwardes, M. (1983), p. 188.
24　Lord Biffen: interview.
25　Edwardes, M. (1983), p. 194.
26　Honda UK Company Report (1993), mimeo, pp. 1–2.
27　BL thought Nissan was bigger than BL and Nissan preferred to greenfield investment.
28　*Scotsman* (1979), 3 April.
29　*Financial Times* (1979), 4 April.
30　Edwardes, M. (1983), pp. 222–3.
31　Hansard (1979), 20 December, col. 885–6.

32 Ibid., col. 892–3.
33 *Financial Times* (1979), 4 April.
34 *Time* (1986), 8 September, p. 35.
35 Mr Atsushi Yamakoshi: interview.
36 Lord Biffen: interview.
37 Sir Michael Edwardes: interview.
38 *Hansard* (1974), 6 December, col. 2116.
39 *Hansard* (1988), 29 March, col. 891.
40 Ibid.
41 Lord Young: interview.
42 *Hansard* (1994), 1 February, col. 737.
43 *Economist* (1988), 5 March, p. 13.
44 Mr Roger King: interview.
45 Fusa, C. (1989), *Financial Weekly*, 20–26 July.
46 *Hansard* (1994), 31 January, col. 619.
47 *Economist* (1988), 16 January, p. 69.
48 Edwardes, M. (1983), p. 203.
49 Borough of Thamesdown Economic and Social Development Group (1989), 'Preliminary Study of the Impact of the Honda Manufacturing Investment on the Swindon Area' (mimeo), p. 5.
50 Ms Lorelei Hunt: interview.
51 Mr Peter McVeigh: interview.
52 Mr Peter McVeigh: interview.
53 Mr Hiroshi Matsumoto: interview in Japanese.
54 'When you enjoy your heyday, you have to prepare cloudy day'.
55 Mr Peter McVeigh: interview.
56 Mr Yasushi Uno: interview.
57 Borough of Thamesdown Economic and Social Development Group (1989), Preliminary Study of the Impact of the Honda Manufacturing Investment on the Swindon Area (mimeo) p. 2.
58 Swindon Economic Development (1994), mimeo paper, 'Issues Arising from the Sale of Rover Group to BMW', p.1.
59 Mr Akio Suzuki: interview.
60 Honda Press Information (mimeo) (1994), p. 6.
61 Swindon Economic Development, 'Issues arising from the sale of Rover Group to BMW', (mimeo), p. 8.
62 Mr Nicolas W.L. Maclean: interview.
63 *Time* (1986), 8 September, p. 34.
64 Honda Press Information (1994) (mimeo), p. 3.
65 Borough of Thamesdown Report (1989) (mimeo).
66 Honda Press Information (1994).
67 Mr Chris Firth: interview.
68 Hunt, L. and Eastwood, K. (1993), 'The Automotive Components Sector in Thamesdown' (mimeo), p. 10.
69 Ms Lorelei Hunt: interview.
70 MITI (1982), *White Paper on International Trade*, p. 21.
71 Williams, K. et al. (1987), *The Breakdown of Austin Rover*, pp. 100–1.
72 MILAN *Report* Visit to AR Plant, Cowley (1986), 1 December (mimeo), pp. 4–5.

73 Lord Biffen: interview.
74 Hunt, L. and Estwood, K. (1993), p. 19.
75 MILAN *Report* (1996), 'Pre-Visit Briefing Note, Honda Assembly Plant Swindon'.
76 *Swindon Business News* (1994), 3 March.
77 House of Lords Select Committee on Science and Technology, *Report* (1991), pp. 3, 43.

Chapter 7

Nissan in the UK: A Case Study in the Politics of FDI Decision-making and Regional Economic Development

One of the most powerful tactics in British industrial policy since the Thatcher period has been its inward FDI strategy, especially from East Asian countries. Britain has been the most favoured country for inward investment by other European and US MNEs. Since the late 1970s, UK was also the top inward investment country for foreign MNEs in the EU, especially from Japan. However, as the Hitachi case[1] showed it had not always been easy.

When Margaret Thatcher came to power, the mutual relations between Britain and Japan changed, but not by any deliberate plan. The burden of suspicion between Japan and Britain arising from World War II was diminished when the Conservative government came in. Thatcher herself experienced a fascinating trip to the Tsukuba Science City on her second visit to Japan in 1984. Her experience caused her to change her mind about Japanese technology and as she said:

> at Tsukuba I saw just how advanced the Japanese were … It was a demonstration that the Japanese not only had advanced electronics: they had managed to develop and apply that technology far more successfully than we had.[2]

After her trip to Japan, she was eager to get inward investment from Japan more than from any other foreign investor. The first task was finding a way on the political level. While she emphasised nationalism in her dealings with Western countries, she took a pragmatic diplomatic attitude towards Japan. I thought Thatcher had the confidence to deal with her government and solve British chronic problems such as over-mighty trade unions and industrial problems, using Japanese management methods. Since that time, Japanese investment, from the Conservative government's point of view, has been regarded as a lifebelt for Britain's manufacturing sectors.[3]

With the government showing a positive approach towards Japanese investors and making a stable foothold in the emerging 'fortress Europe',

Japanese investment in the UK started early in the 1980s. One of the biggest inward FDI projects in UK after 1980 was the Nissan project. In the face of the dramatic decline in manufacturing investment and employment in the UK by domestic firms, it is not surprising that new sources of manufacturing investment were anxiously sought. The Nissan project, which was started in 1984, was a highly political decision rather than an economic one. The Secretary of State for Industry, Patrick Jenkin, was reported:

> ... as threatening to curtail Japanese car imports into the UK if companies such as Nissan do not go ahead with their plan, which was announced rather prematurely two years ago but since postponed, to establish a car manufacturing plant in the UK.[4]

Even the Prime Minister explained that:

> While in Japan I met the President of Nissan, ... We had a useful talk, though I could not at this stage draw from him any explicit commitment. Negotiations were at first known only to a small group. But agreement was finally reached in January 1984. I was convinced that the Nissan project made as much sense for Japan as it did for us.[5]

Despite the fact that this was a private business decision, the investment plan had to be supported by governments, even by the senior levels within each cabinet. While the British government and Thatcher herself did most of the work, the Japanese government shadowed her policy by influencing the Nissan company. In the continuous dumping accusations by EU Committee toward Japanese prime export goods, the Japanese government, especially MITI, devised a plan for direct investment in specific countries within the EU. The role of MITI since the early 1980s has been rather that of political negotiator than that of business promoter, as it had been during the 1960s and 1970s. Naohiro Amaya, Vice Minister at MITI, said that:

> ... whether they lose money or make money is no longer MITI's concern. It's up to the companies themselves. But when their operations bring about too much trade friction it becomes MITI's business.[6]

Since the Nissan UK programme, the UK is dominated by Japanese car makers. Why are all of them here?

Table 7.1   Balance of trade in the car industry

	Cars	CV	Components	Total
1970	2035.5	1397.3	2835.8	7790.8
1975	22.9	1527.4	3470.6	6998.6
1980	-2719.9	549	2192.5	1179.9
1985	-4100.8	-488.1	-116.1	-4270.7
1990	-4175	-214.6	-1017.8	-4580.3
1992	-1960.4	154.7	-659.7	-1863.8

Unit: £ million 1990 prices.

Source: DTI Datastream (mimeo).

Why are all Japanese big three car makers in the UK? I think the answer is simple. Comparing the total of new car registrations and home production, Britain has much room to penetrate the market. Other countries such as the Netherlands, which have no nationalised car industry, will be important markets. Those countries, however, will see severe competition between Japanese car makers and other European makers within relatively small markets. With the size of the potential market, open minded consumer behaviour, and most of all the government's effort to attract inward investment, why did Japanese car makers need to find other countries?[7]

The decline of the UK balance of payments deficit within car trading is largely due to Japanese makers' effort to export.

From the viewpoint of trade balance, the Thatcher government's intentions were largely achieved. During the late 1980s, 25 per cent of UK trade profit came from the car industry. Against this, the level of employment, which is the other issue to consider in connection with inward investment policies, was getting worse. Within the two axes of inward investment theory, the balance of trade and employment have to work simultaneously. Why was one factor a failure despite the other factor's success? The employment policy is a solid economic achievement; the balance of trade is more important for political reasons. Without an effective employment programme to back it up, a further inward investment programme would be ineffective.

Whether the UK escaped deindustrialisation or not, has government saved British manufacturing industry by using foreign help? Is it really true that ownership does not matter? Interestingly, the car industry in the UK has faced all these questions.

Nissan and the Politics of FDI Decision-making

Nissan is the second largest car maker in Japan, and fourth in the world. While Toyota, its main rival in Japan, concentrated upon copying Western technology through the recruitment of top Japanese university engineers, Nissan depended on the transfer of technology from the US or the UK. Compared to Honda, Nissan has its own *keiretsu*. Nissan is a member of the Fuyo group, which was founded 1966 and has 29 companies including Hitachi, Canon, Nippon Oil, and Sapporo Breweries. Its main banks are the Industrial Bank of Japan (IBJ) and the Fuji Bank. One of the notable characteristics of Nissan is its close relation with MITI. MITI and IBJ are one of Nissan's major axes towards the Japanese government. Nissan has regular directors' connections with IBJ, Fuji bank, and MITI. Compared to Honda's close relations with the Ministry of Foreign Affairs, Nissan's international strategy will usually be worked closely in collaboration with MITI.

> The role of MITI towards the FDI plans of the car industries seemed to be successful. The UK is a good example. When Toyota announced their intention to invest in the UK, it was criticised by other government organisations. However, because of the good experience in the UK with Nissan's investment in the car industry, MITI allowed, or maybe, did not object to the Toyota plan. The high level of competition within same market had been proved successful in the domestic market. MITI gave its full support, when car makers designed their FDI plans.[8]

This was corroborated by Lord Tebbit, who commented that:

> When I met a member of MITI, I thought they had prepared very well about each company's FDI plan. Nissan was a good example. Nissan seemed to have two channels; one from their directors, the other from MITI. During the negotiation, we had to balance our approach between staff from MITI and from Nissan.[9]

The general picture of Japanese greenfield investment in the EU was quite different from that of US investment.

> Unlike in the US, where Japanese direct investments were generally straightforward, their investments in Europe were thus compelled to take complicated 'detours'.

> (i)   The existence of many competitive small-car manufacturers, coupled with politically imposed volume restrictions, made it more difficult for Japanese

automobile manufacturers to choose the right models and ascertain adequate sales volume. With the exception of Spain and the UK, Japanese car producers had to get started by way of project-oriented, 'licensed production' approaches, which produced mixed results ...

(ii) Direct investments have been mainly limited to the UK and Spain, where national champions are absent and there are fewer barriers to Japanese participation ...

(iii) The European automobile industry has had a long tradition of car-making and has entertained certain peculiarities in each local market. In order to accommodate diversity as well as reasonable economies of scale, product development activities for choosing the right products play a particularly important role there ...

(iv) Two parallel patterns of Japanese participation are likely to continue. On the one hand, 100 per cent Japanese-owned investments in greenfield-site European transplants are taking place (e.g. Nissan, Honda, and Toyota in the UK). On the other hand, there will continue to be heterogeneous forms of enterprise: project-based collaboration, licensed manufacturing, JV, or acquisition of existing ones.

(v) The auto parts market in Europe has historically been different from that of the US in that a small number of giant component suppliers coexisted with numerous small parts makers. In order to avoid friction with the local supplier group, the dominant investment style of Japanese parts manufacturers has been either licensed manufacturing or acquisition of existing operations.[10]

In Britain, greenfield investment showed particular attention that:

... (i) mobilise the uncritical political and financial support of local authorities in the context of fierce competition between localities to attract inward investors to replace lost jobs; (ii) capitalise on the peculiarities of local labour markets and mass unemployment by focusing recruitment on 'green works' and using intensive selection procedures to recruit a compliant and committed workforce; (iii) exploit the political divisions and competition for membership among British trade unions by encouraging 'beauty contests' and the acceptance of a tightly circumscribed role for workplace trade unionism; and (iv) deploy such management techniques as participation, teamworking, and single status to enhance the commitment of workers to enterprise goals and limit opposition.[11]

Nissan's globalisation plan followed this trajectory closely.

Nissan's vertical structure is the traditional Japanese car manufacturing system. Under the parent company, there is a core group of about 20 key subcontractors in which the main company holds an average 40 per cent equity stake. Under these first subcontractors, there are second and third tiers of subcontractors.

> Until a few years ago the Nissan *keiretsu* had two distinct classes of subcontractors – those primarily loyal to Nissan and the 'independents', firms that had somehow managed to keep control of their own destiny and used that precarious position to conduct business with a variety of different auto makers. In the early 1990s, however, Nissan's profits began a stomach-wrenching downward spiral that led to the firm posting its first red-ink settlement since listing in 1951.
>
> As the company began severe production cutbacks, its captive parts makers were naturally envious of the independents' freedom to turn to other makers for orders. Thus, Nissan merged its second- and third-tier suppliers, the loyalists and the independents alike, into a single organisation, the Nissho-kai, which consists of almost 200 companies.[12]

During these slimming-down restructuring processes, Nissan faced up to its globalisation programme. Between the hammer of Toyota on the top, and the anvil of Honda below, Nissan had to find a more radical project. Between 1982 and 1984 Nissan plunged from Japan's third most profitable company to fourteenth. Earnings also fell sharply. Before tax income, which reached a record $752 million in 1982, fell 32 per cent over the two-year period to $513 million. In the ultra-price competitive domestic market, Nissan saw its sales declining 2.3 per cent to 1,074,936 units in 1985. Of greater concern for the company, its Japanese market share fell close to a full percentage point to 26.8 per cent. In contrast, industry leader Toyota improved its overall standing.

Compared to the relatively horizontal Honda organisation, Nissan has a traditional vertical organisation. The vertical organisation needs to pay much attention towards subcontractors and has to control the traffic between them.

Nissan and Globalisation[13]

Nissan's globalisation plan was initiated by Takashi Ishihara, the Chairman of Nissan in 1980. Since then, Nissan has proved many times that globalisation represents a long-term commitment to the market. It serves and entails localised integration of design engineering, manufacturing, sales, finance, service and other essential functions. Nissan management regards localisation as a five-step process.

> First, local production is created and increased, second; local content is raised through expanded use of locally sourced parts and components; third, local R&D

Table 7.2   Japanese car MNEs' affiliates in the UK

Plant	Honda	Nissan
Type of entry	JV	Sole entry
Established	1979 with Rover1985	1984
Equity share	Japanese company 80% Rover 20%	Japanese company 100%
Location	Swindon	Tyne and Wear
Products	Passenger cars and engine	Passenger cars and engine
Sale	1992	1986
Production per year	200,000 cars	100,000 cars
Employee	2230	4038
Japanese staff	80	28
Trade union	None	AEU
Total investment	$370 million	£1.25 billion

Source: Author derived from company reports and various newspapers.

capabilities are strengthened; fourth, localisation in management functions takes place; fifth, the decision-making process is also localised.[14]

Compared to that of Honda's, the globalisation project of Nissan is at a rather practical stage. While Honda reacted to the BL proposal, Nissan pro-actively moved to occupy 'fortress Europe' by using the Japanese government's negotiating position. Nissan's international strategy was based on future market share. The world's demand for consumer cars was not expected to keep the growth trends of the 1970s and the early 1980s. The annual demand at the mid-1980s was for about 40 million cars, but Nissan forecasted that by the start of the 1990s, it would only have risen to 50 million. That meant, the annual growth of the car market, during the 1990s would be under 2 per cent, compared with the average yearly rise of 3.9 per cent throughout the 1970s. Considering the car exports of developing countries such as Korea, and Malaysia, the developed countries would probably have growth rates of well under 1.7–1.8 per cent or show an actual drop in demand, with the Japanese and East European manufacturers likely to benefit from any subsequent recovery at the expense, in the EU, of the local car manufacturers.

Until the mid-1980s, the Japanese car industries such as Toyota, Nissan and Honda exported over 50 per cent of their production to the US and the EU. It was a quite different picture of that of the US car manufacturers such

Table 7.3   Nissan's globalisation strategy

Stage 1   Increase local production levels and increase jobs
     Nissan Motor Manufacturing Co. Ltd at Australia
     Nissan Mexican SA de CV
     Nissan Motor Iberica SA
     Nissan Motor Manufacturing Ltd at UK
     Nissan Motor Manufacturing Corporation at USA

Stage 2   Raise local content levels at manufacturing operations

Stage 3   Strengthen local R&D functions
     Nissan R&D Inc.
     Nissan Design International Inc.
     Arizona Test Centre Inc.
     Nissan European Technology Centre Ltd.
     Nissan European Technology Centre NV at Brussels
     Nissan Motor Iberica SA

Stage 4   Localise management of subsidiaries
     Ian Gibson at UK
     Thomas D. Mignanelli at USA corporation
     Ivan A. Deveson at Australia
     Juan Echevarria at Spain
     Jerry L. Benefield at USA manufacturing corporation

Stage 5   Localise decision-making on important matters
     Nissan Europe NV
     Nissan North America Inc.

Source: Nissan Motor Information.

as Opel in West Germany, Ford and Vauxhall in the UK. Up until the mid-1970s, the Japanese share of the total European car market was comparatively small, but the situation changed dramatically. At the same time, the growing dumping accusations constricted Japanese car market penetration into Europe. The decision-making about the Nissan investment project towards the EU coincided with dumping accusations from EU Committee.

In 1980 Japanese cars took more than 10 per cent of the total market, a 20 per cent rise over the previous year. With the exception of specially restricted countries such as Spain, France and Italy, sales of Japanese cars had sprung up throughout Europe. Some countries which did not have their own car industries, were finding about 20 per cent or 30 per cent of their car markets taken by Japanese imports. If this penetration had happened in the context of a continued growth in general demand, it would not have been quite so serious. However the increase in Japanese car sales had coincided with a recession in the European car market. Japanese car makers, hence, were suddenly taking a much larger proportion of a market hit by a period of contraction. Then, Japanese exports to Europe were meeting growing resistance.

The strengthened market share of Toyota, and the high rate of import of Honda 'City' cars from US, squeezed Nissan's position in the domestic Japanese market from top to bottom. Within the volume car market, imported cars and Toyota were favoured. Despite Nissan's effort in the field of small cars, the 'March' model failed to reach its target, owing to the Honda 'City' and Mitsubishi 'Mirage'. Also, Nissan's US market share fell behind that of Toyota and Honda. For the European market, production outside Japan was the inevitable solution. Since then, Nissan's strategy was to step up local production in the EU markets. It was the final approach to the third and last market within this century. From the point of view of Nissan's management strategy, they should have been seeking a stable consumer supply company within the EU with substantial support from the Japanese mother company and *keireitsu*. Nissan vice-president Okuma said that 'Nissan's strategy is to step up local production in the US and European market'.[15]

Their first step was the joint venture with Alfa Romeo. It was a 50/50 contract, and called ARNA. It built a body assembly plant near Naples and started building bodies-in-white of a version of the Nissan 'Cherry'. The completed bodies were taken to the nearby Alfasud plant in Pomigliano where they were mated with Alfa Romeo engines and all the innards. Only the body panels were from Japan, and it sold an Alfa Romeo version in Italy, and a Nissan-badged version in the UK and Austria. Compared to the Honda-Rover collaboration, there were no technical or market penetrating innovations. During this joint venture, Nissan had faced criticism from Japanese components industries.

The second option of globalisation was a portfolio investment in Spain. In January 1980, Nissan announced that it had acquired 36 per cent of Motor Iberica, Spain's biggest commercial vehicle manufacturer, and was to participate in the management of the Spanish motor industry. Early in 1982, Nissan increased its share holding to 54.6 per cent. This investment had several attractions for Nissan. Spain was due to join the EEC (now EU), so there was the prospect of a foothold inside the Common Market. From a technical viewpoint, Nissan would benefit from Motor Iberica's truck building experience. Japanese trucks are designed for comparatively short journeys, because of their land conditions. So Nissan stood to gain from Motor Iberica's knowhow in long-distance truck design, both technically and in such basic areas as driver comfort and sleeping accommodation. In return, Motor Iberica would benefit from Nissan's technology and thereby become more competitive when Spain entered the EU.

The other project of Nissan's outward investment was the medium-scale venture with Volkswagen (VW) in February 1984. With Volkswagen, Nissan was to produce the Santana, a new model in the VW Passat range. It would be made in Japan, for sale through Nissan's own dealer network in Japan and for export to South East Asia. The plan was attacked by other European makers and US car makers who found it too difficult to penetrate Japanese market. Nissan and VW's collaboration, however, was a good experiences for Nissan's global management. It was quite different from that of the Honda and Rover collaboration, because the Honda project aimed at the penetration of the EU market using weakened UK car manufacturers, and at the unfamiliar technological area of the Diesel engine system. However Nissan's partner was bigger than that of Honda. Moreover Nissan's capability and knowledge of the car manufacturing industry within the EU was much less than that of VW. In market share, in contrast with VW's market share, Rover's share of the Japanese market was small enough to be neglected from Honda's management viewpoint. If Nissan wanted to set up a joint venture with VW, Nissan had to think about the consequences of the sale of VW cars in the home market using the Nissan dealer system. This would injure Nissan in its domestic market.

Nissan started the largest investment in the US in spring 1983. The company invested US$ 750 million in Smyrna, Tennessee, to build trucks, and Nissan thus started an aggressive penetration of the American market.

Nissan US and Nissan UK greenfield investments were the core of Nissan's globalisation programme. Despite financial difficulties, Nissan put all their effort into these two companies. It was a real cars war between first rank car makers, such as Toyota, Ford and GM, and the runner-up group. Nissan's main objective was to compete with GM outside the US, then to move into the US after its victory. The best place to compete with GM was the UK.[16]

The Decision to Manufacture in the UK

Nissan's first approach to the UK was an agreement to produce the Austin A40 Somerset and later Austin A50 Cambridge cars in Japan under licence between 1952 and 1959. 'Austin was chosen as a partner in this effort because of the British company's stability and long history of technological excellence.'[17] It was ironical that the eclipse of British car industries followed the dramatic rise of the Japanese car industry to world prominence.

Nissan's main project for the EU was to find a proper car production site to compete with the US makers, especially General Motors (GM).[18] Direct competition with GM in the consumer market was expected to be advantageous to Nissan's position. Learning from the contest would decrease the gap between GM and Nissan. There were two reason why Nissan chose GM as a competitor. Because of the conservative marketing habits of the Japanese domestic market, Nissan never expected to catch up its counterpart Toyota. While Toyota dominated in the domestic market, Nissan hoped to increase its international market share. On this strategy, GM had quite a similar model range to that of Nissan. On the other hand, GM has different management methods from Ford's. GM, if they found it necessary, adopted the Japanese system. Mr Takashi Ishihara, president of Nissan emphasised that 'GM had learned truck manufacturing skills from Isuzu, and then they made a one-ton truck called S10, which is outselling Japanese trucks in the US market. I think this case illustrates GM's formidable strengths'.[19]

The same reasoning applied to the choice of competitor in Europe. Nissan's intention to build a passenger car model in the Europe was also focused on GM: a sort of *kamikaze* strategy. If this assumption applied, there were two countries to choose from for Nissan's European manufacturing location. One of the feared points about Japanese car makers' approach to Germany was its high rate of penetration of the Japanese market. The strength of German trade unions power and its restrictive social policy were less of an objection, though they were important factors from the investor's viewpoint. To get a better competitive environment in which to compete with GM, Nissan needed a country with as important a role in the politics of the EU as Germany had, but with an easier competitive environment in the car industry. At the same time, they had to think about the each EU country's car export rate to Japan, for the sake of their own market protection. The host country's inward investment policy was the final stage of their consideration.

The UK came out ahead because of its centrally-assisted local government development strategy, its more attractive incentive policy for inward investment, at that time the expectation of a long-standing Conservative government, the same standing in the EU as France and Germany, and, most of all, a labour force with the longest experience of car manufacturing. Nissan's managers also had a high opinion of the Thatcher government's efforts to restore the

UK economy to health. There were three reasons for the Nissan managers' decision. First, the proportion of locally produced components that the cars made in the projected UK plant would have to reach a certain level. Second, the level of support which Nissan would be able to get from the UK government in grants and industrial subsidies would be attractive. Lastly, industrial relations problems had been solved by the other Japanese industries' successful relations with their employees. After the project established 1982, Nissan's EU project was fulfilled by the announcement of its UK plant in April 1984.

Table 7.4   Nissan in UK: historical approach

Jan. 1980	Nissan acquired equity interest in Spanish vehicle manufacturers, Motor Iberica SA
March 1982	Nissan became the major shareholder in Motor Iberica, Spain
Jan. 1983	Motor Iberica began production of the Patrol
May 1983	Nissan Motor Parts Centre (Europe) BV established in the Netherlands
Feb. 1984	Nissan and HM government signed an agreement to build a car plant in the UK
March 1984	Location of the site for plant announced
April 1984	Nissan Motor Manufacturing (UK) Ltd established
Nov. 1984	Foundation stone laying ceremony took place. Construction work began
April 1985	Single union agreement reached with the Amalgamated Engineering Union (AEU). First group of 22 supervisors joined the company
Dec. 1985	Constructors handed over the completed factory building to Nissan. Project completed within target of 62 weeks
July 1986	First Nissan Bluebird for commercial sale produced at Sunderland
Sept. 1986	Official opening ceremony took place. Nissan announced plans to accelerate the UK manufacturing programme by increasing local content to 60% by 1988 and 80% by 1991, when annual production was projected to be 100,000 units. The first car produced at the plant presented to HRH the Prince of Wales
Jan. 1987	Five-door version of Bluebird introduced to Sunderland's production
Feb. 1987	Sunderland-produced Bluebirds (21 variants) become sole source of supply to UK market
May 1987	Annual production increased to 29,000 Bluebirds. Recruitment plans for 300 jobs brought forward by one year

Nov. 1987	Employment reached 1,100 at the Sunderland plant. Nightshift introduced (8 months ahead of schedule)
Dec. 1987	Nissan announced a further £216 million investment for the Sunderland plant, bringing total investment to £610 million. Plans announced to produce 100,000 Micra-class cars a year
Jan. 1988	60% European content achieved
March 1988	Engine plant and plastic injection moulding facility installed. Britain chosen as location for Nissan's European Technology Centre
May 1988	Employment at the Sunderland plant reached 1,300
Sept. 1988	Computer Aided Design (CAD) network link-up completed between development and production centres in Japan, Europe and the US. Exports began of left-hand drive cars to nine European markets
Feb. 1989	100,000 Nissan Bluebirds completed
June 1989	Ian Gibson appointed managing director and chief executive
May 1990	Production of Nissan Primera began; Bluebird ended
March 1991	Annual production target raised from 100,000 to 120,000
April 1991	Sunderland operations awarded British manufacturers status by SMMT
May 1991	100,000 Primeras completed
July 1991	Production began for Eastern Europe (Hungary, Poland, Romania, Czechoslovakia, Yugoslavia)
Aug. 1991	First shipment of Nissan Primeras to the Far East
Sept. 1991	Recruitment drive began for 1,000 new staff
Jan. 1992	Production target raised to 175,000. Nissan announced a further £200 million investment, raising total investment to £900 million the largest single Japanese inward investment in Europe
March 1992	Nissan announced that Sunderland-built engines will power Nissan Serena
April 1992	Five thousand tonne automatic transfer press installed. Nissan received Queen's Award for Export Achievement. Employment reached 4,000.
May 1992	Nissan announced the Sunderland plant achieved first profit of £18.4 million in 1991
Aug. 1992	Production of Nissan Micra began
Oct. 1992	500,000 vehicles completed
Nov. 1992	Nissan Micra voted European Car of the Year 1993
Jan. 1993	Nissan Micra launched in the UK
April 1993	Nissan received second successive Queen's Award for Export Achievement
June 1993	Nissan presented with RSA Environmental Award for its 'excellence of environmental management' for the production of the Micra

Oct. 1993	Additional £26 million investment announced for the Sunderland plant
Dec. 1993	NMUK received the 1993 Northern Business Exporter of the Year Award
Jan. 1994	Sunderland plant named Britain's biggest car exporter in 1993, when 182,194 Primeras and Micra were exported to 36 world markets
April 1994	Nissan received a third successive Queen's Award for Export Achievement. Nissan adopted NCH Action For Children as its charity partner
May 1994	Sunderland plant announced sponsorship of the Nissan Great North Bike Ride
June 1994	Nissan awarded a Gold Award for excellence in occupational health and safety by the Royal Society for the Prevention of Accidents (RoSPA)
Nov. 1994	Nissan celebrated its tenth year of manufacturing in Sunderland
Jan. 1995	One millionth vehicle produced
April 1995	Nissan began exporting Micra to Australia
July 1995	One millionth engine completed
Sept. 1995	Additional £250 million investment increased commitment in the UK to £1.25 billion

Source: Derived by the author on the basis of original research.

One of the main influencing factors for location in the UK was the successful market penetration of Nissan cars in the UK during the 1970s and 1980s. The UK was Nissan's largest single consumer market outside Japan and the US. A stable market share is one of the main Japanese management objectives for FDI. It has worked for the other Japanese manufacturing sectors, such as electronic goods, and office equipment.

> Continued trade restrictions in Europe had severely restricted the growth in sales of Nissan vehicles and it had become commercially viable to establish manufacturing facilities within the EEC. Britain, as Nissan's largest market in Europe, was the obvious choice.[20]

On 1 February 1984, Mr Takashi Ishihara and Norman Tebbit of the DTI signed a memorandum about a two-stage investment plan. In the first stage Nissan was to build a pilot plant, employ 400–500 employees, and assemble 24,000 cars a year. In the second stage, expected in 1986, it was to go into manufacturing 100,000 cars a year with the initial local content of 60 per cent, eventually 80 per cent, some of which would be exported to other EU countries. During the second stage, employment would reach 2,700 and there would be an grant from the British government of about 10 per cent of the total investment amount, which was estimated at £35 million.

> There is no denying that Thatcher has been a great influence behind this project. She thought Nissan would be a barometer of further Japanese investment in the UK. The government grant was bigger than we expected however there was no objection about this. The real concern of the British government was how to save component industries in the UK.[21]

The Conservative government needed to have an initiative to address the labour and industrial issue, which were expected to be the main issue for next General Election. When Mrs Thatcher heard of the Nissan project, she thought of employment first. She said that:

> On this occasion, my main interest was to press for Nissan to finalise its decision to invest in Britain, which I hoped would create thousands of jobs. Understandably, Mr. Yasuhiro Nakasone's line was that this was a decision for the company. I should add here that it had been reported in the Britain press that Nissan would not have gone ahead with their investment had Labour been elected. This was publicly denied by the company, but it was probably true.[22]

Nevertheless Nissan took far longer than expected to reach a decision. There was three reason for this. The first was the proportion of locally produced components that the cars made in the projected the UK plant would have to contain. From the Thatcher government's position, the strengthening of British component industries by 'Japanisation' was a vital consideration when attracting inward investment from Japanese car makers. It was not only a UK problem, since other EU countries, especially France and Italy, were taking a keen interest in the extent to which these cars would be truly European products.

It was explained by Thatcher herself that:

> I was convinced that the Nissan project made as much sense for Japan as it did for us. By exporting investment to Britain they would undercut protectionist pressure against them, bring in income for years ahead as well, of course, as providing incomes and jobs in the recipient country.[23]

And she did her best to keep this promise after Nissan began its production, which was labelled 'Made in Britain'.

The 'Made in Britain' label impressed Japanese businessmen. The Toyota plan in the UK was mainly affected by the Thatcher government's promise to Nissan. The Thatcher government really did well for inward investment policy.[24]

The second is the level of support Nissan would be able to get from the UK government in grants and industrial subsidies. The UK system had two channels for support. The Invest in Britain Bureau (IBB) gave 'Selective Financial Assistance' and the 'Regional Development Grant' and 'Selective Regional Assistance' (SRA) was distributed by local government. The total grant from the UK side was about 22 per cent of the capital cost of the investment.[25] There was, however, a gap between the Nissan account, which reported a 10 per cent grant after the meeting with Lord Tebbit, and the real grant. If there was only a 10 per cent grant from central government, the rest had to have been made up by local government. According to the author's survey, Nissan reported that there was a high level of assistance from central government for their regional decision-making in the UK. The Regional Development Grant and SRA had financially supported Nissan to about £30 million in total. However, whatever the problems which local government had, was there was no communication with the central government.

As far as inward FDI projects are concerned, we had no right to decide. We were just informed that we should show our manufacturing sites to businessmen from outside Europe. Our task was started when they finished their opening ceremony on the manufacturing site.[26]

One of the more interesting points about Nissan UK's source of finance was the percentage share from the host country. Considering Nissan's difficulties during the early 1980s, British government overcommitted on an inward investment. The overpowered prime minister-led Nissan project was not managed by discussion within the Cabinet or with local government. More importantly, government expenditure on trade, industry and energy had doubled in real terms (at 1989–90 prices), from £5.5 billion in 1978–79 to £11 billion in 1982–83, before falling again by 40 per cent to £6.6 billion in 1989–90, one-fifth higher at the outset.

We had some problems during the Nissan project. It was our first proactive policy in government. I think we had not enough time to design our financial support toward Nissan, which was done mainly by a few cabinet staff.[27]

When the Prime Minister engaged in the details of the investment plan, it usually led to a decision overshadowed by political reasoning rather than a sound industrial strategy.

Table 7.5   Prime ministers judged as being most influential in economic matters (%)

Britain	98
France	73
Ireland	61
Germany	29
Italy	27

Source: Blondel, J. et al. (1993), *Governing Together*, p. 212.

The last and to Nissan the most worrying problem was that of industrial relations, because car manufacturing is heavily dependent on good continuous production methods. The reputation of Japanese cars comes from the good relationship between the manager group and employees on the shop floor. Labour problems would be fatally damaging for the Japanese management techniques which are known as Just-In-Time (JIT), Total Quality (TQ) and the *kanban* system. Vice-president Okuma said about this that:

> ... it might be take some time, but if Nissan could get its way of thinking understood, and could create the sort of atmosphere conducive to good industrial relations, the result would be a smooth-running, contented organisation.[28]

But, they did not have any time to lose. Nissan started from scratch with no traditions of trade union organisation or established shopfloor custom and practice, and had hence been able to experiment from the beginning with a system of its choosing.

When the three troubles were solved, Nissan's thinking about making cars in the UK was straightforward. Nissan needed to sell its products in Europe. Its direct exports to the industrialised countries could not go on growing. Protectionist restrictions could only get worse. A car plant of its own, on the spot in Europe, would put Nissan securely inside Europe ahead of its Japanese rivals, out of danger from import barriers, and able to match its European competitors on an equal footing. The EU recession had tightened its grip since Nissan began its feasibility study early 1981.[29] Fewer Europeans had been buying cars. There was no point in Nissan committing itself to a huge UK plant when demand was falling. On the contrary, the decline in the market had made it easier for the time being for Nissan to meet demand with imports from Japan, which would not be possible in a period of expanding consumption. The lack of sales in Europe was illustrated by the fact that in autumn 1982, Fiat, British Leyland (BL), VW, and German Ford all resorted to short time working, layoffs or temporary production shut downs. And overcapacity continued, with total production capacity exceeding the overall 1981 vehicles sales figure, of over 11 million, by upwards of 10 per cent. In these circumstances the European motor companies had become increasingly antipathetic to a large healthy rival appearing on the scene.

However, there were so many troubles in the EU market that there were many chances to get in. Nissan tried to experiment with this theory in the UK market. Recession in the UK meant unemployment, and therefore a Nissan plant could expect an extremely warm welcome, plenty of financial incentives and an enthusiastic labour force. More importantly, the view of the more cautious members of Nissan's board was that it was wise to hold back at least until demand improved. Accordingly it was to be expected that the overcoming of the recession, and a resulting recovery in the EU markets, should put Nissan in a more optimistic frame of mind about its UK project.

The attractions of a major investment inside the EC – potentially the world's single biggest car markets with 320 million people – immune from trade barriers, thus became compelling: making the vehicles close to the customers would reduce transport costs; a cheap and large supply of labour was available, especially in the depressed regions; and government development grants would diminish the initial costs of setting up a major production operation by up to one-third. This is what the UK had to offer, backed up by government policies against organised labour which were the harshest in Western Europe.[30]

Investment overseas is only attractive if it makes a profit, and Nissan was concerned about how long that might take. It anticipated it being from seven to ten years, assuming that everything else went smoothly such as parts supply arrangements, adequate consumer demand, labour relations both in the factory and nationwide, unrestricted access to other EU market. Nissan had no illusions about the UK plant being a foolproof way to get rich quick. At the first stage the question of profit, and the effects of the recession on overall EU market demand, were cardinal factors in Nissan deferring its decision.

In April 1985, a single union agreement was reached with the Amalgamated Engineering Union (AEU). The first group of 22 Supervisors joined the company. The quality of the Sunderland car was proved in December 1986 when the Nissan Internal Audit Vehicle Evaluation system on first six months' production proved that Bluebirds produced in Sunderland matched the quality level of Japanese-produced vehicles. The relation between the Nissan and sub-automotive industry symbolised the announcement in September 1986 that the local content would rise to 60 per cent by 1988 which was two years earlier than originally expected and 80 per cent by 1991 when annual production was projected to be 100,000 units.

Surprisingly, in May 1992, Nissan announced that its Sunderland plant had achieved its first profit of £18.4 million in 1991 and it exceeded its target for its first stage project. Industrial and labour relations were easier. In connection with the EU, which was expected to be the main market, it happened that in November 1992 after the commencement of the SEM, the Nissan Micra was voted '*European Car of the Year 1993*'. This victorious market penetration was widely supported by Japanese business, and it induced Toyota to build its plant in the UK. The potentially fatal blockade applied to the Nissan Bluebird by the French and Italian governments, was dealt with successfully by the British government's efforts.

> We are successful in the EU because we had unexpectedly high grants from the British government at the initial stage, we established our company out of the reach of the trade unions, which cracked down on trade unions power in the Sunderland plant, and we gathered all the components industries which came from Japan, under the same umbrella. Most of all, Nissan UK succeeded because Nissan could over-run Honda in the EU market, which is one of the difficulties we have faced in the US market.[31]

Has successful market penetration strengthened the competitiveness of the UK component industries? Since the BMW take-over of Rover, British car component industries have been put under severe competition to find new car assembly plants as customers. There is the expectation of Japanese car assembly companies that they will help to promote relations with British component industries, and this is the real hope of British government. Successive stages of inward FDI from first-tier and second-tier industries, and the close relations between local components makers and Japanese assemblers in UK have shown that the impact of inward FDI on local component industries was lower and weaker than expected.

There are two main elements in the explanation. The first is that without some achieved level of local production, about 1 million units, there is no profit in establishing affiliates in the UK. According to Usui Kokusai Sangyo Kaisha Ltd.[32] which started their business in the UK in 1995,

> We faced external and internal pressure. The external pressure is the relation between assembler and its tier company. The car assemblers in the EU member states have been faced with the difficulty of matching owners requirements. Despite their efforts to increase quality and performance, there are increasing difficulties in working together. After experimental periods, assemblers tried to get a further investment from their first and second tiers. Despite the assemblers' inward investment policy, we can not have any confidence to invest. It is our internal problem.[33]

Since the Nissan UK project, the increasing rate of local suppliers in UK has coincided with the increasing rate of FDI investment in the UK. There are about 45 local suppliers to Nissan in UK, totalling 124 component makers in 1996. Further investment in UK has shown clear differences. The successive phases of investment in component industries in the UK were supported by capital from their partner firms. Compared to the technology-intensive indigenous companies, these industries gathered under the umbrella of the assembler company. *This trend weakened the effort to increase British manufacturing competitiveness in car manufacturing sector*. The collapse of small and less competitive components industries in the West Midlands caused successive closures in the British components industries. As Britain failed to protect her nationalised makers during the 1980s, she is likely to fail again in connection with the components sector. Moreover, is there a revival in the local economy from supporting Nissan UK? Is there any Japanese impact in the local area, which is what the British government really expected? Has the Japanisation of the local economy been inspired other areas' component industries?

The Thatcher government's political reason for inward investment aimed to save local economies through the increasing competitiveness of component industries. If there were successful trading in the UK by Nissan, there ought to be a successful local impact in Tyne and Wear. Without regional development, the Thatcher government was shown to have failed in its whole industrial policy. This is discussed in the next section.

Nissan and Regional Economic Development

Between 1981 and 1984, despite some recovery of service sector employment, manufacturing employment in Tyne and Wear continued to shrink rapidly. At this time, Tyne and Wear's manufacturing employment declined by no less than 23 per cent compared with a drop of 20 per cent in the preceding three years from 1978 to 1981, which had been the worst years of the recession. The long-term decline of Tyne and Wear traditional industries continued and accelerated. Mining all but disappeared while shipbuilding saw massive job losses (employment fell from 21,000 in 1978 to about 4,000 in 1987), and heavy engineering struggled to win orders and be competitive.

Also from the central government's viewpoint, the productivity gap between local and national performance has widened. In 1979, productivity in Tyne and Wear's manufacturing industry was 5 per cent below the UK average. However by 1985 it was 15 per cent below the UK average; also, profitability was falling and the only one comfortable thing was the recovery in net investment. The gap between the level of industrialisation in South and North widened during the first term of the Thatcher government. It created political risks for central government. The regional policy and the competitiveness of component industries were the main motives for inward investment in the UK.

The notion that the North has an 'employment culture', with a particular emphasis on public sector employment, rather than an 'enterprise culture', is a common one. The Thatcher government tried many positive policies towards the equalisation of regional performance: RSA, the Enterprise Allowance Scheme, and more positively, strong guidance of local economies using the distribution of inward FDI according to central government policies.

Nissan and the Economy of Tyne and Wear

In February 1984, Nissan signed an agreement with the British government to build a car factory in the UK, and one month later the choice of location of Tyne and Wear was made. There was severe competition between regional development agencies and local governments for the projects. The three principal competing sites were Deeside, Humberside and Tyne and Wear, all outside the traditional British car manufacturing area.

In 1983/84, which was the year of the announcement of the Nissan UK Project by Nissan HQ and the UK government, Tyne and Wear area received around £18.4 million regional policy assistance and by 1985/86 this had fallen to £13.9 million. The timing of the Nissan project, which was politically and economically well designed, was welcomed by UK central and local government. One of difficulties for the Nissan UK project was its financial support. Mr Takashi Ishihara's positive globalisation policy was welcomed by MITI and the British government. According to the interview:

> As far as financial support was concerned, there were more grants from UK government, because of the location of the investment. The location was not a main issue for the management of Nissan, except that they did not want to locate in the West Midlands or the West of England where there was an established car and component industry labour force. When they heard about Northern England, the first emerging negotiation between Nissan and UK government was about how they would employ staff and deal with local trade unions in Nissan.[34]

The reality of Tyne and Wear before the Nissan project was an example of the de-industrialising areas of the Britain.

> Tyne and Wear's manufacturing industry is predominantly externally-owned and externally-controlled. Most of the larger manufacturing establishment in the area are branch plants of national and MNEs with headquarters elsewhere – principally in London. The experience of recent years does suggest that this is a source of weakness. Branch plants are often poorly integrated into the local economy in terms of their inputs and outputs and may be perceived as expendable outputs.[35]

This industrial position made local government very eager to establish an inward investment policy. Both central and local government had been developing and implementing a variety of new policies since the late 1970s. The long-standing central government policy was a regional policy. In the 1980s, Tyne and Wear received regional policy aid, because of its high level of unemployment. The whole Tyne and Wear district had Development Area Status and companies undertaking investment were been able to apply to the DTI for financial subsidies in the form of Regional Development Grant (which was abolished in 1988) and Regional Selective Assistance (RSA) which had a strong emphasis on support for large-scale investment projects and capital-intensive manufacturing industries.

On the local side, inward investment was encouraged by the North of England Development Council, a region-wide promotional organisation financed by central and local government. However, the bulk of local authority economic development expenditure in Tyne and Wear, which was expenditure funded from the Urban Programme and the EU, was largely focused on help for new and small businesses.

> Local authority economic development policies in Tyne and Wear are generally conventional and non-controversial in comparison with the more radical and

interventionist policies of authorities like the old Greater London Council and Sheffield City Council.[36]

As far as any inward FDI policy in local areas was concerned, there was no opportunity for local government to intervene in negotiations between central government and overseas investors.

> Inward FDI policy, during the Thatcher government was designed by DTI and IBB. We had Committees to decide economic projects. They consisted of several ministers and bureaucrats. When we reached the final decision stage, it was passed to a Treasury minister. He scanned it for value-for-money; if he sent it for approval to the Prime Minister, and approval was given, then the project was started by IBB and other parts of government. I don't think there is any room for local government's intervention. Local government's position for inward policy is to make a good environment, such as an education system, leisure facilities, especially golf courses.[37]

Nissan's choice of Tyne and Wear in preference to other manufacturing areas was quite unexpected. When they made the decision to locate in the North of England they hoped to escape traditional union power and hostile industrial action.

> When Nissan made their mind up in the UK, they started to use UK government policy for their benefit. They avoided the traditional car manufacturing areas, such as the West Midlands, they demanded a single union, if there was to be a union in their company, and they wanted a large manufacturing site. The relatively huge site allowed Nissan to put their first-tier component suppliers within the same manufacturing line. And it expected to set up a fully continuous process manufacturing system. This is one of the typical manufacturing systems in Nissan.[38]

The abolition of discrimination between white collar workers and shop floor workers in the company, and single union agreements, were quite unusual things in the British manufacturing sector. According to Nick Tiratsoo:

> one of main factors in the decline of the manufacturing sector in the UK was its discrimination. The highly educated managers took the part of an aristocracy in the shop floor, whereas workers were treated as helots. The gap between manager and shop stewards was the gap between Britain and France. The gap has been too large to ignore.[39]

Nissan's industrial strategy toward Tyne and Wear was quite similar to Honda's behaviour in Swindon. They believed in treating all their employees as first class citizens, with all receiving the same basic conditions of employment. The MILAN report commented on Nissan's relations with the trade unions that:

> The company has an excellent relationship with the AEEU, and has had so since the start of production (*i.e.* AEU) in 1985–1986. This is a single union agreement … Union membership is now in excess of 40 per cent, and is growing steadily. Nissan's Managing Director Ian Gibson positively invites employees to join the trade unions, and the local district secretary visits every Monday at new employee induction to explain the advantages of the union. Nissan does not negotiate with the union, however, but with a Company Council. On this sit directly elected representatives of the workforce, who may or may not be union members. The single union agreement is positively supported as being in 'all our interests'.[40]

Also, a *Guardian* survey showed that:

> The Nissan car factory in Sunderland is an indication of a new style of industrial relations that has been imported from Japan in recent years. The company, which has Japanese directors but only British workers on the factory floor has attempted to avoid an 'us and them' attitude which is common in manufacturing. There is no tradition of division between Nissan management and workers. Everyone uses the same car park and canteen, has the same sickness scheme and perks. There is only one union allowed in the plant – the Amalgamated Engineering Union (AEU), which represents about 35 per cent of the staff. Workers elect representatives to a Company Council to deal with their problems.[41]

The Japanisation was one of the main contributions from Nissan UK.

Nissan's investment decision introduced a new focus to the Tyne and Wear economy, that of car components. Over 40 per cent of Japanese component manufacturers locating a production facility in the UK have chosen join the 120 companies in the North which supply the car industry. Joint ventures, also, are one of the particular business forms in the North area, such as that of Ikeda Hoover and Marley Kanto producing car seats and injection moulded components. Since the Nissan decision in 1984, 28 Japanese companies had chosen to settle in the Northeast by 1992. Of these 10 were car related and the Northeast has seen the largest concentration of Japanese engineering investment in Europe. It was calculated that Japanese investment had created some 9,000 jobs in this area.

Table 7.6   List of Japanese companies in Tyne and Wear area

Name	Activity	Parent company
Calsonic (UK)	Exhaust systems and catalytic converters	Calsonic Japan
Freudenberg Technical Products	Components	*
Hashimoto Ltd (EHQ)	Components	*
Ikeda Hoover Ltd	Car seats and interior trim	Ikeda Hoover
Marley Kansei Ltd	Interior trim components	*
Mi-King Ltd.	Steel stockholding	–
Nissan Trading UK	Trading components	*
Nissan Yamato Engineering Ltd.	Presswork and sub-assembly for motor industry	*
SMC Pneumatics (UK) Ltd	Pneumatic for the automotive industry	*
SP Tyres (UK) Ltd.	Car radial tyres	*

Notes

*   Nissan *keiretsu*
–   Own maker

Source: Tyne and Wear economic paper (mimeo).

One of the differences between Tyne and Wear on the one hand and Swindon on the other is the presence of foreign component industries. There is increasing competition between Japanese second and third tier and other British and European makers in Tyne and Wear. Japanese component industries still dominated the supply chain. Moreover, there has not yet been full open competition between first or second tier Japanese component industries and other European makers, nor could there be because of the habits of Japanese car manufacturers.

The details were that five years after the original decision in which Nissan committed to 3,600 direct jobs, with over £600 million of investment, and 200,000 cars per year, there are 120 suppliers, 97 of which are based in the UK and 14 of these are located in the North East. The local content level has nevertheless reached only 16 per cent instead of the 70 per cent target; this can be compared with the 15 per cent local content achieved by Honda in the US market. Despite further investment in Tyne and Wear, the gap between

Table 7.7   The foreign car component industries in Tyne and Wear

Name	Country	Activity
AE Goetze Ltd	Germany	Piston ring and CI rotor blades
ARD Components Ltd	–	Electrical components
Bundy (Telford) Ltd	–	Prefabricated brake pipes
David Brown Radicon Ltd	–	Gear speed reduction units
Eaton Transmissions UK Ltd		Transmissions, synchronisers parts
Kigass Engineering		Autoparts, air vents
Lucas SEI	UK	Wiring harnesses
Perlos Ltd	Finland	Precision injection moulded plastic components
Pirelli Ltd	Italy	Tyre manufacture
R-Tek Ltd	France	Car dashboard moulding
Sommer Masland Ltd	France	Components
Steels Engineering	Germany	Industrial engineering
Valeo Security Systems	Germany	Automobile security locks
Wacker (GB) Ltd		Industrial engineering
TRW Valves Automotive Systems Ltd	US	Automotive valves
TRW Transportation Electronics Ltd	US	Electronic components for vehicle sector

Source: Tyne and Wear Economic Paper (mimeo).

Japanese makers and other UK or European makers **has widened. More** importantly, the level of satisfaction about UK originated components supplied to the Nissan assembly plant has not yet reached the required standard. This is one good reason for increasing components import from the US, or Japan.

Regional Economic Development: Nissan and Honda Compared

The arrival of Nissan has also led to the creation of a totally new Japanese-style support environment, the first of its kind in the EU. Over 60 per cent of Nissan's European components suppliers are UK based. Many international investors such as Ikeda Hoover, Calsonic and Reydel, have chosen to locate a major production facility in the North East, in order to serve the EU market on their doorstep. Nissan's effect on the local economy was summarised by Mr Balls, the Chief Executive of Tyne and Wear Development Corporation.

Table 7.8   The breakdown of component export from Japan to EU

Country	1990 (million yen)	Compared with same period in previous year (%)
UK	104,340	106.00
France	23,450	118.70
Germany	70,234	114.40
Italy	10,778	129.30
Others	231,576	118.60

Source: JETRO (1992) *Your Market in Japan* (mimeo)

The decision by Nissan to establish its European car manufacturing facility in the Northeast has added a new dimension to our economy. Nissan's experience has been given concrete expression in expansion plans which have exceeded expectations and in the creation of an automotive components sector in the North East, made up of both international investors and local firms who have responded to the new market opportunity.[42]

There is a clear difference between greenfield investment and joint venture. Honda, of course, compared to Nissan, is a much smaller car manufacturer in Japan. Moreover, they are not a member of *keiretsu*. Hence a successive inward FDI policy from Japanese components industries which were in close relations with Honda, was not achieved as it was by Nissan in Tyne and Wear.

In the North East of England they describe the Nissan effect by which the company has acted as a magnet for other non-motor investment into the area simply by virtue of its presence, and it is likely that Honda will have a similar effect on Swindon. It has played a vital role in helping to maintain the number of manufacturing jobs in Swindon at a time when these have been failing both nationally and regionally.[43]

Honda's approach at Swindon was rather simple.

At the initial stage, Honda did not think about further investment in Swindon, because they mainly assembled the imported parts in this area. Despite technology exchange between Rover and Honda, Honda did not need any parts manufacturing company in Swindon, except engine plants. Frankly speaking, Honda in Swindon was a warehouse rather than manufacturing centre.[44]

Each company's overall objectives were quite similar. According to the Economic Section report for Swindon,

> The experience from Nissan indicates an impact in the following areas:
>
> 1. the location of suppliers and component manufacturers
> 2. other engineering and manufacturing organisation in the local economy, and local training practice.[45]

Despite better economic conditions than Swindon, Tyne and Wear still faced the competitive weakness of indigenous components industries. The economic impact on local industries, such as the R&D base or mutual technical knowledge transfer between Japanese and UK makers, has not emerged. On the contrary, the increasing rate of imported parts from other countries worsened the indigenous industries' position in local region. 'The Nissan plant in Sunderland is rapidly becoming an assembly plant first and last, and not an effective magnet to pull high-tech operations into the local economy.'[46]

Japanese FDI and the UK Component Industry

What is Japanisation? The increasingly prominent role of Japanese manufacturing companies as powerful competitors, both as exporters of goods from Japan and as operators of factories across the globe since 1980, has caused considerable debate, among corporate management, trade union, workers, and students. There are various meanings for the concept of Japanisation. When connected with FDI in the Western countries, it appears in three categories.

> Three possible meanings of the term 'Japanisation' can be distinguished each very different in its implications for British industry. Firstly, there is the penetration of the British economy and industry by Japanese firms. We may call this 'direct' Japanisation ... Secondly, there is more or less deliberate or overt copying of Japanese policies and practices by British firms and organisations. Here any effects will be mediated by the orientation of British management and therefore less straightforward in their impact. We refer to this as 'mediated Japanisation'. There are actually at least two variants of this; on the one hand, there are attempts to incorporate the best of Japanese practise and to integrate the new with the old in appropriate ways; on the other hand, there is the practice of using an appeal to Japanese efficiency as a way of legitimating the introduction of indigenous changes

Table 7.9   The model for Japanisation

	Nissan in Tyne and Wear	Honda in Swindon
1 Relations with the central and local government	Strong support from the Thatcher government, ranging from financial support to trade union negotiation. Nissan seen as an economic barometer in this area.	Negotiation between companies rather than negotiations through central or local government. No financial support from UK government.
2 The approach to trade union	Single-union agreement. Nissan hoped in practice to reduce unions' power in production process almost to nothing.	No agreement. Honda employed anyone who never worked in manufacturing sectors. Using new educational system to reduce union power, without a direct attack. Honda did not negotiate at all with trade unions.
3 Industrial environment	Nissan has 733 acres of land without local government's intervention. Large space allowed further components industries cooperative working with Nissan.	Honda's further investment in Swindon is mainly by enlarging its manufacturing site as a warehouse.
4 The relation with local component industries	Huge land allocation allowed Nissan's vertical integration with their components industries within the same area. It achieved efficiency with parts supply and de-unionising of parts suppliers.	Mainly imported from the EU (key parts are imported from Japan in OEM system).
5 Manufacturing system	Nissan brought the major stages in the production process together, such as the synchronous system. It achieved vertical integration from parts to assembling procedure.	Mainly collaborated with Rover until 1994, except on engines. Since then body and engine plants are operating.
6 Human management	Single-unionising. Re-educational system will achieve vital changes in industrial relations.	De-unionising and re-educational system.

Source: Derived by the author on the basis of original research.

that are seen as necessary or desirable. It can be argued that the extent of the influence of Japan on British industry is likely to be rather attenuated in all these cases. Finally, there is the possibility that the British economy is itself actually reproducing Japanese forms of economic structure – as well as other, less central aspects of business organisation, such as production procedures and employment relations. We may call this 'permeated or full Japanisation', and suggest that the effect on British institutions might be extensive were this to occur on any scale.[47]

In Britain, after the first market penetration since the 1970s, the Thatcher government tried to move the British manufacturing sectors towards second and final stage Japanisation. Owing to a good world economic environment, the plan of denationalisation was carried without any difficulty. The confidence given by the success of privatisation allowed the Thatcher government to move the denationalised companies towards Japanisation. The policy's core was the synergic effect in manufacturing sectors, and it was tested by the car industry. The chronically troubled British car industry was one of her main targets.

We [Thatcher and other cabinet colleagues] did not believe in the success of Edwardes' plan. The sale of the British car industry to foreign companies was emotionally difficult. Britain has been a traditional car maker since 1900. But economic utility shows that the British car maker is no longer worth while. We hoped that Honda would take Rover over as a whole, but Honda did not have enough money. We know the future of British car makers, however: we have a world-ranked car components industry. Since the Japanese investment in UK, British car components industries have been increased their competitiveness. It is a real economic utility, not a reason for sadness.[48]

Has the British components industries' competitiveness really increased since the Japanese invasion in UK, as politicians were expecting? While it is politically a good omen, the reality in the local economy proved otherwise.

Components Manufacturing in the UK: Nissan and Honda Compared

Since Nissan's announcement of its 200,000 cars a year project, there were expectations that Japanese car components industries would flood the UK. Within the tradition of Japanese loyalty towards main assemblers, the components industries can work with their close relations using the Japanese methodology.[49] This loyalty triggered the arrival of first and second tier components industries in the UK. This mutual security and dependence moved the component industries close to the same region. Nissan has 11 car OEM makers,[50] about 1400 first and second tier component companies, and 10,000 plus subcontractors. The 1400 component companies supplied 75 per cent of parts and subassemblies with the remainder produced in-house. About 500 component companies are first tier according to the criteria of scale of operation and level of technology and are heavily involved in joint product development.

Owing to its single sourcing policy, Nissan in UK has 150–200 suppliers.

Apart from its size, key tier one suppliers are also characterised by having a substantial R&D capacity. This represents a move towards passing responsibilities for design and long term development of key components or systems from Nissan, and other large automobile producers, onto their major suppliers, or at least sharing the development of systems and components. The twin rationales are key specialisms and cost reduction. The large suppliers are seen as having the key specialisms and product development capabilities and are therefore better equipped to design the car producers. Moreover, with increasingly sophisticated, and therefore expensive systems, key suppliers can spread development costs over work for a number of OEMs.[51]

Nissan's management philosophy concerning components industries is that of the Japanese traditional way. The Nissan company report said that:

The car manufacturing industry is dependent on supply logistics to ensure that the correct parts are available to build the right vehicle at the right time. At Nissan Motor Manufacturing (UK) Ltd., just in time (JIT) concepts are used to maintain low inventories by managing the supply pipeline using material requirements planning based systems ... Nissan operates with inventory levels between 2.0 and 2.5 days for European sourced parts, which means that inventory turnover is approximately 100 times per year. This is significantly better than the accepted European industry standard ... The goal is to get as close as possible to Japanese practice, where inventory levels are measured in hours, and delivery of many parts is synchronised to vehicle build ... In order to maintain this 'synchronous supply' Ikeda Hoover, car seats and interior trim maker, is actually linked to Nissan's process computer which controls the total production sequence schedules at the plant. To operate a synchronous delivery the parts supplier clearly needs to be situated close to the plant ... where the UK differs from Japan is that many of Nissan's suppliers are remotely located from Sunderland operations and, therefor, cannot reasonably be expected to maintain multiple deliveries each shift, especially from mainland Europe. To overcome this, external warehousing facilities are set up close to the plant from which sequenced deliveries can be organised.[52]

In the late 1980s, there were major changes within Japanese component industries.

First, OEMs are encouraging their suppliers to diversify their OEM base in order to achieve greater scale economies ... Secondly, the 'second division' automobile manufacturers such as Mazda and Mitsubishi are moving towards parts sharing and, thirdly, Japanese suppliers are following their OEMs in internationalising production.[53]

Synchronous supply is one of the most fully developed forms of Japanese manufacturing methods. Traditionally, Honda has had difficulty with this process. As Honda US showed, Honda UK expected to link its components with the US.

Nissan is not concentrating on increasing European content simply to satisfy EU or British government regulations. The decision to set up a production facility in EU was a strategic one aimed at maximising the advantages inherent in Nissan's sales position as the number one Japanese marquee in EU. Nissan's clear and stated strategy was to develop an autonomous EU operation encompassing component design and manufacture as well as complete car design engineering and manufacture.

According to Table 7.10, Honda showed the highest local content within the big three. However, since the collapse of collaboration, while the rate of local UK content decreased, there was an increasing rate of imported parts. At the same stage, Honda had imported goods to an extent 10 times greater than Nissan.

Table 7.10   Location of first-tier component and material suppliers among Japanese makers in the UK

	UK	Other EU	Total in EU	Japan/ other	Grand total	Local EU content (%)
Nissan	131	71	202	2 *	204	80%
Honda	148	53	201	20 *	221 *	90%
						(70% UK)
Toyota	105	105	210	0	210	80%

* Estimate.

Source: Nissan, Honda, and Toyota company papers, various years.

Compared to Honda's high rate of dependence on imported components, Nissan has been directly involved in the manufacturing companies. As Nissan's Purchase Director Peter Hill said:

> Our increasing international manufacturing presence put those companies that can demonstrate an ability to meet our standards in a very good position. In the coming years, Nissan is going to be spending a great deal more money in Europe and we are currently working on developing world-wide standards for component and materials suppliers, incorporating a common evaluation standard that will allow both Nissan and its suppliers to clearly understand what is required in terms of cost design and engineering facilities and product quality.[54]

The North has proved to be one of the most successful locations for inward investment in the UK. Over 320 foreign companies employing over 50,000 people have chosen to set up a production or major service facility in this area. A third of total North investment are located in Tyne and Wear. Nissan at Tyne and Wear pioneered what has become known internationally as the Nissan effect. It created a completely new support environment. According to its Company Report the component supply structure at Nissan's Tyne and Wear plant became the first example in the EU of the typical Japanese business environment. From the start of its UK operations, Nissan allegedly achieved 60 per cent of final car value in the form of bought-in components and sourced 80 per cent of its component companies within the EU.

In total, there were over 120 component companies serving the car industry from the North. Nissan itself had major local suppliers for a wide range of components and subassemblies. In selecting component industries, Nissan management emphasised commitment to quality and continued improvement, reliability, technical expertise, and flexibility of response. Nissan said that it had found local suppliers responsive to their exacting standards, rating the standard of quality attained by the UK components industry as 65–70 per cent of the best levels of Japanese suppliers.

Despite successful developments in local region, British component industries did not in fact have a competitive strategy. The relations with local suppliers, which the British government expected to stimulate British component industries, however, did not materialise. The MILAN report said:

> Nissan's target was to have '80 per cent of the car sourced within the EU' (care is taken *not* to use the words 'local content'). Nissan seeks long-term partnerships with suppliers. Suppliers are not replaced lightly, so there is no real chance for new suppliers to replace existing ones. Nissan is conscious that if the UK economy

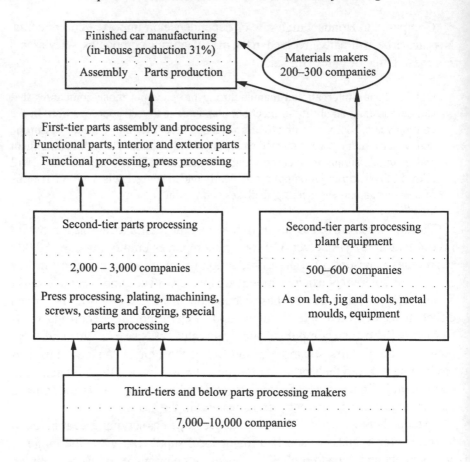

**Figure 7.1   The structure of Japanese car assembler and its
               component makers**

Source: JETRO (1992), *Your Market in Japan* (mimeo), p. 14.

does not pick up, some of its suppliers will go to the wall because of their declining
sales to other customers. Nissan has a free-of-charge 'supplier development team'
that it sends out to suppliers to help them.[55]

Honda, also, has been shown to fail to bring in further FDI from related
components industries. Honda's component supply policies are as follows:

In common with the other two Japanese transplants in the UK, Honda has a policy
using European components suppliers where both quality and competitiveness

can be assured. Much of this has been achieved by partnership, joint venture, and working closely with supplier companies. The Accord contained about 90 per cent from Europe, and the Civic 91 per cent. This is a higher proportion than Honda products assembled in the US ... The reason for this high level of local content is related to the non-competitive value of the *yen*, which encouraged a faster than planned increase in the use of local (European) parts. The process was eased by the collaboration programme with Rover, which gave Honda access to the Rover supplier base. A further factor was the competitive nature of the European component supply structure, and the less vertically integrated structure of the industry, where components are supplied to a variety of customers ... Many key components, however, are still imported direct from Japan, although Honda either complies with or is close to the 80 per cent European content as defined by the DTI.[56]

From local government's side, the lack of further investment from the related companies is a fatal factor. Despite the high rate of local content, Honda has no components industries in Swindon. In Swindon, there are two car-related industries, Clarion Shoji (UK), in car audio equipment, and NCB UK, car paint manufacturers. These were, however, started before Honda's investment. Why did Honda fail to further investment from its related components industries? One of the possible explanations is put forward by Mr Ged Parker, who worked in the Tyne and Wear Development Corporation.

The decision to move depends upon firstly: levels of production – no one is likely to move for 20,000 units a year and 200,000 seems to be a more likely threshold. Secondly: the volume/value ratio of the component. It dose not make sense to transport foam which is 90 per cent air from one end of the country to another. On the other hand the price of a small sophisticated high value electronic component is not really influenced by delivery costs. Thirdly: the tightness of the just-in-time delivery schedule and the ability to guarantee deliveries despite road and rail delays. A fourth issue for overseas suppliers is of course, the exchange rate, which can impact upon the competitive edge of a product.[57]

On a practical basis, there are two main reasons that Honda is not a member of *keiretsu* of Japanese conglomerate. Mr Yasuhiro Fujita, assistant general manager of Sakura Bank in London explained that:

The *keiretsu* is not the whole picture of Japanese manufacturing sectors. But the power of *keiretsu* is normally increased outside Japan. Especially, Japanese manufacturing companies, such as car, electronics and machine tools have close relations between them.

The car makers have several levels of linkage between the main assemblers and their components industries. They are based on long history, close relations, and most of all on the close credit relations between them. The normal arrangement between a main company and its components industries is that goods are paid for when they arrive, but the deal between companies in the same vertical organisation includes a period to pay, between ten days and six months. It was very important for the financial success of FDI. Such relationships were reproduced in the UK. It is more feasible within *keiretsu* than outside them. Honda, which has no particular *keiretsu* support, failed to bring forward further investment, which was expected by the local economy.[58]

One more difficulty, which Swindon faced, was Honda's relationship with Rover. Joint ventures normally caused less inward investment than greenfield investment. Rover, which covered second- and third-tier components, left Honda a freer hand with its components relations. The heavy rate of import of Japanese components, which was pushed by Rover because it hoped to produce new model within visible periods to satisfy political demands, hindered further investment. Despite the 1988 new programme in Honda, there has not been any particular components investment in Swindon. There are 11 companies in Thamesdown, including Rover that supplies to Honda. However, only seven of these could be described as component manufacturers and some of these are second- or third-tier.

Honda's relation with its suppliers do follow the traditional Japanese way. The MILAN report said:

> first tier suppliers are supported 100 per cent by Honda. Other, lower tier suppliers tend not to be supported except on technical issues unless a major problem occurs. The support must come from further down the supply chain ... Local authorities can support the lower tier suppliers through skills training, infrastructure support, and encouragement will assist in this process.[59]

One of the main errors by central and local government in UK is the misunderstanding of the relation between assembler and components industries. As Ms Lorelei Hunt said:

> An early misconception arose from the talk of 'local sourcing' of components for Japanese cars built in the UK. In reality this meant sourcing from Europe rather than from the immediate hinterland of the assembly plant or even from the UK. In order for the cars built by Japanese companies in Britain to be politically acceptable in other European countries they had to include components made in those countries. There appear to be only a small number of key components that are

almost always manufactured close to the assembly plant, which include body panels, seat, paint and glass.[60]

Unlike British or American MNEs, Japanese MNEs rely upon a network of relationships with financial institutions, with suppliers of components, with the labour market and through the labour market with the educational system and with the culture of Japanese society. These relationships are important to attract inward FDI in the local region. Compared to greenfield investment, joint ventures lack these relationships, because the collaboration normally happens in few technical areas only.

After the merger of Rover with BMW, the Honda divisional manager explained that:

> We made two mistakes in Britain: overvaluing government's policy, and undervaluing the relationships with local components makers. We have started a new business in the UK now. One of our main programmes, at this stage, is looking for our second and third tier components suppliers. Technically advanced German products will be favoured, despite the existence of British former suppliers, which were provided by Rover.[61]

Conclusion

Nissan's investment in the UK was regarded as a political triumph for the Thatcher government.

> Thatcher thought Nissan in UK would never have happened under a Labour government. It marked our effort to regenerate our manufacturing sectors, which had not happened since the Second World War because the British car industry enjoyed a period of easy growth. This will be a turning point for our car makers and it must increase their competitiveness in manufacturing skills within the British market. Nissan UK showed the real industrial policy of the Conservative government.[62]

Within the House of Commons, however, the Japanese investment in UK was treated rather pessimistically. It was said that:

> The real reason that Japanese companies come to Britain and have factories here is because, as with Nissan in Sunderland, they can pick up £300 million of taxpayer's money to set up a factory with non-strike agreements, with only 10 per

cent of the work force being trade union members? They pinched the jobs of other car workers in other parts of Britain.

The truth is that the Japanese government have taken the British government for a ride, because our balance of trade deficit with Japan is about three times higher than the value of goods that we send to Japan.[63]

The argument in the House, which was regarded as a political attack, proved right from the viewpoint of the manufacturing sectors. Japanese FDI toward developed countries provided a political solution to the political problem in competitor countries, which regarded the Japanese government as transistor salesmen. From the viewpoint of Japanese MNEs, inward investment, especially developed countries, solved the bottleneck of competition between Japanese makers within the same market. Survivalism, which is the eternal management strategy within Japanese MNEs, is strengthened during the transition period since the 1980s in which regional blocks have been established. The financial support of host governments, stable market share, advantageous negotiation position with trade unions, and most of all, freedom from the political burden which was caused by trade imbalance, were all achieved by FDI.

For the host countries' interests, inward investment had a Midas touch for their economic problems. It was welcomed by the press, which was a political advantage for the ruling party in the region of investment. Sceptical voices in the House of Commons were not heard across the whole country. Was inward FDI successful in Britain?

Nissan's project in the UK was one of the most successful FDI policies by any Japanese MNE towards the EU (until the Toyota project of 1994). From the Japanese government to British government, Nissan did exactly what those governments wanted. Mr Toyohito Shimada told me that:

Nissan is one of the good examples of investment in the EU. Good financial incentives from host government, more favourable local employing negotiations and infra-structure, successive further FDI from sub-contractors, and more importantly, Nissan has cleared all difficulties with which the Japan government has been faced.[64]

From the UK side, Nissan was a lifebelt for the Conservative government's underdeveloped industrial policy.

Nissan in the UK was the perfect success story. I believe it worked properly, it is working now, and it will continue to do so. I know we spent more on the financial package than we expected. Nissan, however, expected to fulfil Thatcher's prediction of impending modernisation and economic recovery. Nissan is regarded as the successful Thatcherite economic and industrial relations project within the country.[65]

One of the main British industrial problems since the war is the result of a failure to invest in the modernisation of capital equipment and technological innovation. Thatcherite industrial policy tried to solve those chronic problems using foreign helpers, which were eager to find a stable place for their business. Since the successful Nissan programme in the UK, Thatcherite policy toward manufacturing sectors started to change. When Thatcher was Leader of the Opposition, she said that: 'It has often been said we must export or die. I would add that we must manufacture or die even quicker.'[66]

However, when she succeeded in her policy of inward FDI in the UK from non-EU member countries, she changed her mind without a clear plan. She had no idea about British manufacturing sectors, moreover she was scared at the fluctuation of the pound. As she used Nissan UK to solve the sterling crisis, she sacrificed manufacturing sectors under the name of monetarism. It was Nissan, which cut the Gordian knot.

The Thatcher government's relationship with industry was paradoxical. The government was, in theory, devoted to the encouragement of business success, yet it cultivated a distant, arm's-length relationship with industry and commerce. The CBI and other bodies whose interest the government purported to be promoting mistrusted ministers who seemed to be more familiar with the works of Adam Smith than with business realities. From the outset Mrs Thatcher's tough monetary policy antagonised industry because it provoked what seemed like an unnecessarily deep recession ... Sir Hector Laing, the Chairman of United Biscuits, told the House of Lords Select Committee in 1985: 'The present Government has in effect made a virtue of not having a vision of the future of British industry and a positive policy of distancing the state from the industrial sector. I think the Government should acknowledge that the nation does have an industrial problem in which it has a serious policy interest. Lord Young, writing after his resignation in 1988, saw the problems as arising from the lack of movement of senior people between government and business: 'We practise a doctrine of separation of experience which appears absolute. Then we wonder why it is that government has an imperfect understanding of the needs of commerce and industry – or even enterprise society'.[67]

The gap between expectation and reality has been satisfied by foreign investors. Nissan UK caused British components industries to work in vain. The government-led business strategy showed a lack of strategic awareness, in that the initiative rapidly moved from assemblers to the first or second tier group of established component suppliers. Especially Japanese movement is faster than that of other European makers.

The Japanese new entrants are focusing attention on radical new styles of operation for all European manufacturers. They entail:

- very long term relationships between the vehicle manufacturers and a limited number of carefully chosen strategic components suppliers.
- a tiered structure in which many 'first tier' suppliers become system builders and take responsibility for managing downstream suppliers.
- the development of more 'transparent' relationships, based on mutual trust and co-operation.
- a steady reduction in costs by suppliers through continuously improved products and manufacturing processes.
- just-in-time (JIT) delivery and continuous quality improvement programmes.
- delegation of design responsibility, involving early involvement of suppliers in model development.[68]

This impact of Japanese further investment in the UK is clearly expected. According to Chris Firth:

Since the decline of British car industries, the competition between British component industries and Japanese ones in the UK was never considered. Thatcher's intention was rather focused on the balance of trade of car industries than on the future of component industries. The responsibility of parts was moved from the assembler to the first tier. The continuous investment by first tier or even second tier towards the UK meant that Japanese makers made another *keiretsu* organisation in the UK.[69]

The 'Japanisation' of British industry was another fallacy that:

However, Japanese transplants in the advanced economies are chiefly assembly operations, dependent on imports of manufactured inputs from Japan, and hence possess a continued reliance on the Japanese economy. Japanese capital not only depends more heavily on disaggregated production, but has also entered global expansion under conditions of free trade, and technological circumstances, which are more conducive to the spatial division of labour. This makes the spread of Japanese best practise to the West different from the 'Americanisation' of Europe because their transplants are more tightly coupled to a logic which suits Japanese capital. In the British case this involves the use of cheap female and male unskilled labour to assemble products for the export market in Europe. Japanese transplants lack a 'full' compliment of engineers, technicians, skilled and semi-skilled workers typical of production at home. These specific features of the Japanese subsidiary constrain transfer or diffusion of practices associated with Japan, because in a real sense we are not comparing like with like when we discuss Nissan UK and Nissan Japan. Therefore any sense of borrowing 'best practice' or the Japanese 'model' is conditioned by a Japanese transnational capital logic and thus it is not open for all societies or firms to participate in an unqualified way.[70]

While the British government put all its efforts towards inward investment, British component industries lost their access to assemblers owing to their weak competitiveness. The problems, which British component industries have faced, are problems which Thatcherite policies never solved.

Notes

1   In 1975, Hitachi considered its manufacturing site in Washington in the North East of England, after Sony and Matsushita in Wales. Owing to the overcapacity and hostility from UK industries, its first intention had to be shelved, and then GEC-Hitachi collaboration was proposed. It had been important factor from Japanese investors until Thatcher's 'Look East' policy.

2   Thatcher, M. (1993), *The Downing Street Years*, p. 497.

3   Mr Nicolas W.L. Maclean: interview.

4   *Observer* (1983), 23 January.

5   Thatcher (1993), p. 497.

6   *Chilton's Automotive Industries* (1986), March, p. 43.

7   Mr Toyohiko Shimada: interview.

8   Mr Toyohiko Shimada: interview in Japanese.

9   Lord Tebbit: interview.

10 Mason, M. and Encarnation, D. (1994), *Does Ownership Matter?*, pp. 389–90.

11 Elger, T. and Smith, C. (ed.) (1994), *Global Japanisation?*, p. 47.

12 Miyashita, K. and Russell, D. (1994), *Keiretsu*, pp. 138–9.

13 According to the Nissan internal paper, Nissan's globalisation was decided when Japan outran the numbers of car producing that of US in 1980. Now Japan stood the largest car producing countries, but where, and how to sell, owing to the high restriction about Japanese cars.

14 The Economist Intelligence Unit (1996), *Japan's Motor Industry*, p. 47.

15 Industry Research and Consultant, *Current Business Conditions of the Nissan Group* (mimeo), p. 6.

16 Mr Atsushi Yamakoshi: interview in Japanese.

17 Nissan Motor Co. Ltd (1983), company paper (mimeo).

18 Mr Takashi Ishihara, president of Nissan said that GM was the company Nissan feared most, and that though Toyota was Nissan's immediate target, GM was Nissan's ultimate competitor; Zakai (1983), *Nissan*, p. 27.

19 Ibid.
20 Nissan Co. Ltd (1987), information pack.
21 Lord Tebbit: interview.
22 Thatcher, *The Downing Street Years*, pp. 299–300.
23 Ibid., p. 497.
24 Mr Yasuhiro Shiraki: interview.
25 Mr Peter Wickens: letter.
26 Ms Lorelei Hunt: interview.
27 Lord Young: interview.
28 *Current Business Condition in Nissan Group*, p. 11.
29 The current situation in the EU car makers and market were rather complicated. Although the EU was the largest car market, there have been only a few true European producers, targeting other than national markets. These include the two US makers, and VW/Audi. The others such as PSA and Renault were trying to catch up but with limited success. Moreover, British maker Rover, despite collaboration with Honda, abandoned the mass markets and identified specific niches in which to become major players. Also, the market was highly fragmented at the luxury or executive level, where indigenous makers had dominance.
30 Garrahan and Steward, p. 22.
31 Nissan Press manager: interview in Japanese.
32 USUI, established in 1941, is a supplier of car and vehicle components. Their main products are important car parts such as brazing pipes, push rods, fan drives and magnet couplings. Most of all, high-pressure fuel injection tube for diesel-engines is becoming a leading product. They are regarded as second-tier suppliers within Nissan.
33 General Manager of Usui (UK): interview in Japanese.
34 Deputy manager of Sakura Bank in London: interview in Japanese.
35 Robinson, F. (ed.) (1988), *Post-Industrial Tyneside*, pp. 46–7.
36 Ibid., p. 51.
37 Lord Young: interview.
38 Senior manager of Industrial Bank of Japan in London: interview in Japanese.
39 Institute Historical Research Conference.
40 MILAN Report (1992), *Inward Investment in Northeast England*, p. 6.
41 *Guardian* (1990), 11 September.
42 Tyne and Wear Development Corporation: Automotive (mimeo).
43 Ms Lorelei Hunt: interview.
44 Mr Chris Firth: interview.
45 Borough of Thamesdown Economic Group (1989), mimeo, p.4.
46 Garrahan and Stewart, p. 56.
47 Askroyd, S. et al. (1988), 'The Japanisation of British Industry?', *Industrial Relations Journal*, pp. 15–16.
48 Lord Biffen: interview.
49 There are several methods by Japanese assemblers of controlling component industries. One of most important way is bidding. There is competitive bidding to select the component makers, though it is usually limited to a few qualified suppliers in the existing companies. The effectiveness of the bidding is enhanced by the car makers' practice of sharing technology among all its suppliers, making then more equal competitors.
50 Each OEM has between 150 and 300 suppliers who are comprised of subsidiaries of the OEMs, affiliates, independent suppliers and occasionally, affiliates of other OEMs. The

majority of suppliers are dedicated to one OEM, 74 per cent in the case of Toyota suppliers and 72 per cent in the case of Nissan, although this is more prevalent of the two largest OEMs than the others. Forty-five supply to both Nissan and Toyota; Morris, J. and Imrie, R. (1992), *Transforming Buyer-Supplier Relations*, p. 66.

51 Ibid., p. 83.
52 Nissan Company Report.
53 Morris and Imrie, *Transforming Buyer-Supplier Relations*, p. 67.
54 Ibid.
55 MILAN Report (1992), 11 November (mimeo).
56 MILAN Report (1996), April 17 (mimeo).
57 Ged Parker (mimeo), p. 7.
58 Mr Yasuhiro Fujita: interview in Japanese.
59 MILAN report (1996), p. 10.
60 Hunt, L. and Eastwood, K. (1993), The Automotive Components Sector in Thamesdown (mimeo), p. 10.
61 Honda local supplier division manager: interview in Japanese.
62 Lord Parkinson: interview.
63 *Hansard* (1993), 10 February, col. 977.
64 Mr Toyohiko Shimada: interview in Japanese.
65 Lord Biffen: interview.
66 Conservative Party Conference (1976), address.
67 Johnson, C. (1991), *The Economy under Mrs Thatcher 1979–1990*, p. 215.
68 DTI (1992), *Supplier Innovation* (mimeo), p. 3.
69 Mr Chris Firth: interview.
70 Elger and Smith, *Global Japanisation?*, p. 36.

Chapter 8

What is to be Done?

In the introduction, a number of questions were posed about the nature of the British government industrial policy, EU inward FDI policy and Japanese FDI policy toward the EU. The case studies, which have used were chosen to respond to the theoretical concerns of some British and Japanese businessmen, car manufacturing employers and employees in the UK and government bureaucrats and politicians. Compared to former governments, the Thatcher government tried to innovate in making policy.

> Politicians sell products in the political market place. That market is changing continuously with evolving tastes and technology. Sometimes the same old product will succeed with some repackaging, like Butskellism in the 1950s and 1960s. Sometimes a political entrepreneur will perceive, or think he perceives, an opportunity for a new product to topple the reigning monopoly. Such is the story of the Thatcher reform programme, at heart an economic reform programme.[1]

What is Thatcherite reform in the manufacturing sector? Did she have any idea or programme towards industry? What was her approach to the place of British manufacturing industry in the world market?

From the early 1990s on, numerous studies have been written relating to the nature of Thatcherism with respect to politics, foreign policy, social policy and economic policy, but few have specifically concerned themselves with investigating issues particular to British manufacturing industries. One of the leading scholars to make this point was John MacInnes, in his study of British industrial relations and economic change during the Thatcher era. MacInnes observed about British industrial policy and the government's role that:

> Work has always taken a central role in Thatcherite ideology. The 1979 general election was fought under the slogan 'Labour isn't working': a comment aimed at the increase in unemployment under Labour, the difficulties Britain had faced and the breakdown of the Social Contract: Labour's attempt to develop a consensus between government, employers and unions about the running of the economy which disintegrated in the 'Winter of Discontent'. Similarly a fundamental theme of the 1987 general election was that Thatcherism had made the British economy 'great' again.[2]

Has it happened? The end of deindustrialisation in Britain coincided with the restructuring process for leaner and fitter manufacturing sectors. Manufacturing has retrenched to a more appropriate base, moreover, manufacturing capacity can confidently be expected to expand in future on a secure footing. Can it be true that British government was consistently under-performing? Under the *laissez-faire* principle of industrial intervention, the effect of the Thatcher government's policy was to concentrate power in the hands of fewer people and to weaken the potential mechanisms of political control over that power.

As Chapter 1 explained, that there is hardly any theoretical discussion of Japanese FDI in the EU. Since Japanese business globalised and the Japanese government faced worldwide criticism about their balance of trade surplus, politico-economic intervention was vital. For this, mutual understanding between two countries is very important. The relationship between the Japanese and UK governments, when the Japanese MNEs were undertaking their FDI towards the UK, was a good example. As Thatcher mentioned in her book, and as the author's interviews with Lord Howe and Lord Young confirmed:

> The Japanese government favoured the British government's approach to the private sector. Whether Nissan had ideas about the UK when they thought about their car manufacturing sector, or not, Thatcher's diplomatic summit meeting in Japan was crucial. Her effort to bring inward Japanese FDI to the UK was much stronger than that of the other G7 countries at the summit meeting in Japan. From the Japanese side, the role of government toward business seemed to be much larger than expected.[3]

There was no exception in the Honda–Rover collaboration. According to Michael Edwardes, compared to the intervention of MITI in the Nissan case, the Ministry of Foreign Affairs was an important factor in the collaboration negotiation.

> Sir Fred Warner was the key negotiator when we started. He had been the British Ambassador to Tokyo, and he is one of the very few British colleagues who could talk with Honda, or the Foreign Office in Japan. The MOFA is one of the participants in *ad hoc* meetings with the Honda managing group. We needed someone to talk with Honda's managers without inhibition, and this was a member of MOFA.[4]

The general picture of Japanese FDI was explained by a member of JETRO London:

We have a role to inform Japanese businessmen about each country's business behaviour. If JETRO's intervention is sufficient for both sides, it will be the means of communication. However if there is a difference between the views of Japanese government and the businessmen, we have a duty to take the government's line, because we think of Japanese national interests first, not simple profits which are the concern of the business group.[5]

In consideration of this, I have demonstrated the existence of 'pull' and 'push' factors between potential investors and host governments. These operate simultaneously but with different impacts. Politically dominated, subject to severe competition, socially sensitive, and with a huge economic impact, the car industry has been a good example to demonstrate the working of these factors.

Chapter 2 shows the more explicit relationship between government and business in Japan. Japanese government and industries during the early 1980s were confronted by internal and external difficulties. Growing demand from employees for social and welfare programmes, the appreciation of the currency, increasing balance of trade surpluses, and emerging regional economic blocs, all demanded changes in the government's attitudes. Did the Japanese government really face all those problems?

The emergence of the world biggest market, the Single European Market, offered a solution for the external problems of the Japanese government and Japanese companies. The globalisation of Japanese MNEs in the EU was an example of government and business collaboration at work. From the government side, the increasing trade friction with EU during the early 1980s pushed her MNEs out of Japan. Facing increasing labour costs and resource prices internally, high levels of protection from the EU and US government externally, car manufacturing was at the heart of the problem. Car manufacturers, on the other hand, were at the take-off stage of globalisation. The globalised programme of production was undertaken in collaboration between the Japanese government and business, for example through MITI for Nissan and MOFA for Honda.

The relationship between globalised business and government organisations is quite common in Japanese society. Nissan and Honda work closely with MITI and MOFA in close informal meetings. Toyota has a freer hand than the other two, but Toyota is a mascot of Japanese manufacturing industries. I think Toyota has access to both government channels for their policy making.[6]

These 'pull and push' factors from both sides made Japanese globalised business in the EU different from that in the US. The strategy adopted by

Japanese MNEs in the EU is more short term profit-seeking, complicated by their relations between assembler and component makers, and more technocratic in their approach to the host country.

As Ozawa mentioned, Japanese FDI has been coincident with Japanese industrial policy. Selective high technology and high-margin goods have been successful in the export trade. Technological transfers and FDI have been both the facilitators and the concomitants of Japan's rapid structural transformation. Within Japanese business, the international economic involvement has proved to be in macroeconomic harmony with Japan's industrialisation and economic growth.

Japanese FDI during the 1980s appears to have been significantly influenced by trade friction and in particular by successful antidumping cases. All these political measures needed political solutions. As far as Japanese MNEs' FDI policies were concerned, Japanese MNEs favoured following government industrial policy rather than company strategy. Especially, in some specific sectors, such as electronic goods, machine tools and car manufacturing, the policies followed MITI's industrial restructuring programme.

According to a senior manager in Sony UK:

> I don't think Japanese MNEs have their own FDI policy. Their FDI policy is part of government industrial policy. It is ambiguous between business plans and government policy. Even Sony, which is regarded as politics-free company, has direct and indirect communication with government when they make investment plans.[7]

The government-led FDI policy needs a counterpart in the host country. Within the Japanese management method, high-level trade agreements are more highly regarded than enterprise-level negotiations. One of the main roles of the Thatcher government towards the Far East during the 1980s was its economic diplomacy. During these periods, the emerging SEM in the EU, the increasing trade disharmony between the EU and Japan, and most of all the strong pull factors demanded by the Thatcher government's industrial policy, all happened at the same time.

Japanese FDI in Car Manufacturing and the 'Fortress Europe' Debate

On this, the answer will be divided into two parts. Has the EU been successful in its 'fortress Europe' policy toward nonmember countries? But also, have the Japanese MNEs' FDI policies in the EU succeeded?

Evaluation of EU Policy

There is one major difference between Continental Western European, and Anglo-American industrial policy. Since the 1980s, the approach to the industrial sector in the EU has been torn between two definitions. One is the Anglo-American dominated capitalistic theory, the other is the so-called Social Market, associated particularly with Germany.

> In Europe, during the 1980s and early 1990s, there were two leading ideologies that jockeyed for dominance and a third at best seemed bereft of purpose and direction. The formers were varieties of free market economies. On the one hand, there was the Anglo-American capitalism hallmarked in Thatcher's Britain of the 1980s and exposing outright competition as a formula for global success. On the other, was the 'social market' capitalism of Germany with its emphasis on consensus, dialogue between government, employees and unions and the insistence on 'social justice'.
>
> These are two very different concepts of how to run a modern economy, and the battle between them has been fierce. However, what is by no means clear is that either is relevant enough in a world of global competition to allow Europe to pull up its industrial competitiveness whether to American or Japanese levels. The Europeans have become the weakest link of the triad.[8]

As mentioned above, the division in the EU industrial sector was not mainly caused by styles of economic ideology, but the governments' attitude towards their industrial sectors. The member countries' government policies have been diversified and complicated. The car manufacturing sector was central to them. During the 1980s, the EU car-makers enjoyed the advantages of national markets in their product technology while the main Japanese car makers strengthened their process technology. Labour productivity was rising roughly twice as fast in Japan as in the EU. The successive restructuring processes such as the automation of production based on electronics and robotics technologies, and the better harmonisation of the various stages of production based on the close human relations, put the Japanese makers far ahead of the EU makers.

One of best solutions of the gap between the EU makers and Japanese competitors was the upgrading and unifying of car manufacturing sectors within the EU regulated area. However, despite continuous negotiations, the attempt to restructure car industries within the EU was seen to fail. After the collapse of unified restructuring processes, each government pushed its nationalised car makers forward as a national champion. Because of intensified market struggle among the member countries' makers, Japanese penetration was promoted in some countries which had weak nationalised car makers within the host countries, or in countries without their own car-makers.

The realisation of weakness in their industrial sectors led to discord between member countries concerning inward FDI policy. The globalisation of business and the commitment to free trade ideology left European manufacturing industries on the brink. From governments' viewpoints, there were two direct options, an internal solution or an external one. The internal solution, such as German-style industrial policy was politically attractive despite its economic cost. There was, moreover, a commitment to the idea that it must have a stable manufacturing capacity and consumer market.

When Thatcher came to power, the German style was regarded as traditional Butskellism. The Thatcherite challenge to traditional ideas made Britain move towards an external solution. Pursuing the external solution, the British government sought to expose domestic industries to free market competition. Privatisation was the initial approach to this, and successive Industrial Acts made British trade unions weaker. Under this pre-condition, the Japanese invasion of UK business happened quite suddenly.

As far as inward FDI policy was concerned, the role of member countries' government policy was the most important factor. Comparing France and the UK, the importance of the role of government can be demonstrated. As a Nissan senior manager expressed it:

> Compared to the electronic goods' MNEs' FDI, car makers' FDI has its own typical pattern. The investor preferred to have qualified component industries, favourable labour regulations, good labour attitudes, and a positive policy from the host government. The UK had shifted component production abroad in response to the decline of domestic demand due to the decline of BL and the changed production base of US car MNEs. However Nissan chose the UK as its manufacturing base, because of the reluctance of the French government to encourage Japanese investment. Madam Edith Cresson's intervention revealed this. As the Toyota case showed clearly in 1997,[9] during the 1980s the UK was the only country to know the real benefit of Japanese FDI in the EU.[10]

After the SEM, there is still ambiguity about Japanese FDI towards the EU. On the one hand, the jobs, capital, technology and competitive stimulus the Japanese MNEs' brought were and are much desired; on other hand, there were fears at the same time that this invasion would be a Trojan Horse, causing a net loss of jobs as domestic manufacturers fell victim to the new Japanese affiliates. All these fears had emerged more clearly during the 1980s. Except in the UK, the car manufacturing sector was the most intensely concerned.

As the Nissan Bluebird case showed, the 'fortress Europe' approach has proved a saga of failure.

> I still wondered about the EU Commission's policy about the manufacturing sector. I thought that the market penetration of Japanese cars to the EU would be faster than the US penetration since the 1960s. There is neither a European nor a national-level policy about the Japanese invasion. The EU Committee and the member countries seem to be muddling through. Especially the Japanese car makers will enjoy a hey-day of export and global production for a couple of decades. After the settling down of Japanese car makers' FDI in the EU, whatever the EU or member government do, the Japanese will survive.[11]

As Table 3.7 showed, there are differences between member countries' interests in regulation of foreign investors. The EU regulation is still far behind that of national governments. Given this tendency, 'the fortress of Europe' will never last long.

Evaluation of Japanese FDI in Europe

> Yes, it is, and it will continue to be.[12]

As far as Japanese car MNEs' are concerned, Japanese penetration has been successful. The Japanese approach to the EU was first described by Prime Minister Hayato Ikeda in the Diet.

> What is worth special attention in the free world today is the fact that the EEC is fast achieving its objectives of economic integration and this objective upholds the traditions and freedoms of European civilisation. The membership of Britain and other like-minded countries in the EEC would produce a new Europe, which would more than equal the US and the Soviet Union. The US is trying to consolidate its economic ties with the Community. The nation is called upon not only economically but in terms of international politics, to address itself to the new developments in the free world.[13]

From the Japanese side, the value of economic return has been more important than diplomatic position. The Japanese penetration of foreign markets had been mainly carried out by export until the early 1980s. The emerging SEM was the turning point of Japanese business policy. FDI has been main business practice since then; however, Japanese FDI is regarded as another form of trade.

Japanese firms come to Europe primarily because the increasing technological sophistication of their products requires them to be closer to their major markets. Their technological and managerial assets enable them to produce behind trade barriers that the EC has erected against them but they would still come to Europe even if no such barriers existed.[14]

The competitiveness of Japanese manufacturing goods allowed her FDI policy to develop under stable conditions in the EU. While the improvement of competitiveness was mainly achieved by business, the Japanese government tried to find more friendly countries within the EU.

The role of JETRO is quite complicated, from market research to direct intervention toward private business. To promote export or to arrange business investment is one of its major tasks.[15]

Compared to the US invasion during the 1960s, Japanese FDI has been faster and easier. There were many factors affecting Japanese FDI such as the increasing volume of MNEs' investment, the globalisation of business, and the free trade world economy. The emerging SEM was against this trend. While there was increasing criticism about EU regionalism from the US and Japan and from developing countries, the Japanese government, on the other hand, sought to find the niche market to penetrate.

Historically, the State assumed an active economic role in Western economies in order to correct what were considered to be the private sector's economic and social failures. Japanese historical tradition, on the other hand, grants to government a legitimate role in shaping and helping to carry out industrial policy. Japanese businessmen share with government leaders and officials a sense of the importance of co-ordinated national development and are generally amenable to and, in fact, expect government intervention to advance this goal. Senior businessmen view government guidance of industry as a normal state of affairs. They may not always enjoy the process or approve of the specific actions but they see the process as legitimate, and in the main, useful.[16]

Compared to other developed countries, the Japanese government's industrial policy is proactive. As her history reveals, there has always been some involvement from the government side.

'Japan Inc.' is a true representation. It will be more true in the EU than in the US, because of the diversification of the EU member countries' interests. Why has Japan been successful in the EU? Because she has two channels. While the government opened diplomatic negotiations, private business penetrated the market proactively. The negotiation would last until the market was established by consumer preference. After that, government negotiation does not matter to business success.[17]

At the first stage, Japanese MNEs faced difficulty in finding any proper and favourable business partner within the EU, despite government support. With car manufacturing, the difficulty was deeper, complicated, and dominated by government policy.

At least in the short term, Japanese car MNEs' FDI in the EU are often just political cosmetics which ease trade friction and deflect the pressure for protection and import controls from member countries. Despite the financial performance and efficiency of Japanese MNEs' FDI in the EU, the Japanese car or even other manufacturing sectors operating in the EU are still in red. However, the success of warehouse operations can be improved in a variety of ways by subsidy of one sort or another. Moreover, despite local content regulations in the EU, many key parts and components for assembly products are still imported from Japan and the US, so that the EU affiliates can maintain their quality standards and competitive advantage in local markets.

One of the major problems, which EU component makers experience in their relations with Japanese assemblers is the role of first-tier component suppliers. The first-tiers chose their second or third tiers within their *keiretsu* relationship. These informal, personal relations are a vital factor in decision-making, rather than technical advantage. The financial advantage is also an important factor to consider.

> We [Japanese second or third tiers] have a two-way payment system. When we get a cheque from assemblers, it will be guaranteed by the same *keiretsu* bank. The assemblers will be protected from money-hungry suppliers.[18]

As far as R&D is concerned, Japanese MNEs are very cautious of revealing their technology. Rather than the transfer of pure technology, Japan's export of technology is limited to that related to the exported products. As a senior manager in Rover told me: 'Japan only exported manufacturing techniques, that is, not *Know-How* but *Know-Why*. In other words, Japan exports quasi-technology only.'[19]

Japanese car makers' penetration into the SEM has proved a most successful story.

By the year 2000 Japanese companies could be producing around 1.7 million cars and 250,000 mainly light, commercial vehicle in Western Europe, of which 1 million could be made by Nissan, Toyota, Honda and others in the UK.[20]

UK Industrial Policy and Japanese FDI in Car Manufacturing

The Thatcher government's industrial policy has received both criticism and applause from businessmen and students. Despite its central importance, there is hardly any Thacherite idea about manufacturing sectors compared with foreign, social or economic policy. One of the complications about industrial policy is the difficulty of the definition of British manufacturing sectors. Some of criticism about British industry is that without a Thatcherite solution to the problems of the manufacturing sector, British industries would have collapsed faster than without her. Others have argued that Britain had been at the bottom since the War, and that regardless of her efforts British industries would regenerate. Whether collapse or regeneration, the question is, did the Thatcher government make an effort to save British industry, as MacInnes mentioned above?

The Thatcher government had two main strands of industrial policy. One was a US-style de-nationalisation plan and other was similar to the Japanese MITI's industrial strategy, namely the search for synergies.

In Britain, the Conservative government followed quickly on the American initiative by similar 'copy-cat' policies in all three sectors. The 'Thatcher' revolution, however, probably went further than the American experience by pioneering a tranche of privatisations throughout the state sector (for example, BAe, British Gas, BA, BT, British Airports Authority, the electricity companies).

The American deregulatory experience was channelled into Europe by the Thatcher government in the UK. In so far as it is useful to talk about an Anglo-American approach to industrial policies, it is this period which demonstrates the two countries working most harmoniously in friendly competition. No other country on the continent has been as influenced by the American example as the British.'[21]

Within the successful denationalisation plan, the emerging question was what to do next?

The denationalisation was easy. However, the emerging problem was how we made the de-nationalised industries competitive. The other European countries have suffered the same mistakes as Britain. The other option was the Japanese style, which was favoured by British politicians.[22]

Compared to the American industrial approach to Britain, Japanese investment in Britain has been more fiercely attacked from the other EU member countries. According to an *Economist* report, Japanese investment in the UK was criticised by Jacques Calvet, president of Peugeot, in that 'by encouraging Japanese car firms to invest there, Britain is becoming an unsinkable aircraft-carrier for Japan'.[23]

To escape this market penetration strategy, British government tried tightly to control local component regulation. However, the real problem was the Thatcher government's failure to recognise British industrial problems, and inability to understand or control local component regulations. As Sir Hector Laing, the Chairman of United Biscuits, told in the House of Lords Select Committee in 1985:

> The present Government has in effect made a virtue of not having a vision of the future of British industry and a positive policy of distancing the state from the industrial sector. I think the Government should acknowledge that the nation does have an industrial problem in which it has a serious policy interests.[24]

When we think about the car industry, the question of local content regulation was more important because of local component industries. Without strong competitiveness of component industries, the local content regulation was not effective. The real problems which British car components makers' faced, were the same that British computer manufacturers experienced a decade ago.[25] The sale of ICL, Britain's last fortress of high technology, was made to Fujitsu in 1990. Where the three leading Japanese computer companies have enjoyed their successful business in the UK, Britain stayed in the role of onlooker. This is real Japanisation of a high technology area. And now this shows the real impact on British car component industries. Despite further investment in the Northwest, the rate of GNP growth and the level of growth in employment has been lower that of the South since the 1980s. Conclusively, the inward investment policy, which was aimed at job creation, has failed. Between 1979 and 1990 employment in the British manufacturing sector fell by over 25 per cent, in Germany by less than 1 per cent.

The *Guardian* explained Japanese penetration into Britain clearly:

> What is at issue is whether Britain is to opt out of the strongest growing areas of high technology to become a provider of services and a maker of low technology

goods. It is a policy which City myopia and government indifference are driving us towards fast.[26]

During the Thatcher government, the manufacturing sector was less valued, made to depend on foreign support and, most of all, made a political scapegoat. One of her intentions about the manufacturing sector was rather the political advantage of reducing trade unions power than the support of industry itself. Her statement in the House of Common proved her conviction that 'the number of people in work has increased by 700,000 since October 1983 ... Yes, many of the jobs have been part-time, and what is wrong with that?'[27] The change from full-time skilled workers to part-time unskilled and women workers weakened the competitiveness of the manufacturing sector. This is widely condemned by foreign investors concerned with the weakening of British manufacturing skill. Among local manufacturers, it has worsened confidence and damaged their ability to compete with Japanese and other European makers.

There were wide gaps between industry's interests and government policy. When they faced severe competition from the EU member countries' makers, British car makers needed a protective government policy. During the Thatcher period, government had to create an appropriate national environment, such as was undertaken by Japanese government during the 1970s. As Japan showed, only after political initiatives have safeguarded the domestic market can management and labour tackle productivity problems, which they can solve and market opportunities which they can exploit.

However, the Thatcher government believed that the British car industry would never survive. The only hope for the British car sector was to save the component industries.

Car makers are eternal money drains. They never made any profits, and, worst of all, car manufacturers are volcanoes of industrial action. To have no nationalised car maker is emotionally difficult, but it proved economically successful. During the 1980s, we had not enough time to think about emotional attitudes toward our manufacturing sectors. We sold it in order to reduce government expenditure and it worked. Our Japanese car makers are better than the chronic British trouble makers. We have balance of trade surplus from our car trade. Does ownership matter?[28]

Thatcher's economic adviser, Professor Alan Walters also, reaffirmed:

... that the closure of BL, whether as the result of a strike or in cold blood, could have a positive effect on the British economy within six months. The short-term impact on regions such as the West Midlands and on the balance of payments might soon be offset, ... by the beneficial effect of the shock of closure on trade unions and employee attitudes across the country. Restrictive practices would be swept away, pay increases would be held down and a more rapid improvement in Britain's competitiveness would thus be achieved through the closure of BL than by any other means available to the government.[29]

As the experience of local economies or the component industries' current situation shows, British competitiveness in the car manufacturing sector never recovered after the closure of BL manufacturing sites and its collaboration with Honda. This was the result of the Thatcherite industrialists' inexperience. As Lord Young said after his resignation:

> We practise a doctrine of separation of experience which appears absolute. Then we wonder why it is that government has an imperfect understanding of the needs of commerce and industry – or even an enterprise society.[30]

To relieve them of a political burden, the Thatcherite industrial programme reorganised the manufacturing sectors under large privatised companies, copying the synergic effect of the Japanese style. The sale of Rover to BAe was a good example. However the result was *Japanese success, British failure.* Overoptimism, ignorance of world demand, overestimation of the British car industry's potential, and lack of government support, all ensured that the government-led restructuring process failed. Moreover, the traditional ignorance about secondary (manufacturing) industries had a significant effect.

> Most aerospace projects involve research-and-development costs, and there are often important considerations for national security and prestige. Both parties had long accepted that, if British aerospace firms were to compete overseas, government should give a helping hand. This was often through 'launch aid' – state money to pay for initial development costs, and which had to be repaid only when the projects went into production.[31]

Mrs Thatcher tried to direct further money toward the aerospace industry using the large discount on the Rover deal. This was the second-choice policy, after the Honda collaboration, and once again British car industries had to be a scapegoat. The synergic effect, which was designed for strengthening manufacturing sectors as in Japan, proved to fail.

Compared to Japanese-style industrial policy, such as tight financial control, prearranged specific sectors, and centrally-controlled government organisation in the form of MITI, Britain experienced a *laissez-faire* industrial policy, with city-based financial control, and weak government control. The fatal mistake during the Thatcher government was over-dependence on foreign investors, especially from Japan.

The manufacturing sector is bound up with all of industry and with the success of industrial policy rather than being a separate part. When the Japanese government put all manufacturing areas together under the *keiretsu*, the government policy was carried out by industry's own agency. By contrast, the UK government's industrial policy showed bipolarity; a problematic issue for public policy and a part of the ambivalence of both major political parties. The differences between the UK and Japanese government in the treatment of the news of companies going bankrupt or suffering some managerial crisis illustrated this clearly. The Japanese government reaction is to analyse the reason behind the crisis and the likelihood of the firm being set back on its feet again. It deals with it as an industrial or economic problem. In contrast to Japan, the UK government calculates the number of jobless because of its social consequences. The fate of each industry at this stage has passed out of the reach of deliberate government action and left to unrestricted market competition. This tradition did not change despite the Thatcher government's 'Britain at Work' policy.

The disappointment for British component industries is all the greater because expectations were pitched so much higher. Mrs Thatcher was too ambitious and did not understand the extent to which the different policy objectives cut across each other. Many of her own interventions caused matters to get worse and not better.[32] She wanted both Japanese assemblers and British component industries and blamed the low competitiveness of British component industries when she found she could not have both. Owing to the frequent ministerial changes at the DTI, intervention by the Prime Minister was higher and long-term continuity of policy was hindered.

> The first element in a successful industrial policy is a creative use and shaping of the market. Industrial policy fails when it overrides or ignores the market and is based upon the presumption that plans and markets are alternative means of economic co-ordination. The purpose is not to substitute the plan for the market but to shape and use markets.[33]

Within the car industries, she did not try to shape or use markets but instead to substitute Japanese manufacturers for British ones.

Japanese FDI and the Decline of Manufacturing Industry in the UK

The Japanese way of thinking depends on the situation rather than principles ... we have no dogma and do not ourselves know where we are going.[34]

There were two axes of the Thatcher government's inward FDI policy: one was the policy for distributing investment between regions, the other was the policy of regenerating component industries. Huge amounts of government subsidy, using good infrastructure and the incentive of free or cheaply provided local services such as utilities, were expected to promote the redevelopment of deindustrialised areas, mainly the assisted areas. The inward investment was regarded as a vital ingredient in the promotion of regional economic development. Since the early 1990, there was hardly a local government in the UK, which did not have the attraction of foreign manufacturing investment as a major objective and commitment. Yet even in regions identified as most successful in attracting new investment, employment in foreign companies' affiliates accounted for well under a tenth of all employment, and often considerably less.

Despite government efforts, the Thatcherite project was largely effective only in the southern part of the country. Inward investment policies tended to favour the deindustrialising areas, but all other aspects of industrial and economic policy allowed the gap between North and South to widen. The impact by Japanese assembly industries upon British component manufacturers was a case in point. The success of a component supplier depends on the relationship between the assemblers' sourcing policies and the domestic content level. Despite components' accounting for half of the total cost of a car, the relationship between assemblers and suppliers was traditionally regarded as 'arm's length'. In the UK, component industries perceived their relative independence, as compared with other European makers, to be a positive advantage. However, the extensive investment by foreign affiliates in the North did not help component manufacturers in that region.

As Lord Biffen explained, the economic utility of inward Japanese car industries in the UK, was its expected effect on the strength of competitiveness of British component industries. However, the British government condoned the mutual relationship between Japanese car makers and component industries. The close interdependence has played an important part in the competitiveness of both Japanese makers and Japanese component industries.

Japanese automakers assign suppliers different roles and given even first-tier suppliers varying levels of responsibility for product development. Only an elite corps of about a dozen first-tiers suppliers enjoy full-blown partnership with their customers. Interestingly, this elite group includes all the big suppliers, such as Nippondenso, Aisin Seiki and Calsonic ... This handful of companies represents all suppliers.[35]

Underestimating such a Japanese industrial relationship, the Thatcher government expected to see the 'Japanisation of British component industries'. Since then, few British component industries have been strong enough to gain on balance from pursuing a more independent stance. Most component makers turned to concentrate on developing closer relationships with UK-based assemblers, such as Ford or Vauxhall.

The inward policy of the UK Conservative government toward Japanese car manufacturers exactly matched the 'push and pull' factors between both governments. Japanese MNEs have their foothold in UK, whereas the UK government tried to regenerate British component industries. Despite greenfield investment in the UK, the Japanese car makers used UK affiliates as an assembly warehouse. It has been argued that the Japanese car MNEs in the UK are little more than 'screwdriver' facilities that simply assemble parts imported from Japan. However, Japanese MNEs insist that their R&D facilities in the EU are making major investments in R&D, design, and engineering to supplement and enhance their expanding production facilities.

Compared to car makers in the US, Japanese car makers in the EU showed two clear characteristics of their business. They put their R&D centres together near the manufacturing site. And highly confidential research is carried by Japanese staff, not even Japanese staff domiciled in the host country. One of the main reasons why every Japanese car MNE favoured big sites is now clear. They hoped to take advantage of the JIT [just in time] philosophy not with the local suppliers but with the suppliers from Japan, which are located on the same site. Real competition between British local manufacturers and Japanese ones never happened under these conditions. This will weaken British components industries, which will become less competitive not more competitive, which was the initial expectation of the UK government.[36]

Louis Turner, Chief Executive of the UK-Japan High Technology Industry Forum concluded that: 'Without R&D facilities in the UK, Japanese car makers merely worked as screwdriver assemblers. Except for Nissan UK, other manufacturers can hardly say that they have full manufacturing facilities.'[37] Even the Nissan R&D facility in Tyne and Wear is mainly concerned with design and development, with particular reference to building-in components. Its pure and intensive technology R&D is still carried in Japan.[38] Nevertheless, without creating new R&D facilities, Japanese manufacturers have made heavy use of the existing Worthing Motor Research Laboratory, and reused the technology in Japan. This is one of the major disadvantages of inward investment to the host country.

Is the British component industry really poor? The demands made by Japanese assemblers on British component industries are very complicated, and this threatens the component suppliers. Systematically, they hinder assembler-suppliers relationship. As Ian Gibson said in the House of Commons Trade and Industry Committee:

> Our concern is perhaps slightly different from the usual one. Clearly we are concerned about external quality indicators such as repair rates, failure rates and cost to us. Those are important considerations. But we are at least as concerned about the insides of their businesses, that is, about their production system, their production reliability, their in-house quality problems as well as their quality problems to us, if any. We are concerned about their internal productivity measures, their internal productivity investment plans, their internal labour relationships. In many ways we are at least as concerned about their business as a business as we are about ours. When I talked about efficiency, I was really including all those indicators … As long as they see those targets and they are going that way, that is fine.[39]

The demands made by Japanese assemblers on British component makers have been criticised by MILAN and the British component makers. According to a local component manufacturer in Tyne and Wear:

> It is well known that Japanese methods are quite unusual among the British component makers. JIT or *Kanban* system, whatever they do, is more demanding than our usual methods. Moreover, when they demanded changes in internal methods, it was regarded not as support but as disruption.[40]

Subsequently, further FDI by second and third tier Japanese component industries will be a natural trend with the support of Japanese assemblers and will make things worse among British component suppliers. The diversification of first tier component industries into the EU will prevent technology transformation from Japanese to British companies. The location of first tier component industries in Germany put the British component industries on the brink of failure. Generally speaking, there is a 50-year mutual relationship between Japanese assemblers and their component industries. If this pattern were adopted in the British situation, there would be no component industries in the UK. Moreover, the real problems which British component industries faced, are the decreasing competitiveness of British products and the increasing import of parts from the other EU member countries.

The emerging question is why British component industries are not attractive to Japanese assemblers, even when they arc located in the UK. The majority of British components suppliers to the Japanese assemblers are manufacturing customised components. Moreover, the clearest evidence of the changes in the component sector is that of a shift from the traditional multi-sourcing of items to a more long-term cooperative relationship with a narrow supplier base. The selected suppliers are given long-term contracts, and are expected to become more involved in new model design and development. This change is typical of the Japanisation of the British component industry. The expected high quality, prompt delivery and lower stockholding are achievable only in a framework of long-term committed relationships. With the increasing electronification of car technology, the technical contribution by specialist suppliers to product design is becoming indispensable.

As Table 8.1 shows, the current situation of British component industries is still far away from the ideal, and the Japanese assemblers in the UK are still reluctant to work with British makers. The British component industries, from the Japanese assemblers' viewpoint, are complex and complicated, because old habits die hard, and because only perseverance with a long-term perspective can transform an adversarial relationship of low trust into a cooperative one of high trust. The just-in-time delivery system, which is the symbol of lean production, has been misused as a means of passing on the burden of stockholding to the supplier, without risk sharing in other aspects by the assembler. Also, a suggestion for a yield-improving design change made by a wiring harness supplier was ignored by its assembler who encourages such suggestions to be made, but whose blue print in reality, once fixed, is hardly ever altered until the next model change.

As the Calsonic and IMI cases illustrated,[41] there has been a second wave of merger or acquisition of British component industries. Robertson made the criticism that 'in order to maintains its quality standards and to achieve 'just-in-time' sourcing while meeting overseas requirements on local content, Nissan has encouraged many of its parts affiliates to set up component feeder plants in the vicinity of its major foreign plants'.[42] All these changes came as a surprise to the British government. The shift towards developing closer

Table 8.1   The mutual relationship between Japanese assembler and suppliers

Assemblers	Suppliers
• Scrutinise each suppliers relationship to determine (a) the status of the relationship, (b) whether you are handling components of a specific complexity consistently, and (c) the most desirable posture to adopt, given the complexity of components and the supplier's capability	• Moving up the ladder from one role to another will require you to take on greater product-development responsibilities
• Assess the technological capabilities of each suppliers, and assign the supplier an appropriate role. More important, monitor each supplier's capabilities routinely, both to benefit from them and to manage the supplier's transition from one role to another	• Make the effort to understand and internalise your customer's product-development cycle. Often this will require assigning your people to work in the customer's organization. Learn to synchronise your new-technology presentations with the customer's development cycle.
• Manage a supplier's involvement in product development, as well as the content and intensity of exchanged information, in a manner that is consistent with the supplier's role.	• Whether you are trying to build a new partnership or maintain an existing relationship, think through the contents of your new-technology presentations.
• Develop a simple, stable product-development process, and communicate it clearly to key suppliers. Be receptive to new technology during the early stages of the development cycle so that suppliers know when to present their suggestions for radical changes.	• Technological competence makes it possible to meet tight deadlines. Some Japanese suppliers have separate manufacturing facilities dedicated to manufacturing prototypes. In-house testing and prototyping capabilities are critical for quick turnarounds during the prototype-testing-and-evaluation stage
• Use carefully considered targets to coordinate and manage your suppliers' development efforts. Make sure your suppliers know the limits of their latitude, because late changes in the targets for one component will reverberate throughout the entire system, affecting the design work of many other suppliers.	• Expenditures on development or on prototyping and testing capabilities are investments in a relationship

Source: Kamath, R.R. and Liker, J.K. (1994), p. 160.

relationships with fewer suppliers on a long-term basis is one more important change. Within the assemblers' interests, it is natural to favour Japanese first- or second tiers components industries. Except for a few globalised British component industries, most British component makers will lose in competition with Japanese makers. This is the paradox which frustrated the Thatcher government's intentions.

> One of the main reasons for inward investment by Japanese car MNEs in the UK was to save our component industries. Because she knew the reality of the British car assemblers' future, she hoped to ensure the survival of our component industries with foreign help, from Japan. If Japanese car makers were successful in Britain, they would use our parts and this must save our component industries.[43]

This was a fallacy. When Thatcher's government abandoned the nationalised car maker by selling Rover to BAe, British industrial policy made one error. And when Japanese car makers abandoned British component industries, a further error was evident.

Conclusively, the EIU report of 1996 demonstrated the current situation of British component industries.

> However, the ravages of the 1970s, and 1980s have run deep and most of the first-tier suppliers to automotive manufacturing in the UK will be foreign-owned. Over the years the decline of the UK components industry's customer base has meant that many major engineering companies in the UK simply took the decision that the UK automotive sector did not offer adequate prospects for shareholder returns, and decided to exit. One major UK components group said that they only stuck with the sector because they were so weak that they lacked the resources to diversity away from automotive. In the words of one purchasing manager; 'it's too late to make UK (owned) first-tier suppliers strong, just as it's too late to make the UK constructors strong'.[44]

The British government made mistakes on the local economy side, in its handling of the collaboration between Japanese car makers and British components industries by misunderstanding the Japanese car manufacturers' culture. Lorelei Hunt, Economic Development Manager in Thamesdown Borough Council argued that:

> ... it is possible to see that there was never likely to be the same level of inward investment from Japanese component manufacturers as had occurred in the USA when Japanese manufacturers began operations there, because the automotive

industry in Europe was never as vertically integrated as that of US. The component supply network was already established in Europe, and Japanese manufacturers had already started to identify their potential component suppliers long before they began to set up manufacturing plants here, in order to avoid the component supply problems they had experienced in the US which led to greenfield investments by Japanese components suppliers.[45]

On the other hand, there is the expectation that the second and third tiers' FDI towards the EU will weaken the more basic components industries in the UK. Mr George Bull, Managing Director of the Anglo-Japanese Economic Institute observed:

> I think there is and will be further FDI from more small-size components industries from Japan to the EU. I think FDI will be located in the EU rather than the UK, because the UK-based assemblers will scatter their suppliers out of the UK to learn new technology and increasing competitiveness. British suppliers will not be able to compete with Japanese second and third tier component suppliers. More attractive markets will be provided by other EU countries such as Germany, France and Italy. And this process is under way already.[46]

Despite the expectation by central and local government in the UK, Japanese car makers will not permit the traditional subcontract relationship with British components industries to grow up. Since the arrival of Nissan in the UK, there have been many studies of Japanisation of UK car components industries such as the DTI 'Learning from Japan Initiative'. However, there is not any direct involvement of R&D or other technical collaboration between Japanese car makers in the UK and British components industries. Because of the extent of forward planning, and the long term relationships that Japanese manufacturers develop with component industries, it is also difficult to see what openings there are for companies who are not already involved to break into this market. The notion of creating opportunities for local companies to supply components to Japanese car makers, however laudable, now seems unrealistic.

One of the more important projects which Japanese car makers undertook in the UK is to control all first-tier components industries within the same manufacturing site. High levels of supplier loyalty, convenient financial arrangements, Japanese-favoured skills, and the fact that the same technology is involved which is involved in Japan at the same time, are reasons for doing this. Honda, and of course Nissan as well, has a larger manufacturing site compared to what it would need for its manufacturing output if it had an

Table 8.2   The breakdown of component suppliers for Japanese assemblers overseas

	Local suppliers	Imported from third country other than Japan %	Imported from Japan %	Total import content of Japanese assemblers
Asia	48.5%	8.9%	37.9%	46.8
US	51.7%	6.2%	42.1%	48.3
EU	29.0%	21.8%	44.4%	66.2
World	46.5%	12.6%	40.9%	53.5

Source: MITI (1992), *Overseas Business Activities of Japanese Corporations* (mimeo).

arm's-length vertical component supply system. Honda since 1992 has tried to copy the Nissan UK management strategy. This is an unexpected impact on the UK components industries. It was clear from the MILAN report about regional trends that the regional trend in British component industries is still dominated by the West Midlands, the South East and the North West, which comprise over 84 per cent of total employment in 1994. This suggests that even if the major Japanese assemblers are creating jobs in the nontraditional regions of Wales and the East Midlands (Toyota), the South West (Honda) and the North (Nissan) nevertheless the main policy emphasis will still need to be focused on the traditional regions. It may be that the policy initiatives required will be related to inward investment in the newer areas while policy should be concentrated on supporting and developing the indigenous industry base in the dominant regions.

The real problems the UK will face within a decade are not problems of employment. Michel Gomez, the Chairman of Thomson Electronics said that

> Britain believes that an infusion of Japanese capital and management through transplants of factories will revitalise British industry. I don't believe a word of it. A few thousand jobs in Wales or Scotland are not the issue. The issue is the repair of the national tissue of technological and managerial competence.
>
> There is not one example – not one – of the Japanese establishing a major R&D lab outside Japan. To the country, they take technology out of other companies. They are buying our scientists and our technology and our high-tech start-ups. They are taking technology out of the US and Europe. How many European managers are working in Japanese transplant factories? If British industry has to be rejuvenated by a transfusion of Japanese manufacturing, it would take

thousands and thousands of British managers and scientists working in Europe *a la Japonaise*, which won't happen.[47]

The EIU report reveals, of Japanisation of the UK components industries, that:

> Their [Japanese car components industries in the UK] rapid growth has been from a low base and they still only employ a few thousand people. Moreover, where investment has been made in technical centres these have often been in Germany, which is the major European components market.[48]

According to the Conservative Party Campaign Guide in 1974: 'All modern governments are involved in economic management and accordingly they cannot fail to take an interest in the workings of industry.'[49] However, since the Thatcher government, they failed to achieve a real industrial policy for its own sake, because of the pursuit of a political result. The over-mighty Thatcher government imposed their own particular burden on a British car industry which was already suffering from the self-inflicted wounds of low skills, poor training and inadequate investment. Her inward investment policy toward component industries has been wholly inimical to industrial success. No government gave uniform support to the competitiveness of the component industries in all its policies, even where it declared the intention of doing so. Each chose initially to pursue those aspects of policy, which were ideologically attractive to it and which, even if relevant to the problem, could only make a partial impact if other policies had a contrary effect. However, during the Thatcher terms, there were to be ten Secretaries of Industry, a rapid succession that if it happened in industry itself would be accounted indifference or incompetence. Moreover, it heavily depended on activity at the prime ministerial level, when there was any negotiation about industrial sectors, especially the inward FDI policy.[50] Under these governments, the British component industries should be left to wither on the vine. While recognising that the factors determining industrial success were complex and varied, precluding the selection of any single policy appeared to be common and to be expected to be successful. She tried to increase competitiveness of component industries with an anti-competitive policy.

The Thatcher government was guilty of inducing over-optimism about the future on the part of British component manufacturers by making exaggerated claims about the improvement in performance by Japanese assemblers. John Dunning in his book observed critically that:

The basic concern over the impact of inward investment on innovatory capacity may be illustrated with reference to the current wave of Japanese manufacturing investment in the UK – although in many ways this is a 'reprise' of some of the anxieties that have been articulated by developing countries for many years now. Here there appear to be two main worries. The first is lest the Japanese undertake only low value-added activities in the UK and centralised their innovatory activities in Japan. The argument then goes on to assume that, by their competitive strategies, they will drive out local firms which perform higher value-added activities. The innovatory base of the UK then becomes eroded, helping the Japanese economy further to strengthen their indigenous capacity and Japanese MNEs better to penetrates global markets. One country's vicious circle of asset decumulation then becomes another's virtuous circle of asset accumulation. The second anxiety has less to do with the way in which Japanese MNEs may or may not control the amount and kind of resources transferred and more with the way in which these are used. The argument is that what is perceived good for the global objectives of Japanese multinationals is not necessary good for the development of the UK economy[51]

This was clearly showed by the car component industries in Britain.

Before entering on the account of my main research, I tried to draw the general picture of foreign direct investment strategy, such as the theoretical approaches, the 'push factors' from Japanese government and 'pull factors' from the EU member countries. Notably, there was severe competition between the big four key countries in the EU, France, German, Spain, and the UK, for inward investment. When we drew a picture of the car industry, the role of government was more significant than in other areas strengthened owing to the domination of the car industry by national champions. Is politico-economy therefore vital to the behaviour the MNEs? Since the business has been globalised, intervention by governments has increased rapidly. Either by direct or indirect intervention, each government has its own master plan toward indigenous multinational enterprises.

'Is (or was) Conservatism working?' Despite Mrs Thatcher's efforts, the impact of inward investment in the UK has not showed yet. Has 'Japanisation in the British manufacturing sector' not happened? From boom to bust, the inward investment policy during the Thatcher era showed the contrary effect in British industries. The British car industry, again, was the victim.

The real impact of Thatcherite industrial policy was reflected a decade later:

Governments, particularly since the Conservative philosophy of privatization took hold, do not run car companies, and Rover is not even a British car company nowadays, having been bought by Germany's BMW when the Conservative Party was in power. If anyone is to blame for the job losses, largely in foreign-owned firms, it is Mr Redwood's party. Successive Conservative administrations were very successful in attracting foreign companies to Britain, and dismal in encouraging domestic investment – as Labour has pointed out for many years. Inward investment has done Britain proud, but it is an uncomfortable truth that an over-reliance on the largesse of foreign firms leaves Britain vulnerable in the case of a downturn in overseas markets over which the UK Government has no control.[52]

Notes

1   Minford, P. (1988), 'Mrs Thatcher's Economic Reform Programme', in *Thatcherism*, p. 93.
2   MacInnes, J. (1987), *Thatcherism at Work*, p. xi.
3   Lord Young and Lord Howe: interview.
4   Sir Michael Edwardes: interview.
5   A member of JETRO in London: interview in Japanese.
6   Yasuhiro Shiraki: interview.
7   A member of Sony UK: interview.
8   Egan, C. and McKiernan, P. (1994), *Inside Fortress Europe*, p. 24.
9   Toyota announced £400 million new investment in Northern France instead of at its plant at Burnaston, Derbyshire. As Hiroshi Okuda Toyota president mentioned that French government effort made its final decision in France.
10 Senior manager of Nissan UK: interview in Japanese.
11 Senior manager in Vauxhall: interview 7 January 1998.
12 Senior manager in Honda UK: interview in Japanese.
13 Diplomatic Blue Book (1962), No. 6, June, p. 6, Annex.
14 Thomsen, S. and Nicolaides, P. (1991), pp. 126–7.
15 Ian Maybin manager in JETRO London: interview.
16 Magaziner, I.C. and Hout, T.M. (1980), *Japanese Industrial Policy*, p. 29.
17 Mr Yasushi Uno: interview at AJBS Conference.
18 Senior manager of Usui Component industry: interview in Japanese.
19 Member of R&D division in Rover at Solihull: interview.
20 National Consumer Council (1990), *Working Papers*, No. 4.
21 Egan and McKiernan, *Inside Fortress Europe*, p. 23.
22 Lord Young: interview.
23 *Economist* (1991), 20 April, p. 81.
24 House of Lords Select Committee (1985), *Report.*
25 In November 1990, ICL, the UK national-champion computer maker became a subsidiary of Fujitsu, the World second largest computer manufacture. With a lack of R&D money and the collapse of national consumer market, ICL made agreement with Fujitsu in October 1981. The agreement, which was supported by the Thatcher government, was quite similar

to the Rover and Honda contract. While ICL had all architecture skill, design, and software of new-range processors, Fujitsu supplied semiconductor design tools, components, and limited manufacturing facilities. According to the agreement, ICL lost their traditional large size computer manufacturing areas. Without government support for the computer industry, and short and medium term turbulent market condition let the British industry under the Japanese hand. The reason of acquisition of ICL has never mentioned. However, there will be two assumptions that one the adoption of ICL's product line for the non-European markets, the other access to the European computer market under the ICL's badge, as Honda did since the mid-1980s. One of common point between ICL, and Rover was lack of government support and muddling through policy toward each industry. The difference was Fujitsu is enough to buy ICL, while Honda failed.

26 *Guardian* (1990), 31 July.
27 *Hansard* (1986), 30 January, col. 1090.
28 Lord Biffen: interview.
29 Edwards, M. (1983), pp. 205–6.
30 Johnson, C. (1991), *The Economy under Mrs Thatcher 1979–1990*, p. 215.
31 Crick, M. (1997), *Michael Heseltine*, p. 166.
32 For example, the imposition of high interest rates in 1980–81 on an economy already experiencing a high exchange rate and recession.
33 Sawyer, M. (1992), 'The Industrial Policy Legacy', in *The Economic Legacy 1979–1992*, p. 332.
34 Chie Nakane (1971), *Newsweek*, 15 October.
35 Kamath, R. and Liker, J. (1994), 'A Second Look at Japanese Product Development', *Harvard Business Review*, November–December, p. 156.
36 Mr Peter McVeigh: interview.
37 Mr Louis Turner: interview.
38 Senior manager in Usui component company: interview in Japanese.
39 Trade and Industry Committee (1987), *The UK Motor Components Industry 3rd Report*, p. 80.
40 A manager of British component industry in Tyne and Wear: interview.
41 When Nissan decided to cut its relation with Japanese component makers from Japan, Calsonic and Nippondensu, main Nissan's suppliers, acquired or joint-ventured British component makers.
42 Robertson, I.L. (1988), *Japan's Motor Industry*, p. 35.
43 Mr Roger King: interview.
44 Chew, E. (1996), *The UK Automotive Components Industry*, p. 27.
45 Hunt, L. and Eastwood, K. (1993), p. 10.
46 Mr George Bull: interview.
47 *Fortune* (1992), 4 May, p. 33.
48 Chew, p. 16.
49 Taylor, R. (1996), 'The Heath Government, Industrial Policy and the "New Capitalism"', *The Heath Government 1970–74*, p. 139.
50 Only Lord Young, among DTI ministers, even mentions inward FDI in his memoirs.
51 Dunning, J.H. (1993), *MNEs and the Global Economy*, p. 318.
52 *The Times* (1998), 28 October.

Epilogue

What is the proper role of a student of international business strategy in a debate about such politically charged issues as UK inward FDI policy and Japanese global business strategy? The traditional theory of FDI itself provides a discipline-neutral framework of analysis. The international business strategy approach allows 'non-economic' factors to be admitted in argument. If, as most Western academics think, the balance of purely international business factors is negative or uncertain in its assessment of foreign direct investment, it may still be quite reasonable to examine the political reasons for such behavior. It still remains important to examine the political factors in international business strategy carefully, and to consider of the peculiar nature of Japanese business policy.

Since the early 1980s, 'globalisation' has been an international slogan associated with success, wealth and the strengthening of national competitiveness. Globalisation was based on two pillars of traditional economic thought: free trade and foreign direct investment. The impressive economic success of several Asian countries, and the collapse of the Soviet-style economic system, have strengthened the approach of a free trade philosophy favoured largely by the United States. Some leading Asian countries, such as Taiwan, Korea and Japan started a US-style projection of their national economies into world markets under the name of foreign direct investment. There has, however, been considerable diversity and even ambiguity in this process.

Globalisation is complex, and in Asian countries has been driven by political and social, as well as economic considerations. A sudden shift towards protection in the European Union, in the form of the Single European Market, forced nonmember countries to change their approach to global competition from export to local manufacturing within tariff walls. Japan was the first country from Asia to adopt a new global strategy for its international business and the government was the key decision-maker during the early stages of the foreign direct investment process, just as it had been in early industrialisation.

Foreign direct investment is a major global business objectives among Japanese manufacturers seeking access to developed countries. However, this 'global Japanisation' has coincided with the restructuring of Japanese manufacturing industry and has generally been designed to favour the 'first runner'. Some companies developed an FDI policy in order to resolve the tension between the Japanese government's industrial policy and their own private sector business strategies. Although potentially competitive as a company, Honda was not favoured by the Japanese government for the participation of motor industry, and undertook its motor manufacturing strategy in the overseas base in order to increase its international reputation and thus its leverage at home. Nissan is good example of the consequences of the Japanese government's FDI strategy in the EU. The long lasting second runner in the Japanese domestic market, Nissan expected its FDI strategy to allow it to compete with Toyota in the international market. The strength of consumer conservatism in Japan drove Nissan into the global market. However, without a stable domestic market share, Nissan was unable to cope with an unexpectedly low rate of market share in the EU, and failed in its objectives.

Compared to other countries' FDI strategy, the Japanese FDI had two different side of their policy. Like Honda case indicated, the globalisation developed against traditional government industrial policy. The globalisation strategy was the part of company's survival strategy. After the two decade of FDI plan, Honda, which was abandoned by Japanese government, has been succeeded, while Nissan faced direct managerial involvement of Renault. This is not the traditional symbol of business bureaucratic system named, 'art of Japanese business: why certain companies dominated the global business areas', which was led by the mind of the industrial strategist in the Japanese government.

The globalisation programs of most Japanese companies are influenced by both government industrial policy and business strategy. FDI, as part of globalisation, has been achieved in large part by government policy. The combined analysis of government industrial policy and business strategy makes Japanese FDI in the EU market comprehensible. However most research about Japanese FDI is restricted to economic considerations. For example, Ford and Strange observe that:

> First, Japanese FDI is attracted to areas of high densities of manufacturing in the appropriate industry and where there are major agglomerations of previous Japanese FDI. Both these findings suggest an active role for industrial policy. Secondly, Japanese FDI is attracted to countries where the workforce is well educated and where there are high levels of innovative and technological ability. These findings suggest an active role for education policy and the promotion of science and technology. Thirdly, Japanese FDI is attracted by low levels of union density and/or high labor force flexibility, suggesting an active role for labor market reform. Fourthly, the fact that Japanese investors favor areas where wage rates are relatively low and where local competition is less effective clearly should not be taken to suggest policies aimed at lowering wages and/or productivity. Fifthly,

the wisdom of any form of active policy depends crucially upon the scale of the net benefits from any inward investment.[1]

However, as this book has shown, Japanese FDI cannot be understood simply as a consequence of company globalisation programmes. When the Japanese government exposed Nissan to free market competition, its relative weakness in manufacturing skill made it vulnerable to takeover by Renault. The case of Rover during the 1980s was not dissimilar: when Rover looked to the UK government for support, it was deflected into an arrangement with a foreign partner.

In the last two years, the UK car industry has once more been a central political issue, because of BMW's decision to sell its Rover subsidiary. Despite its series of internal and external restructurings, the last UK car manufacturer was at risk of disappearance. In a climate of national concern, with the implicit support of the new Labour government, the Phoenix consortium, derived from the UK motor industry and led by John Tower, a former director of Rover, took over the company's assets from BMW. Tower asked the UK government to protect the national consumer market for a limited period to allow Rover to gain strength for international competition. 'Without strong protection for the indigenous manufacturer, there would be no future for Rover. Even the Labour government has to impose some restrictions on the big three Japanese makers in the UK.'[2]

Historically, it is clearly not the case that liberalising a national market without a strong indigenous industrial base has provided the engine for economic development. It was not true of the US, which industrialised behind massive tariff barriers erected in the nineteenth century to keep out competition from more efficient UK industries. Nor was it true of Japan or the newly industrialised countries in the East Asia in the decades after World War II. In the *Guardian*, the economist Dani Rodrik summarised the mismatch between the UK government's dreams and the reality of the international business environment since the 1980s. 'Countries that have achieved long-term economic growth have usually combined the opportunities offered by world market with a growth strategy that mobilizes the capabilities of domestic institutions.'[3]

Globalisation, which has been seen recently as the most powerful economic force transforming national wealth, has continued to boost industrial growth in the developed countries. However there is common thread, which runs through the history of many industrial sectors, that global integration is one of the main causes of rising inequality and the weakening of local industrial competitiveness. This study has shown that in an integrated, laissez-faire economy, the consequence of FDI for a national industry has been relative decline. Moreover, the increased openness of economies widens the already existing divisions between industrialised and industrialising manufacturing sectors.

The 'open multiple competition', which has been taboo of Japanese industrial sector has been strengthened since the globalisation policy. There is no one-side openness for the leading industrial sector. When Japanese companies succeeded into the single European market, her domestic market started to break the mould. It indicated the new wave of government-business relationship, from constructor to provider. Nissan's sell out to Renault and Rover's plan of quasi-nationalisation, in different ways, indicate the pitfalls of government–business cooperation under the name of globalisation. Globalisation enhances the power of businesses, as it causes the state to lose its political ability to discipline domestic capital, and weakens the state's capacity to control and regulate its own economy. At the same time, as the Japanese and the UK cases show, there is still a very close relationship between business strategy and state policy.

Notes

1 *Transnational Corporations* (1999), Vol. 8, No. 1, pp. 133–4.
2 Report from BBC 9 O'clock News, 6 May 1999.
3 *Guardian*, 30 April 2001.

Bibliography

Japanese Government Publications

Economic Planning Agency, *Economic Surveys of Japan 1970–1995*, Tokyo.
Government of Japan (1993), *Reference for FDI in Japan and Technology Importation from Abroad*, Tokyo.
Nikkei Newspaper, Japan Economic Almanac between 1985 and 1997, Tokyo.
The Information Centre of the Mission of Japan to the European Communities, *News and Views from Japan 1990–1996*, Brussels.
Japan External Trade Organisation (JETRO), *JETRO White Paper on International Trade 1970–1995*, Tokyo.
JETRO, *various issues and sources*, Tokyo.
Ministry of Finance, *Annual Report of the International Finance Bureau 1980–1995*, Tokyo.
Ministry of International Trade and Industry (MITI), *Foreign Trade of Japan, 1970–1996*, Tokyo.

UK Government Publications

Agency for Development in the North of England (1996), *A Presentation on the North of England by Northern Development Company*.
Barclay, C. (1987), House of Commons Library Research Division, Research Note 'Rover Group'.
British Business Journal between 1982 and 1988.
Central Policy Review Staff (1975), *The Future of the British Car Industry*, HMSO.
Central Statistical Office (1972), *National Income and Expenditure*, HMSO.
Department of Trade Industry (DTI) (1991), *Supplier Innovation: Opportunities for Small and Medium UK Automotive Component Companies*, London.
DTI and SMMT (1992), *various issues and sources*, HMSO.
Environmental Service Department (1996), *Derbyshire Structure Plan Review Working Paper*, No.7, 'Toyota at Burnaston'.
HMSO (1971), *Japan: its Motor Industry and Market*, HMSO.
House of Common Committee (HCC), quoted various issues (please refer to footnotes).
House of Lords Selective Committee on Overseas Trade (1984–85), *Report and Minutes of Evidence*, HMSO.
House of Lords Selective Committee on Science and Technology (1991), *Report and Minutes of Evidence*, HMSO.

IBB, *Japanese Companies involved in Research, Development and Design in the UK*, London.

Invest in Britain Bureau (IBB), *Automotive Components*, London.

Ministry of Labour, *Labour Gazette*, various years.

Reference Division Central Office of Information (1995),*The UK Motor Vehicle Industry*, HMSO.

Ryder Report (1975), *British Leyland. The Next Decade*, HMSO.

SED (1993), 'The Automotive Components Sector in Thamesdown', by Eastwood, K. and Hunt, L., January SED (1994), 'Issues Arising from the Sale of Rover Group to BMW', March and various issues and sources.

Sunderland, 'The UK's Fastest Growing Automotive Centre'.

Sunderland (1997), 'Current Overseas Investment in Sunderland'.

Sunderland (1997), 'The Right Move'.

Swindon Economic Development (SED) (1992), 'Inward Investment into Swindon in the 1980s and 1990s: The pattern of inward investment into Swindon and its impact on the local economy', June.

TBC (1994–95), 'Annual Review'.

Thamesdown Borough Council (TBC) (1996), 'Thamesdown Unemployment Bulletin 11', April.

Thamesdown Borough (TB) Economic and Social Development Group (1989), 'Preliminary Study of the Impact of the Honda Manufacturing Investment on the Swindon Area' and various issues and sources.

Tyne Wear Development Corporation, 'Automotives: The Driving Force of the New North East'.

Association and Institution Publications

The Anglo-Japanese Economic Institute publication: various issues and sources (please refer to footnotes).

AUEW (TASS) (1978), *BL Cars: Collapse or Growth – An Alternative to Edwardes.*

The British Information Services (BIS) (1962), *British Motor Vehicle Industry*, May.

BIS (1973), *Facts Sheets on British Industry*, November.

BIS (1976), *Facts Sheets on British Industry*, April.

Central Office of Information (1975), *British Industry Today – Motor Vehicle*, August.

Centre for Policy Studies (1983), *BL: Changing Gear*, Policy Studies Institute.

Chamber Patron Profile, *Honda of the UK Manufacturing Ltd.*

CommuniCorp (1997), *Invest in the UK.*

Conservative Party Conference paper (1976).

CPRS report (1975).

The Daiwa Anlglo-Japanese Foundation (1997 and 1998), *UK and Japan: Government and Society Series*, I, II.

EC/EP Forum on the European Automobile Industry (1995), *The Automobile Industry – Current Situation, Challenges, Strategy for the Future and Proposals for Action.*

Economic and Social Consultative Assembly (1991), *Relations between the US and Japan and Between the EC and Japan*, Brussels.

The EU Commission (1988), *Europe 1992: Europe World Partner.*

European Commission, *Examination of Current and Future Excess Capacity in the European Automobile Industry.*

England plc (1995), *North East.*

GATT (1988), *Review of Developments in the Trading System.*

GATT (1991), *Trade Policy Review: The European Communities.*

GATT (1992), *Trade Policy Review: The European Communities.*

Industry Research and Consultant, *Current Business Conditions of the Nissan Group.*

Industrial Research and Information Services (IRIS) News Survey (1966), *The Car Industry*, February.

Industry Forum, *The Newsletter of the SMMT industry Forum, 1993–1997.*

IRIS News Survey (1966), February.

Japan Automobile Manufacturers Association, Inc. (JAMA), *The Motor Industry of Japan, annual report between 1988 and 1998*, Tokyo and various issues and sources (please refer to footnotes).

Japanese Business in the UK (1993).

Motor Industry Local Authority Network (MILAN) (1986), *Visit to Austin Rover Plant, Cowley* and various issues and sources (please refer to footnotes).

National Consumer Council (1990), *Working Papers*, No. 4.

OECD (1983), *Long-term Outlook for the World Automobile Industry*, Paris, OECD.

OECD (1992), *Globalisation of Industrial Activities.*

Panorama (1995), *Motor Vehicles.*

A Report by the Trade Unions Research Unit for the TGWU Automotive Conference (1984), *Cars and Jobs – The Decline of the UK Motor Industry and the Strategic Considerations for Motor Industry Unions*, 5–6 July.

SMMT (1976), *Comment on the CPRS Report* and various issues and sources (please refer to footnotes).

Society of Motor Manufacturers and Traders (SMMT) (1958), *Progress and the Motor Industry.*

A Trade Unions Response to the Edwardes Plan by Leyland Combine Trade Union Council, *BL The Edwardes Plan and Your Jobs.*

TUC (1989), *Europe 1992*, Report Paper.

UN Statistical Year Book, various years.

UN, *World Investment Reports*, various years.

The University of Texas at Austin Graduate School of Business Bureau of Business Research and JETRO (1989), *Understanding Japanese Business.*

The World Bank (1993), *Japanese Foreign Direct Investment: Recent Trends, Determinants and Prospects*, Policy Research Working Paper 1213.

WTO (1992), 'Motor Vehicles', *Trade Policy Review.*
Zaikai (1983), *NISSAN.*

Company Publications

British Leyland annual reports between 1979–87.
EXIM Bank (1996), *EXIM Japan 1996 Survey: The Outlook on Japanese FDI.*
EXIM Bank (1996), *Annual Report.*
Honda Annual Report 1995 and various issues and sources (please refer to footnotes).
Newcastle upon Tyne Development Committee (1996/97), Proposed *Economic Activities.*
Nissan Company File (NCF), *Background: Facts against Fallacy.*
Nissan Motor Manufacturing (UK) Ltd (1997), *Back on Track and Shifting to High Gear: Annual report 1997* and various issues and sources (please refer to footnotes).
Nissan News (1994), *Nissan in Sunderland – A look back over the last 10 years.*
Rover Group Limited (1992), *Report and Accounts.*
Tokai Bank (1994), *Monthly Aurvey about Japanese Affiliates Overseas (Japanese).*
Toyoda, E. (1985), *Toyota: Fifty years in motion*, Tokyo, Kodansh.
Toyota (1995), *The Automobile Industry: Toyota and Japan*, Tokyo and various issues and sources (please refer to footnotes).

Theses or Unpublished Papers

Andriessen, F. (1990), 'Latest EC Thinking Concerning External Aspects of Automotive Trade and Investment', The World Automotive Forum, 23–24 February.
Amako, T., 'Difficulties of Japanese Management Application in Japanese Overseas Firms', paper to be prepared Europe-Japan Economic Research Centre.
Blair, T. (1996), Address to the *keidanren* in Tokyo.
Bowden, S. and Turner, P. (1995), 'The Incomplete Managerial Revolution, Uncertainty and the Competitive Decline of British Motor Industry, 1945–1975', December.
Brittan, L. (1990), 'A Single Market for Motor Vehicle: Why and when?', Cambridge City Conservative Association Business Club, 9 February.
Date, M., 'Japan's Place in a Unified Europe: The Japanese view', joint conference sponsored by the Anglo-Japanese Economic Institute and the Scottish Development Agency on Japanese investment in the UK.
deClercq, Willy (1986), 'Bulletin of the EC', September.
Firth, C. (1992), 'The Impact of Japanese Motor Vehicle Investment on Local and Regional Government Policy in the UK and Europe', *Global Partnership; Local Communities and Japanese Transplants*, Illinois Wesleyan University, Bloomington, Illinois.

Freeman, R., 'The Future of UK Manufacturing'.

Mitsubishi Research Institute (1991), 'Survey'.

Parker, G., 'Toyota in Derbyshire Seminar: The Nissan effect – impact of Japanese companies in the North East'.

Long-Term Credit Bank of Japan (1990), 'The New Europe and the Japanese Response'.

Mackay, D.I., Sladen, J.P. and Holligan, M.J. (1984), *The UK Vehicle Manufacturing Industry – its Economic Significance*, Planning and Economic Consultants, November.

Michael, T. (1973), 'Cross-Country Analysis of the Determinant of US Direct Foreign Investment in Manufacturing in Less-Developed countries', thesis.

Mobious, U. (1991), 'Einfuhr von Industrieprodukten'.

NEDC (1984), 'A News Brief', Summer.

Sazanami, Y. (1992), 'Europe and Japan: Cooperation and Conflict: The economic impacts of antidumping emergency protection and dispute settlement mechanism', 4–6 June, European Policy Unit, European University Institute.

Schutte, H. (1997), 'Regional HQs of Japanese and Western MNCs: A comparative study', paper to be prepared at the 1997 AJBS Conference in Washington, DC.

Tejima, S.(1997), *Globalization/Regionalization, Trilemma and Structural Changes of host and home countries economies through Japanese FDI growth*, Research Institute for International Investment and Development the EXIM Bank of Japan.

Newspapers and Journals

Agarwal, J.P. (1980), 'Determinants of Foreign Direct Investment: A survey', *Wettwirschaftliches Archiv*, No. 16.

Agarwal, S. (1994), 'Socio-cultural Distance and the Choice of Joint Venture: A contingency perspective', *Journal of International Marketing*, Vol. 2, No. 2.

Ahijado, M., Begg, I. and Mayes, D. (1993), 'The Competitiveness of Spanish Industry', *National Institute Economic Review*, November.

Alexander, A. (1989), 'The Decline of Local Government: Does Local Government still matter?', *Contemporary Record*, Summer.

Amin, A. and Smith, I. (1990), 'Decline and Restructuring in the UK Motor Vehicle Components Industry', *Scottish Journal of Political Economy*, Vol. 37.

Asanuma, B. (1985), 'The Contractual Framework for Parts Supply in the Japanese Automotive Industry', *Japanese Economic Studies*, Vol. 15.

Askroyd, S. et al. (1988), 'The Japanization of British Industry?', *Industrial Relations Journal*, Vol. 19, No. 1.

Bachtler, J. (1990), 'Grants for Inward Investors: Giving away money?', *National Westminster Bank Quarterly*, May.

Balasubramanyam, V.N. and Greenway, D. (1992), 'Economic Integration and FDI: Japanese Investment in the EC', *Journal of Common Market Studies* June, No. 2 Vol. 30.

Ball, J. (1989), 'The UK Economy: Miracle or mirage?', *National Westminster Bank Quarterly Review*, February.

Barber, S. (1991), 'Commentary: The Europe of regions – British local government in the new Europe: the driver's cab or the guard's van?', *European Access*, April.

Berggren, C. (1993), 'Lean Production – The End of History', *Work, Employment and Society*, Vol. 7, No. 2.

Birmingham Evening Post (1995), 'BMW sizes up Japanese Market', 31 October.

Blackbourn, A. (1978), 'Multinational Enterprises and Regional Development: A Comment', *Regional Studies*, Vol. 12.

Brittan, L. (1989), 'A Bonfire of Subsidies? A review of state aids in the EC', *European Access*, June.

Brittan, L. (1993), 'Shaping a Framework for Global Trade: The challenge for the EC', *European Access*, No. 3, June.

Buckley, P.J. (1991), '*Kojima*'s Theory of Japanese FDI Revisited', *Hitotsubashi Journal of Economics*, No. 32.

Burnham, P. (1995), 'Rearming for the Korean War: The impact of government policy on Leyland Motor and the British car industry', *Contemporary Record*, Vol. 9, No. 2.

Burton, J. (1995), 'Partnering with the Japanese: Threat or opportunity for European business?', *European Management Journal*, Vol. 13, No. 3, September.

Business Week (1997), 'Can Honda Build a World Car?', 8 September, special issue.

Carr, C. (1992), 'Productivity and Skills in Vehicle Component Manufacturers in Britain, Germany, the USA and Japan', *National Institute Economic Review*, February.

Cassell, M. and Tett, G. (1994), 'Feel the Quality, not the Quantity', *Financial Times*, 29 August.

Caves, R.E. (1993), 'Japanese Investment in the US: Lessons for the economic analysis of foreign investment', *The World Economy*, Vol. 16, No. 3.

Chilton's Automotive Industries (1986), March.

Cleireacain, S. (1990), 'Europe 1992 and Gaps in the EC's Common Commercial Policy', *Journal of Common Market Studies*, March, Vol. 28, No. 3.

Cowling, K. and Sugden, R. (1993), 'Industrial Strategy: A missing link in British economic policy', *Oxford Review of Economic Policy*, Vol. 9, No. 3.

Crouzet, F. (1992), 'Europe and Japan: Cooperation and Conflict – Some French Views of Japan today', European Policy Unit, European University Institute, 4–6 June.

Curtice, J. (1988), 'North and South: The growing divide', *Contemporary Record*, Winter.

Curzon, G. and Curzon, V. (1987), 'Follies in European Trade Relations with Japan', *The World Economy*, Vol. 10, No. 2.

Dahrendorf, R. (1976), 'Listener 96', 14 October.

Dell, E. (1992), 'The Chrysler UK Rescue', *Contemporary Record*, Vol. 6, No. 1.

Dicken, P. (1983), 'Japanese Manufacturing Investment in the UK: A flood or a mere trickle?, *area*, Vol. 15, No. 4.

Dienst, A. (1989), 'Europe Inc.', *Journal of Japanese Trade and Industry*, No. 2, March and April.

Lord Donoughue (1994), 'The 1975 Chrysler Rescue: A political view from Number Ten', *Contemporary Record*, Vol. 8, No. 1.

Dorey, P. (1991), 'Thatcherism's Impact on Trade Unions', *Contemporary Record*, April.

Eltis, W., Fraser, D. and Ricketts, M. (1992), 'The Lesson for Britain from the Suprerior Economic Performance of Germany and Japan', *National Westminster Bank Quarterly Review*, February.

Eltis, W. and Fraser, D. (1992), 'The Contribution of Japanese Industrial Success to Britain and to Europe', *National Westminster Bank Quarterly*, November.

Eltis, W. and Higham, D. (1995), 'Closing the UK Competitiveness Gap', *National Institute Economic Review*, November.

Fujimoto, H. (1992), 'Japan's Automobile *Keiretsu* Changing for the Better', *Tokyo Business Today*, February.

Fujita, N. and James, W.E. (1991), 'Growth Partners of the Japanese Economy in the 1980s: Before and after the Appreciation of the Yen', *Economic System Research*, Vol. 3, No. 4.

Gatsios, C. and Seabright, P. (1989), 'Regulation in the European Community', *Oxford Review of Economic Policy*, Summer, No. 2.

Georgiou, G.C. and Weinhold, S. (1992), 'Japanese Direct Investment in the US', *The World Economy*, Vol. 15, No. 6.

Gerlach, M.L. (1987), 'Twilight of the *Keiretsu*? A Critical Assessment', *Journal of Japanese Studies*, No. 18.

Geroski, P.A. (1989), 'European Industrial Policy and Industrial Policy in Europe', *Oxford Review of Economic Policy*, Vol. 5, No. 2.

Gospel, H.F. (1995), 'The Decline of Apprenticeship Training in Britain', *Industrial Relations Journal*, Vol. 26.

Grabowski, R. (1994), 'The Successful Development State: Where does it come from?', *World Development*, Vol. 22, No. 3.

Greenaway, D. (1993), 'Trade and Foreign Direct Investment', *European Economy*, No. 52.

Guest, D.E. (1990), 'Have British Workers Been Working Harder in Thatcher's Britain? A Re-Consideration of the Concept of Effort', *British Journal of Industrial Relations*, Vol. 28, No. 3.

Hamel, G. (1991), 'Competition for Competence and Inter-partner Learning within International Strategic Alliance', *Strategic Management Journal*, No. 12.

Harvey, J. (1989–90), 'The Determinants of Direct Foreign Investment', *Journal of Post-Keynesian Economics*, Vol. 12.

Hawkesworth, R.I. (1981), 'The Rise of Spain's Automobile Industry', *National Westminster Bank Review*, February.

Heitger, B. and Stehn, J. (1990), 'Japanese Direct Investments in the European Community-Response to the Internal Market 1993', *Journal of Common Market Studies*, September, No. 1.

Hennessy, P. (1994), 'Cabinet Government in the Thatcher Years', *Contemporary Record*, Winter.

Heseltine, M. (1994), 'Competitiveness: What, why and how?', *European Business Journal*, Vol. 6, Issue 3.

Hill, S. and Munday, M. (1992), 'The UK Regional Distribution of Foreign Direct Investment: Analysis and Determinants', *Regional Studies*, Vol. 26.

Hirata, M. (1988), 'Internationalisation Strategy and Globalisation of European Carmakers', *Hitotsubashi Journal of Commerce and Management*, Vol. 23.

Hirata, M. (1990), 'Japanese Corporate Responses to EC Market Unification', *Hitotsubashi Journal of Commerce and Management*, Vol. 25.

Hirata, M. (1993), 'Japanese Overseas Investment in Recent Years and Corporate Responses to the Single EC Market', *Hitotsubashi Journal of Commerce and Management*, Vol. 28.

Hoskynes, J. (1982), 'Whitehall and Westminster: An outsider's view', *Fiscal Studies*, 3 November.

Imai, K. (1992), 'The Global Network of Japanese Firms', *Japanese Economic Studies*, Vol. 21, No. 5.

Industrial Relations Journal (1988), 'Special Edition about Japanization', Vol. 19 No. 1.

Jamieson, B. (1995), 'A Winning Policy Ticket for the Tories', *The Sunday Telegraph*, 8 October.

The Japan Stock Journal (1981), February.

Japan Times Weekly Overseas Edition (1989), 'Toyota Motor Plans to Start Production of Cars in Britain', 11 February.

Jennings, A. (1970), 'Government Policy and the British Motor Industry's Export Performance', *Applied Economics*, Vol. 2.

Kamath, R. and Liker, J. (1994), 'A Second Look at Japanese Product Development', *Harvard Business Review*, November–December.

Keehn, E. (1990), 'Managing Interests in the Japanese Bureaucracy: Informality and Discretion', *Asian Survey*, Vol. XXX, No. 11.

Kilpatrick, A. and Lawson, T. (1980), 'On the Nature of Industrial Decline in the UK', *Cambridge Journal of Economics*, No. 4.

Kissler, L. and Sattel, U. (1985), 'Politics and the Organization of Work in France and the Federal Republic of Germany: A comparison', *Economic and Industrial Democracy*, Vol. 6.

Kojima, K. (1982), 'Macroeconomic versus International Business Approach to Direct Foreign Investment', *Hitotsubashi Journal of Economics*, June.

Krugman, P. (1989), 'Rethinking International Trade', *The Business Economist*, Spring.

Kumon, H. (1993), 'Japanese-Affiliated Auto Plants in the UK', *Journal of International Studies*, No. 7, The Institute of Comparative Economic Studies, Hosei University.

Kumon, H. (1994), 'International Transferability of the Japanese Production System: Japanese-affiliated auto plants in the USA, the UK and Taiwan', *Journal of International Economic Studies*, No. 8.

Lehmann, J. (1992), 'New Directions in the Euro-Japanese Relationship: Economic and geopolitical perspectives', *European Business Journal.*

Mainichi Daily News (1981), 'Honda and Rover Collaboration', 9 May.

Maruyama, M. (1991), 'Japanese Reaction to Management Problems in Europe: Cultural Aspects', *European Management Journal*, Vol. 9, No. 2.

Mason, M. (1994), 'Elements of Consensus: Europe's Response to the Japanese Automobile Challenge', *Journal of Common Market Studies*, December, Vol. 32, No. 4.

Mattoo, A. and Mavroidis, P.C. (1995), 'The EC-Japan Consensus on Cars: Interaction between trade and competition policy', *The World Economy*, Vol. 18, No. 3.

McCrone, G. (1992), 'Subsidiarity: Its implications for economic policy', *National Westminster Bank Quarterly Review*, November.

Melo, J. and Messerlin, P.A. (1988), 'Price, Quality and Welfare Effects of European VERs on Japanese Autos', *European Economic Review*, Vol. 32.

Messerlin, P.A. (1996), 'France and Trade Policy: Is the "French exception" passée?', *International Affair*, Vol. 72, No. 2.

Metcalf, D. (1989), 'Water Notes Dry Up: The impact of the Donovan Reform proposals and Thatcherism at work on labour productivity in British manufacturing industry', *British Journal of Industrial Relations*, Vol. 27.

Middlemas, K. (1988), 'Corporatism: Its rise and fall', *Contemporary Record*, Spring.

Miller, D. (1983), 'The Role of the Motor Car industry in the West Midlands Economy', *Regional Studies*, Vol. 17, No. 1.

Monk, J. (1992), 'Japanese Lessons for British Unions', *Personnel Management*, September.

Monk, J. (1996), 'We're in Danger of Forgetting the Long-term Unemployed', *TUC News*, 19 December.

Morita, A. (1985), 'Japan: Where to go from here', *Japan Times*, 12 March.

Morris, D. and Jepson, D. (1981), 'Coventry and the Motor Vehicle Industry', *National Westminster Bank Review*, May.

Morris, J. (1992), 'Elements of Consensus: Trouble and strife between the EC and Japanese automobile industries', *European Access*, February.

Murata, K. (1990), 'Personnel Management in Japanese Business Enterprises', *Hitosubashi Journal of Commerce and Management*, No. 25.

Murfin, A. and Wright, K. (1994), 'Regional Differences and their Importance for the UK economy', *Bank of England Quarterly Bulletin*, November.

Nitsch, D., Beamish, P. and Makino, S. (1995), 'Characteristics and Performance of Japanese FDI in Europe', *European Management Journal*, Vol. 13, No. 3.

Observer (1983), report 23 January.

Oliver, N. and Wilkinson, B. (1989), 'Japanese Manufacturing Techniques and Personnel and Industrial Relations Practice in Britain: Evidence and implications', *British Journal of Industrial Relations*.

Parsons, A. (1992), 'The Chrysler UK Rescue: A comment', *Contemporary Record*, Vol. 6, No. 3.

Pascale, R.T. (1984), 'Perspectives on Strategy: The real story behind Honda's success', *California Management Review*, Vol. 26, No. 3.

Prais, S.J. and Jones, D.T. (1986), 'Plant Size and Productivity in the Motor Industry', *Oxford Bulletin of Economics and Statistics*.

Press Express (1968), March, No. 41.

Ragazzi, G. (1973), 'Theories of the Determinants of Direct Foreign Investment', *IMF Staff Papers*, No. 20.

Rapoport, C. (1991), 'Why Japan keeps on Winning', *Fortune*, 15 July.

Rhys, D.G. (1974), 'Employment, Efficiency and Labour Relations in the British Motor Industry', *Industrial Relations Journal*, Vol. 5, No. 2.

Rhys, D.G. (1977), 'European Mass-Producing Car Makers and Minimum Efficient Scale: A note', *Journal of Industrial Economics*, Vol. 25, June.

Richardson, J. (1993), 'Parallel Sourcing and Supplier Performance in the Japanese Automobile Industry', *Strategic Management Journal*, Vol. 14, No. 5.

Richardson, K. (1977), *The British Motor Industry, 1896–1939: A social and economic history*, Macmillan.

Richter, F. and Wakuta, Y. (1993), 'Permeable Networks: A future Option for the European and Japanese car industries' *European Management Journal*, Vol. 11, No. 2.

Rose, E. and Wooley, T. (1992), '"Shifting Sands?" Trade Unions and Productivity at Rover Cars', *Industrial Relations Journal*, Vol. 23, No. 4.

Sadowski, D., Schneider, M. and Wagner, K. (1994), 'The Impact of European Integration and German Unification on Industrial Relations in Germany', *British Journal of Industrial Relations*, Vol. 32, No. 4.

Savary, J. (1995), 'The Rise of International Co-operation in the EU Automobile Industry: The Renault case', *European Urban and Regional Studies*, Vol. 2, No. 1.

Schaede, U. (1994), 'Understanding Corporate Governance in Japan: Do classical concepts apply?', *Industrial and Corporate Change*, Vol. 3, No. 2.

Schnedier, F. and Frey, B.S. (1985), 'Economic and Political Determinants of Foreign Direct Investment', *World Development*, Vol. 13.

Shimokawa, K. (1985), 'Japan's *Keiretsu* System: The case of the automobile industry', *Japanese Economic Studies*, Vol. 15.

Silberston, A. (1965), 'The Motor Industry 1955–1964', *Bulletin of the Oxford University, Institute of Economics and Statistics*, November, Vol. 27, No. 4.

Smith, D. (1988), 'The Japanese Example in South West Birmingham', *Industrial Relations Journal*, Vol. 19, No. 1.

Stewart, P. and Garrahan, P. (1995), 'Employment Responses to New Management Techniques in the Auto Industry', *Work, Employment and Society*, Vol. 9, No. 3.

Streeck, W. (1987), 'Industrial Relations and Industrial Change: The structuring of the world automobile industry in the 1970s and 1980s', *Economic and Industrial Democracy*, Vol. 8.

Sutherland, P. (1989), 'Competition Policy in a Single Market', *European Access*, February.

Suzuki, Y. (1994),'The Competitive Advantage of Japanese Industries: Developments, dimensions and directions', *Journal of Far Eastern Business*, Vol. 1, No. 1.

Swamidass, P.M. and Kotabe, M. (1993), 'Component Sourcing Strategies of Multinationals: An empirical study of European and Japanese multinationals', *Journal of International Business Studies*.

Swindon Business News (1994), 'Uncertainty over Honda's plans for Swindon following BMW-Rover deal', 2 March.

Thoburn, T.H. and Takashima (1993), 'Improving British Industrial Performance: Lessons from Japanese subcontracting', *National Westminster Bank Quarterly Review*, February.

Thomsen, S. (1993), 'Japanese Direct Investment in the European Community: The product cycle revisited', *The World Economy*, Vol. 16, No. 3.

Toyo Keizai Inc. (1992), 'Japanese Overseas Investment: A complete listing by firms and countries 1992/1993'.

Toyo Keizai Survey (1992), 'Is Japan's Overseas Corporate Expansion Winding Down?', *Tokyo Business Today*, July.

Tokyo Business Journal (1991), 'Japan Making Inroads into Europe by Strategic Acquisition', January.

Tokyo Business Today (1992), 'Japanese Automakers Rethink Efficiency *vs.* Profit', March.

Tokyo Business Today (1992), 'Japan's Building in EC: Going strong', March.

Tokyo Business Today (1993), 'Wheels Spinning, but Losing Ground'.

Trevor, M. (1991), 'Blending the best of Japan and Europe' *Tokyo Business Today*, June.

Turn, P. (1986), 'The "Japanisation" of British Industrial Relations at Lucas', *Industrial Relations Journal*, Vol. 17, No. 3.

Turn, P. (1988), 'The Limits of "Japanisation": Just-in-time, labour relations and the UK automotive industry', *New Technology, Work and Employment*, Vol. 3, No. 2.

Turnbull, O., Oliver, N. and Wilkinson, B. (1992), 'Buyer-Supplier Relations in the UK Automobile Industry', *Strategic Management Journal*, No. 13.

Uchida, M. (1993), 'The Dictatorship of the Bureaucracy', *Tokyo Business Today*, November.

Usui, C. and Colignon, R.A. (1995), 'Government Elites and *Amakudari* in Japan, 1963–1992', *Asian Survey*, Vol. XXXV, No. 7, July.

Vane, H. (1992), 'The Thatcher Years: Macroeconomic policy and performance of the UK economy, 1979–1988', *National Westminster Bank Quarterly Review*, May.

Verdon-Wortzel, H. and Wortzel, L.H. (1988), 'Globalising Strategies for Multinationals from Developing Countries', *The Columbia Journal of World Business*, Vol. 23, No. 1.

White, D. (1994), 'Foreign Investment: Costs are catching up', *Financial Times*, 11 May.

Whittaker, D.H. (1990), 'The End of Japanese-Style Employment', *Work, Employment and Society*, Vol. 4, No. 3.

Wickens, P. (1985), 'Nissan: The thinking behind the union agreement', *Regional Management*, August.

Wickens, P. (1993), 'Steering the Middle Road to Car Production', *Personnel Management*, June.

Wilkinson, E. (1978), 'Changement des structures des structures des exportations du Japon 1953-1976 et ses complications pour la C.E.', *Chroniques d'Actualite de la SEDEIS*, No. 18.

Willman, P. (1984), 'The Reform of Collective Bargaining and Strike Activity at BL Cars', *Industrial Relations Journal*, Vol. 15, No. 2.

Winters, L.A. (1992), 'Goal and Own Goals in European Trade Policy', *World Economy*, Vol. 15, No. 5.

Wood, S. (1991), 'Japanization and/or Toyotaism', *Work, Employment and Society*, Vol. 5, No. 4.

Wood, S. (1993), 'The Japanization of Fordism', *Economic and Industrial Democracy*, Vol. 14.

Yamashita, T. (1986), 'Making VTRs and Friends in the USA', *Economic Eye*, Vol. 7, No. 1.

Yannopoulos, G.N. (1990), 'FDI and European Integration: The evidence from the formative years of the EC', *Journal of Common Market Studies*, March, Vol. 28, No. 3.

Yannopoulos, G.N. (1990), 'The Effects of the Single Market on the Pattern of Japanese Investment', *National Institute Economic Review*, November.

Young, S., Hood, N. and Wilson, A. (1994), 'Targeting Policy as a Competitive Strategy for European Inward Investment Agencies', *European Urban Regional Studies*.

Books and Published Articles

Abe, E. and Fitzgerald, R. (eds) (1995), *The Origins of Japanese Industrial Power*, Frank Cass.

Abe, E. and Gourvish, T. (eds) (1997), *Japanese Success? British Failure*, Oxford University Press.

Adeney, M. (1988), *The Motor Makers: The turbulent history of Britain's car industry*, Collins.

Aharoni, Y. (1966), *The Foreign Investment Decision Process*, Harvard University Press.

Allen, G.C. (1979), *The British Disease*, IEA.

Altshuler, A., Anderson, M., Jones, D., Roos, D. and Womack, J. (1984), *The Future of the Automobile: The report of MIT's international programme*, Allen and Unwin.

Andersen, C. (1992), *Influencing the European Community: Guidelines for a successful business strategy*, Kogan Page.

Andersson T. (eds) (1993), *Japan: A European Perspective*, St Martin Press.

Andretsch, D.B. (1989), *The Market and the State*, Harvester Weatsheaf.

Artis, M. (1996), *Prest and Coppock's the UK Economy: Annual of Applied Economics*, Oxford University Press.

Bachtler, J. and Clement, K. (1990), *The Impact of the Single European Market on FDI in the UK*, HMSO.

Bacon, R. and Eltis, W. (1978), *Britain's Economic Problems: Too few producers*, Macmillan.

Baglioni, G. and Crouch, C. (1990), *European Industrial Relations: The challenge of flexibility*, SAGE.

Bailey, D., Harte, G. and Sugden, R. (1994), *Transnationals and Governments*, Routledge.

Ball, S. and Seldon, A. (eds) (1996), *The Heath Government 1970–1974: A reappraisal*, Longman.

Barnett, C. (1986), *The Audit of War: The reality and illusion of Britain as a great power*, Macmillan.

Barrell, R. and Pain, N. (1995), *Trade Restrictions and Japanese Direct Investment Flows*, Discussion Paper No. 43, National Institute of Economic and Social Research.

Benn, T., *Diaries*, 5 vols, Hutchinson.

Bhaskar, K. (1979), *The Future of the UK Motor Industry: An economic and financial analysis of the UK motor industry against a rapidly changing background for European and worldwide motor manufacturers*, Kogan Page.

Blackaby, F. (ed.) (1978), *De-Industrialisation*, Heinemann.

Blondel, J. and Muller-Rommel, F. (eds) (1993), *Governing Together: The extent and limits of joint decision-making in Western European cabinets*, St Martin Press.

Bloomfield, G. (1978), *The World Automotive Industry*, David and Charles.

Boddy, M., Lovering, J. and Bassett, K. (1986), *Sunbelt City? A Study of Economic Change in Britain's M4 Growth Corridor*, Clarendon Press.

Boyfield, K. (1983), *BL: Changing gear*, Centre for Policy Studies.

Bratton, J. (1992), *Japanisation at Work: Managerial studies for the 1990s*, Macmillan.

Brech, M. and Sharp, M. (1984), *Inward Investment Policy Options for the UK*, RIIA, Routledge.

Britain, S. (1971), *Government and Market Economy*, IEA.

Browning, P. (1986), *The Treasury Economic Policy 1964–85*, Longman.

Bruton, K. (1994), *The Business Culture in Spain*, Butterworth Heinemann.

Bryant, W.E. (1975), *Japanese Private Economic Diplomacy: An analysis of business–government linkages*, Praeger.

Buckley, P.J. (1989), *The Multinational Enterprise: Theory and applications*, Macmillan.

Buckley, P.J. and Casson M. (1985), *The Economic Theory of the Multinational Enterprise*, Macmillan.

Buckley, P.J. and Casson M. (1991), *The Future of the Multinational Enterprise*, Macmillan.

Burgenmeir, B. and Mucchielli, J.L. (eds) (1991), *Multinationals and Europe 1992: Strategies for the future*, Routledge.

Burton, F., Yamin, M. and Young, S. (eds) (1996), *International Business and Europe in Transition*, Macmillan.

Buxton, T., Chapman, P. and Temple, P. (eds) (1994), *Britain's Economic Performance*, Routledge.

Campbell, N. and Burton, F. (eds) (1994), *Japanese Multinational*, Routledge.

Carr, C. (1990), *Britain's Competitiveness: The management of the vehicle components industry*, Routledge.

Casson, M. (1986), *Multinationals and World Trade*, Allen and Unwin.

Casson, M. (1987), *The Firm and the Market: Studies on MNE and the scope of the firm*, Basil Blackwell.

Castle, B. (1980), *The Castle Diaries 1974–76*, Weidenfeld and Nicolson.

Caves, R. (1982), *MNEs and Economic Analysis*, Cambridge University Press.

Cecchini, P. (1988), *The European Challenge 1992: The benefits of a Single Market*, Aldershot.

Chalmers, N.J. (1989), *Industrial Relations in Japan*, Routledge.

Chan, S. (ed.) (1995), *FDI in a Changing Global Political Economy*, Macmillan.

Chandler, A.D. (1990), *Scale and Scope: The dynamics of industrial capitalism*, Harvard University Press.

Chang, C.S. (1981), *The Japanese Auto Industry and the US Market*, Praeger.

Chew, E. (1996), *The UK Automotive Components Industry*, EIU.

Church, R. (1994), *The Rise and Decline of the British Motor Industry*, Macmillan.

Clutterbuck, D. and Crainer, S. (1988), *The Decline and Rise of British Industry*, Mercury.

Coates, D. (ed.) (1996), *Industrial Policy in Britain*, Macmillan.

Coates, D. and Hillard, J. (eds) (1986), *The Economic Decline of Modern Britain: The debate between Left and Right*, Wheafsheaf.

Coates, D. and Hillard, J. (eds) (1987), *The Economic Revival of Modern Britain: The debate between Left and Right*, Edward Elgar.

Cole, R.E. (1981), *The Japanese Automobile Industry: Model and challenge for the Future*, Michigan, University of Michigan.

Cole, R.E. (ed.) (1983), *Automobiles and the Future*, Michigan, University of Michigan.

Cool, K., Neven, D.J. and Walter, I. (1992), *European Industrial Restructuring in the 1990s*, Macmillan.

Cowling, K. and Sugden, R. (eds) (1992), *Current Issues in Industrial Economic Strategy*, Manchester University Press.

Crafts, N.F.R. (1993), *Can De-industrialisation Seriously Damage Your Wealth?*, IEA.

Crafts, N.F.R. and Toniolo, G. (eds) (1996), *Economic Growth in Europe since 1945*, Cambridge University Press.

Crick, M. (1997), *Michael Heseltine: A biography*, Hamish Hamilton.

Cusumano, M.A. (1985), *The Japanese Automobile Industry: Technology and management at Nissan and Toyota*, Harvard University Press.

Darby, J. (ed.) (1996), *Japan and the European Periphery*, Macmillan.

Davies, T., Mason, C. and Davies, L. (1984), *Government and Labour Market Policy Implementation*, Gower.

de Jong, H.W. (ed.) (1993), *The Structure of European Industry*, Kluwer Academic Publisher.

Deyo, F.C. (ed.) (1987), *The Political Economy of the New Asian Industrialism*, Ithaca, Corneal University Press.

Dicken, P. (1992), *Global Shift: The internationalisation of economic activity*, Paul Chapman Publishing Ltd.

Dintenfass, M. (1992), *The Decline of Industrial Britain 1870–1980*, Routledge.

Dore, R. (1986), *Flexible Rigidities: Industrial policy and structural adjustment in the Japanese economy*, Athlone Press.

Drake, G. (1994), *Issues in the New Europe*, Hodder and Stoughton.

Driver, C. and Dunne, P. (eds) (1992), *Structural Change in the UK Economy*, Cambridge University Press.

Dudley, J.W. (1989), *1992 Strategies for the Single Market*, Kogan Page.

Duncan, W.C. (1973), *US–Japan Automobile Diplomacy*, Ballinger Publication Co.

Dunnet, P.J.S. (1980), *The Decline of the British Motor Industry: The effects of government policy, 1945–1979*, Croom Helm.

Dunning, J.H. (ed.) (1971), *The Multinational Enterprise*, George Allen and Unwin.

Dunning, J.H. (1988), *Explaining International Production*, Unwin Hyman.

Dunning, J.H. and Narula, R. (eds) (1996), *FDI and Governments*, Routledge.

Dunning, J.H. and Narula, R. (eds) (1997), *Governments, Globalisation and International Business*, Oxford University Press.

Dunning, J.H. and Narula, R. (1998), *American Investment in British Manufacturing Industry*, Routledge.

Dunning, J.H. and Robson, P. (eds) (1988), *MNEs and the EC*, Blackwell.

Dunning, J.H. and Robson, P. (eds) (1993), *Multinational Enterprises and the Global Economy*, Addison-Wesley.

Dyer, D., Salter, M.S. and Webber, A.M. (1987), *Changing Alliances*, Boston, Harvard University Press.

Dyker, D. (ed.) (1992), *The National Economies of Europe*, Longman.

The Economist Intelligence Unit (1996), *Japan's Motor Industry*.

Egan, C. and McKiernan, P. (1994), *Inside Fortress Europe*, EIU.

El-Agraa, A.M. (1988), *Japan's Trade Frictions*, Macmillan.

Elger, T. and Smith, C. (eds) (1994), *Global Japanization?: The transnational transformation of the labour process*, Routledge.

Eli, M. (1990), *Japan Inc.: Global strategies of Japanese Trading Corporation*, McGraw-Hill.

Emmott, B. (1993), *Japan's Global Reach*, Arrow.

Ferner, A. and Hyman, R. (eds) (1992), *Industrial Relation in the New Europe*, Blackwell.

Fingleton, E. (1995), *Blindside: Why Japan is still on track to overtake the US by the Year 2000*, Simon and Schuster.

Fitzgerald, R. (ed.) (1994), *The Competitive Advantage of Far Eastern Business*, Frank Cass.

Foreman-Peck, J., Bowden, S. and McKinlay, A. (1995), *The British Motor Industry*, Manchester University Press.

Franko, L.G. (1983), *The Threat of Japanese Multinationals*, Wiley.

Friedman, D. (1988), *The Misunderstanding Miracle: Industrial development and political change in Japan*, Cornell University Press.

Fruin, W.M. (1994), *The Japanese Enterprise System: Competitive strategies and cooperative structures*, Clarendon.

Fucini, J.J. (1992), *Working for the Japanese: Inside Mazda's American auto plant*, Free Press.

Fuss, M.F. and Waverman, L. (1992), *Costs and Productivity in Automobile Production: The challenge of Japanese efficiency*, Cambridge University Press.

Garby, C.C. and Bullock, M.B. (eds) (1994), *Japan: A new kind of Superpower?*, Johns Hopkins University Press.

Garrahan, P. and Stewart, P. (1992), *The Nissan Enigma: Flexibility at work in a local economy*, Mansell.

Genther, P.A. (1990), *A History of Japan's Government–Business Relationship*, Michigan University Press.

Gordon, D.D. (1988), *Japanese Management in America and Britain*, Avebury.

Grimwade, N. (1989), *International Trade: New patterns of trade, production and investment*, Routledge.

Hanabusa, M. (1979), *Trade Problems between Japan and Western Europe*, RIIA.

Harrop, J. (1992), *The Political Economy of Integration in the European Community*, Edward Elgar.

Hayes, J.P. (1993), *Making Trade Policy in the European Community*, Macmillan.

Hayter, T. and Harvey, D. (eds) (1993), *The Factory and the City*, Mansell.

Healey, M.J. and Ilbery, B.W. (1990), *Location and Change: Perspective on economic geography*, Oxford University Press.

Healey, N.M. (ed.) (1993), *Britain's Economic Miracle: Myth or reality*, Routledge.

Healey, N. (ed.) (1995), *The Economics of the New Europe: from Community to Union*, Routledge.

Heidenson, K. (1995), *Europe and World Trade*, Pinter.

Hertner, P. and Jones, G. (eds) (1986), *Multinationals: Theory and history*, Gower.

Heseltine, M. (1989), *The Challenge of Europe: Can Britain win?*, Weidenfeld and Nicolson.

Hill, S. and Munday, M. (1994), *The Regional Distribution of Foreign Manufacturing Investment in the UK*, Macmillan.

Hine, R.C. (1985), *The Political Economy of European Trade*, St Martin Press.

Hoekman, B. and Kostecki, M. (1995), *The Political Economy of the World Trading System: From GATT to WTO*, Oxford University Press.

Holthus, M. and Koopman, G. (1974), *The Extent and Importance of the Operations of Multinational Firms in the EEC*, Institute for International Economics.

Hood, N. and Young, S. (1980), *European Development Strategies of US-owned Manufacturing Companies located in Scotland*, HMSO.

Hook, G.D. and Weiner, M.A. (eds) (1992), *Internationalisation of Japan*, Routledge.

Huber, T.M. (1994), *Strategic Economy in Japan*, Westview Press.

Hufbauer, G.C. (ed.) (1991), *Europe 1992 An American Perspective*, Brookings Institute.

Hughes, K. (ed.) (1993), *The Future of UK Competitiveness and the Role of Industrial Policy*, Policy Studies Institute.

Inkpen, A. (1995), *The Management of International Joint Ventures: An organisational learning perspective*, Routledge.

Inoguchi, T. and Okimoto, D.I. (eds) (1988), *The Political Economy of Japan Vol. 2: The Changing International Context*, Stanford University Press.

Ishikawa, K. (1990), *Japan and the Challenge of Europe 1992*, Pinter.

Jackson, J.H. (1990), *Restructuring the GATT System*, RIIA.

Jackson, T. (1994), *Turning Japanese: The fight for industrial control of the New Europe*, HarperCollins.

James, B.G. (1989), *Trojan Horse: The ultimate Japanese challenge to Western industry*, Mercury Business Books.

Johnson, C. (1991), *The Economy under Mrs Thatcher 1979–1990*, Penguin.

Johnson, C. (1982), *MITI and the Japanese Economic Miracle*, Stanford University Press.

Johnson, C. (1995), *Japan: Who governs?*, Norton.

Johnson, C., Tyson, L.D. and Zysman, J. (eds) (1989), *Politics and Productivity: How Japan's development strategy works*, Ballinger Publishing Co.

Johnson, P. (eds) (1993), *European Industries: Structure, conduct and performance*, Edward Elgar.

Jones, D.T. (1985), *The Import Threat to the UK Car Industry*, Sussex University Policy Research Unit.

Jones, S. (1991), *Working for the Japanese: Myths and realities: British perceptions*, Macmillan.

Katzenstein, P.J. (1989), *Industry and Politics in West Germany*, Cornell University Press.

Kenney, M. and Florida, R. (1993), *Beyond Mass Production: The Japanese system and its transfer to the US*, Oxford University Press.

Kessler, S. and Bayliss, F. (1995), *Contemporary British Industrial Relations*, Macmillan.

Kindleberger, C.P. and Audretsch, P.B. (eds) (1983), *The Multinational Corporation in the 1980s*, MIT Press.

Klein, M.W. and Welfans, P.J.J. (eds) (1992), *Multinationals in the New Europe and Global Trade*, Springer Verlag.

Kojima, K. (1977), *Japan and a New World Economic Order*, Croom Helm.

Kojima, K. and Ozawa, T. (1984), *Japan's General Trading Companies*, OECD.

Komazawa International Symposium (1990), *The Globalisation of Japanese Economy*, Komazawa University Press.

Kono, T. (1984), *Strategy and Structure of Japanese Enterprise*, Macmillan.

Kujawa, D. (1986), *Japanese MNEs in the USA*, Praeger.

Lane, C. (1990), *Management and Labour in Europe: The industrial enterprise in Germany, Britain and France*, Edward Elgar.

Lansbury, M. (1995), *UK Manufacturing Employment since Beverage: The chemical and motor vehicle industries*, Discussion Paper No. 83, National Institute of Economic and Social Research.

Law, C.M. (ed.) (1991), *Restructuring the Global Automobile Industry: National and regional impacts*, Routledge.

Lewchuk, W. (1987), *American Technology and the British Vehicle Industry*, Cambridge University Press.

MacInnes, J. (1987), *Thatcherism at Work*, Open University Press.

Magaziner, I.C. and Hout, T.M. (1980), *Japanese Industrial Policy*, Policy Studies Institute.

Mair, A. (1994), *Honda's Global Local Corporation*, St Martin Press.

Malik, R. (1964), *What's Wrong with British Industry?*, Penguin.

Marsden, D., Morris, T., William, P. and Wood, S. (1985), *The Car Industry: Labour relations and industrial adjustment*, Tavistock.

Marsh, D. and Rhodes, R.A.W. (eds) (1992), *Implementing Thatcherite Policies: Audit of an era*, Open University Press.

Mason, M. and Encarnation, D. (eds) (1995), *Does Ownership Matter? Japanese multinationals in Europe*, Clarendon Press.

Mason, T.D. and Turay, A.M. (eds) (1994), *Japan, NAFTA and Europe: Trilateral cooperation or confrontation*, Macmillan.

Mattsson, L.G. and Stymne, B. (eds) (1991), *Corporate and Industry Strategies for Europe*, Elsevier Science Publishers.

Matsuoka, M. and Rose, B. (1994), *The DIR Guide to Japanese Economic Statistics*, Oxford University Press.

Maxcy, G. (1981), *The Multinational Motor Industry*, Croom Helm.

Maxcy, G. and Silberston, A. (1959), *The Motor Industry*, Allen and Unwin.

Maxton, G.P. and Wormald, J. (1995), *Driving Over a Cliff? – Business Lessons from the World's Car Industry*, Economist Intelligence Unit.

Mayes, D.G. (ed.) (1991), *The European Challenge: Industry's response to the 1992 programme*, Harvester Wheatsheaf.

McCarthy, W.E. (ed.) (1987), *Trade Unions*, Penguin.

McCormick, B. and McCormik, K. (1996), *Japanese Companies – British Factories*, Avebury.

McLeod, J. (1992), *The World Motor Industry*, EIU.

Mikanagi, Y. (1996), *Japan's Trade Policy: Action or reaction*, Routledge.

Mito, S. (1990), *The Honda Book of Management: A leadership philosophy for high industrial success*, Athlone.

Miyashita, K. and Russell, D.W. (1994), *Keiretsu: Inside the hidden Japanese conglomerates*, McGraw-Hill Inc.

Morales, R. (1994), *Flexible Production-Restructuring of the International Automobile Industry*, Polity Press.

Morris, J. (ed.) (1991), *Japan and the Global Economy: Issues and trends in the 1990s*, Routledge.

Morris, J. and Imrie, R. (1992), *Transforming Buyer–Supplier Relations: Japanese-style industrial practices in a Western context*, Macmillan.

Munday, M. (1990), *Japanese Manufacturing Investment in Wales*, University of Wales.

Murata, K. (1991), *How to make Japanese Management Methods Work in the West*, Gower.

Murphy, A. (1990), *The European Community and the International Trading System*, 2 vols, Centre for European Policy Studies.

Murray, G. (1991), *Synergy: Japanese companies in Britain*, PHP Institute Inc.

NEDO (1971), *Japan: Its motor industry and market*, HMSO.

Nomura Research Institute (1988), *Investment Opportunities in Europe*.

Nomura Research Institute (1995), *The New Wave of FDI in Asia*, Institute of Southeast Asian Studies.

Odagiri, H. (1992), *Growth through Competition, Competition through Growth: Strategic management and the economy in Japan*, Clarendon Press.

Okimoto, D.I. (ed.) (1982), *Japan's Economy: Coping with change in the international environment*, Westview Press.

Okimoto, D.I. (1989), *Between MITI and the Market: Japanese industrial policy for high technology*, Stanford University Press.

Oliver, N. and Wilkinson, B. (1992), *The Japanization of British Industry: New developments in the 1990s* (2nd edn), Blackwell.

Ozawa, T. (1979), *Multinationalism, Japanese Style*, Princeton University Press.

Park, S.J. (1989), *Technology and Labour in the Automotive Industry*, Campus Verlag.

Petrochilas, G.A. (1989), *FDI and the Development Process: The case of Greece*, Avebury.

Pinder, J. (1995), *European Community: The building of a union*, Oxford University Press.

Pliatzky, L. (1989), *The Treasury under Mrs Thatcher*, Blackwell.

Plowden, W. (1972), *The Motor Car and Politics in Britain*, Penguin Books.

Porter, M.E. (1990), *The Competitive Advantage of Nations*, Macmillan.

Poynter, T.A. (1985), *Multinational Enterprises and Government Intervention*, Croom Helm.

Rae, J.B. (1982), *Nissan–Datsun: A history of Nissan Motor Corporation in USA 1960–80*, McGraw Hill.

Rajan, A. and Thompson, M. (1989), *Economic Significance of the UK Motor Vehicle Manufacturing Industry*, Institute of Manpower Studies.

Randlesome, C. (1994), *The Business Culture in Germany*, Butterworth Heinemann.

Rhys, D.G. (1972), *The Motor Industry: An economic survey*, Butterworths.

Richardson, H. (1989), *EC–Japan Relations*, Nissan Institute of Japanese Studies.

Robertson, I.L. (1988), *Japan's Motor Industry*, EIU.

Robertson, I.L. (1989), *The UK Car Market*, EIU.

Robinson, F. (ed.) (1988), *Post-Industrial Tyneside: An economic and social survey of Tyneside in the 1980s*, Newcastle-upon-Tyne City Library and Arts.

Robinson, F., Wren, C. and Goddard, J. (1987), *Economic Development Policies: An evaluative study of the Newcastle Metropolitan Region*, Clarendon Press.

Robson, G. (1988), *The Rover Story*, Patrick Stephens.

Rothacher, A. (1983), *Economic Diplomacy between EC and Japan 1959–1981*, Gower.

Rothacher, A. (1993), *The Japanese Power Elite*, Macmillan.

Rugman, A. (ed.) (1982), *New Theories of the MNE*, Croom Helm.

Rugman, A. and Verbeke, A. (1990), *Global Corporate Strategy and Trade Policy*, Routledge.

Sakia, T. (1987), *Honda Motor: The men, the management, the machine*, Kodansa International.

Salmon, K.G. (1991), *The Modern Spanish Economy*, Pinter.

Sato, K. (ed.) (1980), *Industry and Business in Japan*, Croom Helm.

Scarbrough, H. and Terry, M. (1996), *Industrial Relations and the Reorganization of Production in the UK Motor Vehicle Industry: A study of the Rover Group*, Industrial Relations Research Unit, Warwick Business School.

Sekiguchi, S. (1979), *Japanese Direct Foreign Investment*, Allanheld, Osmun and Co.

Servan-Schreiber, J. (1968), *The American Challenge*, Hamish Hamilton.

Sheridan, K. (1993), *Governing the Japanese Economy*, Polity Press.

Shibagaki, K., Trevor, M. and Abo, T. (eds) (1989) *Japanese and European Management: Their international adaptability*, Tokyo, University of Tokyo.

Shimokawa, K. (1994), *The Japanese Automobile Industry: A business history*, Athlone.

Shiomi, H. and Wada, K. (eds) (1995), *Fordism Transformed: The development of production methods in the automobile industry*, Oxford University Press.

Shook, R.L. (1988), *Honda: An American success story*, Prentice Hall.

Sinhh, D. and Siregar, R.Y. (eds) (1995), *ASEAN and KOREA: Emerging issues in trade and investment relations*, Institute of Southeast Asian Studies.

Sked, A. (1987), *Britain's Decline: Problems and perspectives*, Blackwell.

Sleigh, P. (1988), *The UK Automotive Component Industry*, EIU.

Smith, D. (1992), *From Boom to Bust: Trial and error in British economic policy*, Penguin.

Spencer, K., Taylor, A., Smith, B., Mawson, J., Flynn, N. and Batley, R. (1986), *Crisis in the Industrial Heartland: A study of the West Midlands*, Clarendon Press.

Stewart, M. (1978), *Politics and Economic Policy in the UK since 1964*, Pergamon.

Stewart, T. (eds) (1996), *The GATT Uruguay Round: A negotiating history (1986–1992)*, 3 vols, Kluwer.

Stopford, J. and Turner, L. (1985), *Britain and the Multinationals*, John Wiley and Sons.

Strange, R. (1993), *Japanese Manufacturing Investment in Europe: Its impact on the UK economy*, Routledge.

Streeck, W. (1984), *Industrial Relations in West Germany: A case study of the car industry*, Heinemann.

Suzuki, Y. (1991), *Japanese Management Structure 1920–80*, Macmillan.

Takayima, S. and Thurley, K. (1985), *Japan's Emerging MNEs*, University of Tokyo.

Tamames, R. (1986), *The Spanish Economy*, St Martin Press.

Taplin, R. (1995), *Decision-making and Japan: A study of corporate Japanese decision-making and its relevance to Western companies*, Japan Library.

TELESIS (1986), *Competing for Prosperity: Business strategies and industrial policies in modern France*, Policy Studies Institute.

Thatcher, M. (1993), *The Downing Street Years*, HarperCollins.

Thoburn, J.T. and Takashima, M. (1992), *Industrial Subcontracting in the UK and Japan*, Avebury.

Thomsen, S. and Phedon, N. (1990), *Foreign Direct Investment: 1992 and global markets*, RIIA.

Thomsen, S. and Nicolaides, P. (1992), *The Evolution of Japanese Direct Investment in Europe*, Harvester Wheatsheaf.

Tomlinson, J. (1994), *Government and the Enterprise since 1900*, Oxford University Press.

Trevor, M. (1983), *Japan's Reluctant Multinationals*, Macmillan.

Trevor, M. (ed.) (1987), *The Internationalisation of Japanese Business: European and Japanese perspectives*, Westview Press.

Trevor, M. and Christie, I. (1988), *Manufacturers and Suppliers in Britain and Japan*, PSI.

Tsurumi, Y. (1976), *The Japanese Are Coming: A multinational interaction of firms and politics*, Cambridge University Press.

Tugendhat, C. (1977), *The Multinationals*, Penguin.

Turner, C.G. (1991), *Japan's Dynamic Efficiency in the Global Market: Trade, investment, and economic growth*, Quorum Books.

Turner, H.A., Clack, G. and Roberts, G. (1967), *Labour Relations in the Motor Industry: A study of industrial unrest and an international comparison*, Allen and Unwin.

Turner, L. (1987), *Industrial Collaboration with Japan*, RKP.

Turner, L. and Hodges, M. (1992), *Global Shakeout: World market competition – the challenges for business and government*, Century Business.

Turner, R. (ed.) (1995), *The British Economy in Transition*, Routledge.

Vestal, J. (1995), *Planning for Change: Industrial policy and Japanese economic development 1945–1990*, Clarendon.

Vogel, E.F. (ed.) (1975), *Modern Japanese Organisation and Decision-making*, University of California Press.

Vogel, E.F. (1979), *Japan as No. 1: Lessons for America*, Harvard University Press.

Walker, B. (1987), *Motor Industry Local Authority Network*, Birmingham University Press.

Ward, J.C. (1978), *The Automotive Components Industry of the UK: Structure, growth and future*, Economist Intelligent Unit.

Wells, P. and Rawlinson, M. (1994), *The New European Automobile Industry*, Macmillan.

Whitehill, A.M. (1991), *Japanese Management: Tradition and transition*, Routledge.

Whitley, R. (ed.) (1992), *European Business Systems – Firms and Markets in their National Contexts*, Sage.

Wickens, P. (1987), *The Road to Nissan: Flexibility, quality, teamwork*, Macmillan.

Wiener, M.J. (1981), *English Culture and the Decline of the Industrial Spirit 1850–1980*, Penguin.

Wilks, S. (1984), *Industrial Policy and the Motor Industry*, Manchester University Press.

Wilks, S. (1994), *The Revival of Japanese Competition Policy and its Importance for EU-Japan Relations*, RIIA.

Willams, K., Williams, J. and Thomas, D. (1983), *Why Are the British Bad at Manufacturing?*, Routledge and Kegan Paul.

Willams, K., Williams, J., Thomas, D. and Haslam, C. (1987), *The Breakdown of Austin Rover*, BERG.

Willams, K., Williams, J., Thomas, D. Adcroft, A. and Johal, S. (1992), *Factories or Warehouses: Japanese manufacturing FDI in Britain and the US*, University of North London Occasional Papers on Business, Economy and Society.

Willams, K., Williams, J., Thomas, D. Adcroft, A. and Johal, S. (1994), *Cars: Analysis, history, cases*, Berghahn Books.

Willman, P. and Winch, G. (1985), *Innovation and Management Control: Labour relations at BL cars*, Cambridge University Press.

Wilson, H. (1979), *Final Term: The Labour Government 1974–1976*, Weidenfeld and Nicolson.

Wolf, M.J. (1983), *The Japanese Conspiracy: A stunning analysis of the international trade war*, New English Library.

Womack, J.P., Jones, D.T. and Ross, D. (1990), *The Machine that Changed the World*, Rawson Associates.

Wood, C. (1992), *The Bubble Economy: The Japanese economic collapse*, Sidgwick and Jackson.

Wood, J. (1988), *Wheels of Misfortune: The rise and fall of the British motor industry*, Sedgwick and Jackson.

Woolcock, S. and Yamane, H. (1993), *EC-Japanese Trade Relations: What are the rules of the game?*, RIIA.

Wormald, J. and Maxton, G.P. (1995), *Driving Over A Cliff? Business Lessons from the World's Car Industry*, Addison-Wesley.

Woronoff, J. (1990), *Japan as – anything but – Number One*, Yohan Publications Inc.

Woronoff, J. (1992), *Japanese Targeting: Success, failure, lessons*, Macmillan.

Wright, M. (1989), *Government-Industrial Relations in Japan: The role of the bureaucracy*, Manchester Statistical Society.

Yamazawa, I. (1990), *Economic Development and International Trade: The Japanese model*, East-West Centre.

Yanarella, E.J. and Green, W.C. (eds) (1990), *The Politics of Industrial Recruitment: Japanese automobile investment and economic development in the American states*, Greenwood Press.

Yasutomo, D.T. (1995), *The New Multinationalism in Japan's Foreign Policy*, Macmillan.

Yazawa, T. (ed.) (1994), *Japanese Business Success: The evolution of a strategy*, Routledge.

Young, D. (1990), *The Enterprise Years: A businessman in the Cabinet*, HEADLINE.

Yoshino, M.Y. (1976), *Japan's MNEs*, Harvard University Press.

Yoshitomi, M. (ed.) (1990), *Japanese Direct Investment in Europe: Motives, impact and policy implications*, Avebury.

Young, S. and Hamill, J. (eds) (1992), *Europe and the Multinationals: Issues and responses for the 1990s*, Edward Elgar.

Young, S., Hood, N. and Hamill, J. (1988), *Foreign Multinationals and the British Economy: Impact and policy*, Croom Helm.

Yuzawa, T. (eds) (1994), *Japanese Business Success*, Routledge